THE ALASKA
ALMANAC®

FACTS ABOUT ALASKA
17TH EDITION

D0036846

THE ALASKA
ALMANAC®

FACTS ABOUT ALASKA
17TH EDITION

Alaska Northwest Books™
Anchorage • Seattle • Portland

Seventeenth edition
Previously published as *FACTS ABOUT ALASKA: The ALASKA ALMANAC*®

ISBN 0-88240-446-6
ISSN 0270-5370
Key title: The Alaska Almanac

Compiled by Lisa Yeager and Ann Chandonnet
Edited by Carolyn Smith
Layout Design/Editorial Assistance by Fay L. Bartels
Illustrations by Val Paul Taylor and David Berger
Cover illustration by David Berger

Alaska Northwest Books™
An imprint of Graphic Arts Center Publishing Company
Editorial office: 2208 NW Market Street, Suite 300, Seattle, WA 98107
Catalog and order dept.: P.O. Box 10306, Portland, OR 97210
800-452-3032

Printed in the United States of America

Contents

Miscellaneous Facts

Motto: "North to the Future."
State capital: Juneau.
Organized as a territory: 1912.
Entered the union: Jan. 3, 1959; 49th state.
Number of boroughs: 14.
Governor: Walter J. Hickel.
Land area: 586,412 square miles, or about 365,000,000 acres—largest state in the union; one-fifth the size of the Lower 48.
State population: 570,345 from 1991 census.
Largest city in population: Anchorage, population 226,338 from 1990 census.
Largest city in area: Sitka with 4,710 square miles, 1,816 square miles of which is water. Juneau is second, with an area of 3,108 square miles.
Typical Alaskan: According to 1990 census figures, 28.9 years old and male. This compares to 32.3 years for the United States. About 51 percent of Alaskans are male, the highest percentage of any state.
Average household income: $60,853 in 1989, fifth highest in the nation (latest available figures).
Per capita personal income: $21,603 in 1992, eighth highest in the nation.
Area per person: There are approximately 1.02 square miles for each person in Alaska. New York State has .003 square mile per person.
Highest/Lowest temperatures: *Highest* 100°F at Fort Yukon, 1915. *Lowest* –80°F at Prospect Creek Camp, 1971.
Heaviest annual snowfall: 974.5 inches at Thompson Pass near Valdez, during the winter of 1952–53.
Tallest mountain: Mount McKinley, 20,320 feet.
Largest natural freshwater lake: Iliamna, 1,150 square miles.
Longest river: Yukon, 1,400 miles in Alaska; 1,875 total.
Largest glacier: Bering Glacier complex, 2,250 square miles, which includes the Bagley Icefield.
Oldest building: Erskine House in Kodiak, built by the Russians, probably between 1793 and 1796.
Farthest north supermarket: In Barrow; constructed on stilts to prevent snow build-up, at a cost of $4 million.
World's largest and busiest seaplane base: Lake Hood, in Anchorage, accommodating more than 800 takeoffs and landings on a peak summer day.
Largest state park in the nation: Wood-Tikchik State Park, with 1.6 million acres of wilderness.
World's largest concentration of bald eagles: Along the Chilkat River, just north of Haines. More than 3,500 bald eagles gather here in fall and winter months for late salmon runs.
America's biggest earthquake: Occurred March 27, 1964, Good Friday. Measuring 8.6 on the Richter scale (has since been revised upward to 9.2—the strongest ever recorded in North America), the earthquake devasted much of Southcentral Alaska.
Second greatest tide range in North America: 38.9 feet near Anchorage in Upper Cook Inlet.

Agriculture

Agriculture in Alaska ranges from backyard gardens to 2,000-acre barley farms. Volatile weather and a short growing season challenge cultivation in the state, but certain crops—notably potatoes and carrots—thrive in the cool soil temperatures. Overall, climatic conditions are not the greatest impediments to Alaska farming. More significant hurdles are the lack of access to major metropolitan markets, high production costs and competition from the Lower 48.

Alaska's commercial farming is concentrated in two major regions: the Matanuska Valley, northeast of Anchorage, which in 1992 contributed 67 percent of the state's value of farm production; and the Tanana Valley, outside of Fairbanks, which was responsible for 27 percent.

An estimated 15 to 18 million acres in Alaska are believed to be arable, but only 1 million acres—less than one-half of 1 percent of the state—are currently considered land in farms. In 1992, crops covered 23,016 acres; the balance was in pasture or uncleared land.

Total market of Alaska's agricultural products in 1992 was $25,470,000—$1,071,000 less than in 1991. An early winter curtailed harvest of several hundred acres of small grain, hay and potatoes in the fall of 1992. Feed crops accounted for $1.9 million of total market receipts; and vegetables, including potatoes, were $2.53 million of the total. The annual production of eggs declined to 42,000 dozen, down from 58,000 dozen in 1991. The value of egg production was $70,000 in 1992.

Greenhouse and nursery industries—an ever-increasing portion of the state's agricultural picture—amounted to $15.2 million, or 60 percent of total cash receipts for 1992.

The annual milk production in 1992 totaled 12,200,000 pounds, a

TOTAL ACREAGE OF ALASKA FARMLAND BY REGION

Matanuska Valley 40.5%
Tanana Valley 50.3%
Kenai Peninsula 8.8%
Southeast & Southwest Alaska 0.4%

decrease of 1.1 million pounds from 1991. Dairy products brought in $2.39 million in 1992, down from $2.58 million in 1991.

Almost 94 percent of the barley grown in 1992 was harvested in the Tanana Valley. Total production netted 124,000 bushels, yielding 54 bushels per acre. Production value for the 1992 barley crop was roughly $415,000, less than half of the value of the 1991 crop of $838,000. Harvest of oats yielded 44 bushels per acre for a total of only 8,800 bushels at an estimated value of $21,000. This reflects a sizable decrease from 54,900 bushels valued at $143,000 in 1991.

Another agricultural enterprise showing continued success is the raising of reindeer. Officials estimate there are 16 herds in western Alaska, or a total population of approximately 37,000. Most of the reindeer are located on the Seward Peninsula and Nunivak Island, where they contribute heavily to the local economies. Among the by-products of reindeer is the powder made from clipped antlers, much of which is exported to the Far East. Sales related to reindeer were valued

Products*	Acres Harvested	1992 Crop Value
Hay (16.4 tons)*	15,800	$2,870,000
Potatoes (130 cwt.)*	560	2,405,000
Vegetables (except potatoes)	271	940,000
Barley (124 bu.) (for grain)*	2,300	415,000
Silage (3.9 tons)*	1,200	225,000
Oats (8.8 bu.) (for grain)*	200	21,000

*Volume in thousands

at $1,548,000 in 1992, down $473,000 from 1991.

Less encouraging is the state of dairy farming in Alaska. Economic stresses continue to reduce the number of farmers involved in this capital-intensive industry. In 1989, 1,500 cows produced nearly 3 million gallons of milk. By 1992, the number of cows decreased to 700, causing milk production to plummet. Fewer than 10 dairies are now operating in the state.

According to the Alaska Agricultural Statistics Service, the value and volume of the principal agricultural products in 1992 were quoted as shown on page 9.

The small vegetable gardens of the Russian fur traders are believed to constitute the first Alaskan agriculture. Gold rush days saw growing interest in local farming possibilities, but it wasn't until 1935 that there was a concerted effort to introduce commercial growing. President Franklin Roosevelt's New Deal resettlement plan transplanted 200 farm families from the Midwest to the Matanuska Valley, where they were to create a food source for the territory. Valley farmers still supply Anchorage and nearby military installations; dairy farming, including feed crops for cows, is the dominant income source. The growing season is 120 days, and there are up to 19 hours of sunlight in the summer (which help produce giant-sized vegetables).

The Tanana Valley growing season is shorter than that of the Matanuska Valley, with about 90 frost-free days. Because growing season temperatures are warmer in the Tanana Valley, many experts consider the area to have greater agricultural potential. Barley,

oats and wheat are raised for grain and hay. Most Alaska-grown grain is used for domestic livestock feed. Almost all are spring varieties, since few winter types survive the cold.

Beef, hay, eggs and potatoes are produced throughout the Railbelt region. (The Railbelt region consists of the areas linked by the Alaska Railroad, from Seward north to Fairbanks.) Umnak and Unalaska islands provide grazing area for 1,500 sheep, down considerably from 27,000 in 1970.

Across Alaska, the pressure of urban development is reducing the number of acres available for farming. At the same time, the state is attempting to increase the number of farms through sales of smaller tracts. Farming is also used by some individuals as a supplement to other income. In 1992, there were 540 farms with annual sales of $1,000 or more.

Since 1978, state land sales have placed more than 165,000 acres of potential agricultural land into private ownership. Most of this acreage is in the Delta Junction area, where tracts of up to 3,200 acres were sold by lottery for grain farming. The Nenana area is among those under consideration for future agricultural development.

More information is available from the Alaska Agricultural Statistics Service, P.O. Box 799, Palmer 99645.

Air Travel

Alaska is the "flyingest" state in the Union; the only practical way to reach many areas of rural Alaska is by airplane. According to the Federal Aviation Administration, Alaska Region, in mid-1993 there were close to 9,400 registered pilots, 1 out of every 58 Alaskans, and 9,408 registered aircraft, 1 for every 58 Alaskans. Alaska has approximately 6 times as many pilots per capita and 16 times as many airplanes per capita as the rest of the United States.

According to the FAA, Alaska has about 700 airports, including seaplane landing sites and heliports. That puts Alaska seventh, behind Texas, Illinois, California, Pennsylvania, Ohio and Florida, in the number of airports in the state. Of the seaplane bases, Lake Hood in Anchorage is the largest and busiest in the world. On a yearly basis, an average of 234 takeoffs and landings occur daily, and more than 800 on a peak summer day. Merrill Field in Anchorage records more than 230,000 takeoffs and landings each year, making it one of the nation's busiest general aviation airports. Anchorage International Airport saw more than 3.8 million passengers pass through in 1992.

Flying in Alaska, as elsewhere, is not without its hazards. In 1992, there were 21 fatal airplane accidents in which 51 persons lost their lives.

Pilots who wish to fly their own planes to Alaska should have the latest United States government flight information publication, *Alaska Supplement*, and a booklet titled *Flight Tips for Pilots in Alaska* available from the Federal Aviation Administration, 222 W. Seventh Ave., No. 14, Anchorage 99513-7587.

Scheduled passenger service is available to dozens of Alaskan communities (*see* Intrastate Service, this section). Contact the airlines for current schedules and fares.

Air taxi operators are found in most Alaskan communities, and aircraft can be chartered to fly you to a wilderness spot and pick you up later at a prearranged time and location. (Many charter services charge an hourly standby fee if the customer is not on time at the pickup point.) Most charter operators charge an hourly rate either per plane load or per passenger (sometimes with a minimum passenger requirement); others may charge on a per-mile basis. Flightseeing trips to area attractions are often available at a fixed price per passenger. Charter fares range from $140 to $175 per person (four-person and up minimum) for a short flightseeing trip, to $350 an hour for an eight-passenger Cessna 404 (multi-engine planes are generally more expensive to charter than single-engine planes).

A wide range of aircraft is used for charter and scheduled passenger service in Alaska. The larger interstate airlines—Alaska, Continental, Northwest, United and Delta—use jets (Douglas DC-8, DC-10, Boeing 727, 737, 757, 767); Reeve Aleutian flies Electra and YS-11. MarkAir uses 737 and de Havilland Dash-7. Prop jets and single- or twin-engine prop planes on wheels, skis and floats are used for most intrastate travel. A few of these types of aircraft flown in Alaska are: DC-3, 19-passenger de Havilland Twin Otter, 10-passenger Britten-Norman Islander, 7-passenger Grumman Goose (amphibious), 5-passenger Cessna 185, 9-passenger twin-engine Piper Navajo Chieftain, 5- to 8-passenger de Havilland Beaver, 3- to 4-passenger Cessna 180, 5- to 6-passenger Cessna 206 and single-passenger Piper Super Cub.

INTERSTATE SERVICE

U.S. carriers providing interstate passenger service: Alaska Airlines, Continental Airlines, Delta Air Lines, MarkAir, Morris Air, Northwest Airlines, Reeve Aleutian Airways and United Airlines. These carriers also provide freight service between Anchorage and Seattle.

As a result of airspace opening up over the former Soviet Union, several airlines that once served Anchorage now fly more direct routes over Russia. Today, only three international carriers service Alaska through the Anchorage gateway: Aeroflot, China Airlines and Korean Airlines.

INTRASTATE SERVICE
From Anchorage

Alaska Airlines, 4750 International Road, Anchorage 99502. Serves Cordova, Fairbanks, Gustavus/Glacier Bay, Juneau, Ketchikan, Kotzebue, Nome, Petersburg, Prudhoe Bay, Sitka, Wrangell and Yakutat. Additional routes served on a contract basis by local carriers.

Alaska Island Air, P.O. Box 220374, Anchorage 99522. Serves Willow.

Delta Air Lines. Serves Fairbanks.

Era Aviation, 6160 S. Airpark Drive, Anchorage 99502. Serves Homer, Kenai and Valdez.

MarkAir, P.O. Box 196769, Anchorage 99519. Serves Aniak, Barrow, Bethel, Dillingham, Dutch Harbor, Fairbanks, Galena, King Salmon, Kodiak, St. Marys and Unalakleet, with connections into 17 other cities.

Peninsula Airways, 6231 Collins Way, Anchorage 99502. Serves Cold

Bay, Dillingham, King Salmon and Kodiak.

Reeve Aleutian Airways, 4700 W. International Airport Road, Anchorage 99502. Serves the Alaska Peninsula, Aleutian Islands and Pribilof Islands.

Ryan Air, 1205 E. International Airport Road, Suite 201, Anchorage 99518. Serves Bethel, Kotzebue, McGrath, Nome and many other bush communities in Alaska.

Southcentral Air, 135 Granite Point Court, Kenai 99611. Serves Homer, Kenai and Soldotna.

United Airlines. Serves Fairbanks.

From Barrow

Cape Smythe Air, P.O. Box 549, Barrow 99723. Serves Brevig Mission, Elim, Golovin, Shishmaref, Teller, Wales and White Mountain.

From Fairbanks

Frontier Flying Service, 3820 University Ave., Fairbanks 99709. Serves Allakaket, Anaktuvuk Pass and Bettles.

Larry's Flying Service, P.O. Box 2348, Fairbanks 99707. Serves Denali National Park and Preserve (McKinley Park airstrip).

From Glennallen

Gulkana Air Service, P.O. Box 342, Glennallen 99588. Serves Anchorage.

From Haines

L.A.B. Flying Service, P.O. Box 272, Haines 99827. Serves Hoonah, Juneau and Skagway.

From Juneau

Wings of Alaska, 1873 Shell Simmons Drive, Suite 119, Juneau 99801. Serves Angoon, Elfin Cove, Gustavus/Glacier Bay, Haines, Hoonah, Kake, Pelican, Skagway and Tenakee.

From Kenai

Southcentral Air, 135 Granite Point Court, Kenai 99611. Serves Anchorage, Homer, Seward and Soldotna.

From Ketchikan

Ketchikan Air Service, P.O. Box 6900, Ketchikan 99901. Serves Stewart, British Columbia, and Hyder.

Temso Helicopters, Inc., P.O. Box 5057, Ketchikan 99901. Serves Craig, Hydaburg, Klawock, Metlakatla and other Southeast points.

From Nome

Bering Air Inc., P.O. Box 1650, Nome 99762. Serves Kotzebue and points in western Alaska.

From Tanana

Tanana Air Service, P.O. Box 60713, Fairbanks 99706. Serves Eagle, Fairbanks, Huslia, Manley Hot Springs, Nenana, New Minto and Rampart.

From Tok

40-Mile Air Ltd., P.O. Box 539, Tok 99780. Serves Boundary, Chicken, Delta Junction, Eagle, Fairbanks and Tetlin.

Related reading: *In the Shadows of Eagles,* by Rudy Billberg as told to Jim Rearden. An aviation pioneer shares his adventures of flying in the Last Frontier. *Heroes of the Horizon,* by Gerry Bruder. Profiles of daring bush pilots who flew during the "golden age" of Alaska aviation. *See* ALASKA NORTHWEST LIBRARY in the back of the book.

Alaska-Canada Boundary

In 1825, Russia, in possession of Alaska, and Great Britain, in possession of Canada, established the original boundary between Alaska and Canada. The demarcation was to begin at 54°40´ north latitude, just north of the mouth of Portland Canal, follow the canal to 56° north latitude, then traverse the mountain summits parallel to the coast as far as 141° west longitude. From there it would conform with that meridian north to the Arctic Ocean. The boundary line along the mountain summits in southeastern Alaska was never to be farther inland than 10 leagues—about 30 miles.

After purchasing Alaska, the United States found that the wording about the boundary line was interpreted differently by the Canadians. They felt the measurements should be made inland from the mouths of bays, while Americans argued the measurements should be made from the heads of the bays. In 1903, however, an international tribunal upheld the American interpretation of the treaty, providing Alaska the 1,538-mile-long border it has with Canada today. The southeastern Alaska border is 891 miles long, and 181 miles of that border is over water. If the Canadians had won their argument they would have had access to the sea, and Haines, Dyea and Skagway now would be in Canada.

The 20-foot-wide vista—a swath of land cleared 10 feet on each side of the boundary between southeastern Alaska, British Columbia and Yukon Territory—was surveyed and cleared between 1904 and 1914. Portions of the 710-mile-long boundary were again cleared in 1925, 1948, 1978 and 1982 by the International Boundary Commission. Monument and vista maintenance of 1978 and 1982 was conducted by the Canadian section of the commission and by the

U.S. section in 1983, 1984 and 1985.

The Alaska–Canada border along the 141st meridian was surveyed and cleared between 1904 and 1920. Astronomical observations were made to find the meridian's intersection with the Yukon River; then, under the direction of the International Boundary Commission, engineers and surveyors of the U.S. Coast and Geodetic Survey and the Canadian Department of the Interior worked together north and south from the Yukon. The vista extends from Demarcation Point on the Arctic Ocean south to Mount St. Elias in the Wrangell Mountains (from there the border cuts east to encompass southeastern Alaska). This 647-mile stretch is one of the longest straight lines on record, varying less than 50 feet along its entire length.

Monuments are the actual markers of the boundary and are located so they tie in with survey networks of both the United States and Canada. Along the Alaska boundary most monuments are two-and-a-half-foot-high cones of aluminum-bronze set in concrete bases or occasionally cemented into rock. A large pair of concrete monuments with a pebbled finish mark major boundary road crossings. Because the boundary is not just a line but in fact a vertical plane dividing land and sky between the two nations, bronze plates mark tunnel and bridge crossings. Along the meridian, 191 monuments are placed, beginning 200 feet from the Arctic Ocean and ending at the south side of Logan Glacier.

Alaska Highway

(*See also* Highways)

This highway runs 1,520 miles through Canada and Alaska from Milepost 0 at Dawson Creek, British Columbia, through Yukon Territory to Fairbanks, Alaska. This well-traveled link between Alaska and the Lower 48 celebrated its 50th anniversary in 1992, with a year-long calendar of events and attractions. A special celebration, called Alaska Highway Rendezvous '92, hosted activities at local and international levels, including formal opening ceremonies at Dawson

Creek, British Columbia, and rededication of the highway in Soldiers Summit, Yukon Territory, on Nov. 20, 1992. Due in part to the publicity of these events, highway visitation in 1992 was up 20 percent over the previous year.

History

The highway was built to relieve Alaska from the wartime hazards of shipping and to supply a land route for wartime equipment.

By agreement between the governments of Canada and the United States, the highway was built in eight months by the U.S. Army Corps of Engineers and was dedicated in November 1942. Crews worked south from Delta Junction, Alaska, north and south from Whitehorse, Yukon Territory, and north from Dawson Creek, British Columbia.

The building of the highway was recognized as one of the greatest engineering feats of the 20th century. Two major sections of the highway were connected on Sept. 23, 1942, at Contact Creek, Milepost 588.1, where the 35th Engineer Combat Regiment working west from Fort Nelson met the 340th Engineer General Service Regiment working east from Whitehorse. The last link in the highway was completed on Nov. 20, 1942, when the 97th Engineer General Service Regiment, heading east from Tanacross, met the 18th Engineer Combat Regiment, coming northwest from Kluane Lake, at Milepost 1200.9. A ceremony commemorating the event was held at Soldiers Summit on Kluane Lake, and the first truck to negotiate the entire highway left that day from Soldiers Summit and arrived in Fairbanks the next day.

After World War II, the Alaska Highway was turned over to civilian contractors for widening and graveling, replacing log bridges with steel and rerouting at many points. Construction continues on the Alaska Highway today.

Road Conditions

The Alaska Highway is a two-lane road that winds and rolls across the wilderness. Some sections of road have no centerline, and some stretches of narrow road have little or no shoulder. The best driving advice on these sections is to take your time, drive with your headlights on at all times, keep to the right on hills and corners and drive defensively.

There are relatively few steep grades on the Alaska Highway. The most mountainous section of highway is between Fort Nelson and Watson Lake, where the highway crosses the Rocky Mountains.

Almost the entire length of the Alaska Highway is asphalt-surfaced, ranging from poor to excellent condition. Some rugged stretches exist with many chuckholes, gravel breaks, hardtop with loose gravel, deteriorated shoulders and bumps.

On the Alaska portion of the highway, watch for frost heaves. This rippling effect in the pavement is caused by the alternate freezing and thawing of the ground. Drive slowly in sections of frost heaves to avoid breaking an axle or trailer hitch.

Travelers should keep in mind that road conditions are subject to change. Be alert for bumps and holes in the road; some are signed or flagged, but many are not.

Watch for construction crews along the Alaska Highway. Extensive road construction may require a detour, or travelers may be delayed while waiting for a pilot car to guide them through the construction. Motorists may also encounter some muddy roadways at construction areas if there were heavy rains while the roadbed was torn up.

Dust and mud are generally not a problem anymore, except in construction areas and on a few stretches of the highway.

Don't drive too fast on gravel. Gravel acts just like many little ball bearings, and you could lose control of your vehicle. Driving fast on gravel is also hard on your tires, raises dust and throws rocks at oncoming cars. Heavy rain on a gravel road generally means mud. Considerable clay in the road surface means it can be very slippery when wet.

Gas, food and lodging are found along the Alaska Highway on an average of every 20 to 50 miles. The longest stretch without services is about 100 miles. Not all businesses are open year-round, nor are most services available

24 hours a day. Regular, unleaded and diesel gasoline, and propane fuel are available along the highway. Both government campgrounds and commercial campgrounds are located along the Alaska Highway.

Preparation for Driving the Alaska Highway

Make sure your vehicle and tires are in good condition before starting out. An inexpensive and widely available item to include is clear plastic headlight covers to protect your headlights from flying rocks and gravel.

You might also consider a wire-mesh screen across the front of your vehicle to protect paint, grill and radiator from flying rocks. These may be purchased ready-made, or you may manufacture your own.

For those hauling trailers, a piece of $1/4$-inch plywood fitted over the front of your trailer offers protection from rocks and gravel.

You'll find well-stocked auto shops in the North, but may wish to carry the following for emergencies: flares; first-aid kit; trailer bearings; good bumper jack with lug wrench; a simple set of tools, such as crescent wrenches, socket and/or open-end wrenches, hammer, screwdrivers, pliers, wire, pry bar; electrician's tape; small assortment of nuts and bolts; fan belt; one or two spare tires (two spares for traveling any remote road); and any parts for your vehicle that might not be available along the way. Include an extra few gallons of gas and also water, especially for remote roads. You may also wish to carry a can of fluid for brakes, power steering and automatic transmissions. You do not, however, want to overload your vehicle with too many spare parts.

Along the Alaska Highway, dust is at its worst during dry spells, following heavy rain (which disturbs the road surface), and in construction areas. If you encounter much dust, check your air filter frequently. To help keep dust out of your vehicle, try to keep air pressure in the car by closing all windows and turning on the fan. Filtered heating and air-conditioning ducts in a vehicle bring in much less dust than open windows or vents. Mosquito netting placed over the heater/fresh air intake and flow-through ventilation will also help eliminate dust.

Related reading: *Along the Alaska Highway,* photography by Alissa Crandall, text by Gloria J. Maschmeyer. Stunning color photographs and engaging text reveal the people and landscape of this epic highway. *See* ALASKA NORTHWEST LIBRARY in the back of the book.

Alcoholic Beverages

The legal age for possession, purchase and consumption of alcoholic beverages is 21 in Alaska.

Any business that serves or distributes alcoholic beverages must be licensed by the state. The number of different types of licenses issued is limited by the population in a geographic area. Generally one license of each type may be issued for each 3,000 persons or fraction thereof. Licensed premises include bars, some restaurants and clubs. Packaged liquor, beer and wine are sold by licensed package stores. Recreational site licenses, caterer's permits and special events permits allow the holder of a permit or license to sell at special events, and allow nonprofit fraternal, civic or patriotic organizations to serve beer and wine at certain activities.

State law allows liquor outlets to operate from 8 A.M. to 5 A.M., but provides that local governments can impose tighter restrictions.

Local governments may also ban the sale of or otherwise restrict alcoholic beverages. Barrow, Bethel, Kotzebue, Huslia, Iliamna and Nondalton have banned the sale of alcoholic beverages. Communities that have banned possession and/or the sale and importation of alcoholic beverages (knowingly bringing, sending or transporting alcoholic beverages into the community) are:

Akiak	Atka
Alakanuk	Atmautluak
Allakaket	Birch Creek
Ambler	Brevig Mission
Anaktuvuk Pass	Buckland
Angoon	Chalkyitsik

15

Chefornak
Chevak
Deering
Diomede
Eek
ElimEmmonak
Gambell
Golovin
Goodnews Bay
Hooper Bay
Kaktovik
Kasigluk
Kiana
Kipnuk
Kivalina
Kobuk
Kokhanok
Kongiganak
Kotlik
Koyuk
Kwethluk
Kwigillingok
Lower Kalskag
Manokotak
Marshall
Mekoryuk
Minto
Mountain Village
Napakiak
Napaskiak
Newtok
Noatak

Noorvik
Nuiqsut
Nunapitchuk
Pilot Station
Platinum
Point Hope
Point Lay
Quinhagak
Russian Mission
St. Marys
St. Michael
Savoonga
Scammon Bay
Selawik
Shaktoolik
Sheldon Point
Shishmaref
Shungnak
Stebbins
Stevens Village
Tanacross
Tatitlek
Teller
Tetlin
Togiak
Toksook Bay
Tuluksak
Tuntutuliak
Tununak
Upper Kalskag
Wainwright
Wales

Alyeska

Pronounced Al-YES-ka, this Aleut word means "the great land" and was one of the original names of Alaska. Mount Alyeska, a 3,939-foot peak in the Chugach Mountains, is the site of the state's largest ski resort.

Amphibians

In Alaska, there are three species of salamander, two species of frog and one species of toad. In the salamander order, there are the rough-skinned newt, long-toed salamander and northwestern salamander. In the frog and toad order, there are the boreal toad, wood frog and spotted frog. The northern limit of each species may be the latitude at which the larvae fail to complete their development in one summer. While some species of sala-

mander can overwinter as larvae in temperate southeastern Alaska, the shallow ponds of central Alaska freeze solid during the winter. All but the wood frog, *Rana sylvatica*, which with its shortened larval period is found widespread throughout the state and north of the Brooks Range, are found primarily in southeastern Alaska.

Antiquities Laws

State and federal laws prohibit excavation or removal of historic and prehistoric cultural materials without a permit. Nearly all 50 states have historic preservation laws; Alaska's extends even to tidal lands, thereby making it illegal to pick up artifacts on the beach.

It sometimes is difficult to distinguish between historic sites and abandoned property. Old gold-mining towns and cabins, plus areas such as the Chilkoot and Iditarod trails, should always be considered historic sites or private property. Also, cabins that appear to be abandoned may in fact be seasonally used trapping cabins where the structure and possessions are vital to the owner.

Alaska law prohibits the disturbance of fossils, including prehistoric animals such as mammoths.

Archaeology

(*See also* Bering Land Bridge)

Alaska has a long and rich archaeological history. The first human migrants to North and South America some 20,000 to 12,000 years ago came first to Alaska, crossing over the now-submerged ice-age Bering Land Bridge that connected Siberia to Alaska.

The oldest archaeological materials that demonstrate human occupation of Alaska come from Trail Creeks Cave north of Nome, where a 15,000-year-old cracked bison leg bone and bone point were found. Better evidence can be found for human occupation from 11,000 years ago. Small hunting tools have been found throughout Alaska, except Prince William Sound, probably belonging to nomadic hunting and

Barrow

Arctic Circle

Selawik
Fort Yukon

Fairbanks

Anchorage

gathering peoples. The archaeological record becomes more complicated about 4,000 years ago, and reveals cultural patterns characteristic of Alaska Native groups at the time of contact with the white man.

There is still much to discover about Alaska's prehistory. Many archaeological sites are small, representing the camps of wandering hunters and gatherers; some sites, especially along the coast where rich natural resources allowed people to become more sedentary and established, are large and deep. Where permafrost occurs, preservation of even the most perishable organic materials offers a wealth of information on life in the past. While no exact count has been made, there are several thousand known archaeological sites in the state.

Archaeological excavations, or digs, are almost always confined to the summer months. The University of Alaska in both Fairbanks and Anchorage frequently sponsors digs, as do several state and federal agencies. Recent excavations have taken place near Unalaska, Tok, Kodiak, Fairbanks and on the Kenai Peninsula. Volunteers and visitors are frequently welcome, but check first with the anthropology departments at the University of Alaska for active sites and more information.

One of Alaska's archaeological treasures, "Blue Babe," a 36,000-year-old fully preserved Pleistocene bison, was discovered in 1979 in the permafrost near Fairbanks during a mining operation. "Blue Babe" is on display at the Alaska Museum in Fairbanks.

Arctic Circle

The Arctic Circle is the latitude at which the sun does not set for one day at summer solstice and does not rise for one day at winter solstice. The latitude, which varies slightly from year to year, is approximately 66°34´ north from the equator and circumscribes the northern frigid zone.

A solstice occurs when the sun is at its greatest distance from the celestial equator. On the day of summer solstice, June 20 or 21, the sun does not set at the Arctic Circle and because of refraction of sunlight, it appears not to set for four days. Farther north, at Barrow (the northernmost community in the United States), the sun does not set from May 10 to August 2.

At winter solstice, December 21 or 22, the sun does not rise for one day at the Arctic Circle. At Barrow, it does not rise for 67 days.

Arctic Winter Games

The Arctic Winter Games are a biennial event held in mid-March for northern athletes from Alaska, northern Alberta, Yukon Territory and Northwest Territories. The first games were held in 1970 in Yellowknife, Northwest Territories, and have since been held in Fairbanks and Whitehorse, Yukon Territory. The 1994 games will take place March 6–13, in Slane Lake, Alberta. Alaska will host the games in 1996.

In 1992, 53 athletes from Russia and about 40 athletes from Greenland participated in the games. Speed skating and a speed skating-skiing-snowshoeing triathlon were dropped from the games, and dog mushing and Arctic (Dene and Inuit) Sports Games were added. Other competition includes badminton, cross-country skiing, curling, figure skating, basketball, broomball, gymnastics, silhouette shooting, ski biathlon, snowshoeing and volleyball. Participation by people of all ages is encouraged.

Aurora Borealis

The Phenomenon

The aurora borealis is produced by charged electrons and protons striking gas particles in the earth's upper atmosphere. The electrons and protons are released through sunspot activity on the sun and emanate into space. A few drift the one- to two-day course to Earth, where they are pulled to the most northern and southern latitudes by the planet's magnetic forces.

The color of the aurora borealis varies, depending on how hard the gas particles are being struck. Auroras can range from simple arcs to draperylike forms in green, red, blue and purple. The lights occur in a pattern rather than as a solid glow, because electric current sheets flowing through gases create V-shaped potential double layers. Electrons near the center of the current sheet move faster, hit the atmosphere harder and cause the different intensities of light observed in the aurora.

Displays take place as low as 40 miles above the Earth's surface, but usually begin about 68 miles above and extend hundreds of miles into space. They concentrate in two bands roughly centered above the Arctic Circle and Antarctic Circle (the latter known as aurora australis) that are about 2,500 miles in diameter. In northern latitudes the greatest occurrence of auroral displays is in the spring and fall months, owing to the tilt of the planet in relationship to the sun's plane, but displays may occur on dark nights throughout the winter. If sunspot activity is particularly intense and the denser-than-usual solar wind heads to Earth, the resulting auroras can be so great that they cover all but the tropical latitudes. However, the cycle of sunspot activity is such that it will be many years before the numerous, brilliant displays of the late 1950s are regularly seen again.

Some observers claim that the northern lights make a noise similar to the rustle of taffeta, but scientists say the displays cannot be heard in the audible frequency range.

Residents of Fairbanks, which is located on the 65th parallel, see the aurora borealis an average of 240 nights a year.

Photographing the Aurora Borealis

To capture the northern lights on film, you will need a 35mm camera that has both adjustable f-stop and shutter speed, a sturdy tripod, a locking-type cable release (some 35mm cameras have both *time* and *bulb* settings, but most have *bulb only,* which calls for use of the locking-type cable release) and a camera with an f/3.5 lens (or faster).

It is best to photograph the lights on a night when they are not moving too rapidly. And, as a general rule, photos improve if you manage to include recognizable subjects in the foreground—trees and lighted cabins being favorites of many photographers. Set your

f-stop	ASA 200	ASA 400
f1.2	3 sec.	2 sec.
f1.4	5	3
f1.8	7	4
f2	20	10
f2.8	40	20
f3.5	60	30

camera up at least 75 feet back from the foreground objects to make sure that both the foreground and aurora are in sharp focus.

Normal and wide-angle lenses are best. Try to keep your exposures under a minute—a 10- to 30-second exposure is generally best. The lens openings and exposure times are only a starting point, since the amount of light generated by the aurora is inconsistent. (For best results, bracket widely.)

Ektachrome 200 and 400 color film can be push-processed in the home darkroom or by most custom-color labs, allowing use of higher ASA ratings (800, 1200 or even 1600 on the 400 ASA film, for example). Kodak will push-process film if you include an ESP-1 envelope with your standard film-processing mailer. (Consult your local camera store for details.)

A few notes of caution: Protect the camera from low temperatures until you are ready to make your exposures. Some newer cameras, in particular, have electrically controlled shutters that will not function properly at low temperatures. Wind the film slowly to reduce the possibility of static electricity, which can lead to streaks on the film. Grounding the camera when rewinding can help prevent the static-electricity problem. (To ground the camera, hold it against a water pipe, drain pipe, metal fence post or other grounded object.) Follow the basic rules and experiment with exposures.

The first photographs to show the aurora borealis in its entirety were published in early 1982. These historic photographs were taken from satellite-mounted cameras specially adapted to filter unwanted light from the sunlit portion of the earth, which is a million times brighter than the aurora. From space, the aurora has the appearance of a nearly perfect circle.

Baleen

(See also Baskets and Whales and Whaling)

Baleen lines the mouths of baleen whales in long, fringed, bonelike strips. It strains out small fish and plankton, and the tiny, shrimplike creatures called krill from the water. Humpback whales are the largest of the baleen whales, having a coarse baleen similar in thickness to human fingernails. The inside edges of the baleen plates end in coarse bristles that are similar in appearance to matted goat hair. The color of the plates varies from gray to almost black and the bristles from white to grayish white. The number of plates in an adult humpback mouth varies from 600 to 800 (300 to 400 per side); the roof of the mouth is empty of plates. The bowhead whale has 600 plates, the longest of any whale species—some reach 12 feet or more in length. The sei whale has finely textured baleen, and the minkes are the smallest of the baleen whales. Other baleen whales are the right, blue, fin and gray. Baleen was once used for corset stays and buggy whips. It is no longer of significant commercial use, although Alaska Natives use brownish black bowhead baleen to make fine baskets and model ships to sell.

Barabara

Pronounced buh-rah-buh-ruh, this traditional Aleut or Eskimo shelter is built of sod supported by driftwood or whalebone.

Baseball

There are six teams playing baseball in Alaska, making up two leagues. The Alaska Baseball League consists of the Fairbanks Goldpanners, Anchorage Bucs and Hawaiian Island Movers. The Alaska Central Baseball League includes the Anchorage Glacier Pilots, Mat–Su Miners and Kenai Peninsula Oilers.

Baseball season opens in June and runs through the end of July. Each team plays a round-robin schedule with the other Alaska teams, in addition to scheduling games with visiting Lower 48 teams. In 1992, the Anchorage Bucs won their fourth Hawaiian International Tournament. Competition was tough and included teams from Seoul, Korea, and Tokyo, Japan.

The caliber of play in Alaska is some of the best nationwide at the amateur level. Since 1968, Alaska teams have won 10 National Baseball Congress championships, and are a great draw when they travel outside the state. Major league scouts rate Alaska baseball at A to AA, visiting each season to check out the talent for possible recruitment.

Alaska league teams are comprised primarily of college players, including both walk-on and recruited players. Since 1969, Alaska baseball has sent more than 150 players on to careers in major league baseball. However, any college senior drafted by a major league team cannot play in the Alaska league.

The list of those now playing in the major leagues who were once in Alaskan teams is impressive, and includes such stars as Tom Seaver, Chris Chambliss and Dave Winfield. In 1992, Bobby Jones, one of the Anchorage Bucs 1990 season pitchers, was drafted by the New York Mets.

Baskets

(*See also* Baleen *and* Native Arts and Crafts)

Native basketry varies greatly according to materials locally available. Athabascan Indians of the Interior, for example, weave baskets from willow root gathered in late spring. The roots are steamed and roasted over a fire to loosen the outer bark. Weavers then separate the bark into fine strips by pulling the roots through their teeth.

Eskimo grass baskets are made in river delta areas of southwestern Alaska from Bristol Bay north to Norton Sound and from Nunivak Island east to interior Eskimo river villages. The weavers use very fine grass harvested in fall. A coil basketry technique is followed, using coils from ⅛- to ¾-inch wide. Seal gut, traditionally dyed with berries (today with commer-

cial dyes), is often interwoven into the baskets.

Baleen, a glossy, hard material that hangs in slats from the upper jaw of some types of whales, is also used for baskets. Baleen basketry originated about 1905 when Charles D. Brower, trader for a whaling company at Point Barrow, suggested, after the decline of the whalebone (baleen) industry for women's corsets, that local Eskimos make the baskets as a source of income. The baskets were not produced in any number until 1916. The weave and shape of the baskets were copied from the split-willow Athabascan baskets acquired in trade. Men, rather than women, became the basket makers. Later, baleen baskets were also made in Point Hope and Wainwright.

Most birch-bark baskets are made by Athabascan Indians, although a few Eskimos also produce them. Commonly, they are shaped as simple cylinders and are held together with root bindings. Sometimes the birch bark is cut into thin strips and woven into diamond or checkerboard patterns. Birch bark is usually collected in spring and early summer; large pieces free of knots are preferred. Birch-bark baskets traditionally were used as cooking vessels; food was placed in them and hot stones added. Birch-bark baby carriers also are still made.

Among the finest of Alaskan baskets are the tiny, intricately woven Aleut baskets made of rye grass, which in the Aleutians is abundant, pliable and very tough. The three main styles of Aleut baskets—Attu, Atka and Unalaska—are named after the islands where the styles originated. Although the small baskets are the best known, Aleuts also traditionally made large, coarsely woven baskets for utilitarian purposes.

Tlingit, Haida and Tsimshian Indians make baskets of spruce roots and cedar bark. South of Frederick Sound, basket material usually consists of strands split from the inner bark of red cedar. To the north of the sound, spruce roots are used. Maidenhair ferns are sometimes interwoven into spruce root baskets in a technique that looks like embroidery. A large spruce root basket may take months to complete.

Examples of Alaska Native basketry may be viewed in many museums within the state, including the University of Alaska Museum, Fairbanks; the Anchorage Museum of History and Art, Anchorage; the Sheldon Jackson Museum, Sitka; and the Alaska State Museum, Juneau.

Prices for Native baskets vary greatly. A fine-weave, coiled beach grass basket may cost from $60 to $450; birch-bark baskets, which look like trays, may range from $30 to $100; willow root trays may cost $800; finely woven Aleut baskets may cost $200 to $600; cedar-bark baskets may range from $30 to $80; and baleen baskets range in price from $450 to more than $1,100 for medium-sized baskets. These prices are approximate and are based on the weave, material used, size, and decoration added, such as beadwork or ivory.

Beadwork

(*See also* Native Arts and Crafts)

Eskimo and Indian women create a variety of handsomely beaded items. Before contact with Europeans, Indian women sometimes carved beads of willow wood or made them from seeds of certain shrubs and trees. Glass seed beads became available to Alaskan Athabascan Indians in the mid-19th century, although some types of larger trade beads were in use earlier. Beads quickly became a coveted trade item. The *Cornaline d'aleppo,* an opaque red bead with a white center, and the faceted Russian blue beads were among the most popular types.

The introduction of small glass beads sparked changes in beadwork style and design. More colors were available, and the smaller, more easily maneuvered beads made it possible to work out delicate floral patterns impossible with larger trade beads.

Historically, beads were sewn directly onto leather garments or other items with the overlay stitch. Contemporary beadwork is often done on a separate piece of felt that is not visible once the beads are stitched in place.

Alaskan Athabascan beadworkers sometimes use paper patterns, often combining several motifs and tracing their outline on the surface to be worked. The most common designs include flowers, leaves and berries, some in very stylized form. Many patterns are drawn simply from the sewer's environment. Recently, magazines, graphic art, advertising and patriotic motifs have inspired Athabascan beadworkers, although stylized floral designs are still the most popular.

Designs vary regionally, as do the ways in which they are applied to garments or footgear. Women from some areas do beadwork so distinctive it can be recognized at a glance.

Bears

(*See also* Mammals)

Three species of bear inhabit Alaska: the black, the brown/grizzly and the polar bear. Most of Alaska can be considered bear country, and for those wishing to spend time in Alaska's great outdoors, bear country becomes "beware" country. It's good to remember that sows are extremely aggressive if their young are around and bear behavior should always be considered unpredictable. The Alaska Department of Fish and Game publishes *The Bears and You,* recommended reading for hikers and campers. The pamphlet is available from Fish and Game offices and government information centers.

Black Bears. Black bears are usually jet black or brown with a brown-yellow muzzle, and weigh from 100 to 200 pounds as adults. The brown color phase can sometimes be confused with grizzlies, but black bears are generally smaller and lack the grizzly's distinct shoulder hump. Black bear habitat covers three-fourths of Alaska, with high concentrations found in Southeast, Prince William Sound, and the coastal mountains and lowlands of southcentral Alaska. Low to moderate densities are found in interior and western Alaska. Their range coincides with that of semi-open forests, and though omnivorous, their diet consists mainly of vegetation due to the difficulty of getting meat or fish. Black bears often spend their lives within five miles of their birthplace and will frequently return to their home range if transplanted. They easily climb trees, with both cubs and adults using trees as a place of escape. Cubs are generally born in late January or February weighing 8 to 10 ounces, and while average litter size is two cubs, three or four is not unusual. Black bears den up in winter for up to six months, but are not true hibernators. Their body temperature remains high, and they awaken easily—even in midwinter.

Brown/Grizzly Bears. Fur colors of brown/grizzly bears vary from blond to black with shades of brown and gray in between. As adults, they can weigh over 1,000 pounds, but are usually smaller; size depends on sex, age, time of year and geographic location. Coastal bears, referred to as "browns" or "brownies," are the largest living omnivorous land mammals in the world and grow larger than Interior "grizzlies." Browns or grizzlies are found in most of Alaska, with the exception of islands in the extreme southeastern part of the state. The lowest populations are found in the northern Interior and the Arctic. Their range is wherever food is abundant, but they prefer open tundra and grass-lands. Diet consists of a wide variety of plants and animals, including their own kind, and humans under some circumstances. In their realm, grizzlies are king and fear no other animal except man with a firearm. While attacks on humans are the exception, when they occur the results are tragic. These bears are also tremendously strong and have been seen carrying—off the ground—an 800-pound moose. One to two hairless cubs are usually born in late January or February weighing 8 to 10 ounces, and sows have been known to adopt orphaned cubs. Time of year and duration of denning varies with the location and physical condition of the bear, and can be up to six months of the year. Dens are frequently on hillsides or on mountain slopes.

Polar Bears. The only areas on a polar bear not covered with heavy, white fur are its eyes and large, black nose. The bears, seemingly aware that their noses give them away to prey, will hold a paw up to hide it when hunting. An adult polar bear weighs 1,500 pounds or more and has a long neck with a proportionately small head. Their habitat is the Canadian–eastern Alaska Arctic and the western Alaska–eastern Soviet Union, the latter being home to the world's largest polar bears. Their range is the arctic ice cap, and they are more numerous toward the southern edge of the ice pack. Occasionally they will come ashore, but generally stay near the coast. While ashore they eat some vegetation, but their diet consists primarily of ringed seal, walrus, stranded whales, birds and fish. Cannibalism of cubs and young bears by older males is not unusual. Polar bears are natural swimmers, and reports exist of swimming bears seen 50 miles from the nearest land or ice. When swimming, they use their front paws for propulsion and trail their rear paws. Mother bears have been seen with a cub hanging onto their tail getting a tow through the water. Cubs are born in December with two being the common litter size. They weigh about a pound at birth and remain with their mother for about 28 months. Usually only pregnant sows den up, for an average of six months in the winter. Polar bears need stable, cold areas for denning, and dens in Alaska have been found 30 miles inland, along the coast, on offshore islands, on shorefast ice and on drifting sea ice.

Related reading: *The Great Bear: Contemporary Writings on the Grizzly*, edited by John A. Murray. *More Alaska Bear Tales*, by Larry Kaniut. *Grizzly Cub: Five Years in the Life of a Bear*, by Rick McIntyre. *See* ALASKA NORTHWEST LIBRARY in the back of the book.

Bering Land Bridge

The Bering Land Bridge, which joined eastern Siberia and western Alaska, is thought by most archaeologists to be the route by which the New World came to be occupied between 40,000 and 15,000 years ago. The land bridge rose as the formation of massive glaciers during the ice ages caused the sea levels to fall, creating an arctic grassland up to 900 miles wide called Beringia. Early migrants crossed Beringia in pursuit of prey such as the woolly mammoth and mastodon. While the two continents were connected, plants, animals and man migrated into Alaska, and probably down ice-free corridors to populate other parts of the western hemisphere. Even after the glaciers melted and the sea level rose, many of the indigenous peoples on both sides of the Bering Strait remained united by family ties, common traditions and common environments, and into this century used skin boats to cross the 55 miles of ocean separating the two continents.

Recognizing the need to preserve the unique archaeological record, both discovered and undiscovered, that the area holds, the National Park Service created Bering Land Bridge National Preserve. Located just below the Arctic Circle on the Seward Peninsula, the 2.8-million-acre preserve features ecological, geological, anthropological and historical processes rather than places. The low profile of the preserve's landscape gives a sense of unobstructed vastness and exposure to the elements.

Russia also plans to establish a park or preserve on the Chukotka Peninsula west of the Bering Strait. At the June 1990 summit conference, Presidents Gorbachev and Bush endorsed a Beringian Heritage International Park, leading the way for joint research, conservation and management of the region's unique resources.

Berries

Wild berries abound in Alaska with the circumboreal lingonberry/lowbush cranberry (*Vaccinium vitis-idaea*) being the most widespread. Blueberries of one species or another grow in most of the state. Some 50 other species of wild fruit are found in Alaska, including strawberries, raspberries, cloudberries, salmonberries, crowberries, nagoonberries and crabapples. Highbush cranberries (which are not really cranberries) can be found on bushes even in the dead of winter, and the frozen berries provide a refreshing treat to the hiker.

Lingonberry/Lowbush Cranberry, *Vaccinium vitis-idaea* (Reprinted from *Alaska Wild Berry Guide and Cookbook*)

The fruit of the wild rose, or rose hip, is not strictly a berry but is an ideal source of vitamin C for bush dweller and city resident alike. A few hips will provide as much of the vitamin as a medium-sized orange. The farther north the hips are found, the richer they are in vitamin C.

Alaska does have one poisonous berry, the baneberry. Sometimes called doll's eyes or chinaberries, baneberries are extremely bitter to the taste. As few as six berries can induce violent symptoms of poisoning in an adult.

Related reading: *Alaska Wild Berry Guide and Cookbook*. Where to find the berries, what they are, how to recognize them and the best recipes for cooking berries. *See* ALASKA NORTHWEST LIBRARY in the back of the book.

Billiken

This smiling ivory figure with a pointed head, though long a popular Northland souvenir, is not an Eskimo invention. The billiken was patented in 1908 by Florence Pretz of Kansas City. A small, seated, Buddhalike figure, the original billiken was manufactured by the Billiken Company of Chicago and sold as a good luck charm. Thousands of these figurines were sold during the 1909 Alaska-Yukon-Pacific Exposition in Seattle. Billikens vanished soon afterward from most Lower 48 shops; however, someone had brought them to Nome, and the Eskimos of King Island, Little Diomede and Wales began carving ivory replicas of the billikens.

Billikens are still being made elsewhere in the world in such materials as wood, concrete and glass.

A popular notion contends that rubbing a billiken's tummy brings good fortune.

Birds

Authorities at the Anchorage Audubon Society acknowledge 430 bird species in Alaska. If unsubstantiated sightings are included, the species total increases.

Thousands of ducks, geese and swans come north to breeding grounds each spring. Millions of seabirds congregate in nesting colonies on exposed cliffs along Alaska's coastline, particularly on the Aleutian Islands, and on islands in the Bering Sea.

Migratory birds reach Alaska from many corners of the world. Arctic terns travel up to 22,000 miles on their round trip each year from Antarctica. Others come from South America, the South Pacific islands and Asia.

Each May one of the world's largest concentrations of shorebirds funnels through the Copper River Delta near Cordova. Waterfowl such as trumpeter swans and the world's entire flock of dusky Canada geese breed there.

Other key waterfowl habitats include the Yukon–Kuskokwim Delta, Yukon Flats, Innoko Flats and Minto Lakes. During migration, huge flocks gather at Egegik, Port Heiden, Port Moller, Izembek Bay, Chickaloon Flats, Susitna Flats and Stikine Flats.

Raptors, led by the bald eagle, range throughout the state. The largest gathering of eagles in the world takes place in Alaska every winter between October and February. In 1972, the Chilkat Bald Eagle Preserve was set aside to protect the 3,500 eagles that assemble at the site along the Chilkat River near Haines.

Alaska has three subspecies of peregrine falcon: Arctic, American and Peale's. Arctic and American peregrine falcons join the Eskimo curlew, Aleutian Canada goose and short-tailed albatross on the endangered or threatened species list for the state. The Steller's eider and the spectacled eider are now being considered as additions to the endangered or threatened species list by the U.S. Fish and Wildlife Service.

Following is a list of some geographically restricted birds whose origins are in Siberia or Asia, as well as a few of the state's more well-known species:

Aleutian Tern—Breeds in coastal areas, marshes, islands, lagoons, rivers and inshore marine waters. Nests only in Alaska on ground in matted, dry grass. Casual sightings in southeastern Alaska in spring and summer, and in northern Alaska in summer.

Arctic Tern—Breeds in tidal flats, beaches, glacial moraines, rivers, lakes and marshes. Nests in colonies or scattered pairs on sand, gravel, moss or in rocks. The arctic tern winters in Antarctica, bypassing the Lower 48 in its 20,000-mile round-trip migration. Common sightings in southeastern, southcoastal and western Alaska in spring, summer and fall, and in southwestern Alaska in spring and fall.

Arctic Warbler—Found in willow thickets. Nests on the ground in grass or moss in willow thickets. Common sightings in the Alaska Range, the Seward Peninsula and the Brooks Range in spring, summer and fall.

Bald Eagle—Found in coniferous forests, deciduous woodlands, rivers and streams, beaches and tidal flats, rocky shores and reefs. Nests in old-growth timber along the coast and larger mainland rivers. In treeless areas, nests on cliffs or on the ground. There are more bald eagles in Alaska than in all the other states combined, and common sightings occur in southeastern, southcoastal and southwestern Alaska year-round.

Bluethroat—Nests on the ground in shrub thickets in the uplands and the foothills of western and northern Alaska. Casual sightings in south-western Alaska in spring and fall.

Emperor Goose—Nests near water in grassy marsh habitat on islands or banks or in large tussocks. The bulk of the world's population nests in the Yukon–Kuskokwim Delta, with a few others nesting farther north to Kotzebue Sound and a few more in eastern Siberia. Rarely is an emperor goose seen east or south of Kodiak. Common sightings in southwestern Alaska in spring, fall and winter, and in western Alaska in spring, summer and fall.

Horned Puffin—Nests on sea islands in rock crevices or in burrows among boulders, on sea cliffs and on grassy slopes. Breeds inshore, in marine waters and on islands. Common sightings in southwestern and western Alaska in spring, summer and fall.

Pacific Loon—Breeds in coniferous forests or in lakes on tundra, and nests on projecting points or small islands. Folklore credits the loon with magical powers, and several legends abound. Common sightings in southeastern and southcentral Alaska in spring, fall and winter, and in southwestern, central, western and northern Alaska in spring, summer and fall.

Red-faced Cormorant—Habitat includes inshore marine waters. Nests in colonies on ledges of sea cliffs, small piles of rocks and shelves on volcanic cinder cones. In North America this bird appears only in Alaska. Common sightings in southcoastal and southwestern Alaska year-round.

Red-legged Kittiwake—Breeds in the Pribilof Islands, and on Buldir and Bogoslof islands in the Aleutians. Nests on cliff ledges and cliff points. Common sightings near breeding areas in southwestern Alaska in summer.

White Wagtail—Found in open areas with short vegetation usually along the Seward Peninsula coast. Nests near or on the ground in crevices or niches in old buildings. Casual sightings in central Alaska in spring, and in southwestern Alaska in spring and summer.

Yellow Wagtail—Habitat is willow thickets on the tundra. Nests on open tundra under grass or overhanging banks. Common sightings in western Alaska in spring, summer and fall.

About 10 million swans, geese and

ducks also nest in Alaska each year, making the state "critical" habitat for North America's waterfowl. In North America some species and subspecies use Alaska as their exclusive nesting grounds, while over half the North American population of other species nests in the state.

Five chapters of the National Audubon Society are based in Alaska: the Anchorage Audubon Society, Inc. (P.O. Box 101161, Anchorage 99510), the Juneau Audubon Society (P.O. Box 021725, Juneau 99802), the Arctic Audubon Society (P.O. Box 82098, Fairbanks 99708), the Kenai Audubon Society (P.O. Box 3371, Soldotna 99669) and the Kodiak Audubon Society (Box 1756, Kodiak 99615). In addition to trying to help people increase their knowledge of birds, the groups (except for Fairbanks) coordinate over 20 annual Christmas bird counts around the state. The Fairbanks Bird Club (P.O. Box 81791, Fairbanks 99708) conducts the annual Christmas count for that area.

Related reading: *Guide to the Birds of Alaska*. Revised edition, by Robert H. Armstrong. Detailed information on all species of birds found in Alaska. *See* ALASKA NORTHWEST LIBRARY in the back of the book.

Blanket Toss

As effective as a trampoline, the blanket toss (or *nalukataq*) features a walrus hide blanket grasped by a

number of people in a circle. They toss a person on the blanket as high as possible for as long as that person can remain upright. Every true Eskimo festival and many non-Native occasions include the blanket toss, which was originally used to allow Eskimo hunters to spot game, such as walrus and seal, in the distance. Depending on the skill of the person being tossed and the number of tossers, a medium-weight person might typically go 20 feet in the air.

Boating

(*See also* Cruises *and* Ferries)

Travel by boat is an important means of transportation in Alaska, where highways cover only about one-third of the state. Until the advent of the airplane, boats were often the only way to reach many parts of Alaska. Most of Alaska's supplies still arrive by water and in Southeast—where precipitous terrain and numerous islands make road building impossible—water travel is essential.

According to the U.S. Coast Guard, there are 40,300 vessels registered in Alaska. Of these, 20,376 are between 16 and 26 feet, and 3,859 are between 26 and 40 feet.

Moorage

To accommodate the needs of this fleet, there are approximately 8,000 slips available at public small-boat harbors in Alaska. According to the state, actual service capacity is somewhat greater because of the transient nature of many boats and certain management practices allowing "double parking." There are also harbors at various remote locations; no services other than moorage are provided at these harbors.

Local governments have the major responsibility for operating public floats, grids, docks, launching ramps and associated small-boat harbor facilities throughout the coastal areas of the state. Moorage facilities constructed by the state are intended for boats up to a maximum of 100 feet, with a limited number of facilities for larger vessels where large boats are common. With the exception of Ketchikan, Sitka,

Homer and Juneau, there are no private marine facilities.

Recreational Boating

Recreational boating opportunities in Alaska are too numerous and varied to list here; Alaska has thousands of miles of lakes, rivers and sheltered seaways. For information about boating within national forests, parks, monuments, preserves and wildlife refuges, contact the appropriate federal agency. For travel by boat in southeastern Alaska's Inside Passage and the sheltered seaways of southcentral Alaska's Prince William Sound—or elsewhere in Alaska's coastal waters—NOAA nautical charts, pilot guides and tidal current tables are available. (*See* Information Sources)

Sea kayakers from around the world are drawn to Alaska to paddle its sheltered waterways and challenge its open coast. Kayakers in Alaska can visit tidewater glaciers and natural hot springs, meeting whales and sea otters along the way.

Inland boaters will find hundreds of river and lake systems suitable for traveling by boat, raft, kayak or canoe. Canoe routes have been established on the Kenai Peninsula (contact Kenai National Wildlife Refuge, P.O. Box 2139, Soldotna 99669); in Nancy Lake State Recreation Area (contact Superintendent, Mat–Su District, HC32, Box 6706, Wasilla 99687); and on rivers in the Fairbanks and Anchorage areas (contact Bureau of Land Management, 1150 University Ave., Fairbanks 99709 and 222 W. Seventh Ave., #13, Anchorage 99513).

Travel by water in Alaska requires extra caution. Weather changes rapidly and is often unpredictable; it's important to be prepared for the worst. Alaska waters, even in midsummer, are cold. A person falling overboard may become immobilized by the cold water in only a few minutes. And since many of Alaska's water routes are far from civilization, help may be a long way off.

Persons inexperienced in traveling Alaska's waterways might consider hiring a charter boat operator or outfitter. Guides offer local knowledge and provide all necessary equipment. The Division of Tourism (Pouch E, Juneau 99811) maintains current lists of such services. Recreation information on both state and federal lands is available at the three Alaska Public Lands Information Centers: 605 W. Fourth Ave., Suite 105, Anchorage 99501; 250 Cushman St., Suite 1A, Fairbanks 99701; and P.O. Box 359, Tok 99780.

Bore Tide

(*See also* Tides)

A bore tide is a steep, foaming wall of water formed by a flood tide surging into a constricted inlet. In Cook Inlet, where maximum tidal range approaches 40 feet, incoming tides are further compressed in Knik and Turnagain arms and tidal bores may sometimes be seen. Though 1- to 2-foot-high bores are more common, spring tides in Turnagain Arm may produce bore tides up to 6 feet high, running at speeds of up to 10 knots, and even higher bores have been reported when unusually high tides come in against a strong southeast wind. Good spots to view bore tides in Turnagain Arm are along the Seward Highway, between 26 and 37 miles south of Anchorage; they can be expected to arrive there approximately 2 hours and 15 minutes later than the tide book prediction for low tide at Anchorage.

Breakup

(*See also* Nenana Ice Classic)

Breakup occurs when melting snows raise the level of ice-covered streams and rivers sufficiently to cause the ice to break apart and float downstream. Breakup is one of two factors determining the open-water season for river navigation, the second being the depth of the river. Peak water conditions occur just after breakup.

The navigable season for the Kuskokwim and Yukon rivers is June 1 through September 30; the Nushagak River, June 1 through August 31; and the Noatak River, late May through mid-June.

Breakup is a spectacular sight-and-sound show. Massive pieces of ice crunch and pound against each other as they push their way downriver racing for the sea, creating noises not unlike many huge engines straining and grating. The spine-tingling sound can be heard for miles. It marks the finale of winter and the arrival of spring in Alaska.

Sometimes great ice jams occur, causing the water to back up and flood inhabited areas. This natural phenomenon occurred at Fort Yukon in spring 1982 and at McGrath in 1990.

Bunny Boots

Bunny boots, also called vapor barrier boots, are large, insulated rubber boots that protect feet from frostbite. Black bunny boots are generally rated to −20°F, while the more common white bunny boots are even warmer and used in the most extreme conditions, including the heights of Mount McKinley. (The cumbersome boots are adequate for easy climbing but unsuitable for technical mountain climbing.)

Prices for bunny boots range from about $50 for used boots to about $175 for new ones.

Bus Lines

Scheduled bus service is available in summer to and within Alaska, although buses don't run as frequently as in the Lower 48. (Local transit service is also available in some major communities.) Services may be infrequent; consult current schedules.

Alaska–Denali Transit, P.O. Box 4557, Anchorage 99510. Provides service between Anchorage, Talkeetna, Denali National Park and Preserve, Fairbanks, Tok, Haines, Kenai and Homer.

Alaska Intercity Tours, 700 W. Sixth Ave., Anchorage 99501. Provides service between Mount McKinley, Kenai Peninsula, Valdez and Fairbanks.

Alaska Sightseeing Tours, 543 W. Fourth Ave., Anchorage 99501. Provides service between Anchorage, Denali National Park and Preserve, Columbia Glacier, Fairbanks, Golden Circle, Haines and Valdez.

Alaska–Yukon Motorcoaches, 543 W. Fourth Ave., Anchorage 99501. Provides service between Anchorage, Haines/Skagway, Valdez, Fairbanks and Denali National Park and Preserve.

Alaskon Express, 300 Elliott Ave. W., Seattle, WA 98119. Provides service between Anchorage, Fairbanks, Haines, Skagway and Whitehorse.

Atlas Tours Ltd., P.O. Box 4340, Whitehorse, YT, Canada Y1A 3T5. Provides service between Whitehorse and Skagway.

Caribou Express Bus, 501 L St., Anchorage 99501. Provides service between Anchorage, Denali National Park and Preserve, Fairbanks, Tok Junction, Alyeska, Portage Glacier, Homer and Seward.

Denali Express, 405 L St., Anchorage 99501. Provides service between Anchorage, Denali and Fairbanks.

Eagle Custom Tours, 329 F St., Anchorage 99501. Provides service between Anchorage, Portage Glacier, the Matanuska Valley, Mount McKinley, Seward and Talkeetna.

Gray Line of Alaska, 745 W. Fourth Ave., Anchorage 99501. Provides local city sightseeing tours, travel between Anchorage, Fairbanks, Denali National Park, Dawson, Prudhoe Bay, Skagway and Whitehorse.

Norline Coaches (Yukon) Ltd., 2191 Second Ave., Whitehorse, YT, Canada Y1A 4T8. Provides service between Whitehorse and Tok via Dawson City and Fairbanks.

Princess Tours, 519 W. Fourth Ave., Anchorage 99501. Provides sightseeing excursions and tours throughout Alaska.

Seward Bus Lines, P.O. Box 1338, Seward 99664. Provides service between Anchorage and Seward.

Valdez/Anchorage Bus Lines, P.O. Box 101388, Anchorage 99510. Provides service between Valdez and Anchorage via Glennallen.

Westours Motorcoaches, 547 W. Fourth Ave., Anchorage 99501. Provides service throughout Alaska and the Yukon.

White Pass and Yukon Motorcoaches, 300 Elliott Ave. W., Seattle, WA 98119. Provides service between Skagway, Haines, Valdez, Glennallen, Whitehorse and Anchorage.

Bush

Originally used to describe large expanses of wilderness beyond the fringes of civilization, inhabited only by trappers and miners, "bush" has come to stand for any part of Alaska not accessible by road. A community accessible only by air, water, sled or snow machine is considered a bush village, and anyone living there is someone from the bush.

The bush is home to most of Alaska's Native people and to many individuals who live on homesteads, operate mines or work as guides, pilots, trappers or fishermen.

The term "bush" has been adapted to the small planes and their pilots who service areas lacking roads. Bush planes are commonly equipped with floats and skis to match terrain and season. For their oftentimes courageous air service, bush pilots have become the modern frontier hero.

Related reading: *Skystruck: True Tales of an Alaskan Bush Pilot,* by Herman

Lerdahl with Cliff Cernick. *See* ALASKA NORTHWEST LIBRARY in the back of the book.

Cabin Fever

Cabin fever is a state of mind blamed on cold, dark winter weather when people are often housebound. It is characterized by depression, preoccupation, discontent and occasionally violence and has been described as "a 12-foot stare in a 10-foot room." Cabin fever is commonly thought to afflict miners and trappers spending a lonely winter in the wilderness, but, in truth, these people are active and outdoors enough to remain content. It is more likely to strike the snowbound or disabled. The arrival of spring or a change of scene usually relieves the symptoms.

Related reading: *Winter Watch,* by James Ramsey. For 266 days, the author tested himself against an Arctic winter in a remote cabin in the Brooks Range. *See* ALASKA NORTHWEST LIBRARY in the back of the book.

Cabins

(*See also* National Forests *and* State Park System)

Rustic cabins in remote Alaskan places can be rented from the Forest Service, the Bureau of Land Management (BLM), the Alaska State Parks and the U.S. Fish and Wildlife Service. The modest price ($20 to $25 per night per cabin) makes this one of the best vacation bargains in Alaska. Visitors should prepare for rigorous backcountry travel and be ready to provide emergency shelter should they be unable to reach their cabin for any reason.

Almost 200 Forest Service cabins are scattered through the Tongass and Chugach national forests in southeast and southcentral Alaska. Some are located on salt water; others on freshwater rivers, streams or lakes. Some of the cabins can be reached by boat or trail, but because of the remote locations, visitors frequently come by chartered aircraft.

The average cabin is 12 by 14 feet and is usually equipped with a table, an oil or wood stove and wooden bunks without mattresses. Most will accommodate a group of four to six. There is no electricity. Outhouses are down the trail a little way. Visitors need to bring their own food, bedding, cooking utensils and stove fuel. In addition, it's advisable to have a gas or propane stove for cooking, a lantern and insect repellent. Splitting mauls are provided on site for cutting firewood. Since firewood is scarce and often wet, visitors should carry a supply of dry wood.

Reservations may be made in person or by mail. Payment must accompany the reservation. Permits for use are issued on a first-come, first-served basis, up to 179 days in advance. Length of stay for some cabins is limited.

For reservations and information on **Chugach National Forest** cabins, contact: Alaska Public Lands Information Center (APLIC), 605 W. Fourth Ave., Anchorage 99501; phone (907) 271-2737.

For reservations and information on **Tongass National Forest** cabins, contact: USDA Forest Service Information Center, 101 Egan Drive, Juneau 99801.

The **Forest Service** recommends that visitors contact the Information Center and request a copy of the Recreation Cabins booklet. It's a good idea to do this at least six months before the date of desired occupancy. The booklet contains the applications for cabin use plus tips on planning a stay.

The **Bureau of Land Management** has eight public-use cabins in the White Mountains National Recreation area east of Fairbanks. These are used primarily by winter recreationists.

Cabins must be reserved prior to use and a fee is required. Contact the Fairbanks Support Center Public Room, 1150 University Ave., Fairbanks 99709-3844, phone (907) 474-2350.

The **U.S. Fish and Wildlife Service** maintains public-use cabins within Kodiak National Wildlife Refuge. Contact the Refuge Manager, 1390 Buskin River Road, Kodiak 99615.

The **Alaska Division of Parks and Outdoor Recreation** maintains 21 public-use cabins throughout the state. For reservations and information contact the following regional offices: *Southcentral,* P.O. Box 107005, Anchorage 99510-7005, phone (907) 762-2617; *Southeast,* 400 Willoughby Ave., Juneau 99801, phone (907) 465-4563; *Northern Region,* 3700 Airport Way, Fairbanks 99709, phone (907) 451-2695; and *Kodiak State Park,* SR Box 3800, Kodiak 99615, phone (907) 486-6339.

Cache

Pronounced *cash,* this small storage unit is built to be inaccessible to marauding animals. A cache resembles a miniature log cabin mounted on stilts. It is reached by a ladder that bears, dogs, foxes and other hungry or curious animals can't climb. Extra precautions include wrapping tin around the poles to prevent climbing by clawed animals and extending the floor a few feet in all directions from the top of the poles to discourage those clever enough to get that high.

Squirrels are the most notorious of Alaska's cache-marauding critters. To be truly animal-proof, a cache should be built in a clearing well beyond the 30-foot leaping distance a squirrel can manage from a treetop.

Bush residents use the cache as a primitive food freezer in winter. A cache may also contain extra fuel and bedding. Size is determined by need. Sometimes a cache will be built between three or four straight trees growing close together.

Calendar of Events

JANUARY

Anchorage—Nastar Ski Races, Alyeska Ski Resort; Sled Dog Races; Hatcher Cup Series, Hatcher Pass Lodge; Torchlight Ski Parade; All Alaska Juried Art Show. *Anchor Point*—Snow Rondi Fest. *Bethel*—Sled Dog Races. *Fairbanks*—Ski Joring and Sled Dog Races. *Glennallen*—Copper Basin 300 Sled Dog Race. *Haines*—Snow Machine Rally; Dalton Trail 30 Sled Dog Race. *Homer*—Snow Machine Races. *Juneau*—Rainier Downhill Challenge Cup; Alascom Ski Challenge; State legislature convenes. *Kodiak*—Russian Orthodox Starring Ceremony; Russian Orthodox Masquerade Ball. *Seward*—Polar Bear Jump-off. *Sitka*—Russian Christmas and Starring; Alaska Airlines Basketball Tournament. *Soldotna*—Winter Games; Sled Dog Races. *Willow*—Winter Carnival.

FEBRUARY

Anchorage—Fur Rendezvous; Iron Dog Iditarod; Sled Dog Races; Northern Lights Women's Invitational; Ice Carving Competition; World Masters Cross Country Ski Championships. *Big Lake*—Winter Carnival. *Cordova*—Iceworm Festival. *Fairbanks*—Ski Joring and Sled Dog Races; Festival of Native Arts; Yukon Quest Sled Dog Race. *Homer*—Winter Carnival. *Juneau*—Taku Rendezvous; Alascom Divisional Championships. *Ketchikan*—Festival of the North. *Knik*—Iditabike; Iditaski Nordic Ski Race. *Nenana*—Ice Classic Tripod Raising Festival; Tour de Minto Sled Dog Race. *Nome*—Dexter Creek Sled Dog Race; Heart Throb Biathlon; Gold Rush Classic Snow Machine Race. *Palmer*—Sled Dog Races. *Petersburg*—Devil's Thumb Days Festival. *Sitka*—Basketball Tournament. *Soldotna*—Winter Games; Ski Joring; Sled Dog Races. *Tok*—Sled Dog Races. *Valdez*—Winter Carnival; Ice Climbing Festival. *Wasilla*—Iditarod Days. *Whitehorse*—Sourdough Rendezvous; Yukon Quest Sled Dog Race. *Wrangell*—Tent City Days.

MARCH

Anchorage—Iditarod Sled Dog Race begins; International Ice Carving Competition; Native Youth Olympics. *Chatanika*—Chatanika Days. *Dillingham*—Beaver Round Up. *Fairbanks*—Arctic Winter Games; Festival of Native Arts; Winter Carnival; Ice Festival; Sled Dog Races; Athabascan Old-Time Fiddling Festival. *Juneau*—Sourdough Pro/Am Ski Race; Southeast Championships; Rainier Downhill Challenge Cup. *Kodiak*—Pillar Mountain Golf Classic; Comfish Alaska. *Nome*—Ice Golf Classic on the Bering Sea; Month of Iditarod; Sled Dog Races; Snow Machine Race; Dog Weight Pull; Basketball Tournament. *North Pole*—Winter Carnival. *Skagway*—Windfest Winter Festival; Buckwheat Ski Classic. *Tok*—Race of Champions Sled Dog Race. *Valdez*—Winter Carnival. *Wasilla*—Iditarod Days.

APRIL

Anchorage—Alyeska Spring Carnival; Native Youth Olympics. *Barrow*—Spring Festival. *Cordova*—Copper Day Celebrations. *Fairbanks*—Curling Bonspiel. *Haines*—Alaska State Community Theater Festival. *Juneau*—Folk Festival; Ski to Sea Race. *Kotzebue*—Arctic Circle Sunshine Festival.

Unalaska—Tanner Crab Roundup Festival. *Valdez*—World Extreme Ski Championships. *Whittier*—Crab Festival.

MAY

Anchor Point—Anchor River King Salmon Derby. *Delta Junction*—Buffalo Wallow Square Dance Jamboree. *Homer*—Center for Alaska Coastal Studies Beach Walk; Halibut Derby. *Juneau*—Jazz and Classics Festival; Ski to Sea Relay Race. *Kodiak*—Crab Festival and Fishing Derby; Chad Ogden Ultramarathon. *Nome*—Annual Polar Bear Swim in the Bering Sea; Firemen's Ball. *Palmer*—Colony Days. *Petersburg*—Little Norway Festival; Salmon Derby. *Savoonga*—Walrus Festival, St. Lawrence Island. *Seldovia*—Fishing Derby. *Seward*—Exit Glacier Run. *Sitka*—Salmon Derby. *Talkeetna*—Miners' Day Festival. *Valdez*—Salmon Derby; Prince William Sound Regatta of Ships.

JUNE

Anchorage—Alaska Women's Run; Renaissance Faire; Tent City Festival; Mayor's Midnight Sun Marathon; Basically Bach Festival; Festival of Music. *Barrow*—Nalukataq Whaling Festival. *Fairbanks*—Tanana River Raft Classic; Yukon 800 Marathon River Boat Race; Midnight Sun Run; Midnight Sun Baseball Game; Air Show. *Homer*—Halibut Derby. *Kodiak*—Freedom Days. *Nenana*—River Daze. *Nome*—Midnight Sun Softball Tournament, Festival and Raft Race; ARCO–Jesse Owens Games. *Palmer*—Colony Days. *Sitka*—Salmon Derby; All Alaska Logging Championships; Writer's Symposium; Summer Music Festival. *Skagway*—Summer Solstice. *Valdez*—Halibut Derby; Whitewater Weekend. *Whitehorse*—Dog Show.

JULY

Fourth of July celebrations take place in most towns and villages. *Anchorage*—Freedom Days Festival; Tent City Festival; Bluegrass and Folk Festival. *Big Lake*—Regatta Water Festival; Fishing Derby. *Chugiak*—Bear Paw Festival. *Dawson City*—Yukon Gold Panning Championship. *Delta Junction*—Softball Tournament. *Fairbanks*—World Eskimo-Indian Olympics; Renaissance Faire; Golden Days; Summer Arts Festival. *Homer*—Halibut Derby. *Hope*—EMS 5-K Run and Crafts Bazaar. *Kodiak*—Freedom Days. *Kotzebue*—Northwest Native Trade Fair. *Nome*—Anvil Mountain Run. *North Pole*—Summer Festival. *Seward*—Mount Marathon Race; Softball Tournaments; Halibut Tournament; Silver Salmon Derby. *Sitka*—Fourth of July Celebration (four days). *Skagway*—Soapy Smith's Wake. *Soldotna*—Progress Days. *Talkeetna*—Salmon Derby; Moose Dropping Festival. *Valdez*—Silver Salmon Derby; Gold Rush Days. *Wasilla*—Water Festival. *Wrangell*—Logging Show.

AUGUST

Anchorage—Air Show. *Anchor Point*—Salmon Derby. *Copper Valley*—Kenny Lake Fair. *Cordova*—Silver Salmon Derby. *Dawson City*—Discovery Days. *Dillingham*—Silver Salmon Derby. *Eagle River*—Alaskan Scottish Highland Games. *Fairbanks*—Tanana Valley Fair; Iditafoot Race; Summer Arts Festival. *Haines*—Bald Eagle Music Festival; Southeast Alaska State Fair. *Juneau*—Golden North Salmon Derby. *Ketchikan*—Alaska Seafest; Silver Salmon Derby; Blueberry Festival. *Kodiak*—Cry of the Wild Ram (outdoor historical pageant); Rodeo and State Fair; Pilgrimage to St. Herman's Monks Lagoon. *Ninilchik*—Kenai Peninsula State Fair. *Palmer*—Alaska State Fair. *Seward*—Silver Salmon Derby; Tok Run; Softball Tournament. *Skagway*—Dyea Dash. *Soldotna*—Silver Salmon Derby. *Talkeetna*—Bluegrass Festival. *Tanana*—Valley Fair. *Tok*—Mainstreet Alaska Sourdough Potlatch. *Unalaska*—Pink Salmon Derby. *Valdez*—Gold Rush Days; Silver Salmon Derby.

DECEMBER

Anchorage—Seawolf Hockey Classic; Christmas Tree Lighting Ceremony. *Barrow*—Christmas Festival. *Cordova*—North Country Faire. *Fairbanks*—Ski Joring and Sled Dog Races. *Ketchikan*—Festival of Lights. *Kodiak*—Harbor Stars Boat Parade. *Nome*—Firemen's Carnival. *North Pole*—Candle Lighting Ceremony. *Palmer*—Colony Christmas. *Sitka*—Christmas Boat Parade. *Talkeetna*—Christmas Lighting; Bachelor Society Ball and Wilderness Women Contest. *Whittier*—Animals' Christmas.

Camping

(*See also* Cabins; Hiking; National Forests; National Parks, Preserves and Monuments; National Wildlife Refuges; *and* State Park System)

Numerous public and privately operated campgrounds are found along Alaska's highways. Electrical hookups and dump stations are scarce. The dump station at Russian River campground is available for Chugach National Forest visitors. Alaska's backcountry offers virtually limitless possibilities for wilderness camping. Get permission before camping on private land. If the land is publicly owned, it's worthwhile to contact the agency that manages the land regarding regulations and hiking/camping conditions.

The U.S. Forest Service (Alaska Regional Office, U.S. Forest Service, P.O. Box 21628-RN, Juneau 99802) maintains 25 campgrounds in the Tongass and Chugach national forests, most with tent and trailer sites and minimum facilities. All campgrounds are available on a first-come, first-served basis, and stays are limited to 14 days. Campground fees vary, from $6 to $8 per night depending upon facilities, which can include firegrates, pit toilets, garbage pickup, picnic tables and water. Most campgrounds are open from Memorial Day through Labor Day, weather permitting.

The National Park Service (Alaska Regional Office, 2525 Gambell St., Anchorage 99503) at Denali National Park and Preserve offers one walk-in campground, three campgrounds accessible by private vehicles and three

Wrangell—Coho Derby. *Yukon*—Fireweed Festival.

SEPTEMBER

Anchorage—Oktoberfest; UAA Crafts Fair. *Cordova*—Salmon Derby. *Dillingham*—Fall Fair. *Fairbanks*—Tanana–Rampart Labor Day Race; Equinox Marathon. *Kenai*—Silver Salmon Derby. *Ketchikan*—Salmon Derby. *Kodiak*—Silver Salmon Derby; State Fair and Rodeo. *Nome*—Great Bathtub Race. *Petersburg*—Salmon Derby. *Seward*—Silver Salmon Run. *Skagway*—Klondike Trail of '98 Road Relay. *Valdez*—Silver Salmon Derby. *Whittier*—Silver Salmon Derby. *Wrangell*—Silver Salmon Derby.

OCTOBER

Anchorage—Quiana Alaska. *Fairbanks*—Oktoberfest. *Haines*—Alaska Day Fest. *Petersburg*—October Arts Festival. *Sitka*—Alaska Day Festival.

NOVEMBER

Anchorage—Great Alaska Shootout; Symphony of Trees. *Cordova*—Community Christmas Festival. *Delta Junction*—Winter Carnival. *Fairbanks*—Northern Invitational Curling Spiel; Athabascan Old-Time Fiddling Festival; Sled Dog Races. *Juneau*—Public Market. *Kenai*—Christmas Comes to Kenai Celebration. *Ketchikan*—Christmas Festival of Lights; Singing in the Rain Festival.

campgrounds accessible only by shuttle bus. All of them require a $12 fee per night. Most campsite permits and shuttle bus coupons are issued at the Visitor Access Center located at the entrance to Denali National Park and Preserve. Campsites may be reserved *in person only* on a first-come, first-served basis up to two days in advance. Allow two to three days during peak season (June through August) to obtain campground permits or bus coupons.

The Alaska Public Lands Information Centers in Fairbanks and Anchorage reserve a *limited number* of campground permits and shuttle bus coupons for Denali. Reservations must be made *in person*; no reservations will be accepted by telephone. Campground reservations can be made seven to 21 days in advance; shuttle bus reservations can be made one to 21 days in advance. These advance reservations are usually filled within hours of becoming available. All camping and park entrance fees are collected in advance when making reservations, and there are no refunds.

Situated near the park entrance and open year-round are Riley Creek, for tents and trailers, and Morino, for walk-in tent campers. The other campgrounds are open between May and September, depending on weather. Brochures may be obtained from Denali National Park and Preserve, P.O. Box 9, Denali Park 99755.

Glacier Bay and Katmai national parks each offer one campground for walk-in campers, and Katmai now requires reservations. Backcountry camping is permitted in Denali, Glacier Bay, Katmai and Klondike Gold Rush parks, as well as other national parks and monuments.

Alaska Division of Parks (P.O. Box 107005, Anchorage 99510) maintains the most extensive system of roadside campgrounds and waysides in Alaska. All are available on a first-come, first-served basis. Fees are charged and a yearly pass is offered.

U.S. Fish and Wildlife Service (State Office, 1011 E. Tudor, Anchorage 99503) has several wildlife refuges open to campers, although most are not accessible by highway. The Kenai National Wildlife Refuge, P.O. Box 2139, Soldotna 99669, however, has several campgrounds accessible from the Sterling Highway linking Homer and Anchorage.

The Bureau of Land Management (222 W. Seventh Ave., No. 13, Anchorage 99513) maintains 10 campgrounds in interior Alaska; fees for the Paxton campground are $3 for walk-ins, $6 for RV and drive-in sites; all other campgrounds are free. Brochures describing BLM campgrounds are also available.

The Alaska Public Lands Information Centers provide information on all state and federal campgrounds in Alaska, along with state and national park passes and details on wilderness camping. Visit or contact one of the following centers: 605 W. Fourth Ave., Anchorage 99501; P.O. Box 359, Tok 99780; 250 Cushman, Suite 1A, Fairbanks 99701.

Chambers of Commerce

(*See also* Convention and Visitors Bureaus and Information Centers)

Alaska State Chamber, 217 Second St., Suite 201, Juneau 99801; phone (907) 586-2323; 415 E St., Suite 201, Anchorage 99501; phone (907) 278-2722.

Anchor Point Chamber, P.O. Box 610, Anchor Point 99556; phone (907) 235-2600.

Anchorage Chamber, 437 E St., Suite 300, Anchorage 99501; phone (907) 272-2401.

City of Barrow, P.O. Box 629, Barrow 99723; phone (907) 852-5222.

Bethel Chamber, P.O. Box 329, Bethel 99559; phone (907) 543-2911.

Big Lake Chamber, P.O. Box 520067, Big Lake 99652; phone (907) 892-9230.

Chugiak–Eagle River Chamber, P.O. Box 770353, Eagle River 99577-0353; phone (907) 694-4702.

Greater Copper Valley Chamber, P.O. Box 469, Glennallen 99588; phone (907) 822-5555.

Cordova Chamber, P.O. Box 99, Cordova 99574; phone (907) 424-7260.

Delta Junction Chamber, P.O. Box 987, Delta Junction 99737; phone (907) 895-5068.

Dillingham Chamber, P.O. Box 348, Dillingham 99576; phone (907) 842-5115.

Dutch Harbor Chamber, P.O. Box 833, Dutch Harbor 99692; phone (907) 581-2190.

Greater Fairbanks Chamber, 709 Second Ave., Fairbanks 99707; phone (907) 452-1105.

Funny River Chamber, HC 1, Box 1424, Soldotna 99669; phone (907) 262-7711.

Haines Chamber, P.O. Box 518, Haines 99827; phone (907) 766-2202.

Homer Chamber, P.O. Box 531, Homer 99603; phone (907) 235-7740.

Greater Juneau Chamber, 124 W. Fifth St., Juneau 99801; phone (907) 586-6420.

Kenai Chamber, P.O. Box 497, Kenai 99611; phone (907) 283-7989.

Greater Ketchikan Chamber, P.O. Box 5957, Ketchikan 99901; phone (907) 225-3184.

Kodiak Chamber, P.O. Box 1485, Kodiak 99615; phone (907) 486-3760.

City of Kotzebue, P.O. Box 46, Kotzebue 99752; phone (907) 442-3401.

City of Nenana, P.O. Box 00070, Nenana 99760; phone (907) 832-5441.

Nome Chamber, P.O. Box 251, Nome 99762; phone (907) 443-5535.

North Peninsula Chamber, P.O. Box 8053, Nikiski 99635; phone (907) 776-8369.

North Pole Chamber, P.O. Box 55071, North Pole 99705; phone (907) 488-2242.

Greater Palmer Chamber, P.O. Box 45, Palmer 99645; phone (907) 745-2880.

Petersburg Chamber, P.O. Box 649, Petersburg 99833; phone (907) 772-3646.

Greater Prince of Wales Chamber, P.O. Box 89, Craig 99921; phone (907) 826-2927.

Seldovia Chamber, Drawer F, Seldovia 99663; phone (907) 234-7643.

Seward Chamber, P.O. Box 749, Seward 99664; phone (907) 224-3046.

Greater Sitka Chamber, P.O. Box 638, Sitka 99835; phone (907) 747-8604.

Skagway Chamber, P.O. Box 194, Skagway 99840; phone (907) 983-2854.

Soldotna Chamber, P.O. Box 236, Soldotna 99669; phone (907) 262-9814.

Sutton Chamber, P.O. Box 24, Sutton 99674; phone (907) 745-4527.

Talkeetna Chamber, P.O. Box 334, Talkeetna 99676; phone (907) 733-2330.

Tok Chamber, P.O. Box 389, Tok 99780; phone (907) 883-5887.

Valdez Chamber, P.O. Box 512, Valdez 99686; phone (907) 835-2330.

Greater Wasilla Chamber, 1801 Parks Highway, Wasilla 99687; phone (907) 376-1299.

Wrangell Chamber, P.O. Box 49, Wrangell 99929; phone (907) 874-2010.

Cheechako

Pronounced chee-CHA-ko, or chee-CHA-ker by some old-time Alaskans, the word means tenderfoot or greenhorn. According to *The Chinook Jargon*, a 1909 dictionary of the old trading language used by traders from the Hudson's Bay Company in the early 1800s, the word cheechako comes from combining the Chinook Indian word *chee,* meaning new, fresh or "just now," with the Nootka Indian word *chako,* which means to come, to approach or to become.

Chilkat Blankets

Dramatic, bilaterally symmetrical patterns, usually in black, white, yellow and blue, adorn these heavily fringed ceremonial blankets.

The origin of the Chilkat dancing blanket is Tsimshian. Knowledge of the weaving techniques apparently diffused north to the Tlingit, where blanket-making reached its highest form among the Chilkat group. Visiting traders coined the blanket's name during the late 19th century.

Time, technical skill and inherited privileges were required to weave Chilkat blankets and other ceremonial garments. Both men and women wore the blankets and heavily decorated aprons and tunics.

Yarn for Chilkat dancing blankets was spun primarily from the wool of the mountain goat. The designs woven into Chilkat blankets consist of geometric totemic shapes that can be reproduced by the method known as twining. (Early blankets are unadorned or display geometric patterns lacking curvilinear elements.) Often, totemic crests on painted house posts and the designs woven into garments were quite similar. Weavers reused pattern boards of wood painted with a design.

A few weavers are producing the blankets today.

Chilkoot Trail

The Chilkoot Trail, which spans 33 miles from Dyea, just north of Skagway, over Chilkoot Pass to Lake Bennett, British Columbia, was one of the established routes taken by would-be prospectors to Yukon Territory gold-fields during the Klondike gold rush of 1897–98. Thousands of gold stampeders climbed the tortuous trail over Chilkoot Pass that winter. Those who reached Lake Bennett built boats to float down the Yukon River to Dawson City.

Today, the Chilkoot Trail is part of Klondike Gold Rush National Historical Park and is climbed each year by hundreds of backpackers. The Chilkoot Trail begins about 8 miles from Skagway on Dyea Road. There are a dozen campgrounds along the trail and ranger stations on both the Alaska and British Columbia portions of the trail (the trail crosses the international border at 3,739-foot Chilkoot Pass, 16.5 miles from the trailhead). The trail ends at Bennett, site of a White Pass and Yukon Route railway station. For more information, contact Klondike Gold Rush National Historical Park, Box 517, Skagway 99840.

Related reading: *Chilkoot Pass: The Most Famous Trail in the North*, by Archie Satterfield. This revised and expanded edition is a historical guide to the hiking trail and includes photos. *See* ALASKA NORTHWEST LIBRARY in the back of the book.

Chill Factor

The wind's chill factor can lower the effective temperature many degrees. While Alaska's regions of lowest temperatures also generally have little wind, activities such as riding a snowmobile or even walking can produce the same effect on exposed skin.

Temperature (Fahrenheit)	Wind Chill Temperature at Selected mph			
	10	20	30	45
40	28	18	13	10
30	16	4	–2	–6
20	4	–10	–18	–22
10	–9	–25	–33	–38
0	–21	–39	–48	–54
–10	–33	–53	–63	–70
–20	–46	–67	–79	–85
–30	–58	–82	–94	–102
–40	–70	–96	–109	–117

The wind's chill factor, when severe, can lead to frostnip (the body's early-warning signal of potential damage from cold—a "nipping" feeling in the extremities), frostbite (formation of small ice crystals in the body tissues) or hypothermia (dangerous lowering of the body's core temperature). Other factors that combine with wind chill and bring on these potentially damaging or fatal effects are exposure to wetness, exhaustion and lack of adequate clothing.

Chitons

Chitons are oval-shaped marine mollusks with shells made up of eight overlapping plates. The gumboot and the Chinese slipper chiton are favorite Alaskan edible delicacies. The gumboot, named for the tough, leathery, reddish-brown covering that hides its plates, is the largest chiton in the world. It has long been traditional food for southeastern Alaska Natives.

Climate

(See also Winds)

Alaska's climate zones are maritime, transition, continental and arctic. With the exception of the transition zone along western Alaska, the zones are divided by mountain ranges that form barriers to shallow air masses and modify those deep enough to cross the ranges. The Brooks Range inhibits southward movement of air from the Arctic Ocean, thus separating the arctic climate zone from the Interior. The Chugach, Wrangell, Aleutian and Alaska mountain ranges often limit northward air movement and dry the air before it reaches the Interior's continental zone.

Other meteorologic/oceanographic factors affecting Alaska's climate zones are air temperature, water temperature, cloud coverage, and wind and air pressure. The amount of moisture that air can hold in a gaseous state is highly dependent on its temperature. Warm air can contain more water vapor than cold air. Therefore, precipitation, as rain or snow or in other forms, is likely to be heavier from warm than from cold air. Water temperatures change more slowly and much less than land temperatures. For this reason, coastal area temperatures vary less than those farther inland.

Climate Zones

The maritime climate zone includes Southeast, the Northern Gulf Coast and the Aleutian Chain. Temperatures are mild—relatively warm in the winter and cool in summer. Precipitation is heavy, 50 to 200 inches annually along the coast and up to 400 inches on mountain slopes. Storms are frequently from the west and southwest, resulting in strong winds along the Aleutian Islands and the Alaska Peninsula. Amchitka Island's weather station has recorded the windiest weather in the

state, followed by Cold Bay. Frequent storms with accompanying high winds account for rough seas with occasional waves to 50 feet in the Gulf of Alaska, particularly in fall and winter.

The transition zone is, in effect, two separate zones. One is the area between the coastal mountains and the Alaska Range, which includes Anchorage and the Matanuska Valley. Summer temperatures are higher than those of the maritime climate zone, with colder winter temperatures and less precipitation. Temperatures, however, are not as extreme as in the continental zone.

Another transition zone includes the west coast from Bristol Bay to Point Hope. This area has cool summer temperatures that are somewhat colder than those of the maritime zone, and cold winter temperatures similar to the continental zone. Cold winter temperatures are partly due to the sea ice in the Chukchi and Bering seas.

The continental climate zone covers the majority of Alaska except the coastal fringes and the Arctic Slope. It has extreme temperatures and low precipitation. There are fewer clouds in the continental zone than elsewhere, so there is more warming by the sun during the long days of summer and more cooling during the long nights of winter. Precipitation is light because air masses affecting the area lose most of their moisture crossing the mountains to the south.

The Arctic, north of the Brooks Range, has cold winters, cool summers and desertlike precipitation. Prevailing winds are from the northeast off the arctic ice pack, which never moves far offshore. Summers are generally cloudy and winters are clear and cold. The cold air allows little precipitation and inhibits evaporation. Because continuous permafrost prevents the percolation of water into the soil, the area is generally marshy with numerous lakes. *(See also* Permafrost.)

The chart on pages 38–39 shows normal monthly temperatures and precipitation for 14 communities in Alaska. Included are mean seasonal snowfall and annual temperatures and precipitation. The chart is based on

(Continued on page 40)

37

AVERAGE TEMPERATURES (FAHRENHEIT) AND PRECIPITATION (INCHES)							
	ANCHORAGE	BARROW	BETHEL	COLD BAY	FAIRBANKS	HOMER	JUNEAU
January							
Temperature	14.9	–13.4	6.7	28.6	–10.1	22.7	24.2
Precipitation	0.80	0.20	0.81	2.71	0.55	2.23	3.98
February							
Temperature	18.7	–17.8	6.0	27.4	–3.6	24.7	28.4
Precipitation	0.86	0.18	0.71	2.30	0.41	1.78	3.66
March							
Temperature	25.7	–15.1	13.3	29.9	11.0	28.0	32.7
Precipitation	0.65	0.15	0.80	2.19	0.37	1.57	3.24
April							
Temperature	35.8	–2.2	23.6	33.3	30.7	35.4	39.7
Precipitation	0.63	0.20	0.65	1.90	0.28	1.27	2.83
May							
Temperature	46.6	19.3	39.9	39.6	48.6	42.8	47.0
Precipitation	0.63	0.16	0.83	2.40	0.57	1.07	3.46
June							
Temperature	54.4	34.0	50.5	45.7	59.8	49.3	53.0
Precipitation	1.02	0.36	1.29	2.13	1.29	1.00	3.02
July							
Temperature	58.4	39.3	55.0	50.5	62.5	53.4	56.0
Precipitation	1.96	0.87	2.18	2.50	1.84	1.63	4.09
August							
Temperature	56.3	37.9	52.9	51.5	56.8	53.3	55.0
Precipitation	2.31	0.97	3.65	3.71	1.82	2.56	5.10
September							
Temperature	48.4	30.5	45.2	47.7	46.5	47.6	49.4
Precipitation	2.51	0.64	2.58	4.06	1.02	2.96	6.25
October							
Temperature	36.6	13.5	29.4	39.6	25.1	37.5	42.2
Precipitation	1.86	0.51	1.48	4.45	0.81	3.41	7.64
November							
Temperature	21.2	–1.7	16.8	34.4	2.7	28.6	33.0
Precipitation	1.08	0.27	0.98	4.33	0.67	2.74	5.13
December							
Temperature	16.3	–11.2	8.5	31.0	–6.5	24.3	27.1
Precipitation	1.06	0.17	0.95	3.16	0.73	2.71	4.48
Annual							
Temperature	35.9	9.4	29.0	38.3	26.9	37.4	40.6
Precipitation	15.37	4.67	16.90	35.84	10.37	24.93	52.86
Mean Seasonal Snowfall (inches)	69.0	28.0	47.0	62.0	68.0	58.0	100.0

KETCHIKAN	KING SALMON	KODIAK	MCGRATH	NOME	PETERSBURG	VALDEZ	
							January
33.9	14.9	29.9	–8.7	7.0	27.6	20.5	Temperature
14.01	1.11	9.52	0.81	0.88	9.31	5.63	Precipitation
							February
38.9	14.8	30.5	–2.6	3.9	31.1	24.1	Temperature
12.36	0.82	5.67	0.74	0.56	7.85	5.08	Precipitation
							March
38.9	22.4	32.9	10.2	8.6	34.7	29.2	Temperature
12.22	1.06	5.16	0.75	0.63	7.19	4.06	Precipitation
							April
42.8	30.2	37.5	26.5	17.6	40.4	37.1	Temperature
11.93	1.07	4.47	0.73	0.67	6.94	2.89	Precipitation
							May
48.6	42.4	43.5	44.5	35.6	47.2	45.2	Temperature
9.06	1.25	6.65	0.84	0.58	5.92	2.74	Precipitation
							June
54.0	50.0	49.6	55.3	45.9	53.0	51.8	Temperature
7.36	1.54	5.72	1.56	1.14	5.00	2.64	Precipitation
							July
58.0	54.7	54.4	58.7	51.5	55.8	54.9	Temperature
7.80	2.10	3.80	2.16	2.18	5.36	3.77	Precipitation
							August
58.4	53.9	55.2	54.3	50.2	55.0	53.5	Temperature
10.60	2.96	4.03	2.87	3.20	7.57	5.73	Precipitation
							September
53.6	47.2	50.0	44.2	42.5	50.3	47.2	Temperature
13.61	2.75	7.18	2.19	2.59	11.15	7.99	Precipitation
							October
46.3	32.4	40.7	24.7	28.0	43.5	38.1	Temperature
22.55	1.98	7.85	1.24	1.38	16.83	8.23	Precipitation
							November
39.0	22.0	34.4	4.4	15.9	35.6	27.4	Temperature
17.90	1.45	6.89	1.18	1.02	11.99	6.09	Precipitation
							December
35.4	15.9	30.8	–6.0	7.3	30.5	22.9	Temperature
15.82	1.19	7.39	1.12	0.82	10.66	6.65	Precipitation
							Annual
45.5	33.5	40.8	25.5	26.2	42.1	37.7	Temperature
155.22	19.28	74.33	16.18	15.64	105.77	61.50	Precipitation
37.0	46.0	80.0	93.0	56.0	102.0	320.0	Mean Seasonal Snowfall (inches)

(Continued from page 37)
data from NOAA and the Alaska state climatologist.

Climate Records

Highest temperature: 100°F, at Fort Yukon, June 27, 1915.

Lowest temperature: –80°F, at Prospect Creek Camp, Jan. 23, 1971.

Most precipitation in one year: 332.29 inches, at MacLeod Harbor (Montague Island), 1976.

Most monthly precipitation: 70.99 inches at MacLeod Harbor, November 1976.

Most precipitation in 24 hours: 15.2 inches, in Angoon, Oct. 12, 1982.

Least precipitation in a year: 1.61 inches, at Barrow, 1935.

Most snowfall in a season: 974.5 inches, at Thompson Pass, 1952–53.

Most monthly snowfall: 297.9 inches, at Thompson Pass, February 1953.

Most snowfall in 24 hours: 62 inches, at Thompson Pass, December 1955.

Least snowfall in a season: 3 inches, at Barrow, 1935–36.

Highest recorded snow pack (also highest ever recorded in North America): 356 inches on Wolverine Glacier, Kenai Peninsula, after the winter of 1976–77.

Highest recorded wind speed: 139 mph, at Shemya Island, December 1959.

Coal

(See also Minerals and Mining)

About half of the coal resource of the United States is believed to be in Alaska. The demonstrated coal reserve base of the state is over 6 billion short tons, identified coal resources are about 160 billion short tons, and hypothetical and speculative resource estimates range upward to 6 trillion short tons. The provinces containing the most coal are northwestern Alaska, Cook Inlet–Susitna Lowland and the Nenana Trend. Geologists estimate that perhaps 80 percent of Alaska's coal underlies the 23 million-acre National Petroleum Reserve on the North Slope. Although the majority of the coals are of bitumi-

nous and subbituminous ranks, anthracite coal does occur in the Bering River and Matanuska fields. In addition to the vast resource base and wide distribution, the important selling points for Alaska coal are its extremely low sulfur content and access to the coast for shipping.

Exploration, technology and economics will ultimately determine the marketability of Alaska's coal resources. Large-scale exploration programs have been conducted in most of Alaska's coalfields by private industry and state and federal governments. Maxus Energy, Inc., and Placer–Dome U.S. are working to develop the Beluga coalfield west of Anchorage on Cook Inlet. Wishbone Hill Mine is in the permit phase and is scheduled to produce 1 million metric tons of clean coal per year. Exploration continues in the Nenana coalfield. The Arctic Slope Regional Corporation is working to develop its coal reserves in northwestern Alaska.

Alaska's production of coal in 1992 was 1.54 million tons and came exclusively from the Usibelli Coal Mine near Healy. Of that estimate, one-half was burned in interior Alaska power plants, and the remainder was shipped to Korea.

Coal production value in Alaska was over $38.3 million in 1992.

Conk

Alaskans apply this term to a type of bracket fungus. The platelike conks grow on dead trees. When dry and hard, conks are snapped off and used to paint on.

Constitution of Alaska

One of the most remarkable achievements in the long battle for Alaskan statehood was the creation of the constitution of the state of Alaska in the mid-1950s. Statehood supporters believed that creation of a constitution would demonstrate Alaska's maturity and readiness for statehood, so in 1955 the territorial legislature appropriated $300,000 for the cost of holding a Constitutional Convention in Fairbanks.

For 73 days in 1955–1956, a total of 55 elected delegates from all across the territory of Alaska met in the new Student Union Building (now called Constitution Hall) on the University of Alaska campus. William A. Egan, a territorial legislator and former mayor of Valdez, who later became the first governor of the state of Alaska, was president of the convention. Under his leadership, the disparate group of Alaskans hammered out a document that is considered a model for a state constitution.

The National Municipal League said that the brief 14,000-word document drafted by the convention delegates was "one of the best, if not the best, state constitutions ever written." By an overwhelming margin the people of Alaska approved the new constitution at the polls in 1956, paving the way for the creation of the 49th state in 1959.

Continental Divide

(*See also* Mountains)

The Continental Divide extends into Alaska. Unlike its portions in the Lower 48, which divide the country into east-west watersheds, the Continental Divide in Alaska trends through the Brooks Range, separating watersheds that drain north into the Arctic Ocean and west and south into the Bering Sea.

According to *Alaska Science Nuggets*, geologists used to regard the Brooks Range as a structural extension of the Rocky Mountains. Recent thinking, however, assumes the range to be 35 million to 200 million years older than the Rockies. The Alaska Range is comparatively young, only about 5 million years old.

Convention and Visitors Bureaus and Information Centers

Anchorage Convention and Visitors Bureau, 1600 A St., Suite 200, Anchorage 99501; phone (907) 276-4118.

Begich–Boggs Visitors Center, P.O. Box 129, Girdwood 99587; phone (907) 783-2326.

Bethel Visitor Center, P.O. Box 388, Bethel 99559; phone (907) 543-2798.

Big Lake Visitor Information Center, P.O. Box 520067, Big Lake 99652; phone (907) 892-9030.

Greater Copper Valley Visitor Information Center, P.O. Box 469, Glennallen 99588; phone (907) 822-5555.

Cordova Visitors Center, P.O. Box 391, Cordova 99574; phone (907) 424-7443.

Delta Junction Visitor Information Center, P.O. Box 987, Delta Junction 99737; phone (907) 895-5068.

Eagle River Visitor Center, P.O. Box 7001, Anchorage 99510; phone (907) 694-2108.

Fairbanks Convention and Visitors Bureau, 550 First Ave., Fairbanks 99701; phone (907) 456-5774.

Haines Visitor Information Center, City of Haines, P.O. Box 518, Haines 99827; phone (907) 766-2234.

Juneau Convention and Visitors Bureau, 369 S. Franklin St., Juneau 99801; phone (907) 586-1737.

Kenai Visitor Information Center, P.O. Box 497, Kenai 99611; phone (907) 283-7989.

Ketchikan Convention and Visitors Bureau, 131 Front St., Ketchikan 99901; phone (907) 225-6166.

Kodiak Island Convention and Visitors Bureau, 100 Marine Way, Kodiak 99615; phone (907) 486-4782.

Matanuska–Susitna Convention and Visitors Bureau, HCO-1, Box 6616J21, Palmer 99645; phone (907) 746-5000.

Nome Convention and Visitors

Bureau, P.O. Box 251, Nome 99762; phone (907) 443-5535.

Petersburg Visitor Information, P.O. Box 649, Petersburg 99833; phone (907) 772-3975.

Seward Visitor Information Cache, P.O. Box 749, Seward 99664; phone (907) 224-3094.

Sitka Convention and Visitors Bureau, P.O. Box 1226, Sitka 99835; phone (907) 747-5940.

Skagway Convention and Visitors Bureau, P.O. Box 415, Skagway 99840; phone (907) 983-2854.

Tok Visitor Center, P.O. Box 389, Tok 99780; (907) 883-5775.

Valdez Convention and Visitors Bureau, P. O. Box 1603, Valdez 99686; phone (907) 835-2984.

Wrangell Convention and Visitors Bureau, P.O. Box 1078, Wrangell 99929; phone (907) 874-3800.

Coppers

(*See also* Potlatch)

Coppers (*tinnehs*) are beaten copper plaques that were important symbols of wealth among the Pacific Northwest Coast Natives. Coppers are shaped something like a keyhole or a shield, are usually 2 or 3 feet long and weigh approximately 40 pounds. Coppers varied in value from tribe to tribe.

Early coppers were made of ore from the Copper River area, although western traders quickly made sheet copper available. Some scholars believe that Tlingit craftsmen shaped placer copper into the desired form themselves, while others maintain that coppers were formed by Athabascans. The impressive plaques were engraved or carved in relief with totemic crests.

The value of coppers increased as they were traded or sold, and their transfer implied that a potlatch would be given by the new owner. Coppers were given names, such as "Cloud," "Point of Island" or "Killer Whale," and were spoken of in respectful terms. They were thought of as powerful, and their histories were as well known as those of the noblest families.

Coppers were often broken and destroyed during public displays and distribution of wealth. Some parts of the coppers were valued nearly as much as the whole.

To this day, certain coppers that have been part of museum collections for years are still valued highly by some tribes, and are used as symbols of wealth and prestige during marriage ceremonies and potlatches.

Cost of Living

(*See also* Income)

Alaska is an expensive place to live for a variety of reasons. The main mode of transportation in the state is by air travel or by sea. Alaska's sheer size, lack of a comprehensive road network and distance from the contiguous 48 states make personal and business transportation costly. Air travel, which may be a luxury for residents in other states, becomes a necessity for Alaskans living in places such as Barrow, Sitka or Nome. A typical living cost for these residents usually includes the high cost of transportation just to leave town.

Likewise, shipping goods as well as providing services and medical care to more remote areas in Alaska is expensive, especially when there is little or no competition to keep prices down. And because agriculture and industry in Alaska is limited, most consumption items are shipped in from Outside, adding to their cost.

Food: In a June 1992 Cost of Food study conducted by the University of Alaska Cooperative Extension Study, the U.S. Department of Agriculture and SEA Grant Cooperating, food prices fluctuated greatly among cities and towns within the state. Prices on the average were less expensive in the larger cities, such as Anchorage, and very expensive in rural communities. Food costs for the more isolated communities of Bethel and Dillingham can range between 50 percent and 70 percent more than Anchorage. For example, a week's worth of groceries for a family of four (with elementary schoolchildren) in June 1992 cost $98.41 in Anchorage, $143.85 in Bethel and $129.57 in Kodiak.

Housing: Though housing costs are considered high in Alaska, other states nationwide reflect comparable prices. According to the Cost of Living Index for the fourth quarter of 1992 compiled by the American Chamber of Commerce Researchers Association (ACCRA), the sample purchase price of a house in Anchorage was $159,246; Fairbanks, $138,750; Juneau, $138,750; Ketchikan, $163,333; and Kodiak $185,049.

Gasoline: The average cost for one gallon of gasoline (from a fourth quarter 1992 ACCRA survey) was: Juneau, $1.62; Anchorage, $1.16; Fairbanks, $1.22; Ketchikan, $1.57; Kodiak, $1.47.

Taxes: City and borough taxes (compiled in 1992) were: Juneau, 4 percent sales; Anchorage, none; Fairbanks, none; Nome, 4 percent sales; Dillingham, 5 percent sales. There is no state income tax in Alaska.

Personal income: The cost of living in Alaska is high, and so is personal income. In 1992, the annual per capita personal income for Alaska was $21,603, which positioned Alaska as the eighth highest in the nation in income standings.

Courts

The Alaska court system operates at four levels: the supreme court, court of appeals, superior court and district court. The Alaska judiciary is funded by the state and administered by the supreme court.

The five-member supreme court, established by the Alaska Constitution in 1959, has final appellate jurisdiction of all actions and proceedings in lower courts. It sits monthly in Anchorage and Fairbanks, quarterly in Juneau and occasionally in other court locations.

The three-member court of appeals was established in 1980 to relieve the supreme court of some of its ever-increasing caseload. The supreme court retained its ultimate authority in all cases, but concentrated its attention on civil appellate matters, giving authority in criminal and quasi-criminal matters to the court of appeals. The court of appeals has appellate jurisdiction in certain superior court proceedings and jurisdiction to review district court decisions. It meets regularly in Anchorage and travels occasionally to other locations.

The superior court is the trial court, with original jurisdiction in all civil and criminal matters and appellate jurisdiction over all matters appealed from the district court. The superior court has exclusive jurisdiction in probate and in cases concerning minors. There are 31 superior court judges.

The district court has jurisdiction over misdemeanor violations and violations of ordinances of political subdivisions. In civil matters, the district court may hear cases for recovery of money, damages or specific personal property if the amount does not exceed $50,000. The district court may also inquire into the cause and manner of death, as well as issue marriage licenses, summons, writs of habeas corpus and search and arrest warrants. District court criminal decisions may be appealed directly to the court of appeals or the superior court. There are 17 district court judges.

Administration of the superior and district courts is divided by region into four judicial districts: First Judicial District, Southeast; Second Judicial District, Nome-Kotzebue; Third Judicial District, Anchorage-Kodiak-Kenai; and Fourth Judicial District, Fairbanks.

District magistrates serve rural areas and help ease the work load of district courts in metropolitan areas. In criminal matters, magistrates may enter judgment of conviction upon a plea of guilty to any state misdemeanor and may try state misdemeanor cases if the defendant waives his right to a district court judge. Magistrates may also hear municipal ordinance violations and state traffic infractions without the consent of the accused. In civil matters, magistrates may hear cases for recovery of money, damages or specific personal property if the amount does not exceed $5,000.

Selection of Justices, Judges and Magistrates

Supreme court justices and judges of the court of appeals, superior court and district court are appointed by the governor from candidates submitted by the Alaska Judicial Council. All justices and judges must be citizens of the United

States and have been residents of Alaska for at least five years. A justice must be licensed to practice law in Alaska at the time of appointment and have engaged in active law practice for eight years. A court of appeals judge must be a state resident for five years immediately preceding appointment, have been engaged in the active practice of law not less than eight years immediately preceding appointment and be licensed to practice law in Alaska. Qualifications of a superior court judge are the same as for supreme court justices, except that only five years of active practice are necessary. A district court judge must be 21 years of age, a resident for at least five years, and (1) be licensed to practice law in Alaska and have engaged in active practice of law for not less than three years immediately preceding appointment, or (2) have served for at least seven years as a magistrate in the state and have graduated from an accredited law school.

The chief justice of the supreme court is selected by majority vote of the justices, serves a three-year term and cannot succeed him or herself.

Each supreme court justice and each judge of the court of appeals is subject to approval or rejection by a majority of the voters of the state on a nonpartisan ballot at the first general election held more than three years after appointment. Thereafter, each justice must participate in a retention election every 10 years. A court of appeals judge must participate every eight years.

Superior court judges are subject to approval or rejection by voters of their judicial district at the first general election held more than three years after appointment. Thereafter, it is every sixth year. District court judges must run for retention in their judicial districts in the first general election held more than two years after appointment and every fourth year thereafter.

District magistrates are appointed for an indefinite period by the presiding superior court judge of the judicial district in which they will serve.

The Alaska State Supreme Court, 1959–1992: Justices and Tenure

Jay A. Rabinowitz , 1965–
Chief Justice, 1972–1975; 1978–1981; 1984–1987; 1990–1992
Edmond W. Burke, 1975–
Chief Justice, 1981–1984
Allen T. Compton, 1980–
Warren W. Mathews, 1977–
Chief Justice, 1987–1990
Daniel A. Moore, Jr., 1983–
Chief Justice, 1992-
John H. Dimond, 1959–1971
Walter H. Hodge, 1959–1960
Buell A. Nesbett, 1959–1970
Chief Justice, 1959–1970
Harry O. Arend, 1960–1965
George F. Boney, 1968–1972
Chief Justice, 1970–1972
Roger G. Connor, 1968–1983
Robert C. Erwin, 1970–1977
Robert Boochever, 1972–1980
Chief Justice, 1975–1978
James M. Fitzgerald, 1972–1975

The Alaska State Court of Appeals, 1980–1992: Judges and Tenure

Alexander O. Bryner, 1980–
Chief Judge, 1980–
Robert G. Coats, 1980–
David Mannheimer, 1990–
James K. Singleton, Jr., 1980–1990

Cruises

(*See also* Boating *and* Ferries)

There are many opportunities for cruising Alaska waters, aboard either charter boats, scheduled boat excursions or luxury cruise ships.

Charter boats are readily available in southeastern and southcentral Alaska. Charter boat trips range from day-long fishing and sightseeing trips to overnight and longer customized trips or package tours. There is a wide range of charter boats, from simple fishing boats to sailboats, yachts and mini-class cruise ships.

In summer, scheduled boat excursions—from day trips to overnight cruises—are available at the following locations: Ketchikan (Misty Fiords); Sitka (harbor and area tours); Bartlett Cove and Gustavus (Glacier Bay); Valdez and Whittier (Columbia Glacier, Prince William Sound); Seward (Resurrection Bay, Kenai Fjords); Homer (Kachemak Bay); and Fairbanks (Chena and Tanana rivers).

For details and additional information on charter boat operators and scheduled boat excursions, contact the Alaska Division of Tourism, P.O. Box E, Juneau 99811.

From May through September, luxury cruise ships carry visitors to Alaska via the Inside Passage. There are 24 ships to choose from and almost as many itineraries. There's also a bewildering array of travel options. Both round-trip and one-way cruises are available, or a cruise may be sold as part of a packaged tour that includes air, rail and/or motorcoach transportation.

Various shore excursions may be included in the cruise price or available for added cost. Ports of call may depend on length of cruise or time of sailing.

Because of the wide variety of cruise trip options, it is wise to work with your travel agent.

Following is a partial list of cruise ships serving Alaska in the 1993–94 season:

Alaska Sightseeing/Cruise West, Suite 700, Fourth & Battery Building, Seattle, WA 98121; phone (206) 441-8687. *Sheltered Seas* (35 passengers); 5- or 6-day daylight cruise between Ketchikan and Juneau. *Spirit of Glacier Bay* (49 passengers); 3-day cruise between Juneau and Glacier Bay. *Spirit of Alaska* and *Spirit of Discovery* (82 passengers) and *Spirit of '98* (101 passengers); 7-night cruises between Seattle and Juneau.

Clipper Cruise Lines, 7711 Bonhomme Ave., St. Louis, MO 63105-1965; phone 1-800-326-0010. *Yorktown Clipper* (138 passengers); 7- and 14-day round-trip cruise between Juneau and Ketchikan.

Costa Cruises, Inc., World Trade Center, 80 SW Eighth St., Miami, FL 33130; phone (305) 358-7325. MTS *Daphne* (420 passengers); 7-night round-trip cruises from Vancouver, British Columbia.

Cunard/NAC Lines, 555 Fifth Ave., New York, NY 10017; phone (212) 880-7500. *Sagafjord* (618 passengers); 11-day cruise between Vancouver, British Columbia and Anchorage.

Holland America Line, 300 Elliott Ave. W., Seattle, WA 98119; phone (206) 281-3535. MS *Nieuw Amsterdam* (1,214 passengers), MS *Noordam* (1,214 passengers), SS *Rotterdam* (1,114 passengers) and the *Westerdam*; 3-, 4- and 7-night round-trip cruises from Vancouver, British Columbia. The *Rotterdam* also offers 7-night cruises between Vancouver, British Columbia, and Seward.

Princess Cruises, 10100 Santa Monica Blvd., Suite 1800, Los Angeles, CA 90067; phone (213) 553-1770. *Dawn Princess* (850 passengers); 10-day round-trip from San Francisco. *Regal Princess* and *Crown Princess* (1,590 passengers); 7-day cruises between Vancouver, British Columbia, and Anchorage. *Sky Princess* (1,200 passengers) and *Star Princess* (1,470 passengers); 7-day round-trip Inside Passage cruise from Vancouver, British Columbia.

Regency Cruises, 260 Madison Ave., New York, NY 10016; phone (212) 972-4499. MV *Regent Sea* (729 passengers) and *Regent Sun* (836 passengers); 7 days between Vancouver, British Columbia, and Whittier.

Royal Caribbean Cruise Line, 903 South America Way, Miami, FL 33132. *Sun Viking* (726 passengers); 7 days between Vancouver, British Columbia, and Skagway.

Royal Cruise Line, 1 Maritime Plaza, San Francisco, CA 94111; phone 1-800-227-4534. *Golden Odyssey* (450 passengers); 7-day cruises between Vancouver and Anchorage.

Special Expeditions, 720 Fifth Ave., New York, NY 10019. *Sea Bird* (70 passengers) and *Sea Lion* (70 passengers); 11-day wilderness cruises between Prince Rupert, British Columbia, and Sitka.

World Explorer Cruises, 555 Montgomery St., San Francisco, CA 94111; phone 1-800-854-3835. SS *Universe* (554 passengers); 14-day round-trip cruises between Vancouver, British Columbia, and Seward.

Dalton Highway

(*See also* Highways)

This all-weather gravel road bridges the Yukon River, crosses the Arctic Circle, climbs the Brooks Range and passes through tundra plains before reaching the Prudhoe Bay oil fields at Deadhorse on the coast of the Arctic Ocean.

The highway was named for James Dalton, a post–World War II explorer who played a large role in the development of North Slope oil and gas industries. It was built as a haul road for supplies and to provide access to the northern half of the 800-mile trans-Alaska oil pipeline during construction.

Originally called the North Slope Haul Road, it is still referred to as the "Haul Road."

The Dalton Highway has been partially opened by the state for public use. The public may drive the road's first 211 miles to Disaster Creek at Dietrich. North of Dietrich, the highway is closed to the public. In 1991, Governor Hickel moved to open the highway to Deadhorse, but the opening was postponed. Contact the Department of Transportation regarding the current status of the highway. At present, permits to travel north of Disaster Creek are issued only for commercial or industrial purposes. Permits may be obtained from the Alaska Department of Transportation and Public Facilities.

Fuel, limited food services and tire repairs, as well as wrecker service at $5 per mile, are available (for cash) at the Yukon Bridge and at Coldfoot. Travelers are advised that dust clouds, large trucks traveling fast and sometimes narrow, rough road surfaces may make stopping along the roadway dangerous. Also, because safe drinking water is not available along the road, travelers should carry their own.

The 414-mile-long Dalton Highway begins at Milepost 73.1 on the Elliott Highway.

Daylight Hours

(*See also* Arctic Circle)

Maximum (At Summer Solstice, June 20 or 21)

	Sunrise	Sunset	Hours of Daylight
Barrow	May 10	August 2	84 days continuous
Fairbanks	1:59 a.m.	11:48 p.m.	21:49 hours
Anchorage	3:21 a.m.	10:42 p.m.	19:21 hours
Juneau	3:51 a.m.	10:09 p.m.	18:18 hours
Ketchikan	4:04 a.m.	9:33 p.m.	17:29 hours
Adak	6:27 a.m.	11:10 p.m.	16:43 hours

Minimum (At Winter Solstice, December 21 or 22)

	Sunrise	Sunset	Hours of Daylight
Barrow	*	*	0:00 hours
Fairbanks	10:59 a.m.	2:41 p.m.	3:42 hours
Anchorage	10:14 a.m.	3:42 p.m.	5:28 hours
Juneau	9:46 a.m.	4:07 p.m.	6:21 hours
Ketchikan	9:12 a.m.	4:18 p.m.	7:06 hours
Adak	10:52 a.m.	6:38 p.m.	7:46 hours

*For the period November 18 through January 24—67 days—there is no daylight in Barrow.

Diamond Willow

Fungi, particularly *Valsa sordida Nitschke*, are generally thought to be the cause of diamond-shaped patterns in the wood grain of some willow trees. There are 33 varieties of willow in Alaska, of which at least five can develop diamonds. They are found throughout the state, but are most plentiful in river valleys. Diamond willow, stripped of bark, is used to make lamps, walking sticks and novelty items.

Dog Mushing

(*See also* Iditarod Trail Sled Dog Race *and* Yukon Quest International Sled Dog Race)

In many areas of the state where snow machines had just about replaced the working dog team, the sled dog has made a comeback, due in part to a rekindled appreciation of the reliability of nonmechanical transportation. In addition to working and racing dog teams, many people keep two to 10 sled dogs for recreational mushing.

Sled dog racing is Alaska's official state sport. Races ranging from local club meets to world championships are held throughout the winter.

The speed, or championship, races are usually run over two or three days, with the cumulative time for the heats deciding the winner. Distances for the heats vary from about 12 to 30 miles. The size of dog teams also varies, with mushers using anywhere from seven to 20 dogs in their teams. Since racers are not allowed to replace dogs in the team, most finish with fewer than they started with (attrition may be caused by anything from tender feet to sore muscles).

Sprint mushing is divided into limited and open classes. Limited class ranges from three to 10 dogs and from 3 to 12 miles. Open class racing has no limit on the number of dogs and ranges from 10 to 30 miles.

Long-distance racing (the Yukon Quest, the Iditarod) pits racers not only against each other, but also against the elements. Sheer survival can quickly take precedence over winning when a winter storm catches a dog team in an exposed area. Stories abound of racers giving up their chance to finish "in the money" to help out a fellow musher who has gotten into trouble. Besides the weather, long-distance racers also have to contend with moose attacks on the dogs, sudden illness, straying off the trail and sheer exhaustion. With these and other threats to overcome, those who finish have truly persevered against the odds.

Purses range from trophies for the club races to $75,000 for the largest sprint purse at the World Championship Sled Dog Race (including heat money) for the championships. A purse is split between the finishers. The richest purse in sled dog racing is the Iditarod, with a $400,000 purse in 1993.

Statistics for two of the biggest championship races follow on page 48. Other major races around the state include:

Alaska State Championship Race, Kenai to Soldotna. Two heats in two days, 15.4 miles each day. Held in February.

All-Alaska Sweepstakes, Nome to Candle, round-trip. The Nome Kennel Club sponsors this 408-mile race. Held in March, not an annual event.

Clark Memorial Sled Dog Race, Soldotna to Hope, 100 miles. Held in January.

Iditarod Trail Sled Dog Race. (*See* Iditarod Trail Sled Dog Race)

Junior World Championship Race, Anchorage. Three heats in three days. Held in February.

Kusko 300, Bethel to Aniak. Held in January.

Tok Race of Champions, Tok. Two heats in two days, 20.5 miles a day. Held in March.

Willow Winter Carnival Race, Willow. Two heats in two days, 18 miles each day. Held in January.

Women's World Championship Race, Anchorage. Three heats in three days, 12 miles each day. Held in February.

Yukon Quest International Sled Dog Race. (*See* Yukon Quest International Sled Dog Race)

Related reading: *Iditarod: The Great Race to Nome.* Photography by Jeff Schultz, text by Bill Sherwonit. A powerful visual record of the animal and human participants of the race, accompanied by compelling narrative that chronicles the grueling 1,100-mile journey from Anchorage to Nome. *See* the ALASKA NORTHWEST LIBRARY at the back of the book.

WORLD CHAMPIONSHIP SLED DOG RACE, ANCHORAGE

Held in February. Best elapsed time in three heats over three days, 25 miles each day.

	Day 1	Day 2	Day 3	Total	Purse
		Elapsed Time (minutes:seconds)			
1974 Roland Lombard	105:32	108:34	101:36	310:10	$10,000
1975 George Attla	98:09	107:01	104:18	309:28	12,000
1976 George Attla	98:39	102:64	102:32	303:35	12,000
1977 Carl Huntington	97:42	105:29	*	201:11	12,000
1978 George Attla	102:59	108:38	107:11	318:48	15,000
1979 George Attla	99:51	97:23	99:07	296:21	15,000
1980 Dick Brunk	83:25	82:35	*	166:00	15,000
1981 George Attla	90:04	85:43	91:34	267:21	20,000
1982 George Attla	73:19	75:36	76:56	225:51	20,000
1983 Harris Dunlap	82:29	88:58	89:05	260:32	25,000
1984 Charlie Champaine	82:55	84:06	85:03	254:04	26,000
1985 Eddy Streeper	83:08	85:32	88:36	251:16	30,000
1986—Race canceled for the first time due to lack of snow					
1987 Eddy Streeper	87:07	88:36	86:05	261:48	30,000
1988 Charlie Champaine	103:53	92:00	89:33	285:26	30,000
1989 Roxy Wright-Champaine	87:30	90:32	89:22	266.84	50,000
1990 Charlie Champaine	89:00	96:13	94:01	279:14	50,000
1991 Charlie Champaine	89:10	94:49	95:43	279:42	70,000
1992 Roxy Wright-Champaine	87:30	89:35	92:22	269:42	70,000
1993 Roxy Wright-Champaine	87:44	90:45	93:21	271:50	75,000

*Trail conditions shortened race

OPEN NORTH AMERICAN SLED DOG CHAMPIONSHIP, FAIRBANKS

Held in March. Best elapsed time in three heats over three days; 20 miles on Days 1 and 2; 28 miles on Day 3.*

	Day 1	Day 2	Day 3	Total	Purse
		Elapsed Time (minutes:seconds)			
1974 Alfred Attla	72:00	74:25	108:29	254:54	$ 9,000
1975 George Attla	69:56	70:16	104:05	244:17	9,000
1976 Harvey Drake	72:00	73:43	116:00	261:43	10,000
1977 Carl Huntington	71:20	71:40	109:00	252:00	12,000
1978 George Attla	71:07	68:05	106:53	246:07	15,000
1979 George Attla	68:41	70:07	104:44	243:32	15,000
1980 Harvey Drake	63:48	66:49	94:30	225:07	15,000
1981 Peter Norberg	73:01	70:55	109:07	253:03	15,000
1982 Harris Dunlap	69:17	72:14	105:43	247:14	15,000
1983 Gareth Wright**	65:43	68:31	99:36	233:50	15,000
1984 Doug McRae	68:35	67:80	98:89	235:04	17,500
1985 Eddy Streeper	61:88	64:16	98:52	224:56	25,000
1986 George Attla	63:95	65:99	103:07	233:01	25,000
1987 George Attla	63:50	68:10	97:21	229:03	25,000
1988 Marvin Kokrine	63:52	66:16	95:42	225:49	30,000
1989 Roxy Wright-Champaine	62:10	62:42	92:07	216:59	44,000
1990 Charlie Champaine	62:47	67:38	95:40	226:05	45,000
1991 Ross Saunderson	60:12	63:53	97:44	221:50	46,000
1992 Roxy Wright-Champaine	66:17	65:59	94:29	226:46	52,000
1993 Roxy Wright-Champaine	64:48	64:06	95:36	224:31	58,000

*Until 1987, racing times were measured in minutes and hundredths of minutes. Times have been rounded off.
**This was Wright's second win of this race. He took his first championship in 1950.

Earthquakes

(*See also* Waves)

Between 1899 and mid-1993, 10 Alaska earthquakes occurred that equaled or exceeded a magnitude of 8 on the Richter scale. During the same period, more than 75 earthquakes took place that were of magnitude 7 or greater, the most recent occurring in the Gulf of Alaska on March 6, 1988, and registering 7.6 on the Richter scale.

According to the Alaska Tsunami Warning Center, earthquake activity in Alaska typically follows the same pattern from month to month, interspersed with sporadic swarms, or groups of small earthquakes, and punctuated every decade or so by a great earthquake and its aftershocks. Alaska is the most seismic of all the 50 states, and the most seismically active part of the state is the Aleutian Islands arc system. Seismicity related to this system extends into the Gulf of Alaska and northward into interior Alaska to a point near Mount McKinley. These earthquakes are largely the result of underthrusting of the North Pacific plate, with most seismic activity taking place along the Aleutian Island chain. Many earthquakes resulting from this underthrusting occur in Cook Inlet—particularly near Mount Illiamna and Mount Redoubt—and near Mount McKinley. North of the Alaska Range, in the central interior, most earthquakes are of shallow origin.

An earthquake created the highest seiche, or splash wave, ever recorded on the evening of July 9, 1958, when a quake with a magnitude of 7.9 on the Richter scale rocked the Yakutat area. A landslide containing approximately 40 million cubic yards of rock plunged into Gilbert Inlet at the head of Lituya Bay. The gigantic splash resulting from the slide sent a wave 1,740 feet up the opposite mountain side, denuding it of trees and soil down to bedrock. It then fell back and swept through the length of the bay and out to sea. One fishing boat anchored in Lituya Bay at the time was lost with its crew of two; another was carried over a spit of land by the wave and soon after foundered, but its crew was saved. A third boat anchored

in the bay miraculously survived intact. A total of four square miles of coniferous forest was destroyed.

The most destructive earthquake to strike Alaska occurred at 5:36 p.m. on Good Friday, March 27, 1964—a day now referred to as Black Friday. Registering between 8.4 and 8.6 on the Richter scale in use at the time, its equivalent moment magnitude has since been revised upward to 9.2, making it the strongest earthquake ever recorded in North America. With its primary epicenter deep beneath Miners Lake in northern Prince William Sound, the earthquake spread shock waves that were felt 700 miles away. The earthquake and seismic waves that followed killed 131 persons, 115 of them Alaskans. The death tally from tsunamis was: Chenega, 23; Kodiak 12; Point Nowell, 1; Point Whitshed, 1; Port Ashton, 1; Port Nellie Juan, 3; Seward, 12; Valdez, 32; Whittier, 12; Kalsin Bay, 6; Cape St. Elias, 1; Spruce Cape, 1; Shoup Bay, 1. Of the 131 deaths, 119 were caused by the tsunami that resulted from the earthquake.

The 1964 earthquake released 10 million times more energy than the atomic bomb that devastated Hiroshima in World War II, and 80 times the energy of the San Francisco earthquake of 1906. It also moved more earth farther, both horizontally and vertically, than any other earthquake ever recorded except the 1960 Chilean earthquake. In the 69-day period after the main quake, there were 12,000 jolts of 3.5 magnitude or greater.

The highest sea wave caused by the 1964 earthquake occurred when an undersea slide near Shoup Glacier in Port Valdez triggered a wave that toppled trees 100 feet above tidewater and deposited silt and sand 220 feet above salt water.

Economy

Few states in the union have experienced the boom–and–bust cycles that have characterized Alaska's resource-rich economy. Driven by the oil, timber, mining, fishing and tourism industries, Alaska's economy expands when it is able to export its goods and

49

services abroad or to the Lower 48. The peaks and troughs in Alaska's economy are seasonal and often dependent upon events outside the state's borders.

The oil and gas industry is by far the major player in the Alaskan economy. In terms of revenue to the state, no industry is as important to Alaska's economy as oil. About $2 billion a year, or 85 percent of every state dollar, is generated by taxes and royalties on North Slope crude oil. When oil prices are high, so are state revenues. For every $1 per barrel increase in the price of oil, the state collects $150 million from royalty and severance taxes. Nearly 85 percent of the state budget is paid for by oil revenues and more than 20 percent of all jobs in the state are directly dependent on state government spending. The Alaska economy suffered a major blow with the drop in oil prices in 1986; few industries were spared during the recession. The recovery that began in 1989 was spurred on in part by higher oil prices. The *Exxon Valdez* oil spill cleanup effort added about $2 billion to the state's economy over 18 months. The fortunes of Alaska's oil industry, and therefore many sectors of the economy, are dependent on world oil prices.

Alaska's economy experienced a slow expansion in 1992 led by a retail trade boom, a rebounding services sector and continued growth in the seafood processing industry. The downside of the Alaska economy was seen in the contraction of the oil and gas industry, a continued decline in the timber industry and a significant job loss resulting from the closure of the *Anchorage Times*.

The biggest negative in the state's 1992 economy was in oil and gas. Restructuring undertaken by major oil producers resulted in the loss of 1,400 jobs on an annual basis—the largest annual job loss in the industry's history in the state. Two major oil producers announced consolidation efforts in 1992. ARCO and Unocal trimmed their work forces. BP cut nearly a quarter of its work force in the state. A lessening of exploration activity on the North Slope also contributed to job loss in the industry.

The impact of the closure of three sawmills in 1991 and continued cutbacks in logging activity brought another year of job losses to Alaska's wood products sector.

The fastest-growing sector of Alaska's economy in 1992 was general merchandise and apparel. Several large retail outlets, including Sears, Eagle Hardware and Costco, opened in Anchorage and Fairbanks. Nearly every type of retailer experienced gains in employment.

Employment in the services sector grew by 3.9 percent with a gain of 2,000 jobs in the state. More than a quarter of new jobs were generated by health-care services at private hospitals and other health-care businesses. Tourism in Alaska has experienced a steady annual growth of about 4 percent per year, attracting close to 600,000 visitors in 1992. Tourist-related services and businesses such as hotels and motels continued to benefit from another good year in tourist trade.

Alaska's economy received a boost from the fishing industry. Recovering salmon prices, a rebounding crab harvest and continued expansion of the bottomfish industry contributed to job growth in the seafood industry.

Transportation, one of the fastest-growing industries in 1991, continued to grow in 1992, but at a slower rate. On the plus side, air cargo activity helped keep the industry growing. On the negative side, international passenger traffic dropped off and the domestic side of the industry began to suffer financial losses. Both MarkAir and Alaska Airlines announced work-force cutbacks in 1992. And Alaska Airlines cancelled construction of a $45 million maintenance hangar.

Government employment grew, with increases in both local and federal jobs. Average state government employment remained at about 1991 levels. Most of the growth in the public sector came from education-related employment at the University of Alaska or local school districts.

The outlook for Alaska's economy in 1993–94 calls for continued slow but steady growth. This will be driven by the retail and services sectors. In the next two years KMart and Walmart will open new stores around the state, giving a boost to Alaska's construction industry. Oil and gas mining should turn around, pushed ahead by the construction of the gas-handling facility GHX-2, along with increased exploration and development activity on the North Slope and Cook Inlet. But according to the May 1993 issue of *Alaska Economic Trends,* this relatively steady and predictable growth could be upset at any time: "History shows that when Alaska's economy is getting predictable, some incident occurs and changes the complexion of the economy overnight."

Education

(*See also* School Districts *and* Universities and Colleges)

According to the 1992–93 *Alaska Education Directory,* Alaska has 469 public schools and approximately 186 private and denominational schools. The Bureau of Indian Affairs operated schools in Alaska until 1985.

The state Board of Education has seven members appointed by the governor. (In addition, two nonvoting members are appointed by the board to represent the military and public school students.) The board is responsible for setting policy for education in Alaska schools and appoints a commissioner of education to carry out its decisions. The 469 public schools are controlled by 54 school districts, and each school district elects its own school board. There are 21 Regional Education Attendance Areas that oversee education in rural areas outside the 33 city and borough school districts.

Any student in grades kindergarten through 12 (K–12) may choose to study at home through the unique state-operated Centralized Correspondence School, which also serves traveling students, GED students, migrant students and students living in remote areas. Home study has been an option for Alaskan students since 1939.

The state Department of Education also operates the Alaska Vocational Technical Center at Seward and a number of other education programs ranging from adult basic education to literacy skills.

Alaskans between 7 and 16 years old are required to attend school. According to state regulations, a student must earn a minimum of 21 high school credits to receive a high school diploma. The state Board of Education has stipulated that four credits must be earned in language arts, three in social studies, two each in math and science, and one in physical education. Local school boards set the remainder of the required credits.

Since 1976, the state has provided secondary school programs to any community in which an elementary school is operated and one or more children of high school age wish to attend high school. This mandate was the result of a class action suit initiated on behalf of a high-school-age student. Prior to the so-called Molly Hootch Decree, high school–age students in villages without a secondary school attended high school outside their village. Of the 127 villages originally eligible for high school programs under the Molly Hootch Decree, only a few remain without one.

There were approximately 8,500 teachers and administrators in the public schools and approximately 115,000 students enrolled in K–12 in public schools in 1991–92. The size of schools in Alaska varies greatly, from a 1,900-student high school in Anchorage to one- or two-teacher, one-room schools in remote rural areas.

Of the school district's operating fund, 69 percent is provided by the state, 24 percent by local governments and 7 percent by the federal government. Alaska's average salary for teachers is among the highest in the nation.

Employment

(*See also* Economy)

Alaska's economy continued to grow slowly in 1992, showing a modest 1.8 percent employment growth rate. This rate has steadily decreased since the 1989 surge in Alaska's economy. A higher rate of unemployment accompanied the decline in employment growth. Alaska's annual average unemployment rate increased from 8.5 percent in 1991 to 9.3 percent in 1992.

The number of nonagriculture wage

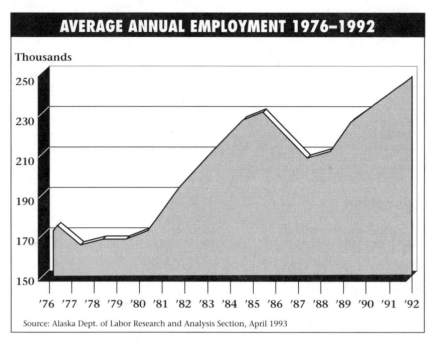

AVERAGE ANNUAL EMPLOYMENT 1976–1992

Thousands

Source: Alaska Dept. of Labor Research and Analysis Section, April 1993

and salary jobs in Alaska in 1991 was about 247,200 jobs, an annual increase of about 4,400 jobs. The fastest-growing segment in the Alaska economy in 1992 was in general merchandise and apparel stores. Major retailers such as Eagle Hardware, KMart and Costco led the retail boom, opening new large retail outlets in Anchorage and Fairbanks. Nearly every type of retailer experienced employment gain.

The services sector added 2,000 jobs in 1992, growing at a rate of 3.9 percent. Health-care services, membership organizations and social services accounted for the majority

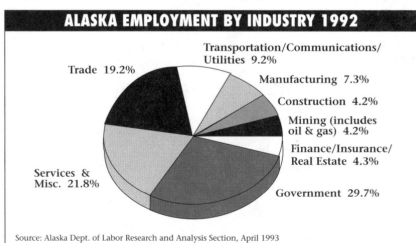

ALASKA EMPLOYMENT BY INDUSTRY 1992

Trade 19.2%

Transportation/Communications/ Utilities 9.2%

Manufacturing 7.3%

Construction 4.2%

Mining (includes oil & gas) 4.2%

Finance/Insurance/ Real Estate 4.3%

Government 29.7%

Services & Misc. 21.8%

Source: Alaska Dept. of Labor Research and Analysis Section, April 1993

ALASKA EMPLOYMENT BY MONTH 1988-1992

Employment (Thousands)

270
260
250
240
230
220
210
200
190

J F M A M J J A S O N D J F M A M J J A S O N D J F M A M J J A S O N D J F M A M J J A S O N D J F M A M J J A S O N D

1988   1989   1990   1991   1992

Source: Alaska Dept. of Labor Research and Analysis Section, April 1993

of the growth in services employment.

Recovering salmon prices, a good crab harvest and continued expansion of the bottomfish industry fueled job growth in the seafood industry.

In the public sector, most job growth came from education-related employment at the University of Alaska and at local school districts expanding employment to accommodate Alaska's growing school-age population.

On the downside, Alaska's oil and gas industry experienced the biggest annual job loss in the industry's history in the state. Due to restructuring, the industry lost about 1,400 jobs on an annual basis—a 10.9 percent decline in employment. This decline, however, came on the heels of two years of record-high employment levels for the industry.

Employment in the timber industry continued to decline following the closure of three sawmills in 1991. Overall, lumber and wood products experienced a 7.7 percent decline in employment.

The largest manufacturing sector in

Alaska outside of wood and seafood products is printing and publishing. More than 400 jobs were lost when the *Anchorage Times* closed its doors in 1992. This was the second-largest employer loss in Anchorage's history.

According to the May 1993 *Alaska Economic Trends,* the 1993–94 employment forecast for Alaska should be slow but steady, continuing the present employment growth rate in the 1.8 to 2 percent range. Retail expansion that began in late 1991 will continue to be a source of job gains.

Alaska's unemployment rate is best characterized by a very seasonal labor market. Increased activity of all types in the summer makes unemployment fairly low, while a lack of activity in the winter months pushes up the unemployment rate. In addition, unemployment figures vary dramatically from one region to another. High unemployment rates in Alaska's rural areas are common. In the Gulf Coast region, for example, the unemployment rate approaches 20 percent in the winter months. On the other hand, bustling seaports such as Kodiak experience unemployment rates below 3 percent during the summer.

Unemployment figures for January 1993 were 10.4 percent statewide; 7.7 percent for Anchorage; 11.6 percent for Fairbanks; 8.4 percent for Juneau; 16.8 percent for Kodiak; 12.6 percent for Nome; 15.4 percent for Ketchikan; 15 percent for Yukon–Koyukuk.

If you're seriously considering a move to Alaska to seek a job, first make a visit and explore the possibilities yourself. Jobs are scarce in Alaska and housing is expensive—there are now, and will be in the foreseeable future, plenty of Alaska residents out of work and anxious to find jobs. For additional information, write: Alaska Department of Labor, Alaska State Employment Service, P.O. Box 3-7000, Juneau 99802. Employment offices are located in most major communities.

Energy and Power

For the purposes of classifying power usage, the state of Alaska can be divided into three major regions, each having similar energy patterns, problems and resources: the Extended Railbelt region; the Southeast region; and the bush region. The Extended Railbelt region consists of major urban areas linked by the Alaska Railroad (Seward, Anchorage and Fairbanks). The southcentral area of this region uses relatively inexpensive natural gas in Cook Inlet and hydroelectrical power plants for electrical production and heating. The Fairbanks–Tanana Valley area uses primarily coal, and also oil, to meet its electrical needs. Future electrical demand for the Railbelt region will be met by a combination of

hydropower and coal- and gas-fired generators. The Southeast region relies on hydropower for a large portion of its electrical generation. (Most of the existing hydroelectric power projects in Alaska are located in the Southeast region.) In the smaller communities, diesel generators are used.

The bush region includes all communities that are remote from the major urban areas of the Extended Railbelt and Southeast regions. Electricity in bush communities is typically provided by small diesel generators. Where wind projects are feasible, such as at Lolo Bay and Unalakleet, wind power can be a viable, fuel-saving alternative to diesel-powered generators. Thermal needs in the bush are currently being met almost entirely by heating oil. Wood and kerosene heaters are used to a limited extent. Natural gas is available in Barrow.

Eskimo Ice Cream

Also called *akutak* (Yup'ik Eskimo word for Eskimo ice cream), this classic Native delicacy, popular throughout Alaska, is traditionally made of whipped berries, seal oil and snow. Sometimes shortening, raisins and sugar are added. In different regions, variations are found. One uses the soopalallie berry, *Shepherdia canadensis* (also called soapberry), a bitter species that forms a frothy mass like soapsuds when beaten.

Ferries

(*See also* Boating *and* Cruises)

The state Department of Transportation and Public Facilities, Marine Highway System, provides year-round scheduled ferry service for passengers and vehicles to communities in southeastern, southcentral and southwestern Alaska. The Southeast Alaska ferry system does not connect with southcentral and southwestern Alaska.

A fleet of six ferries on the southeastern system connects Bellingham, Washington, and Prince Rupert, British Columbia, with the southeastern Alaska ports of Hyder/Stewart,

Ketchikan, Metlakatla, Hollis, Petersburg, Wrangell, Kake, Sitka, Angoon, Pelican, Hoonah, Tenakee Springs, Juneau, Haines and Skagway. These southeastern communities—with the exception of Hyder, Haines and Skagway—are accessible only by boat, ferry or airplane. The six vessels of the southeastern system are the *Aurora, Columbia, LeConte, Malaspina, Matanuska* and *Taku.*

Southwest and southcentral Alaska are served by two ferries. The *Tustumena* serves Seward, Port Lions, Kodiak, Homer, Seldovia, Cordova and Valdez, with limited summer service to Chignik, Sand Point, King Cove, Cold Bay and Dutch Harbor. In summer, the *Bartlett* provides service between Valdez, Cordova and Whittier.

Scheduled state ferry service to southeastern Alaska began in 1963; ferry service to Kodiak Island began in 1964. The first three ferries of the Alaska ferry fleet were the *Malaspina, Matanuska* and *Taku.*

Reservations should be made for all sailings. Senior Citizen and Handicapped rates are available. The address of the main office of the Alaska Marine Highway System is P.O. Box 25535, Juneau 99802-5535; phone (907) 465-3941; or toll free, 1-800-642-0066 (U.S.), 1-800-585-8445 (WA state), 1-800-665-6414 (Canada).

Alaska State Ferry Data

Aurora: (235 feet, 14.5 knots), 250 passengers, 44 vehicles, no cabins. Began service in 1977.

Bartlett: (193 feet, 12 knots), 190 passengers, 41 vehicles, no cabins. Began service in 1969.

Columbia: (418 feet, 17.3 knots), 625 passengers, 158 vehicles, 91 cabins. Began service in 1974.

LeConte: (235 feet, 14.5 knots), 250 passengers, 44 vehicles, no cabins. Began service in 1974.

Malaspina: (408 feet, 16.5 knots), 500 passengers, 107 vehicles, 84 cabins. Began service in 1963 and was lengthened and renovated in 1972.

Matanuska: (408 feet, 16.5 knots), 500 passengers, 108 vehicles, 108 cabins. Began service in 1963.

Taku: (352 feet, 16.5 knots), 475 passengers, 83 vehicles, 44 cabins. Began service in 1963.

Tustumena: (296 feet, 13.3 knots), 210 passengers, 42 vehicles, 26 cabins. Began service in 1964.

Embarking Passenger and Vehicle Totals (in thousands) on Alaska Mainline Ferries*

Southeastern System

	Passengers	Vehicles
1965	123.7	25.8
1970	137.2	28.5
1972	162.7	39.4
1973	162.7	38.4
1974	174.7	41.4
1975	184.5	45.9
1976	181.7	46.3
1977	148.5	40.0
1978	222.1	53.7
1979	244.7	58.2
1980	275.8	63.2
1981	281.6**	65.6**
1982	299.5	73.2
1983	307.8	75.4
1984	311.5	80.0
1985	313.1	79.8
1986	296.1	76.0
1987	326.6	83.5
1988	344.2	90.7
1989	344.4	89.8
1990	363.1	94.7
1991	368.8	95.2
1992	372.7	97.2

Southwestern System

	Passengers	Vehicles
1970	6.9	3.2
1971	25.8	7.7
1972	35.9	9.9
1973	40.7	11.3
1974	44.6	12.4
1975	45.0	12.8
1976	44.4	11.7
1977	38.8	12.5
1978	46.6	13.2

Southwestern System *(continued)*

	Passengers	Vehicles
1979	49.4	13.9
1980	49.5	14.0
1981	55.8	15.1
1982	54.5	15.6
1983	55.5	15.9
1984	55.8	15.5
1985	56.3	16.5
1986	51.8	16.0
1987	52.0	16.5
1988	50.3	16.6
1989	44.2	15.7
1990	50.5	16.5
1991	36.2	12.8
1992	47.8	15.7

*Mainline ports for Southeast are: Seattle (until 1989), Bellingham (since 1989), Vancouver (1970 to 1973 only), Prince Rupert, Ketchikan, Wrangell, Petersburg, Sitka, Juneau, Haines and Skagway. Mainline ports for southwestern Alaska are: Anchorage (1970 to 1973 only), Cordova, Valdez, Whittier, Homer, Seldovia, Kodiak, Seward and Port Lions.
**Does not include totals of passengers (9.5) and vehicles (2.9) on the MV *Aurora*.

NAUTICAL MILES BETWEEN PORTS
Southeastern System
Bellingham–Ketchikan, 600
Prince Rupert–Ketchikan, 91
Ketchikan–Metlakatla, 16
Ketchikan–Hollis, 40
Hollis–Petersburg, 122
Hollis–Wrangell, 95
Ketchikan–Wrangell, 89
Wrangell–Petersburg, 41
Petersburg–Juneau, 108
Petersburg–Kake, 59
Kake–Sitka, 110
Sitka–Angoon, 66
Angoon–Tenakee, 33
Tenakee–Hoonah, 47
Angoon–Hoonah, 60
Hoonah–Juneau (Auke Bay), 45
Sitka–Hoonah, 115
Hoonah–Pelican via South Pass, 58
Hoonah–Juneau, 68
Juneau–Haines, 91
Haines–Skagway, 13
Juneau (Auke Bay)–Haines, 68
Petersburg–Juneau (Auke Bay), 120
Petersburg–Sitka, 156
Juneau (Auke Bay)–Sitka, 136

Southwestern System
Seward–Cordova, 146
Seward–Valdez, 143
Cordova–Valdez, 73
Valdez–Whittier, 84
Seward–Kodiak, 175

Southwestern System *(continued)*
Kodiak–Port Lions, 27
Kodiak–Homer, 126
Homer–Seldovia, 16
Kodiak–Sand Point via Sitkinak Strait, 353

Fires on Wild Land

The 1993 fire season marked 54 years of fire fighting in Alaska. In 1939, fire guards covered only 4 percent of the area needing protection. Today, no area goes unprotected. Village crews make up the backbone of Alaska's fire-fighting operations.

Fire season starts in April or May, when winter's dead vegetation is vulnerable to any spark. Lightning is the leading cause of wild land fires in Alaska. In June, thunderstorms bring as many as 3,000 lightning strikes a day to the Alaska Interior. By mid-July in a normal year, rainfall in interior Alaska increases.

When wildfires threaten inhabited areas, the Bureau of Land Management's (BLM) Alaska Fire Service (in the northern half of the state) and the State of Alaska Division of Forestry (in the southern half of the state) provide fire protection to lands managed by the BLM, National Park Service, U.S. Fish and Wildlife Service, Native corporations and the state.

All land management agencies in Alaska have placed their lands in one of four protection categories—critical, full, modified and limited. These protection levels set priorities for fire fighting.

With its 586,000 square miles of land, Alaska is more than twice the size of Texas. Most of this vast area has no roads, and transportation for fire fighters is usually by airplane. Fire camps are remote. Mosquito repellent is a necessity, but headlamps are not required since the midnight sun shines all night. Aircraft bring in all supplies, even drinking water. Radios are the only means of communication with headquarters.

Black spruce is a fire-dependent species and burns very quickly. Fire fighters use chain saws to cut the trees and pulaskis to cut through the underlying vegetation. It is nearly impossible to transport heavy equipment to fires in remote areas. Bulldozers are not used because they damage the delicate permafrost layer, leading to dramatic erosion.

Fire fighters no longer depend on lookout towers in the wilderness to spot wildfires. Today, computers detect the ionization from a lightning strike anywhere in the state, determine the latitude and longitude of the strike and display it on a computer screen. Detection specialists then fly to the areas of greatest risk.

When a fire is reported, computers tell the dispatcher which agency manages the land and whether the fire should be aggressively attacked.

Remote automatic weather stations report weather conditions all over Alaska, enabling weather forecasters to predict thunderstorms in any part of the state. Smokejumpers and fire-retardant airplanes are pre-positioned close to the predicted thunderstorm activity.

The largest single fire ever reported in Alaska burned 1,161,200 acres 74 miles northwest of Galena in 1957. In 1977, the Bear Creek fire was the largest in the United States that year, consuming 361,000 acres near the Farewell airstrip. Unusually dry weather in 1990 made it the most severe fire season on record in Alaska. Lightning was the primary cause of more than 900 fires with an average of 2,000 strikes a day occurring between June 26 and July 5.

Calendar Year	No. of Fires	Acres Burned
1959	320	596,574
1960	238	87,180
1961	117	5,100
1962	102	38,975
1963	194	16,290
1964	164	3,430
1965	148	7,093
1966	256	672,765
1967	207	109,005
1968	442	1,013,301
1969	511	4,231,820
1970	487	113,486
1971	472	1,069,108
1972	641	963,686
1973	336	59,816
1974	869	662,960
1975	344	127,845
1976	622	69,119
1977	681	2,209,408
1978	356	7,757
1979	620	432,425
1980	417	188,778
1981	556	758,335
1982	283	70,798
1983	800	109,187*
1984	845	122,901*
1985	261	372,230
1986	396	395,169
1987	706	158,851*
1988	639	2,167,795*
1989	485	68,893*
1990	932	3,189,427*
1991	760	1,667,965*
1992	472	150,056

*Combined AFS (federal) and state coverage.

Calendar Year	No. of Fires	Acres Burned
1956	226	476,593
1957	391	5,049,661
1958	278	317,215

Fish Wheel

The fish wheel is a machine fastened to a river shore and propelled by current, which scoops up fish heading upstream to spawn. Widely used for subsistence salmon fishing, the fish wheel provides an easy and inexpensive way of catching salmon without injuring them. Contrary to popular belief, Alaska Natives did not invent the fish wheel. Non-natives apparently first introduced the fish wheel on the Tanana River in 1904. Soon after, it appeared on the Yukon River, where it was used by both settlers and Natives. It first appeared on the Kuskokwim in 1914, when prospectors introduced it for catching salmon near Georgetown.

Today, subsistence fishing with the use of a fish wheel is allowed on the Copper River, as well as the Yukon River and its tributaries. Currently, there are 166 limited-entry permits for the use of fish wheels by commercial salmon fishermen on the Yukon River system—the only district where commercial and subsistence fishermen use the same gear. Fishing times with the wheels are regulated.

Prior to its appearance in Alaska, the fish wheel was used on the East Coast, on the Sacramento River in California and on the Columbia River in Washington and Oregon.

Fishing

COMMERCIAL

Alaska's commercial fish production is greater in value than that of any other state in the country and first in volume, according to the state Department of Fish and Game.

Commercial fisheries in Alaska during 1991 harvested approximately 5.58 billion pounds of seafood, worth about $1.6 billion. The breakdown on the various commercial fisheries is as follows:

Salmon

The 1992 Alaska commercial salmon harvest of over 136 million salmon was in line with the state's most recent 10-year average catches. The ex-vessel value of the 1992 harvest was the second largest on record, however, as fishermen around the state landed a catch worth over $575 million. This

compares to the record ex-vessel value of about $750 million in 1988.

The 1992 season produced a record sockeye catch of over 58 million fish worth over $445 million. That value alone far exceeds the entire 1991 all-species, commercial salmon harvest value of $310 million. Sockeye accounted for about 43 percent of the statewide harvests, and this year's record catch was fueled by the second-largest catch in Upper Cook Inlet's history, and the third-largest catch in Bristol Bay's history. About 60 million pink salmon were taken commercially around the state, accounting for about 44 percent of the total salmon landings—down considerably from the 128 million pink record established in 1991. Chum landings continued a recent downward trend, and represented about 7 percent of the Alaska harvest. Coho and chinook catches contributed 5 percent and less than 1 percent to the statewide total, respectively.

There are approximately 12,000 limited-entry salmon permits in the state. The 1992 season again presented a mixed bag for those permit holders. Most drift fishermen willing to do battle in Bristol Bay's Egegik District did exceptionally well. Cook Inlet drifters and eastside setnetters took advantage of a sockeye return far stronger than anticipated. Southeast seiners targeted on a strong return of pinks. However, for others the season was a major disappointment. Pink salmon failed to show in projected numbers in Prince William Sound, Lower Cook Inlet and Kodiak. Weak fall chum salmon returns to Yukon prevented any commercial fishery during the fall season. Some setnetters in Cook Inlet and Bristol Bay had little opportunity because of the nature of salmon returns to the river systems they fished.

Shellfish

The 1992 (1991–92) shellfish season produced a harvest of aproximately 380 million pounds, worth over $300 million to participating fishermen. This is a slight decrease from the previous year record, as both king and Tanner crab landings decreased. Bering Sea C. *opilio* Tanner crab catches once again dominated all catches with over 315 million pounds taken in about four months.

Herring

The 1992 commercial herring harvests set new records. The sac roe fisheries accounted for over 64,000 tons of the 73,523-ton herring total. This catch was significantly greater than any previous season. The value of the 1992 herring fisheries, which include sac roe, food and bait, and spawn on kelp fisheries, was about $30 million, up slightly from the previous year. Poorer prices contributed to lower values despite larger catches.

Halibut

The 1992 commercial halibut fisheries in Alaska produced a catch of approximately 51 million pounds, worth about $49 million according to the International Pacific Halibut Commission. Halibut fisheries in Alaska may change from the present "24-hour derby style," to an Individual Fishing Quota (IFQ) system in the next several years. The new system could provide nearly year-round opportunities for the qualifying fleet.

Groundfish

According to statistics compiled by the National Marine Fisheries Service, over 4.3 billion pounds of groundfish

Value and Volume of Alaska Fish and Shellfish Landings*

Year	Value	Volume (in lbs.)
1982	$575,569,000	878,935,000
1983	543,941,000	963,765,000
1984	509,300,000	1,002,909,000
1985	590,751,000	1,184,807,000
1986	752,417,000	1,236,062,000
1987	941,690,000	1,697,547,000
1988	1,339,394,000	2,639,250,000
1989	1,332,000,000	5,213,100,000
1990	1,500,000,000	5,920,000,000
1991	1,216,482,000	5,144,800,000
1992	1,577,421,000	5,637,937,000

*Source: National Marine Fisheries Service, U.S. Department of Commerce

were harvested during the 1992 season. Most was pollock from the Bering Sea. Estimates place the value at more than $600 million for Alaska's groundfish fisheries. Both volume and total value increased from the previous year.

Alaska's $1.6 billion fishing industry faces some hard choices in the future. Too many boats are chasing too few fish, according to some experts. Highly efficient trawlers with huge capacities have emphasized speed and volume fishing, increasing pressure for more and more fish to be harvested. In 1970, for example, halibut in the Gulf of Alaska were caught during a three-month fishing season by just 211 boats. In 1991, more than 2,500 boats competed for the halibut harvest, compressing the season to just two days.

Nowhere in the industry has the race for fish been as frenzied as for Alaska's groundfish, for which the number of harvesting permits has grown 700 percent in the last 10 years. Not so long ago, groundfish such as pollock and cod were considered low-value species. Groundfish today is a $600 million piece of the fisheries pie.

There is growing concern that over-exploitation of Alaska's fisheries could result in biological devastation of some species—a problem that New England fisheries now face. In the quest for quick, high-yield catches, there is significant accidental by-catch waste of species such as halibut, salmon and crab. An estimated 3 percent of the halibut taken from the North Pacific in 1989 was the result of waste. Illegal fishing, questions about the effects of concentrated harvesting during spawning season and habitat pollution add to the potential biological difficulties that the Alaska fishing industry could face. The prospect is serious enough that regulators are considering an end to open access fishing by imposing a moratorium on the granting of new commercial permits and instituting a system of individual quotas. Instead of a short derby-style fishing season, individual fishermen would be allowed a set amount of fish to harvest each year.

Following are Alaska Department of Fish and Game ex-vessel value figures:

Value of Alaska's Commercial Fisheries to Fishermen (in millions of dollars)

Species	1985	1986	1987	1988	1989	1990	1991	1992*
Salmon	$389.0	$414.0	$457.9	$744.9	$505.0	$546.8	$312.3	$575
Shellfish	106.3	186.4	213.5	235.6	274.0	352.0	301.4	301
Halibut	40.3	63.2	60.9	66.1	76.1	85.0	91.6	49
Herring	38.0	38.5	41.8	56.0	20.3	27.0	28.6	30
Groundfish	137.5**	197.9**	324.3	441.1	456.6	482.8	482.6	625

*Preliminary estimates.
**Includes international, joint-venture landings not previously shown in table.

1992 Preliminary Commercial Salmon Harvest (in thousands of fish)

Region	King	Red	Silver	Pink	Chum	Total
Southeast	233	2,665	3,685	34,959	4,964	46,506
Central (Prince William Sound, Cook Inlet, Kodiak,Chignik and Bristol Bay)	164	48,485	1,844	14,934	2,511	67,938
Arctic–Yukon– Kuskokwim	196	197	887	91	1,467	2,838
Western (Alaska Peninsula and Aleutian Islands)	19	6,991	596	10,045	1,685	19,336
Total	612	58,338	7,012	60,029	10,627	136,618

Note: Preliminary statistics are from Alaska Department of Fish and Game, 1993.

SPORT

There are 12 sportfishing management areas in Alaska, with varying bag and possession limits and possible special provisions. Current copies of *Alaska Sport Fishing Regulations Summary* are available from the Department of Fish and Game, Box 3-2000, Juneau 99802, or any sport-fishing office in the state.

Regulations

A sportfishing license is required for residents and nonresidents 16 years of age or older. (Alaskan residents 60 years of age or more who have been residents one year or more do not need a sportfishing license as long as they remain residents; a special identification card is issued for this exemption.)

Resident sportfishing licenses cost $10, valid for the calendar year issued (nonresident, $50; 1-day nonresident, $10; 3-day nonresident, $15; 14-day nonresident, $30). A resident is a person who has maintained a permanent place of abode within the state for 12 consecutive months and has continuously maintained a voting residence in the state. Military personnel on active duty permanently stationed in the state and their dependents can purchase a nonresident military sportfishing license ($10).

An additional tag is required for those wishing to fish for king salmon. Cost for residents is $10, for nonresidents, $20.

Nearly all sporting goods stores in Alaska sell fishing licenses. They are also available by mail from the Alaska Department of Revenue, Fish and Game License Section, 1111 W. Eighth St., Room 108, Juneau 99801.

The following sport fish species information includes the best bait or lure and the state record fish weight in pounds and ounces:

Arctic char: spoons, eggs, 17 lbs. 8 oz.
Arctic grayling: small spinners, flies, 4 lbs. 13 oz.
Burbot: bait, 24 lbs. 12 oz.
Chum salmon: spoons, 32 lbs.
Cutthroat trout: eggs, spinners, flies, 8 lbs. 6 oz.
Dolly Varden: eggs, spinners, flies, 17 lbs. 8 oz.
Halibut: octopus, herring, 450 lbs.
King salmon: eggs, herring, 97 lbs. 4 oz.
Kokanee: spinners, eggs, 2 lbs.
Lake trout: spoons, plugs, 47 lbs.

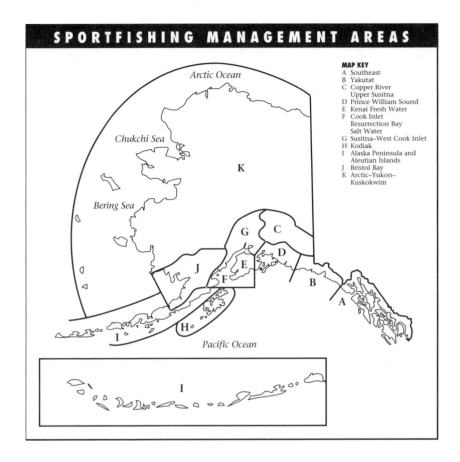

MAP KEY
A Southeast
B Yakutat
C Copper River
  Upper Susitna
D Prince William Sound
E Kenai Fresh Water
F Cook Inlet
  Resurrection Bay
  Salt Water
G Susitna–West Cook Inlet
H Kodiak
I Alaska Peninsula and
  Aleutian Islands
J Bristol Bay
K Arctic–Yukon–
  Kuskokwim

Northern pike: eggs, spoons, spinners, 38 lbs.

Pink salmon: small spoons, 12 lbs. 9 oz.

Rainbow/Steelhead trout: flies, lures, eggs, 42 lbs. 3 oz.

Red salmon: flies, 16 lbs.

Sheefish: spoons, 53 lbs.

Silver salmon: herring, spoons, 26 lbs.

Whitefish: flies, eggs, 9 lbs.

Furs and Trapping

According to the state furbearer biologist, the major sources of harvested Alaska furs are the Yukon and Kuskokwim valleys. The Arctic provides limited numbers of arctic fox, wolverine and wolf, but the Gulf Coast areas and Southeast are more productive. Southeast Alaska is a good source of mink and otter.

Trapping is seasonal work, and most trappers work summers at fishing or other employment. (Licenses are required for trapping. See Hunting section for cost of licenses.)

State-regulated furbearers are beaver, coyote, red fox (includes cross, black or silver color phases), arctic fox (includes white or blue), lynx, marmot, marten, mink, muskrat, raccoon, river (land) otter, squirrel (parka or ground, flying and red), weasel, wolf and wolverine. Very little harvest or use is made of parka squirrels and marmots.

Flying squirrels are not caught deliberately, nor are raccoons, introduced in a couple of coastal locations years ago.

Prices for raw skins are widely

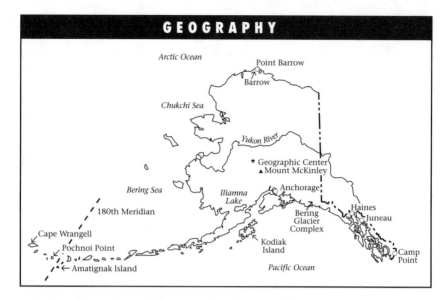

variable and depend on the buyer, quality, condition and size of the fur. Pelts accepted for purchase are beaver, coyote, lynx, marten, mink, muskrat, otter, red and white fox, red squirrel, weasel (ermine), wolf and wolverine. Check with a buyer for current market prices.

Related reading: *Trapline Twins*, by Julie and Miki Collins. Identical-twin sisters trap, canoe, dogsled and live off the land. *See* ALASKA NORTHWEST LIBRARY in the back of the book.

Geography

State capital: Juneau.
State population: 570,000
Land area: 586,412 square miles, or about 365,000,000 acres—largest state in the union; one-fifth the size of the Lower 48. Alaska is larger than the three next largest states in the United States combined.
Area per person: Approximately 1.02 square miles per person.
Diameter: East to west, 2,400 miles; north to south, 1,420 miles.
Coastline: 6,640 miles, point to point; as measured on the most detailed maps available, including islands, Alaska has 33,904 miles of shoreline.

Estimated tidal shoreline, including islands, inlets and shoreline to head of tidewater, is 47,300 miles.
Adjacent salt water: North Pacific Ocean, Bering Sea, Chukchi Sea, Arctic Ocean.
Alaska–Canada border: 1,538 miles long; length of boundary between the Arctic Ocean and Mount St. Elias, 647 miles; Southeast border with British Columbia and Yukon Territory, 710 miles; water boundary, 181 miles.
Geographic center: 63°50′ north, 152° west, about 60 miles northwest of Mount McKinley.
Northernmost point: Point Barrow, 71°23′ north.
Southernmost point: Tip of Amatignak Island, Aleutian Chain, 51°13′05″ north.
Easternmost and westernmost points: It all depends on how you look at it. The 180th meridian—halfway around the world from the prime meridian at Greenwich, England, and the dividing line between east and west longitudes—passes through Alaska. According to one view, Alaska has both the easternmost and westernmost spots in the country! The westernmost is Amatignak Island, 179°10′ west; and the easternmost, Pochnoi Point, 179°46′ east. On the other hand, if you are facing north, east is to your right

and west to your left. Therefore, the westernmost point is Cape Wrangell, Attu Island, 172°27' east; and the easternmost is near Camp Point, in southeastern Alaska, 129°59' east.

Tallest mountain: Mount McKinley, 20,320 feet, and the tallest mountain in North America. Alaska has 39 mountain ranges, containing 17 of the 20 highest peaks in the United States.

Largest natural freshwater lake: Iliamna, 1,150 square miles. Alaska has more than three million lakes more than 20 acres in size.

Longest river: Yukon, 1,400 miles in Alaska; 1,875 total. There are more than 3,000 rivers in the state. The Yukon River ranks third in length of U.S. rivers, behind the Mississippi and Missouri rivers.

Largest island: Kodiak, in the Gulf of Alaska, 3,588 square miles. There are 1,800 named islands in the state, 1,000 of which are located in Southeast Alaska.

Largest glacier: Bering Glacier complex, 2,250 square miles, which includes the Bagley Icefield. Ice fields cover about 5 percent of the state, or 29,000 square miles.

Largest city in population: Anchorage, population 226,338 (1990 census).

Largest city in area: Sitka, with 4,710 square miles, 1,816 square miles of which are water. Juneau is second, with 3,108 square miles.

Glaciers and Ice Fields

The greatest concentrations of glaciers are in the Alaska Range, Wrangell Mountains, and the coastal ranges of the Chugach, Coast, Kenai and St. Elias mountains, where annual precipitation is high. All of Alaska's well-known glaciers fall within these areas. (See map on page 64.)

Glaciers cover approximately 29,000 square miles—or 5 percent—of Alaska, which is 128 times more area covered by glaciers than in the rest of the United States. There are an estimated 100,000 glaciers in Alaska, ranging from tiny cirque glaciers to huge valley glaciers.

Glaciers are formed where, over a number of years, more snow falls than melts. Alaska's glaciers fall roughly into five general categories: alpine, valley, piedmont, ice fields and ice caps. Alpine (mountain and cirque) glaciers head high on the slopes of mountains and plateaus. Valley glaciers are an overflowing accumulation of ice from mountain or plateau basins. Piedmont glaciers result when one or more glaciers join to form a fan-shaped ice mass at the foot of a mountain range. Ice fields develop when large valley glaciers interconnect, leaving only the highest peaks and ridges to rise above the ice surface. Ice caps are smaller glaciers perched on plateaus.

Alaska's better-known glaciers accessible by road are: Worthington (Richardson Highway), Matanuska (Glenn Highway), Exit (Seward Highway), Portage (Seward Highway) and Mendenhall (Glacier Highway). In addition, Childs and Sheridan glaciers may be reached by car from Cordova, and Valdez Glacier, also accessible by car, is only a few miles from the town of Valdez. The sediment-covered terminus of Muldrow Glacier in Denali National Park and Preserve is visible at a distance along several miles of the park road.

Many spectacular glaciers in Glacier Bay National Park and Preserve and in Prince William Sound are accessible by tour boat.

Glacier ice often appears blue because its great density absorbs all the colors of the spectrum except blue, which is reflected back.

Other facts about glaciers:

• About three-fourths of all the fresh water in Alaska is stored as glacial ice. This is many times greater than the volume of water stored in all the state's lakes, ponds, rivers and reservoirs.

• Longest tidewater glacier in North America is Hubbard, 76 miles in length (heads in Canada). In 1986, Hubbard rapidly advanced and blocked Russell Fiord near Yakutat. Later in the year, the ice dam gave way.

• Longest glacier is Bering (including Bagley Icefield), more than 100 miles in length.

• Southernmost active tidewater glacier in North America is LeConte.

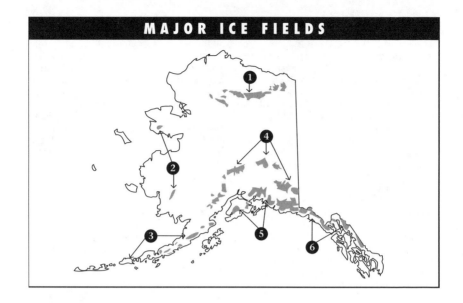

• Greatest concentration of tidewater-calving glaciers is in Prince William Sound, with 20 active tidewater glaciers.

• Largest piedmont lobe glacier is Malaspina, 850 square miles; the Malaspina Glacier complex (including tributary glaciers) is approximately 2,000 square miles in area. The largest glacier is the Bering Glacier complex, about 2,250 square miles in size, which includes Bagley Icefield.

• La Perouse Glacier in Glacier Bay National Park is the only calving glacier in North America that discharges icebergs directly into the open Pacific Ocean.

• Iceberg production in Prince William Sound has increased fourfold recently because Columbia Glacier is retreating.

• There are more than 750 glacier-dammed lakes in Alaska; the largest at the present time is 28-square-mile Chakachamna Lake west of Anchorage.

According to the U.S. Geological Survey, distribution of glacier ice is as follows (see map above):

Region	Sq. Miles (approx.)
1 **North**: Brooks Range	279
2 **West**: Seward Peninsula	2
Kilbuk Mountains	89
3 **Southwest**: Aleutian Islands	371
Alaska Peninsula	483
4 **Interior**: Alaska Range	5,367
Talkeetna Mountains	309
Wrangell Mountains	3,205
5 **Southcentral**: Kenai Mtns	1,776
Chugach Mountains	8,340
6 **Southeast**: St. Elias Mtns	4,556
Coast Mountains	4,055
Total	28,832

Gold

(*See also* Minerals and Mining)

The largest gold nugget ever found in Alaska was discovered near Nome. The nugget, weighing 155 troy ounces, was found Sept. 29, 1903, on Discovery Claim on Anvil Creek, Nome District. The nugget was 7 inches long, 4 inches wide and 2 inches thick.

Four other large nuggets have been found in Alaska, one of which also came from the Discovery Claim on Anvil Creek in 1899. It was the largest Alaska nugget found up to that time, weighing 82.2 troy ounces, and was 6^1/4 inches long, 3^1/4 inches wide, 1^3/8 inches thick at one end and ^{1}/2 inch thick at the other.

In 1914, the second-largest nugget mined, weighing 138.8 troy ounces, was found near Discovery Claim on Hammond River, Wiseman District. Two of the top five nuggets have been discovered within the last ten years, with one coming from Lower Glacier Creek, Kantishna District, in 1984, weighing 91.8 troy ounces, and the other from Ganes Creek, Innoko District, in 1986, weighing 122 troy ounces.

According to *Alaska's Mineral Industry 1992*, a publication of the Alaska Division of Geological and Geophysical Surveys, major operators produced 262,500 troy ounces of gold in 1992.

Following are volumes (in troy ounces) and value figures for recent years of Alaska gold production:

Gold Production in Alaska, 1980–92

Year	Vol. (in troy oz.)	Value
1980	75,000	$32,000,000
1981	134,000	55,200,000
1982	174,900	69,960,000
1983	169,000	67,600,000
1984	175,000	63,000,000
1985	190,000	61,175,000
1986	160,000	60,800,000
1987	229,700	104,500,000
1988	265,500	112,837,000
1989	297,900	113,796,000
1990	231,700	89,204,000
1991	243,900	88,291,000
1992	262,500	88,463,000

The following chart shows the fluctuation in the price of gold after the gold standard was lifted in 1967. Note that these are average annual prices and do not reflect the highest or lowest prices during the year.

Average Annual Price of Gold, per Troy Ounce

1934 to 1967—$35.00	1980—$569.73
1968— 39.26	1981— 548.90
1969— 41.51	1982— 461.00
1970— 36.41	1983— 400.00
1971— 41.25	1984— 360.00
1972— 58.60	1985— 325.00
1973— 97.81	1986— 380.00
1974—159.74	1987— 447.00
1975—161.49	1988— 425.00
1976—125.32	1989— 381.98
1977—148.31	1990— 385.00
1978—193.55	1991— 362.03
1979—307.50	1992— 337.00

If you are interested in gold panning, sluicing or suction dredging in Alaska—for fun or profit—you'll have to know whose land you are on and familiarize yourself with current regulations.

Panning, sluicing and suction dredging on private property, established mining claims and Native lands is considered trespassing unless you have the consent of the owner. On state and federal lands, contact the agency for the area you are interested in for current restrictions on mining.

You can pan for gold for a small fee by visiting one of the commercial gold-panning resorts in Alaska. These resorts rent gold pans and let you try your luck on gold-bearing creeks and streams on their property.

If you want to stake a permanent claim, the state Department of Natural Resources has a free booklet, *Regulations and Statutes Pertaining to Mining Rights of Alaska Lands,* which can be obtained by contacting the department office in Juneau, (907) 465-2400; Fairbanks, (907) 451-2790; and Anchorage, (907) 762-2518.

Gold Strikes and Rushes

1848—First Alaska gold discovery (Russian River on Kenai Peninsula)

1861—Stikine River near Telegraph Creek, British Columbia

1872—Cassiar district in Canada (Stikine headwaters country)

1872—Near Sitka

1874—Windham Bay near Juneau

1880—Gold Creek at Juneau

1886—Fortymile discovery

1887—Yakutat beach areas and Lituya Bay

1893—Mastodon Creek, starting Circle City

1895—Sunrise district on the Kenai Peninsula

1896—Klondike strike, Bonanza Creek, Yukon, Canada

1898—Anvil Creek near Nome; Atlin district

1898—British Columbia

1900—Porcupine rush out of Haines

1902—Fairbanks (Felix Pedro, Upper Goldstream Valley)

1906—Innoko
1907—Ruby
1908—Iditarod
1913—Marshall
1913—Chisana
1914—Livengood

Related reading: *Chilkoot Pass: The Most Famous Trail in the North,* revised and expanded edition, by Archie Satterfield. *See* ALASKA NORTH-WEST LIBRARY in the back of the book.

Government

(*See also* Courts *and* Officials)

Alaska is represented in the U.S. Congress by two senators and one representative. The capital of Alaska is Juneau.

A governor and lieutenant governor are elected by popular vote for four-year terms on the same ticket. The governor is given extensive powers under the constitution. He administers 15 major departments: Administration, Commerce and Economic Development, Community and Regional Affairs, Corrections, Education, Environmental Conservation, Fish and Game, Health and Social Services, Labor, Law, Military and Veterans Affairs, Natural Resources, Public Safety, Revenue, and Transportation and Public Facilities.

The legislature is bicameral, with 20 senators elected from 14 senate districts for four-year terms, and 40 representatives from 27 election districts for two-year terms. Under the state constitution, redistricting is accomplished every 10 years, after the reporting of the decennial federal census. The latest redistricting occurred in 1981 and was carried out by the governor's office with assistance of an advisory apportionment board. The judiciary consists of a state supreme court, court of appeals, superior court, district courts and magistrates.

Alaska is unique among the 50 states in that most of its land mass has not been organized into political subdivisions equivalent to the county form of government. Local government is by a system of organized boroughs, much like counties in other states. Several areas of the state are not included in any borough because of sparse population. Boroughs generally provide a more limited number of services than cities. There are three classes. First- and second-class boroughs have three mandatory powers: education, land use planning, and tax assessment and collection. The major difference between the two classes is in how they may acquire other powers. Both classes have separately elected borough assemblies and school boards. A third-class borough has two mandatory powers: operation of public schools and taxation. All boroughs may assess, levy and collect real and personal property taxes. They may also levy sales taxes.

Incorporated cities are small units of local government, serving one community. There are two classes. First-class cities, generally urban areas, have six-member councils and a separately elected mayor. Taxing authority is somewhat broader than for second-class cities and responsibilities are broader. A first-class city that has adopted a home rule charter is called a home rule city; adoption allows the city to revise its ordinances, to the extent that the powers it assumes are those not prohibited by law or charter. Second-class cities, generally places with fewer than 400 people, are governed by a seven-member council, one of whom serves as mayor. Taxing authority is limited.

A borough and all cities located within it may unite in a single unit of government called a unified municipality.

There are 246 federally recognized tribal governments in Alaska and one community organized under federal law. Originally an Indian reservation, Metlakatla was organized so municipal services could effectively be provided to its residents.

In 1991, there were 15 organized boroughs and unified home rule municipalities: three unified home rule municipalities, four home rule boroughs, seven second-class boroughs and one third-class borough.

Alaska's 150 incorporated cities include: 12 home rule cities, 22 first-class cities and 116 second-class cities. One city, Metlakatla, is organized under federal law.

BOROUGH ADDRESSES AND CONTACTS
Aleutians East Borough
P.O. Box 349, Sand Point 99661; phone (907) 383-5334
Municipality of Anchorage
Contact: Mayor's Office or Manager's Office, P.O. Box 196650, Anchorage 99519; phone (907) 343-4431
Bristol Bay Borough
Contact: Borough Clerk, P.O. Box 189, Naknek 99633; phone (907) 246-4224
Denali Borough
Contact: Mayor, P.O. Box 480, Anderson 99744; phone (907) 683-1330.
Fairbanks North Star Borough
Contact: Clerk, P.O. Box 71267, Fairbanks 99707; phone (907) 459-1000
Haines Borough
Contact: Borough Secretary, P.O. Box 1209, Haines 99827; phone (907) 766-2611
City and Borough of Juneau
Contact: City-Borough Manager, 155 S. Seward St., Juneau 99801; phone (907) 586-5240
Kenai Peninsula Borough
Contact: Borough Clerk, 144 N. Binkley St., Soldotna 99669; phone (907) 262-4441
Ketchikan Gateway Borough
Contact: Borough Manager, 344 Front St., Ketchikan 99901; phone (907) 225-6625
Kodiak Island Borough
Contact: Borough Mayor or Borough

Clerk, 710 Mill Bay Road, Kodiak 99615; phone (907) 486-5736
Lake and Peninsula Borough
P.O. Box 495, King Salmon 99613; phone (907) 276-3421
Matanuska–Susitna Borough
Contact: Borough Manager, 350 E. Dahlia Ave., Palmer 99645-6488; phone (907) 745-4801
North Slope Borough
Contact: Borough Mayor, P.O. Box 69, Barrow 99723; phone (907) 852-2611
Northwest Arctic Borough
P.O. Box 1110, Kotzebue 99752; phone (907) 442-2500
City and Borough of Sitka
Contact: Administrator, 304 Lake St., Room 104, Sitka 99835; phone (907) 747-3294

Highways

(*See also* Alaska Highway *and* Dalton Highway)

As of June 1993, the state Department of Transportation and Public Facilities estimated total public road mileage in Alaska at 13,632 miles, including those in national parks and forests (2,539). The state also operates 2,229 miles of ferry routes.

Highways in Alaska range from four-lane paved freeways to one-lane dirt and gravel roads.

Approximately 47 percent of the roads in the Alaska Highway system are paved, with the exception of the following major highways that are gravel: Steese (Alaska Route 6), Taylor (Alaska Route 5), Elliott (Alaska Route 2), Dalton (Alaska Route 12) and Denali (Alaska Route 8). Alaska's relative sparseness of roadway is accentuated by a comparison to Austria, a country only one-eighteenth the size of Alaska but with nearly twice as many public roads.

The chart on page 68 lists each major highway in Alaska, its route number, the year the highway opened to vehicle traffic and its total length within Alaska (most of the Alaska Highway, Haines Highway and Klondike Highway 2 lie within Canada). Also indicated is whether the highway is open all year or closed in winter:

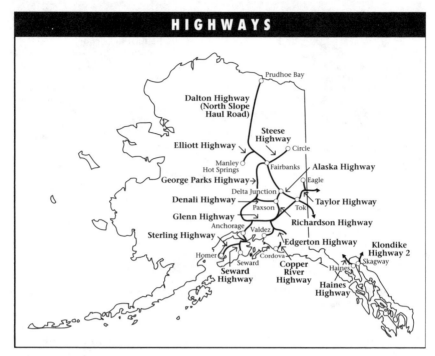

	Alaska Route	Year Opened	Total Length (miles) Paved	Gravel	Open
Alaska	2	1942	298.2*		All year
Copper River	10 **		12.4	35.7	Apr.–Oct.
Dalton	12	1974		414	All year
Denali	8	1957	21	115	Apr.–Oct.
Edgerton	10	1923	35		All year
Elliott	2	1959	28	124	All year
George Parks	3	1971	322.7		All year
Glenn	1	1942	328*		All year
Haines	7	1947	40.5		All year
Klondike	2	1978	14.9		All year
Richardson	4	1923	368*		All year
Seward	1&9	1951	127		All year
Steese	6	1928	43.8	118.2	All year
Sterling	1	1950	135.8		All year
Taylor	5	1953		161	Apr.–Oct.

*The Richardson shares a common alignment with the Alaska Highway (for 98 miles) and with the Glenn (for 14 miles).
**Construction on the Copper River Highway—which was to link up with Chitina on the Edgerton—was halted by the 1964 Good Friday earthquake, which damaged the Million Dollar Bridge, and local Cordova citizens who desired semi-isolation.

Hiking

Developed trails suitable for all ability levels may be found near Alaska's larger cities and towns. However, most of Alaska's public recreation lands are wilderness. Trails are nonexistent and hikers must chart their own course using topographic maps and compass. Using both maps and tide tables, it is also feasible to hike along ocean shorelines at low tide.

Hikers in Alaska must plan for cold, wet and rapidly changing weather. Take rain gear. If staying overnight in the back country, carry a tent, backpacking stove, first-aid kit and emergency flares. Snow can be encountered at any time of year.

Bears inhabit most of Alaska. Read all bear safety information and follow proper procedures for camping and hiking in bear country. You must be completely self-sufficient and responsible for your own safety. (*See* Bears)

Plan to bring everything you need with you, as there are few businesses that rent outdoor equipment. Back country guides often furnish equipment on escorted expeditions.

Information on hiking in Alaska's national parks and monuments is available from the Alaska Public Lands Information Centers: 605 W. Fourth Ave., Suite 105, Anchorage 99501; 250 Cushman St., Suite 1A, Fairbanks 99701; and P.O. Box 359, Tok 99780; or from park headquarters for the area you're interested in. (*See* National Parks, Preserves and Monuments)

The Alaska Division of Parks (*see* State Park System) has information on hiking on the lands managed by that agency.

History

(*See also* Russian Alaska)

6,000–11,000 years ago—Human culture in southeastern, Aleutians, Interior and northwestern Arctic Alaska.

6,000 years ago—Most recent migration from Siberia across the land bridge. Earliest migration believed to have taken place up to 20,000 years ago.

3,000–5,000 years ago—Human culture present on the Bering Sea coast.

1725—Vitus Bering sent by Peter the Great to explore the North Pacific.

1741—On a later expedition, Bering in one ship and Alexei Chirikof in another ship, sights Alaska. Chirikof probably sees land on July 15, a day ahead of his leader, who was perhaps 300 miles or more to the north. Georg Steller goes ashore on Kayak Island, becoming the first white man known to have set foot on Alaska soil.

1743—Russians begin concentrated hunting of sea otter, continuing until the species is almost decimated; fur seal hunting begins later.

1774–94—Explorations of Alaska waters by Juan Perez, James Cook and George Vancouver.

1784—First Russian settlement in Alaska established at Three Saints Bay, Kodiak Island.

1794—Vancouver sights Mount McKinley.

1799—Alexander Baranof establishes the Russian post known today as Old Sitka. A trade charter is granted to the Russian–American Company.

1821—Russians prohibit trading in Alaska waters by other nations, making the Russian–American Company the sole trading firm.

1824–42—Russian exploration of the mainland leads to the discovery of the Kuskokwim, Nushagak, Yukon and Koyukuk rivers.

1847—Fort Yukon is established by Hudson's Bay Company.

1848—First mining begins in Alaska, on the Kenai Peninsula.

1853—Russian explorers-trappers find the first oil seeps in Cook Inlet.

1857—Coal mining begins at Coal Harbor, Kenai Peninsula, to supply steamers.

1859—Baron Edoard de Stoecki, minister and chargé d'affaires of the Russian delegation to the United States, is given authority to negotiate the sale of Alaska.

1867—United States under President Andrew Johnson buys Alaska from Russia for $7.2 million; the treaty is signed March 30 and formal transfer takes place on October 18 at Sitka. Fur seal population begins to stabilize. U.S.

Army is given jurisdiction over the Department of Alaska the following year.

1869-70—The *Sitka Times,* first newspaper in Alaska, published.

1872—Gold is discovered near Sitka. Later discoveries include Windham, 1874; Juneau, 1880; Fortymile, 1886; Circle City, 1893; Sunrise District (Kenai Peninsula), 1895; Nome, 1898; Fairbanks, 1902; Innoko, 1906; Ruby, 1907; Iditarod, 1908; Marshall, 1913; Chisana, 1913; and Livengood, 1914.

1878—First salmon canneries established at Klawock and Old Sitka.

1882—First commercial herring fishing begins; U.S. Navy destroys the Tlingit village of Angoon.

1887—Tsimshians, under Father William Duncan, arrive at Metlakatla from British Columbia.

1891—First oil claims staked in Cook Inlet area.

1897-1900—Klondike gold rush in Yukon Territory; heavy traffic through Alaska on the way to the goldfields.

1902—First oil production, at Katalla. Telegraph from Eagle to Valdez is completed.

1906—Peak gold production year. Alaska is granted a nonvoting delegate to Congress.

1911—Copper production begins at Kennicott.

1912—Territorial status for Alaska; first territorial legislature is convened the following year.

1913—First airplane flight in Alaska, at Fairbanks; first automobile trip from Fairbanks to Valdez.

1914—President Wilson authorizes construction of the Alaska Railroad.

1916—First bill proposing Alaska statehood is introduced in Congress; peak copper production year.

1922—First pulp mill starts production at Speel River, near Juneau.

1923—President Warren Harding drives spike completing the Alaska Railroad.

1930—The first "talkie" motion picture is shown in Fairbanks, featuring the Marx Brothers in *The Cocoanuts.*

1935—Matanuska Valley Project, which establishes farming families in Alaska, begins. First Juneau-to-Fairbanks flight.

1936—All-time record salmon catch in Alaska—126.4 million fish.

1940—Military buildup in Alaska; Fort Richardson, Elmendorf Air Force Base are established. At this point there are only about 40,000 non-Native Alaskans and 32,458 Natives. Pan American Airways inaugurates twice-weekly service between Seattle, Ketchikan and Juneau, using Sikorsky flying boats.

1942—Dutch Harbor is bombed and Attu and Kiska islands are occupied by Japanese forces. Alaska Highway is built—first overland connection to Lower 48.

1943—Japanese forces are driven from Alaska.

1944—Alaska–Juneau Mine shuts down.

1953—Oil well is drilled near Eureka, on the Glenn Highway, marking the start of modern oil history; first plywood mill at Juneau; first big pulp mill at Ketchikan.

1957—Kenai oil strike.

1958—Statehood measure is passed by Congress; statehood is proclaimed officially on Jan. 3, 1959. Sitka pulp mill opens.

1964—Good Friday earthquake, March 27, causes heavy damage throughout the Gulf Coast region; 131 people lose their lives.

1967—Alaska Centennial celebration; Fairbanks flood.

1968—Oil and gas discoveries at Prudhoe Bay on the North Slope; $900 million North Slope oil lease sale the following year; pipeline proposal follows.

1971—Congress approves Alaska Native Claims Settlement Act, granting title to 40 million acres of land and providing more than $900 million in payment to Alaska Natives.

1974—Trans-Alaska pipeline receives final approval; construction buildup begins.

1975—Population and labor force soar with construction of pipeline; Alaska Gross Products hits $5.8 billion—double the 1973 figure.

1976—Voters select Willow area for new capital site.

1977—Completion of the trans-Alaska pipeline from Prudhoe Bay to Valdez; shipment of first oil by tanker from Valdez to Puget Sound.

1978—A 200-mile offshore fishing limit goes into effect. President Jimmy Carter withdraws 56 million acres of federal lands in Alaska to create 17 new national monuments.

1979—State of Alaska files suit to halt the withdrawal of 56 million acres of Alaska land by President Carter under the Antiquities Act.

1980—Special session of the Alaska legislature votes to repeal the state income tax and provides for refunds of 1979 taxes. Legislature establishes a Permanent Fund as a repository for one-fourth of all royalty oil revenues for future generations. Census figures show Alaska's population grew by 32.4 percent during the 1970s. The Alaska Lands Act of 1980 puts 53.7 million Alaska acres into the national wildlife refuge system, parts of 25 rivers into the national wild and scenic rivers system, 3.3 million acres into national forest lands and 43.6 million acres into national park land.

1981—Legislature puts on the ballot a constitutional amendment proposal to limit state spending. Secretary of the Interior James Watt initiates plans to sell oil and gas leases on 130 million acres of Alaska's nonrestricted federal land and announces a tentative schedule to open 16 offshore areas of Alaska as part of an intense national search for oil and gas on the outer continental shelf.

1982—Oil revenues for state decrease. Vote for funds to move state capital from Juneau to Willow is defeated. First permanent fund dividend checks of $1,000 each are mailed to every six-month resident of Alaska.

1983—Time zone shift. All Alaska, except westernmost Aleutian Islands, moves to Alaska Standard Time, one hour west of Pacific Standard Time. Record-breaking salmon harvest in Bristol Bay. Building permits set a record at just under $1 billion.

1984—State of Alaska celebrates its 25th birthday.

1985—Anchorage receives the U.S. bid for the 1994 Olympics. Iditarod Sled Dog Race is won by Libby Riddles, the first woman to win in the history of the race.

1986—Mount Augustine in lower Cook Inlet erupts. World Champion-

Mount Augustine

ship Sled Dog Race held during Fur Rendezvous is canceled for the first time due to lack of snow. Iditarod Sled Dog Race is again won by a woman, Susan Butcher of Manley.

1987—Alaska is retained as America's choice for the 1994 Olympics. Iditarod Sled Dog Race is won by Susan Butcher for the second straight year.

1988—The first successful solo winter ascent of Mount McKinley by Vern Tejas of Anchorage. The Iditarod Sled Dog Race is won by Susan Butcher for the third year in a row. Anchorage loses its bid to Norway for the 1994 Olympics.

1989—Worst oil spill in U.S. history occurs in Prince William Sound. Record-breaking cold hits entire state, lasting for weeks. Soviets visit Alaska, and the Bering Bridge Expedition crosses the Bering Strait by dogsled and skis. Mount Redoubt begins erupting in December.

1990—Valdez sets a new record for snowfall. Susan Butcher wins her fourth Iditarod Sled Dog Race. Election upset as Walter J. Hickel becomes governor.

1991—Fairbanks sets a new record for snowfall. Rick Swenson claims fifth Iditarod win.

1992—Alaska celebrates 50th anniversary of the Alaska Highway; one of Alaska's oldest newspapers, the *Anchorage Times*, shuts down; Mount Spurr erupts.

1993—Exxon releases its scientific study on the effect of the oil spill in Prince William Sound; the Department of Fish and Game announces a plan to allow aerial hunting of wolves; springtime comes early to the Interior, making April the second warmest on record.

71

Holidays 1994

New Year's Day........................January 1
Martin Luther King Day......January 17
President's Day
—holiday...............................February 21
—traditional.........................February 22
Seward's Day*.........................March 28
Memorial Day............................May 30
Independence Day.......................July 4
Labor Day...........................September 5
Alaska Day**........................October 17
Veterans Day....................November 11
Thanksgiving Day............November 24
Christmas Day..................December 25

*Seward's Day commemorates the signing of the treaty by which the United States bought Alaska from Russia, signed on March 30, 1867.
**Alaska Day is the anniversary of the formal transfer of the territory and the raising of the U.S. flag at Sitka on Oct. 18, 1867.

Homesteading

(*See* Land Use)

Hooligan

Smelt, also known as eulachon or candlefish (because these oily little fish can be burned like candles), are known as "ooligan" in southeastern Alaska. Natives once used hooligan for trading. Hooligan are caught by dip-netting as they travel upriver to spawn.

Hospitals and Health Facilities

(*See also* Pioneers' Homes)
Alaska has numerous hospitals, nursing homes and other health facilities. The only hospital in the state currently offering specialized care units is Providence Hospital in Anchorage, with its thermal unit (burn and frostbite), cancer treatment center and neonatal intensive care nursery.

A list of emergency medical services on Alaska's highways and marine highways is provided in a brochure available from the Office of Emergency Medical Services, Division of Public Health, Dept. of Health and Social Services, P.O. Box H, Juneau 99811.

MUNICIPAL, PRIVATE AND STATE HOSPITALS

Anchorage
Alaska Psychiatric Institute (176 beds), 2900 Providence Drive, 99508

Alaska Regional Hospital (238 beds), 2801 DeBarr Road, P.O. Box 143889, 99514

Providence Hospital (341 beds), 3200 Providence Drive, P.O. Box 196604, 99519

Cordova
Cordova Community Hospital (23 beds), Box 160, 99574

Fairbanks
Fairbanks Memorial Hospital (166 beds), 1650 Cowles St., 99701

Glennallen
Cross Road Medical Center (6 beds), Box 5, 99588

Homer
South Peninsula Hospital (39 beds), 4300 Bartlett St., 99603

Juneau
Bartlett Memorial Hospital (51 beds), 3260 Hospital Drive, 99801

Juneau Recovery Unit (15 alcoholism treatment beds), 3250 Hospital Drive, 99801

Ketchikan
Ketchikan General Hospital (92 beds), 3100 Tongass Ave., 99901

Kodiak
Kodiak Island Hospital (44 beds), 1915 E. Rezanof Drive, 99615

Palmer
Valley Hospital (36 beds), P.O. Box 1687, 99645

Petersburg
Petersburg General Hospital (25 beds), Box 589, 99833

Seward
Seward General Hospital (32 beds), Box 365, 99664

Sitka
Sitka Community Hospital (24

beds), 209 Moller Drive, P.O. Box 500, 99835

Soldotna
Central Peninsula General Hospital (62 beds), 250 Hospital Place, 99669

Valdez
Harborview Developmental Center (state-operated residential center for the mentally handicapped; 80 beds), Box 487, 99686

Valdez Community Hospital (15 beds), Box 550, 99686

Wrangell
Wrangell General Hospital (22 beds), Box 1081, 99929

U.S. PUBLIC HEALTH SERVICE PHYSICIANS
Anchorage
Alaska Native Medical Center (170 beds), Box 107741, 99510

Barrow
PHS Alaska Native Hospital (14 beds), 99723

Bethel
Yukon–Kuskokwim Delta Regional Hospital (51 beds), P.O. Box 287, 99559

Dillingham
Bristol Bay Area Kanakanak Hospital (15 beds), P.O. Box 130, 99576

Fairbanks
Chief Andrew Issac Health Center, 1638 Cowles, 99701

Juneau
SEARHC Medical Clinic, 3245 Hospital Drive, 99801

Ketchikan
PHS Alaska Native Health Center, 3289 Tongass Ave., 99901

Kodiak
Kodiak Area Native Association, 402 Center St., 99619

Kotzebue
Maniilaq Medical Center (31 beds), P.O. Box 256, 99752

Metlakatla
Annette Island Service Unit, P.O. Box 439, 99926

Nome
Norton Sound Regional Hospital (22 beds), P.O. Box 966, 99762

Sitka
SEARHC Regional Health Hospital (78 beds), 222 Tongass Drive, 99835

MILITARY PHYSICIANS
Adak
Branch Hospital, Adak, PSC 486, Box 1211, FPO AP 96506-1211

Eielson Air Force Base
Eielson Air Force Base Clinic, 99702

Elmendorf AFB
Headquarters Third Medical Centers, 24800 Hospital Drive, 99506

Fort Greely
Fort Greely Health Clinic, APO AP 96508

Fort Richardson
U.S. Army Troop Medical Clinic, 99505

Fort Wainwright
Bassett Army Community Hospital, 99703

Ketchikan
Coast Guard Dispensary, 99901

Kodiak
USCG Support Center, Rockmore-King Medical Center, Box 195002, 99619

Mount Edgecumbe
Sitka Coast Guard Air Station, Box 6-5000, 99835

NURSING HOMES AND HEALTH CARE FACILITIES
Anchorage
Alaska Surgery Center, 4001 Laurel St., 99508

Charter North Hospital (80 beds), 2530 DeBarr Road, 99514

Hope Cottage Interim Care Facility (40 beds), 540 W. International Airport Road, 99518

Mary Conrad Center (60 beds), 9100 Centennial Drive, 99504

North Star Hospital (34 beds), 1650 S. Bragaw, 99508

Our Lady of Compassion (224 beds), 4900 Eagle, 99503

Fairbanks
Denali Center (101 beds), 1949 Gillam Way, 99701

Glennallen
Cross Road Medical Center, P.O. Box 5, 99588

Juneau
Saint Ann's Nursing Home (45 beds), 415 Sixth St., 99801

Ketchikan
Island View Manor (46 beds), 3100 Tongass Ave., 99901

Seward
Wesleyan Nursing Home (66 beds), Box 430, 99664

Soldotna
Heritage Place (45 beds), 232 Rockwell Ave., 99669

Valdez
Harborview Development Center (80 beds), P.O. Box 487, 99686

Hostels

Alaska has 12 hostels, located in the following communities:

Alyeska International Home Hostel, P.O. Box 10-4099, Anchorage 99510; phone (907) 783-2099. Located 40 miles south of Anchorage on Alpina in Girdwood.

Anchorage International Hostel, 700 H St., Anchorage 99501; phone (907) 276-3635. Located on the corner of Seventh and H streets.

Bear Creek Camp and Hostel, P.O. Box 334, Haines 99827; phone (907) 766-2259. Located at Mile 2 of Small Tract Road.

Delta Youth Hostel, P.O. Box 971, Delta Junction 99737; phone (907) 895-5074. Located three miles from Milepost 272 on Richardson Highway.

Fairbanks Youth Hostel, P.O. Box

2196, 1641 Willow St., Fairbanks 99707; phone (907) 456-4159. Located near Tanana Valley Fairgrounds.

Juneau International Hostel, 614 Harris St., Juneau 99801; phone (907) 586-9559. Located four blocks northeast of the capitol building.

Ketchikan Youth Hostel, P.O. Box 8515, Ketchikan 99901; phone (907) 225-3319. Located in United Methodist Church, Grant and Main streets.

Sheep Mountain Lodge, SRC Box 8490, Palmer 99645; phone (907) 745-5121. Located at Mile 113.5 of the Glenn Highway.

Sitka Youth Hostel, P.O. Box 2645, Sitka 99835; phone (907) 747-8356. Located in United Methodist Church, Edgecumbe and Kimsham streets.

Skagway Home Hostel, Box 231, Skagway 99840; phone (907) 983-2131. Located on Third Avenue near Main Street.

Snow River International Hostel, HRC 64, Box 425, Seward 99664. Located at Mile 16 of the Seward Highway.

Tok International Youth Hostel, P.O. Box 532, Tok 99780. Located one mile south of Mile 1322.5 of the Alaska Highway on Pringle Drive.

The hostels in Alyeska, Anchorage, Haines, Juneau, Skagway and Seward are open year-round. All others are open only in the summer, and all of the hostels accept reservations by mail. Opening and closing dates, maximum length of stay and hours vary.

Hostels are available to anyone with a valid membership card issued by one of the associations affiliated with the International Youth Hostel Federation. Membership is open to all ages. By international agreement, each youth hostel member joins the association of his own country. A valid membership card, which ranges from $10 to $250 (life), entitles a member to use hostels.

Hostel memberships and a guide to American Youth Hostels can be purchased from the state office (Alaska Council, AYH, Box 240347, Anchorage 99524; phone (907) 562-7772), national office (American Youth Hostels, 1332 I St. N.W., Suite 800, Washington, D.C. 20005) or from most local hostels. For more information regarding Alaska

International Hostels, write the Alaska Council at the address listed above.

Hot Springs

The U.S. Geological Survey identifies 79 thermal springs in Alaska. Almost half of these hot springs occur along the volcanic Alaska Peninsula and Aleutian Chain. The second greatest regional concentration of such springs is in southeastern Alaska. Hot springs are scattered throughout the Interior and western Alaska, as far north as the Brooks Range and as far west as the Seward Peninsula.

Early miners and trappers were quick to use the naturally occurring warm waters for baths. Today approximately 25 percent of the recorded thermal springs are used for bathing, irrigation or domestic use. However, only a handful can be considered developed resorts.

Resorts (with swimming pools, changing rooms and lodging) are found at Chena Hot Springs, a 62-mile drive east from Fairbanks; and Circle Hot Springs, 136 miles northeast by road from Fairbanks. The less-developed Manley Hot Springs, in the small community of the same name at the end of the Elliott Highway, is privately owned, and the primitive bathhouse is used mainly by local residents. Developed, but not easily accessible, are the hot springs at Melozi Hot Springs Lodge, some 200 miles northwest of Fairbanks by air. The community of Tenakee Springs on Chichagof Island in southeastern Alaska maintains an old bathhouse near the waterfront. The state Marine Highway System provides ferry service to Tenakee Springs. Goddard Hot Springs near Sitka on Baranof Island was at one time owned by the Territory and operated as a Pioneers' Home for Alaska women. The temperature of the hot springs at Goddard Hot Springs is about 106°F/41°C. Also on Baranof Island is Baranof Hot Springs on the east shore of the island. Both Goddard and Baranof hot springs are accessible by private boat or by air; both have bathhouses.

Hunting

There are 26 game management units in Alaska with a wide variety of seasons and bag limits. Current copies of the *Alaska Game Regulations* with maps delineating game unit boundaries are available from the Alaska Department of Fish and Game (P.O. Box 3-2000, Juneau 99802) or from Fish and Game offices and sporting goods stores throughout the state.

Regulations

A hunting or trapping license is required for all residents and nonresidents with the exception of Alaska residents under 16 years or older than 60 years of age. A special identification card is issued for the senior citizen exemption.

A resident hunting license (valid for the calendar year) costs $25; trapping license (valid until September 30 of the year following the year of issue), $15; hunting and trapping license, $40; hunting and sportfishing license, $40; hunting, trapping and sportfishing license, $55.

A nonresident (U.S. citizen) and alien hunting license (valid for calendar year) costs $85; hunting and sportfishing license, $135; hunting and trapping license, $250.

Military personnel stationed in Alaska may purchase a small game hunting license for $25, and a small game hunting and sportfishing license for $40. Military personnel must purchase a nonresident hunting license at full cost ($85) and pay nonresident military fees for big game tags (one-half the nonresident rate), unless they are hunting big game on military property.

Licenses may be obtained from any designated issuing agent or by mail from the Alaska Department of Fish and Game, Licensing Section, P.O. Box 3-2000, Juneau 99802. Licenses are also available at Fish and Game regional offices in Anchorage, Fairbanks, Juneau and Kodiak.

Big game tags and fees are required for residents hunting musk-oxen and brown/grizzly bear and for nonresidents and aliens hunting any big game animal. These nonrefundable, non-transferable, metal locking tags (valid for calendar year) must be purchased prior to the taking of the animal. A tag may be used for any species for which the tag fee is of equal or less value. Fees quoted below are for *each* animal.

All residents (regardless of age), nonresidents and aliens intending to hunt brown/grizzly bear must purchase tags (resident, $25; nonresident, $500; alien, $650). Residents, nonresidents and aliens are also required to purchase musk-oxen tags (resident, $500 each bull taken on Nunivak Island, $25 each bull from Nelson Island or in Arctic National Wildlife Refuge, $25 cow; nonresident, $1,100; alien, $1,500).

Nonresident tag fees for other big game animals are as follows: deer, $150; wolf or wolverine, $175; black bear, $225; elk or goat, $300; caribou, $325; moose, $400; bison, $450; sheep, $425.

Nonresident alien tag fees for other big game animals are as follows: deer, $200; wolf or wolverine, $250; black bear, $300; elk or goat, $400; caribou, $425; moose, $500; bison, $650; and sheep, $550.

Nonresidents hunting brown/grizzly bear, Dall sheep or mountain goat are required to have a guide or be accompanied by an Alaska resident relative over 19 years of age within the second degree of kinship (includes parents, children, sisters or brothers). Nonresident aliens hunting big game must have a guide. A current list of registered Alaska guides is available for $5 from the Department of Commerce, Guide Licensing and Control Board, P.O. Box D-LIC, Juneau 99811.

Residents and nonresidents 16 years of age or older hunting waterfowl must have a signed federal migratory bird hunting stamp (duck stamp) and a state waterfowl conservation stamp. The Alaska duck stamp is available from agents who sell hunting licenses or by mail from the Alaska Department of Fish and Game, Licensing Section.

Trophy Game

Record big game in Alaska as recorded by the Boone and Crockett Club in the latest (1988) edition of *Records of North American Big Game* are as follows:

Black bear: Skull 13 $7/16$ inches long, 8 $6/16$ inches wide (1966).

Brown bear (coastal region): Skull 17 $15/16$ inches long, 12 $13/16$ inches wide (1952).

Grizzly bear (inland): Skull 16$4/16$ inches long, 10$5/16$ inches wide (1983).

Polar bear: Skull 18$1/2$ inches long, 11$7/16$ inches wide (1963). It is currently illegal for anyone but an Alaskan Eskimo, Aleut or Indian to hunt polar bear in Alaska.

Bison: Right horn 18$1/8$ inches long, base circumference 15 inches; left horn 21 inches long, base circumference 15$1/4$ inches; greatest spread 31$7/8$ inches (1977).

Barren Ground caribou: Right beam 51$1/4$ inches, 22 points; left beam 51$5/8$ inches, 23 points (1967).

Moose: Right palm length 49$5/8$ inches, width 20$3/4$ inches; left palm length 49$6/8$ inches, width 15$5/8$ inches;

right antler 18 points, left 16 points; greatest spread 77 inches (1978).

Mountain goat: Right horn 11⁵/₈ inches long, base circumference 5³/₄ inches; left horn 11⁵/₈ inches long, base circumference 5⁵/₈ inches (1933).

Musk-oxen: Right horn 26³/₄ inches; left horn 26¹/₂ inches; tip-to-tip spread 27 inches (1985).

Dall sheep: Right horn 48⁵/₈ inches long, base circumference 14⁵/₈ inches; left horn 47⁷/₈ inches long, base circumference 14³/₄ inches (1961).

Related reading: *Northwest Sportsman Almanac.* The best works of writers and photographers are gathered in an informative guide to outdoor recreation. *See* ALASKA NORTHWEST LIBRARY in the back of the book.

Hypothermia

(*See also* Chill Factor)

Hypothermia develops when the body is exposed to cold and cannot maintain normal temperatures. In an automatic survival reaction, blood flow to the extremities is shut down in favor of preserving warmth in the vital organs. As internal temperature drops, judgment and coordination become impaired. Allowed to continue, hypothermia leads to stupor, collapse and death. Immersion hypothermia occurs in cold water.

Ice

(*See* Glaciers and Ice Fields *and* Icebergs)

Icebergs

Icebergs are formed in Alaska wherever glaciers reach salt water or a freshwater lake. Some accessible places to view icebergs include Glacier Bay, Icy Bay, Yakutat Bay, Taku Inlet, Endicott Arm, portions of northern Prince William Sound (College Fiord, Barry Arm, Columbia Bay), Mendenhall Lake and Portage Lake.

If icebergs contain little or no sediment, approximately 75 percent to 80 percent of their bulk may be under-water. The more sediment an iceberg contains, the greater its density, and an iceberg containing large amounts of sediment will float slightly beneath the surface. Glaciologists of the U.S. Geological Survey believe that some of these "black icebergs" may actually sink to the bottom of a body of water. Since salt water near the faces of glaciers may be liquid to temperatures as low as 28°F, and icebergs melt at 32°F, some of these underwater icebergs may remain unmelted indefinitely.

Alaska's icebergs are comparatively small compared to the icebergs found near Antarctica and Greenland. One of the largest icebergs ever recorded in Alaska was formed in May 1977, in Icy Bay. Glaciologists measured it at 346 feet long, 297 feet wide and 99 feet above the surface of the water.

Sea Ice

Sea water typically freezes at –1.8°C or 28.8°F. The first indication that sea water is freezing is the appearance of frazil—tiny needlelike crystals of pure ice—in shallow coastal areas of low current or areas of low salinity, such as near the mouths of rivers. Continued freezing turns the frazil into a soupy mass called grease ice and eventually into an ice crust approximately four inches thick. More freezing, wind and wave action thicken the ice and break it into ice floes ranging from a few feet to several miles across. In the Arctic Ocean, ice floes can be 10 feet thick. Most are crisscrossed with 6- to 8-foot-high walls of ice caused by the force of winds.

Sea salt that is trapped in the ice during freezing is leached out over time, making the oldest ice the least saline. Meltwater forming in ponds on multi-year-old ice during summer months is a freshwater source for native marine life.

Refreezing of meltwater ponds and the formation of new ice in the permanent ice pack (generally north of 72° north latitude) begins in mid-September. While the ice pack expands southward, new ice freezes to the coast (shorefast ice) and spreads seaward. Where the drifting ice pack grinds against the relatively stable shorefast ice, tremendous walls or ridges of ice are formed, some observed to be 100 feet thick and grounded in 60 feet of water. They are impenetrable by all but the most powerful icebreakers. By late March the ice cover has reached its maximum extent, approximately from Port Heiden on the Alaska Peninsula in the south to the northern Pribilof Islands and northwestward to Siberia. In Cook Inlet, sea ice, usually no more than two feet thick, can extend as far south as Anchor Point and Kamishak Bay on the east and west sides of the inlet, respectively. The ice season usually lasts from mid-November to mid-March.

The Navy began observing and forecasting sea ice conditions in 1954 in support of the construction of defense sites along the Arctic coast. In 1969, the National Weather Service began a low-profile sea ice reconnaissance program, which expanded greatly during the summer of 1975 when, during a year of severe ice, millions of dollars of materials had to be shipped to Prudhoe Bay. Expanded commercial fisheries in the Bering Sea also heightened the problem of sea ice for crabbing and bottom fish trawling operations. In 1976, headquarters for a seven-day-a-week ice watch was established at Fairbanks; it was moved to Anchorage in 1981.

The National Weather Service operates a radio facsimile broadcast service that makes current ice analysis charts, special oceanographic charts and standard weather charts available to the public via standard radios equipped with "black box" receivers. Commercial fishing operators, particularly in the Bering Sea, use the radio-transmitted charts to steer clear of problem weather and troublesome ice formations. More information is available from the National Weather Service in Kodiak or Anchorage.

Ice Fog

Ice fog develops when air just above the ground becomes so cold, it can no longer retain water vapor and tiny, spherical ice crystals are formed. Ice fog is most common in arctic and subarctic regions in winter when clear skies create an air inversion, trapping cold air at low elevations. It is most noticeable when man-made pollutants are also contained by the air inversion.

Iceworm

Although often regarded as a hoax, iceworms actually exist. These small, thin, segmented black worms, usually less than one inch long, thrive in temperatures just above freezing. Observers as far back as the 1880s reported that at dawn or dusk or on overcast days, the tiny worms, all belonging to the genus *Mesenchytraeus,* may literally carpet the surface of glaciers. When sunlight strikes them, they burrow back down into the ice.

The town of Cordova commemorates its own version of the iceworm each February in the Iceworm Festival, when a 150-foot-long, multilegged "iceworm" marches in a parade down Main Street.

IDITAROD TRAIL

—— Iditarod Trail ——
- - -Alternate Route - - -

Map Location

Nome
FINISH
Safety
Roadhouse
Norton
Sound

White
Mountain
Golovin
Elim
Shaktoolik
Unalakleet

Koyuk
Nulato
Kaltag

Ruby
Slatna Crossing
Cripple

Yukon River
North Fork

Beaver Creek
Shageluk
Ophir
Iditarod
Takotna
Rohn Roadhouse
Rainy Pass Lodge

McGrath
Nikolai
Farewell Station
Finger Lake
Skwentna

RANGE

Yukon River
Kuskokwim
River

ALASKA

Susitna Station
Knik
Wasilla
Eagle
River
Anchorage
START

Cook Inlet

Scale
100 miles
100 kilometers

Iditarod Trail
Sled Dog Race

(*See also* Dog Mushing *and* Yukon Quest
International Sled Dog Race)

Two of the longest sled dog races in
the world take place in Alaska: the
Yukon Quest and the Iditarod. The first
Iditarod Trail Sled Dog Race, conceived
and organized by Joe Redington, Sr., of
Knik, and historian Dorothy Page, of
Wasilla, was run in 1967 and covered
only 56 miles. The race was lengthened
in 1973, and the first ever 1,100-mile
sled dog race began in Anchorage on
March 3, 1973, and ended April 3 in
Nome. Of the 34 who started the race,
22 finished. The Iditarod has been run
every year since its inception. In 1976,
Congress designated the Iditarod as a
National Historic Trail.

Following the old dog team mail

route blazed in 1910 from Knik to
Nome, the trail crosses two mountain
ranges, follows the Yukon River for
about 150 miles, runs through several
bush villages and crosses the pack ice of
Norton Sound.

Strictly a winter trail because the
ground is mostly spongy muskeg
swamps, the route attracted national
attention in 1925 when sled dog mushers, including the famous Leonhard
Seppala, relayed 300,000 units of life-
saving diphtheria serum to epidemic-
threatened Nome. However, as the
airplane and snowmobile replaced
the sled dog team, the trail fell into
disuse. Thanks to Redington and Page,
the trail has been assured a place in
Alaska history.

Each year the Iditarod takes a
slightly different course, following an
alternate southern route in odd years
(*see* map). The route is traditionally

described as 1,049 miles long (a figure that was selected because Alaska is the 49th state), but the actual distance run each year is close to 1,100 miles. Part of it is run on frozen river ice. The official length of the Iditarod National Historic Trail System, including northern and southern routes, is 2,350 miles.

The majority of the Iditarod purse is divided among the first 20 finishers. In 1993, Jeff King was awarded $3,000 in silver ingots for being the first musher to cross the halfway checkpoint at Iditarod ahead of all other racers. Martin Buser won the Seppala Humanitarian Award. Other awards went to both Keizo Funaizu and Jason Barron for Rookie of the Year; and Dee Dee Jonrowe won the Most Inspirational Musher Award. Jeff King enjoyed the

1993 Results

Place Musher	Days	Hrs.	Min.	Sec.	Prize
1. Jeff King, Denali Park	10	15	38	15	$50,000
2. DeeDee Jonrowe, Willow	10	16	10	50	43,000
3. Rick Mackey, Nenana	10	18	07	55	37,000
4. Susan Butcher, Manley	10	22	02	40	32,000
5. Tom Osmar, Kasilof	10	22	07	00	27,000
6. Martin Buser, Big Lake	11	00	47	39	22,000
7. Matt Desalernos, Nome	11	05	47	03	19,000
8. Doug Swingley, Simms, MT	11	06	38	28	18,000
9. Rick Swenson, Two Rivers	11	03	14	45	17,000
10. Bruce Lee, Denali Park	11	12	00	35	16,000
11. Vern Halter, Trapper Creek	11	13	04	15	15,000
12. Joe Runyan, Nenana	11	13	06	12	14,000
13. Claire Philip, By Thomery, France	11	13	15	45	13,000
14. Kathy Swenson, Two Rivers	11	15	10	30	12,500
15. John Barton, Big Lake	11	15	59	03	12,000
16. Joe Garnie, Willow	11	18	42	20	11,500
17. Linwood Fiedler, Willow	11	21	02	50	11,000
18. Sonny Lindner, Fairbanks	11	23	49	40	10,500
19. Bill Cotter, Nenana	11	23	49	50	10,000
20. Kate Persons, Nomak River	11	23	50	20	9,500

Winners and Times

Year Musher	Days	Hrs.	Min.	Sec.	Prize
1973 Dick Willmarth, Red Devil	20	00	49	41	$12,000
1974 Carl Huntington, Galena	20	15	02	07	12,000
1975 Emmitt Peters, Ruby	14	14	43	45	15,000
1976 Jerry Rilen, Nenana	18	22	58	17	7,000
1977 Rick Swenson, Eureka	16	16	27	13	9,600
1978 Dick Mackey, Wasilla	14	18	52	24	12,000
1979 Rick Swenson, Eureka	15	10	37	47	12,000
1980 Joe May, Trapper Creek	14	07	11	51	12,000
1981 Rick Swenson, Eureka	12	08	45	02	24,000
1982 Rick Swenson, Eureka	16	04	40	10	24,000
1983 Dick Mackey, Wasilla	12	14	10	44	24,000
1984 Dean Osmar, Clam Gulch	12	15	07	33	24,000*
1985 Libby Riddles, Teller	18	00	20	17	50,000
1986 Susan Butcher, Manley	11	15	06	00	50,000
1987 Susan Butcher, Manley	11	02	05	13	50,000
1988 Susan Butcher, Manley	11	11	41	40	30,000
1989 Joe Runyan, Nenana	11	05	24	34	50,000
1990 Susan Butcher, Manley	11	01	53	23	50,000
1991 Rick Swenson, Two Rivers	12	16	34	39	50,000
1992 Martin Buser, Big Lake	10	19	17	15	50,000
1993 Jeff King, Denali Park	10	15	38	15	50,000**

*Does not include $2,000 in silver ingots for reaching the halfway checkpoint first.
**Does not include $3,000 in silver ingots for reaching the halfway checkpoint first.

celebration dinner at Anvik and the $3,500 cash prize for being the first musher to the Yukon River. Jerry Austin and Dave Olesen shared the Eukanuba Sportsmanship Award for the efforts to keep up the spirits of a large group of musher who were detained in White Mountains.

In 1993, 68 mushers started the world's longest and richest sled dog race. Of those, 54 finished the Anchorage-to-Nome ordeal. Jeff King of Denali Park won the Iditarod race, shaving off more than five hours from the previous record-winning time. Jeff King was awarded the Golden Harness Award for the outstanding performance of his lead dog. King also received the first-place check of $50,000 from a $400,000 purse. The 1993 race had the largest purse in the race's history and in dog mushing. There were no $1,000 checks issued to finishers beyond position 20.

Related reading: *Iditarod: The Great Race to Nome.* Photographs by Jeff Schultz, text by Bill Sherwonit. *Travelers of the Cold: Sled Dogs of the Far North,* by Dominique Cellura. *See* ALASKA NORTHWEST LIBRARY at the back of the book.

Igloo

Also known as snowhouses, these snow block structures provided temporary shelter for Arctic Alaska Eskimos. Igloos are built in a spiral with each tier leaning inward at a greater angle. The entrance is a tunnel with a cold trap in front of the sleeping platform. A vent at the top allows for ventilation, and an ice window lets in light.

Imports and Exports

Alaska's most important trading region is Asia, to which it sent 91 percent of its exports in 1992. Other significant regions were Europe (3.9 percent) and Americas (0.31 percent). Alaska imports for 1992 were valued at $1.3 billion. The largest importer to the state was Japan at $427 million, followed by Singapore ($280 million) and Taiwan ($125 million).

Exports for 1992 were valued at $4.84 billion by the Alaska Center for International Business. Of this total, the state's most valuable exports were fish (39.7 percent), timber (11.6 percent) and petroleum products (7.6 percent).

Income

(*See also* Cost of Living)

On a per capita income basis, Alaska was ranked eighth in the nation at $21,603 per person in 1992, a slight gain from $21,144 per capita income in 1991. More than 70 percent of Alaska's personal income comes from earnings, which represents a larger portion than the rest of the nation. One reason could be that a larger percentage of Alaska's working age population is in the labor force and earning income from employment.

The average monthly wage reached $2,540 in 1991, the highest it has ever been in nominal terms. In the major industry groups, mining still reflects the highest average monthly wage at $5,689, according to a 1991 report from the Alaska Department of Labor, Research and Analysis Section. Roughly 88 percent of these mining jobs are supplied through the oil and gas industry. Construction followed at $3,504 per month. The lowest average monthly wage remains in the retail trade at $1,411.

Median household income in Alaska in 1989 (latest available statistics) was $41,408, which ranks Alaska second in the nation. In terms of the number of Alaskans who live in poverty, the U.S. Census Bureau reported 9 percent of Alaska's population lived below the poverty level in 1991. The figure nationwide was 13.1 percent. Taking Alaska's higher cost of living into account, the Alaska Department of Labor reports that 12.4 percent of the population is below 125 percent of poverty level (ranking 26th).

Though Alaska's per capita income increased in 1992, the increase in cost of living was greater. But on a positive note, Alaskans still hold on to more of their income after taxes than residents in most other states.

Information Sources

Agriculture: Agricultural Statistics Service, P.O. Box 799, Palmer 99645; Cooperative Extension Service, University of Alaska, Fairbanks 99701.

Alaska Natives: Alaska Federation of Natives, 411 W. Fourth Ave., Anchorage 99501.

Boating, Canoeing and Kayaking: Alaska Dept. of Transportation and Public Facilities, P.O. Box Z, Juneau 99811; State of Alaska, Division of Parks and Outdoor Recreation, 3601 C St., Suite 1200, Anchorage 99503.

Business: Alaska Department of Commerce and Economic Development, P.O. Box D, Juneau 99811; State Chamber of Commerce, 217 Second St., Suite 201, Juneau 99801.

Camping and Hiking: U.S. Forest Service, P.O. Box 21628, Juneau 99802; Bureau of Land Management, 222 W. Seventh Ave., #13, Anchorage 99513; Supervisor, Chugach National Forest, 201 E. Ninth Ave., Suite 206, Anchorage 99501; National Park Service, 2525 Gambell St., Anchorage 99503; Supervisor, Tongass National Forest, P.O. Box 21628, Juneau 99802; U.S. Fish and Wildlife Service, 1011 E. Tudor Road, Anchorage 99503.

Census Data: Alaska Department of Labor, Research and Analysis, P.O. Box 107018, Anchorage 99510.

Climate: State Climatologist, University of Alaska, Arctic Environmental and Data Center, 707 A St., Anchorage 99501.

Education: Alaska Department of Education, P.O. Box F, Juneau 99811.

Gold Panning: State Division of Geological and Geophysical Surveys, Mines Information Office, 3601 C St., Anchorage 99503; Alaska Miners Association, 501 W. Northern Lights Blvd., Suite 203, Anchorage 99503.

Health: State Department of Health and Social Services, Division of Public Health, P.O. Box H, Juneau 99811.

Housing: State Housing Authority, P.O. Box 10080, Anchorage 99510.

Hunting and Fishing Regulations: State Department of Fish and Game, P.O. Box 3-2000, Juneau 99802.

Job Opportunities: State Employ-ment Service, P.O. Box 3-7000, Juneau 99802.

Labor: State Department of Labor, P.O. Box 25501-5501, Juneau 99802.

Land: State Division of Lands, P.O. Box 107005, Anchorage 99510; Bureau of Land Management, 222 W. Seventh Ave., #13, Anchorage 99513; Alaska Public Lands Information Centers, 605 W. Fourth Ave., Suite 105, Anchorage 99501; 250 Cushman St., Suite 1A, Fairbanks 99701; P.O. Box 359, Tok 99780.

Legislature: Legislative Information Office, 3111 C St., Anchorage 99503.

Libraries: Alaska State Libraries, Archives and Museums, P.O. Box 6, Juneau 99811.

Made in Alaska Products: Alaska Association of Manufacturers, P.O. Box 142831, Anchorage 99514.

Maps (topographic): U.S. Geological Survey, 4230 University Drive, Room 101, Anchorage 99508; 101 12th Ave., Room 126, Fairbanks 99701.

Military: Department of the Air Force, Headquarters, Alaskan Air Command, Elmendorf Air Force Base 99506; Department of the Army, Headquarters, 6th Infantry Brigade (Alaska), Fort Richardson 99505; State Department of Military Affairs, Office of the Adjutant General, 3601 C St., Anchorage 99503; Department of Transportation, U.S. Coast Guard, 17th Coast Guard District, P.O. Box 3-5000, Juneau 99802.

Mines and Petroleum: State Division of Geological and Geophysical Surveys, 3601 C St., Anchorage 99503; Petroleum Information Corp., P.O. Box 102278, Anchorage 99510; Alaska Miners Association, 501 W. Northern Lights Blvd., Suite 203, Anchorage 99503.

River Running: National Park Service, 2525 Gambell St., Anchorage 99503; U.S. Dept. of the Interior, Fish and Wildlife Service, 1011 E. Tudor Road, Anchorage 99503; Bureau of Land Management, 222 W. Seventh Ave., #13, Anchorage 99513.

Travel and Visitor Information: State Division of Tourism, P.O. Box E, Juneau 99811; Alaska Visitors Association, 501 W. Northern Lights Blvd., Anchorage 99503.

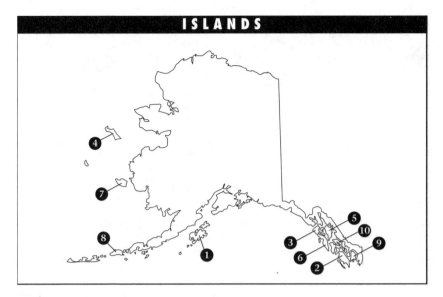

Islands

Southeastern Alaska contains about 1,000 of the state's 1,800 named islands, rocks and reefs; several thousand remain unnamed. The Aleutian Island chain, stretching southwest from the mainland, contains more than 200 islands.

Of the state's 10 largest islands, six are in southeastern Alaska. Of the remainder, Unimak is in the Aleutians, Nunivak and Saint Lawrence are in the Bering Sea off the west coast of Alaska, and Kodiak is in the Gulf of Alaska (*see* map above). The state's 10 largest islands, according to U.S. Geological Survey figures, are:

1. Kodiak, 3,588 sq. mi.
2. Prince of Wales, 2,731 sq. mi.
3. Chichagof, 2,062 sq. mi.
4. Saint Lawrence, 1,780 sq. mi.
5. Admiralty, 1,709 sq. mi.
6. Baranof, 1,636 sq. mi.
7. Nunivak, 1,600 sq. mi.*
8. Unimak, 1,600 sq. mi.
9. Revillagigedo, 1,134 sq. mi.
10. Kupreanof, 1,084 sq. mi.

*Estimate

Ivory

Eskimos traditionally carved ivory to make such implements as harpoon heads, dolls and ulu (fan-shaped knife) handles. For the past 80 years, however, most carvings have been made to be sold. Etching on ivory originally was done with hand tools and the scratches were filled in with soot. Today power tools supplement the hand tools and carvers may color the etching with India ink, graphite, hematite or commercial coloring.

The large islands of the Bering Sea—Saint Lawrence, Little Diomede and Nunivak—are home to the majority of Alaska's ivory carvers. Eskimos from King Island, renowned for their carving skill, now live in Nome along with talented artists from many other villages.

The bulk of the ivory used today comes from walrus tusks and teeth, seasoned for a few months. Old walrus ivory, often mistakenly called fossil ivory, is also used. This ivory has been buried in the ground or has been on beaches for years, and contact with various minerals has changed it from white to tan or any of a multitude of colors. Some highly prized old ivory exhibits rays of deep blue or areas of brown and gold that shine. Most old ivory comes from ancient sites or beaches on Saint Lawrence Island and is sold by the pound to non-Native buyers, generally for use in some kind of artwork.

Mastodon tusks are often unearthed in the summer by miners or found eroding on river cutbanks where they have been buried for thousands of years. Although these tusks are enormous and their colorations often beautiful, the material cannot be used efficiently because it dries and then separates into narrow ridges.

Various federal prohibitions govern the collection of old walrus, mammoth and mastodon ivory. Such materials may be gathered from private or reservation lands, but may not be traded or sold if found on public lands. The taking of fresh walrus ivory is prohibited to non-Natives in accordance with the Marine Mammal Protection Act of 1972.

In the 19th century, Native artists who came in contact with whalers etched realistic scenes on sperm whale teeth. Today, with the ban on the taking of sperm whales, this type of ivory is not available to Native scrimshanders.

Walrus may be taken only by Alaska Natives (Aleuts, Eskimos and Indians) who dwell on the coast of the North Pacific Ocean or the Arctic Ocean, for subsistence purposes or for the creation and sale of authentic Native articles of handicrafts or clothing.

Raw walrus ivory and other parts can be sold only by an Alaska Native to an Alaska Native within Alaska, or to a registered agent for resale or transfer to an Alaska Native within the state. Only authentic Native-processed ivory articles of handicrafts or clothing may be sold or transferred to a non-Native, or sold in interstate commerce.

Beach ivory, which is found on the beach within a quarter of a mile of the ocean, may, however, be kept by anyone. This ivory must be registered by all non-Natives with the U.S. Fish and Wildlife Service (USFWS) or the National Marine Fisheries Service within 30 days of discovery. Beach-found ivory must remain in the possession of the finder even if carved or scrimshawed.

Carved or scrimshawed walrus ivory (authentic Native handicraft) or other marine mammal parts made into clothing or other authentic Native handicrafts may be exported from the United States to a foreign country, but the exporter must first obtain an export permit from the USFWS. Even visitors from the Lower 48 simply traveling through, or stopping in Canada on their way home, are required to have a USFWS export and/or transit permit. Cost is $25. Mailing the carved ivory home will avoid the need for an export/transit permit. Importation of walrus or other marine mammal parts is illegal, except for scientific research purposes or for public display once a permit is granted.

For further information contact: Special Agent-in-Charge, U.S. Fish and Wildlife Service, 1011 E. Tudor Road, Anchorage 99503; phone (907) 786-3311; or Senior Resident, U.S. Fish and Wildlife Service, 1412 Airport Way, Fairbanks 99701; phone (907) 456-0239.

Jade

Most Alaskan jade is found near the Dall, Shungnak and Kobuk rivers, and Jade Mountain, all north of the Arctic Circle. The stones occur in various shades of green, brown, black, yellow, white and even red. The most valuable are those that are marbled black, white and green. Gem-quality jade, about one-fourth of the total mined, is used in jewelry making. Fractured jade is used for clock faces, table tops, book ends and other items. Jade is the Alaska state gem.

Kuspuk

A *kuspuk* is an Eskimo woman's parka, often made with a loosely cut back so that an infant may be carried piggyback-style. Parkas are made from rabbit or fox skins; traditionally, the fur lining faces inward. The ruffs are generally made of wolverine or wolf fur. An outer shell, called a *qaspeg,* is worn over a fur parka to keep it clean and to prevent wear. This outer shell is usually made of brightly colored corduroy, cotton print or velveteenlike material, and may be trimmed with rickrack.

Labor and Employer Organizations

The Alaska State AFL–CIO *Alaska Labor Union Directory* lists the following organizations:

Anchorage
Alaska Federation of Teachers Local 8050

Alaska Metal Trades Council

Alaska Public Employees Association

Alaska State AFL-CIO

Alaska State District Council of Laborers

Alaska State Employees Association, AFSCME Local 52

American Federation of Government Employees, Anchorage Council, Local 121

Anchorage Central Labor Council

Anchorage Joint Crafts Council

Anchorage Municipal Employees Association

Anchorage Musicians Association Local 650

Anchorage Typographical Union Local 823

Asbestos Workers Local 97

Associated General Contractors of America

Boilermakers Local 502

Bricklayers and Allied Craftsmen Local 1

Brotherhood of Railroad Carmen of U.S.A. and Canada

Central and Southeastern Alaska District Council of Carpenters

Graphic Communications International Union Local 327

Hotel Employees, Restaurant Employees Union Local 878

International Alliance of Theatrical Stage Employees Local 918

International Association of Bridge, Structural and Ornamental Workers Local 751

International Association of Firefighters Local 1264

International Association of Machinists and Aerospace Workers Local 601

International Brotherhood of Electrical Workers Local 1547

International Brotherhood of Painters and Allied Trades Local 1140

International Brotherhood of Teamsters, Chauffeurs, Warehousemen and Helpers Local 959

International Union of Operating Engineers Local 302

Laborers International Union of North America Local 341

Laundry and Dry Cleaning Union Local 333

National Electrical Contractors Association

Operative Plasterers and Cement Masons Local 867

Piledrivers, Bridge, Dock Builders and Drivers Local 2520

Public Employees Local 71

Roofers and Waterproofers Local 190

Sheetmetal Workers International Association Local 23

United Association of Plumbers and Steamfitters Local 367

United Brotherhood of Carpenters and Joiners Local 1281

United Food and Commercial Workers Union Local 1496

United Transportation Union Local 1626

Western Alaska Building and Construction Trades Council

Cordova
Cordova District Fishermen United
International Longshoremen's and Warehousemen's Union Local 200

Craig
International Longshoremen's and Warehousemen's Union Local 200

Dillingham
Western Alaska Cooperative Marketing Association

Fairbanks
Alaska Public Employees Association
Fairbanks Building and Construction Trades
Fairbanks Central Labor Council
Fairbanks Firefighters Association Local 1324
Fairbanks Joint Crafts Council
Hotel Employees, Restaurant Employees Union Local 879
International Association of Bridge, Structural and Ornamental Workers Local 751
International Brotherhood of Electrical Workers Local 1547
International Brotherhood of Painters and Allied Trades Local 1555
International Brotherhood of Teamsters, Chauffeurs, Warehousemen and Helpers Local 959
International Printing and Graphic Communications Union Local 704
International Union of Operating Engineers Local 302
Laborers International Union of North America Local 942
Operative Plasterers and Cement Masons Local 867
Public Employees Local 71
Sheetmetal Union Local 72
United Association of Journeymen and Apprentices of the Plumbing and Pipefitting Industry Local 375
United Brotherhood of Carpenters and Joiners Local 1243
United Food and Commercial Workers Union Local 1496

Haines
International Longshoremen's and Warehousemen's Union Local 200

Juneau
Alaska Public Employees Association
Alaska State District Council of Laborers
Hotel Employees, Restaurant Employees Union Local 878
Inland Boatmen's Union of the Pacific, Alaska Region
International Association of Machinists and Aerospace Workers Local 2263
International Brotherhood of Electrical Workers Local 1547
International Brotherhood of Teamsters, Chauffeurs, Warehousemen and Helpers Local 959
International *Longshoremen's* and Warehousemen's Union Local 200
International Longshoremen's and *Warehousemen's* Union Local 200
International Union of Operating Engineers Local 302
Juneau Building and Construction Trades Council
Juneau Central Labor Council
Laborers International Union of North America Local 942
National Education Association
National Federation of Federal Employees Local 251
Operative Plasterers and Cement Masons Local 867
Public Employees Local 71
United Association of Journeymen and Apprentices of the Plumbing and Pipefitting Industry Local 262
United Brotherhood of Carpenters and Joiners Local 2247
United Fishermen of Alaska

Kenai
Hotel Employees, Restaurant Employees Union Local 878
International Brotherhood of Electrical Workers Local 1547
International Brotherhood of Teamsters, Chauffeurs, Warehousemen and Helpers Local 959
Kenai Peninsula Central Labor Council
Laborers International Union of North America Local 341

Ketchikan
Alaska Loggers Association
Associated Western Pulp and Paper Workers Local 783
Hotel Employees, Restaurant Employees Union Local 878

Inland Boatmen's Union of the Pacific, Alaska Region
International Brotherhood of Electrical Workers Local 1547
International *Longshoremen's* and Warehousemen's Union Local 200
International Longshoremen's and *Warehousemen's* Union Local 200
International Woodworkers of America Local 3-193
Ketchikan Building and Construction Trades Council
Ketchikan Central Labor Council
Laborers International Union of North America Local 942
United Brotherhood of Carpenters and Joiners Local 1501

Kodiak

Firefighters Local 3054
Hotel Employees, Restaurant Employees Union Local 878
Inland Boatmen's Union of the Pacific, Alaska Region
International Longshoremen's and Warehousemen's Union Local 200
Kodiak Labor Council
Laborers International Union of North America Local 341

Palmer

Laborers International Union of North America Local 341

Pelican

International Longshoremen's and Warehousemen's Union Local 200

Seward

International Longshoremen's and Warehousemen's Union Local 200

Sitka

Hotel Employees, Restaurant Employees Union Local 873
International Longshoremen's and Warehousemen's Union Local 200
United Brotherhood of Carpenters and Joiners Local 466

Unalaska

International Longshoremen's and Warehousemen's Union Local 200

Valdez

Hotel Employees, Restaurant Employees Union Local 878
Laborers International Union of

North America Local 341

Ward Cove

Associated Western Pulp and Paper Workers Local 783

Wrangell

International Longshoremen's and Warehousemen's Union Local 200
United Paperworkers Local 1341

Lakes

There are 94 lakes with surface areas of more than 10 square miles among Alaska's more than 3 million lakes. According to the U.S. Geological Survey, the 10 largest natural freshwater lakes in square miles are: Iliamna, 1,150; Becharof, 458; Teshekpuk, 315; Naknek, 242; Tustumena, 117; Clark, 110; Dall, 100; Upper Ugashik, 75; Lower Ugashik, 72; and Kukaklek, 72.

Land Use

At first glance it seems odd that such a huge area as Alaska has not been more heavily settled. Thousands of acres of forest and tundra, miles and miles of rivers and streams, hidden valleys, bays, coves and mountains, are spread across an area so vast that it staggers the imagination. Yet, more than two-thirds of the population of Alaska remains clustered around two major centers of commerce and survival. Compared to the settlement of the western Lower 48, Alaska is not settled at all.

Visitors flying over the state are impressed by immense areas showing no sign of humanity. Current assessments indicate that approximately 160,000 acres of Alaska have been cleared, built on or otherwise directly altered by man, either by settlement or resource development, including mining, pipeline construction and agriculture. In comparison to the 365 million acres of land that make up the total of the state, the settled or altered area currently amounts to less than one-twentieth of 1 percent.

There are significant reasons for this lack of development in Alaska. Frozen for long periods in the dark of the

Arctic, much of the land cannot support quantities of people or industry. Where the winters are "warm," the mountains, glaciers, rivers and oceans prevent easy access for commerce and trade.

The status of land is constantly changing, especially in Alaska. In most places, the free market affects patterns of land ownership, but in Alaska, all land ownership patterns until recently were the result of a century-long process of a single landowner, the United States government.

The Statehood Act signaled the beginning of a dramatic shift in land ownership patterns. It authorized the state to select a total of 104 million of the 365 million acres of land and inland waters in Alaska. (Under the Submerged Lands Act, the state has title to submerged lands under navigable inland waters.) In passing the Statehood Act, Congress cited economic independence and the need to open Alaska to economic development as the primary purposes for large Alaska land grants.

Alaska Native Claims Settlement Act

The issue of the Native claims in Alaska was cleared up with the passage of the Alaska Native Claims Settlement Act (ANCSA) on Dec. 18, 1971. This act of Congress provided for the creation of Alaska Native village and regional corporations, and gave the Alaska Eskimos, Aleuts and Indians nearly $1 billion and the right to select 44 million acres from a land "pool" of some 115 million acres.

Immediately after the settlement act passed, and before Native lands and National Interest Lands were selected, the state filed to select an additional 77 million acres of land. In September 1972, the litigation initiated by the state was resolved by a settlement affirming state selection of an additional 41 million acres.

Section 17 of the settlement act, in addition to establishing a Joint Federal–State Land Use Planning Commission, directed the secretary of the interior to withdraw from public use up to 80 million acres of land in Alaska for study as possible national parks, wildlife refuges, forests, and wild and scenic rivers. These were the National Interest Lands Congress was to decide upon, as set forth in Section 17(d)(2) of the settlement act, by Dec. 18, 1978. The U.S. House of Representatives passed a bill (HR39) that would have designated 124 million acres of national parks, forests and wildlife refuges, and designated millions of acres of these and existing parks, forests and refuges as wilderness. Although a bill was reported out of committee, it failed to pass the Senate before Congress adjourned.

In November 1978, the secretary of the interior published a draft environmental impact supplement, which listed the actions that the executive branch of the federal government could take to protect federal lands in Alaska until the 96th Congress could consider the creation of new parks, wildlife refuges, wild and scenic rivers and forests. In keeping with this objective, the secretary of the interior, under provisions of the 1976 Federal Land Policy and Management Act, withdrew about 114 million acres of land in Alaska from most public uses. On Dec. 1, 1978, the president, under the authority of the 1906 Antiquities Act, designated 56 million acres of these lands as national monuments.

In February 1980, the House of Representatives passed a modified HR39. In August 1980, the Senate passed a compromise version of the Alaska lands bill that created 106 million acres of new conservation units and affected a total of 131 million acres of land in Alaska. In November 1980, the House accepted the Senate version of the Alaska National Interest Lands Conservation Act (ANILCA), which President Jimmy Carter signed into law on Dec. 2, 1980. This is also known as the d-2 lands bill or the compromise HR39. (*See also* National Parks, Preserves and Monuments; National Wilderness Areas; National Wildlife Refuges; National Forests; *and* National Wild and Scenic Rivers.)

Alaska's land ownership was complicated even further in 1982, when advocates for mental health programs in Alaska filed suit against the state of Alaska. Prior to statehood, Alaska was granted title to 1 million acres of federal land, with the provision that some revenues from the mental health trust were to be used to fund mental health programs for Alaskans.

In 1978, the legislature waived the trust status of mental health lands. In return, the mental health trust was to receive 1.5 percent of all income from state lands. However, this funding was not appropriated, and mental health advocates sued the state.

As of mid-1993, a settlement of the lawsuit was pending before the court, and the state legislature was considering additional legislation. The proposed settlement of the lawsuit has greatly curtailed the sale or exchange of state land for the forseeable future.

Land use in Alaska will continue to be a controversial and complex subject for some time. Implementation of the d-2 bill, and distribution of land to the Native village and regional corporations, the state of Alaska and private citizens in the state will require time. Much of this work is being done by the Bureau of Land Management, which also surveys federal land before a patent is issued. The passage of ANILCA 13 years ago set the stage for long-term management of resources, and the BLM is now moving forward to establish fish, wildlife and recreation resources as critical and necessary ingredients in a multiple-use mix. Balancing the needs of people, wildlife and the land itself will continue to challenge land use and management policies in the coming years.

Acquiring Land for Private Use

The easiest and fastest way to acquire land for private use is by purchase from the private sector, through real estate agencies or directly from individuals. Because of speculation, land claim conflicts and delays involving Native, state and federal groups, however, private land is considered by many people to be in short supply and often is very expensive.

Private land in Alaska, excluding land held by Native corporations, is estimated to be more than 1 million acres, but less than 1 percent of the state. Much of this land passed into private hands through the federal Homestead Acts and other public land laws, as well as land disposal programs of the state, boroughs or communities. Most private land is located along Alaska's small road network. Compared to other categories of land, it is highly accessible and constitutes some of the prime settlement land.

All laws related to homesteading on federal land (as opposed to state land) in Alaska were repealed as of 1986. Federal land is not available for homesteading or trade and manufacturing sites.

Following are programs that are in effect for the sale of state land. A one-year residency (except for the auction program) and an age of at least 18 is required for all programs.

Auction: The state has been selling land by public auction since statehood. The state may sell full surface rights, lease of surface or subsurface rights, or restricted title at an auction. There is a minimum bid of fair market value and the high bidder is the purchaser. Participants must be 18.

Homesite: The homesite program was passed in 1977 by the state legislature. Under its provisions, each Alaskan household is eligible for up to five acres. A person who has a homesite entry permit, purchase contract or patent may not apply for another homesite, and neither can any member of that person's household. The land is free, but the individual must pay the cost of the application filing fee ($10), survey and platting, and appraisal, if purchasing. Persons enrolled in this program must live on the homesite for 35 months within seven years of entry and construct a permanent, single-family dwelling on the site within five years (this is called "proving up" on the land). After the dwelling is completed and approved by the division, the permit holder may purchase the land at fair market value at the date of purchase. The occupancy requirement is then waived.

Remote Parcels: This remote parcel program replaced the old open-to-entry program. It permitted entry upon designated areas to stake a parcel of up to 5, 20 or 40 acres, depending on the area, and to lease the area for five years with an option for a five-year renewal.

Remote parcels ended July 1, 1984, when the program was replaced by the 1983 homesteading bill. Alaskans leasing remote parcels, but who have not yet purchased them, may continue under the remote parcel lease agreement program to obtain patent.

Lottery: One year of residency is required to participate in the lottery program. Successful applicants are determined by a drawing and pay the appraised fair market value of the land. They repay the state over a period of up to 20 years, with interest set at the current federal land loan bank rate. Lotteries require a 5 percent down payment.

The state offered 100,000 acres of land to private ownership in each fiscal year from July 1, 1979, to July 1, 1982. Disposal levels from that time forward have been based on an annual assessment of the demand for state land. There are no land sales scheduled for 1993.

On April 1, 1983, the Department of Natural Resources discontinued a program that provided Alaska residents who were registered voters a 5-percent-per-year-of-residency discount (up to $25,000) on the sale of land purchased from the state. Recent legislation has changed U.S. military veteran benefits. A 90-day service now qualifies the veteran. It used to be that 15-year veteran residents had been eligible for up to $37,500 on this one-time program.

Homestead: Under state law, any resident of at least one year, who is 18 years or older and a U.S. citizen, has a chance to receive up to 40 acres of nonagricultural land or up to 160 acres of agricultural land without paying for the acreage itself. To receive title, however, the homesteader must pay a $10 application fee and either survey or reimburse the state for survey costs; brush and stake the parcel boundary, build a dwelling, and occupy and improve the land in certain ways within specific time frames. This is called "proving up" on the homestead.

The state homestead act also allows homesteaders to purchase parcels at fair market value without occupying or improving the land. This option requires only that nonagricultural land be staked, brushed and surveyed, and that parcels designated for agricultural use also meet clearing requirements. There is a two-year purchase option available on the homesteads, or a five-year purchase option, which also requires a habitable dwelling to be built by the third year of the permit. Currently, there are no homesteads available.

Whether the homesteader chooses to prove up or purchase, all applicable requirements such as brushing, survey and agricultural clearing must be met. After homesteading areas have been designated, homesteaders must stake the corners and flag the boundaries of the land, pay a fee of $5 per acre and personally file a description of the land with the state. In order to acquire title to the land, homesteaders must brush the boundaries within 90 days after issuance of the entry permit, complete an approved survey of the land within two or five years (depending on purchase option), erect a habitable permanent dwelling on the homestead within three years, live on the parcel for 25 months within five years and, if the land is classified for agricultural use, clear and either put into production or prepare for cultivation 25 percent of the land within five years.

Up-to-date information and applications for state programs are available from the Department of Natural Resources Public Information Office:

Northern Region, 3700 Airport Way, Fairbanks 99709

Southcentral Region, 3601 C St., Suite 200, Anchorage 99503

Southeastern Region, 400 Willoughby Ave., Suite 400, Juneau 99801

Following is the amount of Alaska land owned by various entities as of April 1991:

Owner	Acreage (millions of acres)
U.S. Bureau of Land Management	...92.4
State	84.7
U.S. Fish and Wildlife	75.4
National Park Service	50.6
Native	35.1
Forest Service	23.2
Military and other Federal	2.6
Private	1.0

(Source: U.S. Bureau of Land Management)

Languages

Besides English, Alaska's languages include 20 Native languages. Fifteen of these Native languages are at risk of extinction: Han, Haida, Eyak, Tanana, Tlingit, Dena'ina (or Tanaina), Ahtna, Ingalik, Holikachuk, Tsimshian, Koyukon, Upper Kuskokwim, Upper Tanana, Kutchin and Aleut. The Eskimo language group—Yup'ik, Central Yup'ik, Siberian Yup'ik and Inupiaq—are widely spoken by many Natives in western and northern Alaska.

Mammals

Large Land Mammals

Black bear—Highest densities are found in Southeast, Prince William Sound, and southcentral coastal mountains and lowlands. Black bears also occur in interior and western Alaska, but are absent from Southeast islands north of Frederick Sound (primarily Admiralty, Baranof and Chichagof) and Kodiak archipelago. They are not commonly found west of about Naknek Lake on the Alaska Peninsula, in the Aleutian Islands or on the open tundra sloping into the Bering Sea and Arctic Ocean. (*See also* Bears)

Brown/grizzly bear—These large omnivores are found in most of Alaska. The grizzly is not found in the Southeast islands south of Frederick Sound and in the Aleutians (except for Unimak Island). (*See also* Bears)

Polar bear—There are two groups in Alaska's Arctic rim: an eastern group found largely in the Beaufort Sea and a western group found in the Chukchi Sea between Alaska and Siberia. The latter group are the largest polar bears in the world. Old males can exceed 1,500 pounds. (*See also* Bears)

American bison—In 1928, 23 bison were transplanted from Montana to Delta Junction to restore Alaska's bison population, which had died out some 500 years before. Today, several hundred bison graze near Delta Junction; other herds range at Farewell, Chitina and along the lower Copper River.

Barren Ground caribou—There are at least 13 distinct caribou herds, with some overlapping of ranges: Adak,

Alaska Peninsula, Arctic, Beaver, Chisana, Delta, Kenai, McKinley, Mentasta, Mulchatna, Nelchina, Porcupine and Fortymile. Porcupine and Fortymile herds range into Canada.

Sitka black-tailed deer—Sitka black-tailed deer range the coastal rain forests of southeastern Alaska. They have been successfully transplanted to the Yakutat area, Prince William Sound, and Kodiak and Afognak islands.

Roosevelt elk—Alaska's only elk occur on Raspberry and Afognak islands and result from a 1928 transplant of Roosevelt elk from the Olympic Peninsula in Washington state. Other transplant attempts have failed.

Moose—Moose occur from the Unuk River in Southeast to the Arctic Slope, but are most abundant in second-growth birch forests, on timberline plateaus and along major rivers of Southcentral and Interior. They are not found on islands in Prince William Sound or Bering Sea, on most major islands in Southeast or on Kodiak or Aleutians groups.

Mountain goat—These white-coated animals are found in mountains throughout Southeast, and north and west along coastal mountains to Cook Inlet and Kenai Peninsula. They have been successfully transplanted to Kodiak and Baranof islands.

Musk-oxen—These shaggy, long-haired mammals were eliminated from Alaska by hunters by 1865. The species was reintroduced and first transplanted to Nunivak Island, and from there to the Arctic Slope around Kavik, Seward Peninsula, Cape Thompson and Nelson Island. (*See also* Musk-Oxen)

Reindeer—Introduced from Siberia just before the 20th century, reindeer roamed much of the Bering Sea Coast

region but are now confined to the Seward Peninsula and Nunivak Island.

Dall sheep—The only white, wild sheep in the world, Dall sheep are found in all major mountain ranges in Alaska except the Aleutian Range south of Iliamna Lake.

Wolf—Wolves are protected and managed as big game and valuable furbearers. Wolves are found throughout Alaska except Bering Sea islands, some Southeast and Prince William Sound islands, and the Aleutian Islands. The wolf succeeds in a variety of climates and terrains.

Wolverine—Shy, solitary creatures, wolverines are found throughout Alaska and on some Southeast islands; they are abundant in the Interior and on the Alaska Peninsula. They are not abundant in comparison with other furbearers.

Furbearers

Beaver—These large vegetarian rodents are found in most of mainland Alaska from the Brooks Range to middle of the Alaska Peninsula. Abundant in some major mainland river drainages in the Southeast and on Yakutat forelands, they have also been successfully transplanted to the Kodiak area. Beaver dams are sometimes destroyed to allow salmon upstream; however, the beavers can rebuild their dams quickly and usually do so on the same site.

Coyote—The coyote is a relative newcomer to Alaska, showing up shortly after the turn of the century, according to old-timers and records. They are not abundant on a statewide basis, but are common in Tanana, Copper, Matanuska and Susitna river drainages and on Kenai Peninsula. The coyote is found as far west as Alaska Peninsula and the north side of Bristol Bay.

Fox—*Arctic* (white and blue phases): Arctic foxes are found almost entirely along the Arctic coast as far south as the northwestern shore of Bristol Bay. They have been introduced to Pribilof and Aleutian islands, where the blue color phase, most popular with fox farmers, predominates. The white color phase occurs naturally on Saint Lawrence and Nunivak islands. *Red:* Their golden fur coveted by trappers, the red fox is found throughout Alaska except for most areas of Southeast and around Prince William Sound.

Lynx—These shy night-prowlers' main food source is the snowshoe hare. The lynx is found throughout Alaska, except on the Yukon–Kuskokwim Delta, southern Alaska Peninsula and along coastal tidelands. It is relatively scarce along the northern Gulf Coast and in southeastern Alaska.

Hoary marmot—Present throughout most of the mountain regions of Alaska and along the Endicott Mountains east into Canada, the hoary marmot lives in the high country, especially the warm slopes near and above timberline.

Marten—The marten must have climax spruce forest to survive, and its habitat ranges throughout timbered Alaska, except north of the Brooks Range, on treeless sections of the Alaska Peninsula, and on the Yukon–Kuskokwim Delta. It has been successfully introduced to Prince of Wales, Baranof, Chichagof and Afognak islands in this century.

Muskrat—Muskrats are found in greatest numbers around lakes, ponds, rivers and marshes throughout all of mainland Alaska south of the Brooks Range except for the Alaska Peninsula west of the Ugashik lakes. They were introduced to Kodiak, Afognak and Raspberry islands.

River otter—A member of the weasel family, the river otter occurs throughout the state except on Aleutian Islands, Bering Sea islands and the Arctic coastal plain east of Point Lay. They are most abundant in southeastern Alaska, in Prince William Sound coastal areas and on the Yukon–Kuskokwim Delta.

Raccoon—The raccoon is not native to Alaska and is considered an undesirable addition because of impact on native furbearers. It is found on the west coast of Kodiak Island, on Japonski and Baranof islands, and on other islands off Prince of Wales Island in Southeast.

Squirrel—*Northern Flying:* These small nocturnal squirrels are found in interior, southcentral and southeastern Alaska where coniferous forests are sufficiently dense to provide suitable habitat. ***Red:*** These tree squirrels inhabit spruce forests, especially along rivers, from Southeast north to the Brooks Range. They are not found on the Seward Peninsula, Yukon–Kuskokwim Delta and Alaska Peninsula south of Naknek River.

Weasel—Least weasels and short-tailed weasels are found throughout Alaska, except for Bering Sea and Aleutian islands. Short-tailed weasels are brown with white underparts in summer, becoming snow-white in winter (designated ermine).

Other Small Mammals

Bat—There are five common bat species in Alaska.

Northern hare (arctic hare or tundra hare)—This large hare inhabits western and northern coastal Alaska, weighs 12 pounds or more and measures 2½ feet long.

Snowshoe hare (or varying hare)—In winter, these animals become pure white; in summer, their coats are grayish to brown. The snowshoe hare occurs throughout Alaska except for the lower portion of Alaska Peninsula, the Arctic coast and most islands; it is scarce in southeastern Alaska. Cyclic population highs and lows of hares occur roughly every 10 years. Their big hind feet, covered with coarse hair in winter, make for easy travel over snow.

Brown lemming—Lemmings are found throughout northern Alaska and the Alaska Peninsula; they are not present in Southeast, Southcentral or the Kodiak archipelago.

Collared lemming—Resembling large meadow voles, collared lemmings are found from the Brooks Range north and from the lower Kuskokwim River drainage north.

Northern bog lemming (sometimes called lemming mice)—These tiny mammals, rarely observed, occur in meadows and bogs across most of Alaska.

Deer mouse—These rodents inhabit timber and brush in southeastern Alaska.

House mouse—Extremely adaptive, familiar house mice are found in Alaska seaports and large communities in southcentral Alaska.

Meadow jumping mouse—These mice can jump six feet and are in the southern third of Alaska from Alaska Range to Gulf of Alaska.

Collared pika—Members of the rabbit family, pikas are found in central and southern Alaska; they are most common in the Alaska Range.

Porcupine—These rodents are slow-moving animals that prefer forests and are found in most wooded regions of mainland Alaska.

Norway rat—The Norway rat came to Alaska on whaling ships to Pribilof Islands in the mid-1800s, especially thriving in the Aleutians (the Rat Islands group is named for the Norway rats). They are now found in virtually all Alaska seaports, and in Anchorage and Fairbanks and other population centers with open garbage dumps.

Shrew—Seven species of shrew range in Alaska.

Meadow vole (or meadow mouse)—Extremely adaptive, there are seven species of meadow vole attributed to Alaska that range throughout the state.

Red-backed vole—The red-backed vole prefers cool, damp forests and is found throughout Alaska from Southeast to Norton Sound.

Woodchuck—These large, burrowing squirrels, also called groundhogs,

are found in the eastern Interior between Yukon and Tanana rivers, from east of Fairbanks to the Alaska–Canada border.

Bushy-tailed woodrat—Commonly called pack rats because they tend to carry off objects to their nests, woodrats are found along the mainland coast of southeastern Alaska.

Marine Mammals

Marine mammals found in Alaska waters are: **dolphin** (Grampus, Pacific white-sided and Risso's); **Pacific walrus; porpoise** (Dall and harbor); **sea otter; seal** (harbor, larga, northern elephant, northern fur, Pacific bearded or *oogruk*, ribbon, ringed and spotted); **Steller sea lion;** and **whale** (Baird's beaked or giant bottlenose, beluga, blue, narwhal, bowhead, Cuvier's beaked or goosebeaked, fin or finback, gray, humpback, killer, minke or little piked, northern right, pilot, sei, sperm and Bering Sea beaked or Stejneger's beaked).

The Marine Mammal Protection Act, passed by Congress on Dec. 21, 1972, provided for a complete moratorium on the taking and importation of all marine mammals. The purpose of the act was to give protection to population stocks of marine mammals that "are, or may be, in danger of extinction or depletion as a result of man's activities." Congress further found that marine mammals have "proven themselves to be resources of great international significance, aesthetic and recreational as well as economic, and it is the sense of the Congress that they should be protected and encouraged to develop to the greatest extent feasible commensurate with sound policies of resource management and that the primary objective of their management should be to maintain the health and stability of the marine ecosystem. Whenever consistent with this primary objective, it should be the goal to obtain an optimum sustainable population keeping in mind the carrying capacity of the habitat."

At the present time, the U.S. Fish and Wildlife Service (Department of the Interior) is responsible for the management of polar bears, sea otters and walrus in Alaska. The National Marine Fisheries Service (Department of

Commerce) is responsible for the management of all other marine mammals. The state of Alaska assumed management of walrus in April 1976, and relinquished it back to the USFWS in July 1979. However, an amendment to the Marine Mammal Protection Act in 1981 makes it easier for states to assume management of marine mammals, and Alaska is currently going through the necessary steps to assume management of its marine mammals.

Masks

(*See also* Native Arts and Crafts)

Masks are integral to the cultures of the Eskimos, coastal Indians and Aleuts of Alaska.

Eskimo

Eskimo masks rank among the finest tribal art in the world. Ceremonialism and the mask-making that accompanied it were highly developed and practiced widely by the time the first Russians established trading posts in southeast Alaska in the early 1800s. By the early part of the 20th century, masks were made much less frequently and were rarely made for ceremonial use.

The shaman used masks during certain ceremonies, sometimes in conjunction with wooden puppets, in ways that frightened and entertained participants. Dancers wore religious masks in festivals that honored the spirits of animals and birds to be hunted or that needed to be appeased. Each spirit was inter-preted visually in a different mask and each mask was thought to have a spirit, or *inua,* of its own. This *inua* tied the mask to the stream of spiritual beliefs present in Eskimo religion. Not all masks were benign; some were surrealistic pieces that represented angry or dangerous spirits.

The skill of ceremonial mask-making has remained popular in some regions, notably among King Islanders, on Nunivak Island and in other areas of southwest Alaska.

Indian

Several types of masks existed among the coastal Indians of Alaska, including simple single-face masks, occasionally having an elaborately carved totemic border; a variation of the face mask with the addition of moving parts; and transformation masks, which have several faces hidden behind the first.

Masked dancers were accompanied by a chorus of tribal singers who sang songs associated with the masks and reflecting the wealth of the host. Masks were the critical element in portraying the relationship of the tribe with spirits and projecting their power to spellbind their audiences.

Masks were always created to be worn, but not all members of the tribe held sufficient status or power to wear them. Ceremonial use of masks generally took place in the fall or winter, when the spirits of the other world were said to be nearby.

Crudely carved masks created for

fun were occasionally made among the Kwakiutl.

Northwest Coast Indian mask-makers primarily used alder, though red and yellow cedar were used at times.

Aleut

Examples of masks used on various islands of the Aleutian Chain for shamanistic and ceremonial purposes are reported as early as the mid-18th century. Some of these early masks were described as bizarre representations of various animals, but many were apparently destroyed after use and none survive today. Aleut legends maintain that some masks were associated with ancient inhabitants of the region, a people apparently considered unrelated.

On the Shumagin Islands, a group of cavelike chambers yielded important examples of Aleut masks late in the 19th century. A number of well-preserved masks, apparently associated with the burials of Aleut whalers, were found. All of them had once been painted. Some of them had attached ears and pegs where tooth grips for wearing the masks would have been placed. Other pegs and holes were used for inserting feathers or carved wooden appendages similar to those of Eskimo masks of southern Alaska today. Fragments of composite masks, those decorated with feathers, appendages or movable parts, have been found on Kagamil Island with earlier remains.

Early accounts of masked Aleut dances say each dance was accompanied by special songs. Most masks were apparently hidden in caves or secret places when the ceremony ended, possibly for good luck. Bone masks worn by members of burial parties in some regions were broken and discarded at the gravesite when funeral rites were completed.

Today, no Aleut mask-makers in the old tradition survive, so further explanation of the use and significance of masks already collected depends on future archaeological investigation.

Medal of Heroism

By a law established in 1965, the Alaska governor is authorized to award, in recognition of valorous and heroic deeds, a state medal of heroism to persons who have saved a life or, at risk to their lives, have served the state or community on behalf of the health, welfare or safety of other persons. The heroism medal may be awarded posthumously. Following are recipients of the Alaska Medal of Heroism:

Albert Rothfuss (1965), Ketchikan. Rescued a child from drowning in Ketchikan Creek.

Randy Blake Prinzing (1968), Soldotna. Saved two lives at Scout Lake.

Nancy Davis (1971), Seattle. A flight attendant who convinced an alleged hijacker to surrender to authorities.

Jeffrey Stone (1972), Fairbanks.

Saved the lives of two youths from a burning apartment.

Gilbert Pelowook (1975), Savoonga. An Alaska state trooper who aided plane crash victims on Saint Lawrence Island.

Residents of Gambell (1975). Provided aid and care for plane crash victims on Saint Lawrence Island.

George Jackinsky (1978), Kasilof. Rescued two persons from a burning aircraft.

Mike Hancock (1980), Lima, Ohio. In 1977, rescued a victim of a plane crash that brought down high-voltage lines.

John Stimson (1983), Cordova. A first sergeant in the Division of Fish and Wildlife Protection who died in a helicopter accident during an attempt to rescue others.

Robert Larson (1983), Anchorage. A Department of Public Safety employee who flew through hazardous conditions to rescue survivors of the crash that took John Stimson's life.

David Graham (1983), Kenai. Rescued a person from a burning car.

Darren Olanna (1984), Nome. Died while attempting to rescue a person from a burning house.

Esther Farquhar (1984), Sitka. Tried to save other members of her family from a fire in their home; lost her life in the attempt.

Billy Westlock (1986), Emmonak. Rescued a youngster from the Emmonak River.

Lt. Cmdr. Whiddon, Lt. Breithaupt, ASM2 Tunks, AD1 Saylor, AT3 Milne (1987), Sitka. Rescued a man and his son from their sinking boat during high seas.

Army and Air National Guard (1988), Gambell, Savoonga, Nome and Shishmaref. Searched for seven missing walrus hunters.

Evans Geary, Johnny Sheldon, Jason Rutman, Jessee Ahkpuk Jr. and Carl Hadley (1989), Buckland. These youth rescued two friends who, while ice skating on a frozen pond, had fallen through the ice.

Robert Cusack (1991), Lake Iliamna. Rescued a woman and a child who were trapped inside a floatplane that crashed and sank in Lake Iliamna.

Clifford Comer, Robert Yerex, Gary Strebe, David Schron, Jeffery Waite (1992), Air Station Kodiak. Rescued a four-man fishing crew in adverse conditions.

Metric Conversions

As in the rest of the United States, metrics are slow in coming to Alaska. The conversion formulas on page 98 will help you to prepare for the metric system and to understand measurements in neighboring Yukon Territory.

Mileage Chart

See chart on page 99.

Military

(*See also* National Guard)

Until the rapid escalation of war in Europe in 1940–41, Congress saw little need for a strong military presence in Alaska. Spurred by World War II and a growing realization that Alaska could shorten the route to Asia for friend and foe, the government built and still maintains units of the Air Force, Army, *(Continued on page 99)*

Approximate conversions from customary to metric and vice versa:

	When you know:	You can find:	If you multiply by:
Length	inches	millimeters	25.4
	feet	centimeters	30.5
	yards	meters	0.9
	miles	kilometers	1.6
	millimeters	inches	0.04
	centimeters	inches	0.4
	meters	yards	1.1
	kilometers	miles	0.6
Area	square inches	square centimeters	6.5
	square feet	square meters	0.09
	square yards	square meters	0.8
	square miles	square kilometers	2.6
	acres	square hectometers (hectares)	0.4
	square centimeters	square inches	0.16
	square meters	square yards	1.2
	square kilometers	square miles	0.4
	square hectometers (hectares)	acres	2.5
Weight	ounces	grams	28.4
	pounds	kilograms	0.45
	short tons	megagrams (metric tons)	0.9
	grams	ounces	0.04
	kilograms	pounds	2.2
	megagrams (metric tons)	short tons	1.1
Liquid Volume	ounces	milliliters	29.6
	pints	liters	0.47
	quarts	liters	0.95
	gallons	liters	3.8
	milliliters	ounces	0.03
	liters	pints	2.1
	liters	quarts	1.06
	liters	gallons	0.26
Temperature	degrees Fahrenheit	degrees Celsius	5/9 (after subtracting 32)
	degrees Celsius	degrees Fahrenheit	9/5 (then add 32)

98

DRIVING MILEAGES BETWEEN PRINCIPAL POINTS	Anchorage, AK	Dawson City, YT	Dawson Creek, BC	Fairbanks, AK	Haines, AK	Homer, AK	Prince Rupert, BC	Seattle, WA	Skagway, AK	Valdez, AK	Whitehorse, YT
Anchorage, AK		515	1608	358	775	226	1605	2435	832	304	724
Dawson City, YT	515		1195	393	578	741	1192	2022	435	441	327
Dawson Creek, BC	1608	1195		1486	1135	1834	706	827	992	1534	884
Fairbanks, AK	358	393	1486		653	584	1483	2313	710	284	602
Haines, AK	775	578	1135	653		1001	1132	1962	359	701	251
Homer, AK	226	741	1834	584	1001		1831	2661	1058	530	950
Prince Rupert, BC	1605	1192	706	1483	1132	1831		1033	989	1531	881
Seattle, WA	2435	2022	827	2313	1962	2661	1033		1819	2361	1711
Skagway, AK	832	435	992	710	359	1058	989	1819		758	108
Valdez, AK	304	441	1534	284	701	530	1531	2361	758		650
Whitehorse, YT	724	327	884	602	251	950	881	1711	108	650	

(Continued from page 97)
Navy and Coast Guard at dozens of installations across the state and on floating units in Alaskan waters. At the state level are Air National Guard and Army National Guard units.

U.S. ARMY

The Alaska District Corps of Engineers (COE) has three offices in Alaska: the Alaska District Office at Elmendorf Air Force Base, the Denali Area Office at Fort Richardson and the Fairbanks Resident Office at Fort Wainwright. There are also several offices across the state at Corps construction sites.

The Alaska District COE plans and designs military structures, runways and roads, utilities and other facilities for the Army, the 11th Air Force and the Alaska National Guard (Army and Air Force). Clear, Alaska, is the site of one of three Ballistic Missile Early Warning System (BMEWS) stations, which has been in operation since 1961. The two other BMEWS are in Greenland and England. The BMEWS station has three 400-foot-wide, 165-foot-high radar screens that scan the skies from the North Pole to China. The BMEWS supplies assistance to the Distant Early Warning (DEW) Line, which was originally designed to detect bombers crossing into North American air space. The Alaska sector of the DEW Line System is still in full operation.

The 6th Infantry Division (Light) is the primary Army unit in Alaska. The headquarters at Fort Richardson was moved to Fort Wainwright in 1990. In March 1993, it was announced that the division would be downsized by October 1994 to a brigade task force with 2,800 fewer soldiers. In May 1993, this reduction of 2,800 soldiers was modified to 2,650. The brigade task force commander, a colonel, and his staff, will be located at Fort Wainwright. The senior Army commander in Alaska, a major general, and his staff, will be at Fort Richardson.

Besides combat and combat support forces at those two posts, the division has research facilities and training grounds at Fort Greely. The division, supervised by a two-star general, must be prepared to move quickly to support other troops as needed. In late 1990 and early 1991, more than 200 Alaska-based soldiers were deployed to the Persian Gulf.

The primary units within the division include the 1st and 2nd Infantry Brigades in Alaska, and the 205th Infantry Brigade, which is a U.S. Army Reserve unit at Fort Snelling in St. Paul, Minnesota. In the event of a national emergency, the 205th will deploy to Alaska to "round out" the division. Other major units include the Aviation Brigade, Division Support Command, 6th Signal Battalion, the 6th Engineer Battalion and the 106th Military Intelligence Battalion.

In addition, the 59th Signal Battalion

oversees all Army communications in the state; the Northern Warfare Training Center at Fort Greely trains soldiers, guardsmen and representatives from other services in arctic combat and survival; and the Cold Regions Test Center, also at Fort Greely, tests equipment for cold weather use.

The 6th Infantry Division (Light) conducts major midwinter exercises every other year. Other training includes unit-level exercises in Alaska, training at the Joint Readiness Training Center at Fort Chaffee, Arkansas, and at the National Training Center at Fort Irwin, California. The division also participates in exercises in Thailand and Japan.

United States Army helicopters are stationed at Fort Wainwright (Fairbanks), Fort Richardson (Anchorage) and Fort Greely (Delta Junction). From these installations, Army aircraft participate in search and rescue operations. Medical evacuations of military and civilians in need are performed by the Military Assistance to Safety and Traffic (MAST) unit, which has teams at both forts Wainwright and Greely. The High Altitude Rescue Team (HART) flies specially equipped Chinook (CH-47) helicopters in support of rescues on Mount McKinley and other remote peaks. Army helicopters also transport and train with the Alaska National Guard throughout the state.

U.S. AIR FORCE

The majority of forces comprising Alaskan Command's Air Force component belong to 11th Air Force, a numbered Air Force under Pacific Air Forces (PACAF). The 11th Air Force, with headquarters located at Elmendorf Air Force Base (AFB), is the largest component in Alaska and provides support to all other Air Force units in the state. The 11th Air Forces' largest subordinate units are the 3rd Wing at Elmendorf AFB and the 343rd Wing at Eielson AFB. Another unit under 11th Air Force is the 11th Air Control Wing (ACW) Elmendorf AFB. The 11th ACW controls the 523rd Support Squadron at Galena Airport, the 643rd Support Squadron at King Salmon Airport, the 673rd Air Base Group at Shemya AFB and the network of Air Force radar sites located through-

out Alaska. The 11th Air Force provides combat-ready forces to preserve the sovereignty of the United States' lands, waters and air space and to defend U.S. interests overseas.

Other major Air Force components in Alaska include the Strategic Air Command with its KC-135 tanker fleet and other activities, Military Airlift Command with its fleet of C-130 Hercules cargo aircraft, Tactical Air Command with its E-3 Airborne Warning and Control System (AWACS) aircraft at Elmendorf AFB and radar installations along the northern seacoast, Air Force Space Command performing missile warning and space surveillance, and AF Intelligence Command.

NAVY AND MARINE CORPS

U.S. Navy officers and enlisted personnel are assigned to the Alaskan Command Headquarters staff. Although the Naval Component of the Alaskan Comman, U.S. Naval Forces Alaska (USNAVAK), is primarily composed of 17th Coast Guard District personnel and forces, there are eight active-duty U.S. Navy personnel assigned to the USNAVAK staff. There are no Marines assigned to the Alaskan Command Headquarters or units.

The Navy and Marine Corps have commands and detachments located in Anchorage. Commands located in Anchorage include the Naval Security Group Activity; Military Sealift Command Office; Naval Reserve Center; Personnel Support Detachment, Company E, 4th Recon Battalion, 4th Marine Division; as well as several other small detachments. Naval Air Station Adak is host command for many organizations, including the Naval Security Group Activity; Naval Facility; Naval Investigative Service Office; and Naval Electronics Center Detachment.

U.S. COAST GUARD

The U.S. Coast Guard has been a part of Alaska since the mid-1800s, when it patrolled its extensive and unforgiving coastline with the wooden sailing and steam ships of its predecessor, the Revenue Cutter Service.

Since those early days, the service has changed names and those wooden
(Continued on page 102)

MILITARY INSTALLATIONS

Map Key/Installation/Personnel

Air Force
1 Elmendorf AFB, 6,751
2 Campion AFS*
3 Cape Lisburne AFS*
4 Cape Newenham AFS*
5 Cape Romanzof AFS*
6 Clear AFS, 122
7 Cold Bay AFS*
8 Eielson AFB, 3,282
9 Fort Yukon AFS*
10 Galena Airport, 309
11 Indian Mountain AFS*
12 King Salmon, 275
13 Kotzebue AFS*
14 Murphy Dome AFS*
15 Shemya AFB, 598
16 Sparrevohn AFS*
17 Tatalina AFS*
18 Tin City AFS*

Army
19 Fort Richardson, 4,400

*Now operated by civilian personnel.

20 Fort Greely, 425
21 Fort Wainwright, 4,900

Navy
22 Adak, 1,677

Coast Guard
23 17th District Office Juneau, 170
24 Kodiak Support Center, 287
25 Base/Group Ketchikan, 101
26 Air Station Kodiak, 352
27 Air Station Sitka, 124
28 LORAN Station Attu, 24
29 LORAN Station Saint Paul, 21
30 LORAN Station Port Clarence, 27
31 LORAN Station Kodiak, 14
32 LORAN Station Tok, 7
33 LORAN Station Shoal Cove, 15
34 Communication Station Kodiak, 94
35 Marine Safety Detachment Sitka, 2
36 Marine Safety Office Anchorage, 25
37 Marine Safety Office Juneau, 12
38 Marine Safety Detachment
   Unalaska, 2

Map Key/Installation/Personnel

(continued)

39 Marine Safety Office Valdez, 40
40 Marine Safety Detachment
   Ketchikan, 2
41 Marine Safety Detachment Kenai, 4
42 Marine Safety Detachment Kodiak,2
43 Station Juneau, 14
44 Seasonal Air Facility Cordova, 4
45 Civil Engineering Unit Juneau, 26

46 Electronics Support Unit Kodiak, 20
47 Coast Guard Station Ketchikan, 17
48 Coast Guard Aids to Navigation
   Team, 12

U.S. Coast Guard Cutters/Personnel

Anacapa, 16; *Elderberry,* 6; *Firebush,* 55; *Ironwood,* 55; *Liberty,* 16; *Mustang,* 16; *Naushon,* 16; *Planetree,* 55; *Sedge, Roanoke Island,* 55; *Storis,* 75; *Sweetbrier,* 56; *Woodrush,* 55; *Yocona,* 82

Total Military Expenditures in Alaska by Agency for Fiscal Year 1990 (in millions of dollars)*

Service	Pay	Construction	Operations & Maintenance	Other Procurement	Total
Air Force	$363.9	$ 36.6	$270.8	$97.3	$768.6
Army	393.1	15.6	155.2	2.0	565.9
Coast Guard	65.9	7.1	45.9	9.5	128.4
Corps of Engineers	22.7	0.0	7.7	23.9	54.3
National Guard	71.3	10.0	25.8	0.0	107.1
Navy**	67.7	39.8	32.7	0.1	140.3
Total	$903.6	$160.2	$514.4	$149.2	$1,727.4

*Latest available figures
**Includes Marine Corps

Military Expenditures in Alaska for Fiscal Years 1985–1990 (in millions of dollars)*

	1985	1986	1987	1988	1989	1990
Military Payroll	$ 503.1	$ 516.0	$ 567.5	$ 595.5	$605.3	$649.8
Civilian Payroll	189.7	181.5	212.4	204.9	204.0	214.8
Operations & Maintenance	389.1	493.3	645.3	485.1	527.1	514.4
Construction	204.0	180.3	204.9	167.6	227.0	160.2
Subtotal Appropriated Funds	$1,285.9	$1,371.1	$1,630.1	$1,453.1	$1,563.4	$1,539.2
Exchange & Nonappropriated Payrolls	32.8	35.7	32.5	29.5	30.7	39.0
Other Procurement	136.9	149.5	105.4	194.5	176.7	149.2
Subtotal Other	$169.7	$185.2	$137.9	$224.0	$207.4	$188.2
DOD Retirement	113.1	122.3	130.4	139.5	146.4	175.9
Total	$1,568.7	$1,678.6	$1,898.4	$1,816.6	$1,917.2	$1,903.3

*Latest available figures

(Continued from page 100)
ships have been replaced by today's modern fleet of ships, boats and aircraft, operated and maintained by Alaska's Coast Guard men and women.

The 17th Coast Guard District encompasses the entire state of Alaska, or 33,904 miles of coastline—more than all other states combined. As the nation's smallest military service, the U.S. Coast Guard performs its many missions in Alaska with 2,100 military and civilian employees at 38 units. District headquarters are located in Juneau, and the largest Coast Guard base and air station in the country is in Kodiak.

Major responsibilities in Alaska include enforcing the 200-mile fisheries conservation zone where the majority of the fish caught are sold to foreign countries. Search and rescue in Alaska is another task performed by Coast Guard units. The service maintains aids to navigation, including Long-Range Aids to Navigation (LORAN) lighthouses and buoys. Marine environmental pollution is also a major responsibility. The Coast Guard served as the Federal On-Scene Coordinator for the cleanup of the *Exxon Valdez* oil spill that occurred in Prince William Sound in 1989.

The Coast Guard also has an active role in the defense of Alaska. The District Commander has recently been designated the Naval Component Commander for the Alaskan Command in addition to his responsibility as Commander, Maritime Defense Zone Sector Alaska. The Alaskan Command Naval component commander's mission complements that of Maritime Defense Zone Sector Alaska and Sector Aleutians.

MILITARY POPULATION

The total population of the uniformed services in Alaska as of September 1991 (latest available figures) was approximately 77,201, or about 13 percent of Alaska's total population. Population figures include active-duty personnel, Department of Defense Civil Service employees, Nonappropriated Fund and Exchange personnel, and dependents. Of the total, 25,420 were active-duty uniformed personnel and 4,690 were Civil Service employees of the Department of Defense.

Military services stood as the third largest industry in the state in 1991. Total expenditures on behalf of the military services in Alaska had an estimated $2.7 billion impact on the Alaskan economy.

On a per capita basis, Alaska's veterans population is one of the largest of any state. The Division of Veterans Affairs was established in 1984, as the state's official veterans advocate and coordinator of veterans issues and programs. It is also the liaison with federal and state agencies, veterans organizations, other states' veterans affairs organizations and the state's administration. The division ensures that Alaska's veterans and their dependents are aware of every state and federal benefit available to them and assists them in taking advantage of those benefits.

Minerals and Mining

(*See also* Coal; Gold; Oil and Gas; *and* Rocks and Gems)

In 1992, there were an estimated 3,492 people employed in mineral-related mining sectors in Alaska, according to the state Division of Geological and Geophysical Surveys. The early years of the 1970s were relatively quiet in the industry, with exploration primarily limited to geological reconnaissance. Late in 1974, restrictions on gold in the United States were lifted and the price of gold soared, spurring a revival of gold mining in the state.

By 1981, several large deposits containing minerals such as copper, chromite, molybdenum, nickel and uranium were the subject of serious exploration. Estimated exploration costs were in excess of $100 million for 1981, and more than 3,000 people were employed in the industry.

In 1992, the total value of Alaska's mineral industry, as measured by the sum of exploration and development expenditures and mineral production, amounted to $660.8 million, up 3 percent from 1991. During 1992, employment in the hard-rock mining industry declined by 4 percent, due mainly to lower exploration expenditures.

Zinc was the most valuable mineral commodity in 1992, accounting for more than half of Alaska's total mineral production revenues. Overall, metallic mineral production accounted for 80 percent of total mineral values, versus nonmetallic materials such as coal, sand and gravel, stone, peat and jade, which account for the remaining 20 percent of the values.

Usibelli Coal Mines near Healy continue as the state's only commercial coal mine. Production of coal in 1992 was estimated at 1.54 million tons, nearly unchanged from 1991. Of that total, about half was burned in interior Alaska power plants and the other half was shipped to Korea. During 1992, Usibelli completed its 50th year of operation and shipped its 10 millionth ton of coal through the Port of Seward.

During 1992 the Valdez Creek placer mine reported a record year, producing 86,052 ounces of gold from a year-round operation east of Cantwell. That's about one-third of the state's total gold production, which increased from 244,000 ounces in 1991 to 262,500 in 1992.

Placer mines are by far the biggest employers in Alaska's mining industry. In 1992 placer mines employed 1,251 people out of the mining industry's total work force of 3,492. The average price of gold in 1992 was $337 an ounce.

Greens Creek Mine on Admiralty Island produces silver, along with some lead, zinc and gold, and is the largest silver source in North America. In early 1993, it was announced that the Greens Creek Mine would close in April, laying off 230 employees. Red Dog Mine in the Northwest Arctic Borough is the largest zinc producer in the western world with production of more than 250,000 tons of zinc concentrates. Red Dog Mine also announced in 1993 that it will seek cost-cutting measures due to low metal prices. In spite of low metal prices, developers still sought permits in 1993 for the Kensington and A–J mines in Juneau and the Fort Knox project near Fairbanks.

Miss Alaska

The legislature has declared that the young woman selected as Miss Alaska of the Miss America pageant each year will be the state's official hostess. Holders of the title are selected in Anchorage each spring in a competition sponsored by the nonprofit Miss Alaska Scholarship Pageant organization.

1959—Alansa Rounds Carr, Ketchikan
1960—June Bowdish, Anchorage
1961—Jean Ann Holm, Fairbanks
1962—Mary Dee Fox, Anchorage
1963—Colleen Sharon Kendall,
       Matanuska Valley

1964—Karol Rae Hommon, Anchorage
1965—Mary Ruth Nidiffer, Alaska
       Methodist University
1966—Nancy Lorell Wellman,
       Fairbanks
1967—Penny Ann Thomasson,
       Anchorage
1968—Jane Haycraft, Fairbanks
1969—Gwen Gregg, Elmendorf Air
       Force Base
1970—Virginia Walker, Kotzebue
1971—Linda Joy Smith, Elmendorf Air
       Force Base
1972—Deborah Wood, Elmendorf Air
       Force Base
1973—Virginia Adams, Anchorage
1974—Darby Moore, Kenai
1975—Cindy Suryan, Kodiak
1976—Kathy Tebow, Anchorage
1977—Lisa Granath, Kenai
1978—Patty-Jo Gentry, Fairbanks
1979—Lila Oberg, Matanuska Valley
1980—Sandra Lashbrook,
       Chugiak–Eagle River
1981—Laura Trollan, Juneau
1982—Kristan Sapp, Wasilla
1983—Jennifer Smith, Soldotna
1984—Marilin Blackburn, Anchorage
1985—Kristina Christopher Taylor,
       Palmer
1986—Jerri Morrison, Anchorage
1987—Teresa Murton, Anchorage
1988—Launa Middaugh, Anchorage
1989—Christine Rae McCubbins, Kenai
1990—Holly Ann Salo, Kenai
1991—Beth Gustafson, Anchorage
1992—Keri Baumgardner, Chugiak
1993—Rebecca Nyboer, Anchorage

Mosquitoes

At least 25 species of mosquito are found in Alaska (the number may be as high as 40), the females of all species feeding on people, other mammals or birds. Males and females eat plant sugar, but only the females suck blood, which they use for egg production. The itch that follows the bite comes from an anticoagulant injected by the mosquito. No Alaska mosquitoes carry diseases. The insects are present from April through September in many areas of the

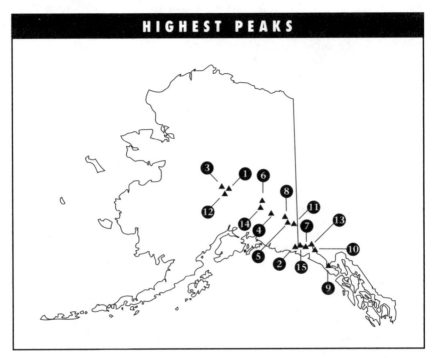

state. Out in the bush they are often at their worst in June, tapering off in July. The mosquito plague usually passes by late August and September. From Cook Inlet south, they concentrate on coastal flats and forested valleys. In the Aleutian Islands, mosquitoes are absent or present only in small numbers. The most serious mosquito infestations occur in moist areas of slow-moving or standing water, of the type found in the fields, bogs and forests of interior Alaska, from Bristol Bay eastward.

Mosquitoes are most active at dusk and dawn; low temperatures and high winds decrease their activity. Mosquitoes can be controlled by draining their breeding areas or spraying with approved insecticides. When traveling in areas of heavy mosquito infestations, it is wise to wear protective clothing, carefully screen living and camping areas and use a good insect repellent.

Mountains

Of the 20 highest mountains in the United States, 17 are in Alaska, which has 19 peaks over 14,000 feet. The U.S. Geological Survey lists them as follows:

Map Key/Elevation
1 McKinley, South Peak, 20,320 feet*
1 McKinley, North Peak, 19,470 feet*
2 Saint Elias, 18,008 feet**
3 Foraker, 17,400 feet
4 Bona, 16,500 feet
5 Blackburn, 16,390 feet
6 Sanford, 16,237 feet
1 South Buttress, 15,885 feet
7 Vancouver, 15,700 feet**
8 Churchill, 15,638 feet
9 Fairweather, 15,300 feet**
10 Hubbard, 15,015 feet**
11 Bear, 14,831 feet
1 East Buttress, 14,730 feet
12 Hunter, 14,573 feet
13 Alverstone, 14,565 feet**
1 Browne Tower, 14,530 feet
14 Wrangell, 14,163 feet
15 Augusta, 14,070 feet**
*Note: The two peaks of Mount McKinley are known collectively as the Churchill Peaks.
**On Alaska–Canada border.

105

Other Well-Known Alaska Mountains/Elevation

Augustine Volcano, 4,025 feet
Deborah, 12,339 feet
Devils Paw, 8,584 feet
Devils Thumb, 9,077 feet
Doonerak, 7,610 feet
Drum, 12,010 feet
Edgecumbe, 3,201 feet
Hayes, 13,832 feet
Kates Needle, 10,002 feet
Marcus Baker, 13,176 feet
Shishaldin, 9,372 feet

Mountain Ranges/Elevation

Ahklun Mountains, 1,000–3,000 feet
Alaska Range to 20,320 feet
Aleutian Range to 7,585 feet
Askinuk Mountains to 2,342 feet
Baird Mountains to 4,300 feet
Bendeleben Mountains to 3,730 feet
Brabazon Range to 5,515 feet
Brooks Range, 4,000–9,000 feet
Chigmit Mountains to 5,000 feet
Chugach Mountains to 13,176 feet
Coast Mountains to 18,000 feet
Darby Mountains to 3,083 feet
Davidson Mountains to 5,540 feet
De Long Mountains to 4,886 feet
Endicott Mountains to 7,000 feet
Fairweather Range to 15,300 feet
Igichuk Hills to 2,000 feet
Kaiyuh Mountains, 1,000–2,844 feet
Kenai Mountains to 6,000 feet
Kiglapak Mountains to 1,070 feet
Kigluaik Mountains to 4,714 feet
Kuskokwim Mountains to 3,973 feet
Lookout Range to 2,400 feet
Mentasta Mountains, 4,000–7,000 feet
Moore Mountains to 3,000 feet
Nutzotin Mountains, 5,000–8,000 feet
Ray Mountains, 2,500–5,500 feet

Mountain Ranges/Elevation
(continued)

Romanzof Mountains to 8,700 feet
Saint Elias Mountains to 18,000 feet
Schwatka Mountains to 8,800 feet
Shublik Mountains to 4,500 feet
Sischu Mountains to 2,422 feet
Talkeetna Mountains, 6,000–8,800 feet
Waxell Ridge, 4,000–10,000 feet
White Mountains to 5,000 feet
Wrangell Mountains to 16,421 feet
York Mountains to 2,349 feet
Zane Hills to 4,053 feet

Mount McKinley

Mount McKinley in the Alaska Range is the highest mountain on the North American continent. The South Peak is 20,320 feet high; the North Peak has an elevation of 19,470 feet. The mountain was named in 1896 for William McKinley of Ohio, who at the time was the Republican candidate for president. An earlier name had been Denali, an Athabascan word meaning "the high one." The state of Alaska officially renamed the mountain Denali in 1975 and the state Geographic Names Board claims the proper name for the mountain is Denali. However, the federal Board of Geographic Names has not taken any action and congressional legislation has been introduced to retain the name McKinley in perpetuity.

Mount McKinley is within Denali National Park and Preserve (formerly Mount McKinley National Park). The park entrance is about 237 miles north of Anchorage and 121 miles south of

Fairbanks via the George Parks Highway. (A 90-mile gravel road runs west from the highway through the park; vehicle traffic on the park road is restricted.) The park is also accessible via the Alaska Railroad and by aircraft.

The mountain and its park are one of the top tourist attractions in Alaska. The finest times to see McKinley up close are on summer mornings. August is best, according to statistics based on 13 summers of observation by park ranger Rick McIntyre. The mountain is rarely visible the entire day. The best view is from Eielson Visitor Center, located about 66 miles from the park entrance and 33 miles northeast of the summit. The center, open from early June through the second week in September, is accessible via free shuttle bus provided by the park.

Eleven climbers perished on Mount McKinley in May 1992, making it the deadliest climbing season in the mountain's history. The 11 climbers, including one American mountaineering guide, died in five separate incidents on the mountain. Since 1932 when the National Park Service began keeping records of climbers attempting to reach the summit of Mount McKinley, 76 climbers have been killed on the mountain (one in 1993). The five deadliest years on the mountain were 1981 and 1989, when six mountaineers were killed; 1967 and 1980, when eight mountaineers were killed, in addition to 1992, when 11 died.

The peak year for climbing the mountain was 1993, when over 1,100 mountaineers scaled its heights. In 1992, 1,070 persons attempted to climb Mount McKinley. The West Buttress remains the most popular route, used by 77 percent or 831 climbers in 1992.

Americans made up the largest segment of the climbers, with 634 attempting the climb and 269 Americans reaching the summit. Foreign climbers numbered 436 with 22 countries represented. The largest number of foreign mountaineers came from Switzerland, with 68 climbers. The 1992 mountaineering season on Denali began with a storm the National Weather Service accurately predicted in early May as the "worst storm to hit the mountain in 10 years." This storm brought in excess of 60 inches of snow at the 7,200-foot base camp in a 24-hour period, and winds over 110 mph at 14,000 feet. This adverse weather halted most summit attempts for several weeks and necessitated a number of rescues. Both guides and climbers assisted the mountaineering rangers at the 14,200-foot ranger station during these rescues, which were carried out throughout intense weather conditions. In a 10-day period from the start of the storm, seven people died and six were rescued.

The 1992 climbing season marked the most intense period of rescues in the mountain's history. Twenty-two rescue or recovery missions involving 28 climbers were conducted by the Talkeetna ranger staff and volunteers. Rescue costs incurred by the National Park Service for Mount McKinley totalled $206,000, double the 1991 expenditure.

In 1991, the National Park Service contracted an Areospatiale Lama helicopter to be stationed in Talkeetna for the mountaineering season. The Lama has been successfully used on several major rescue missions. Its worthiness was proven after it was used for two successful rescues above 18,000 feet.

Registration is required for all Mount McKinley climbs and expeditions. Beginning in 1994, all climbers must preregister by Feb. 15 of the year they plan to climb. This will allow the park service to better plan for mountain patrols for increasing numbers of climbers.

Related reading: *To the Top of Denali*, by Bill Sherwonit. A collection of Mount McKinley climbing stories. *See* ALASKA NORTHWEST LIBRARY in the back of the book.

Mukluks

Mukluks are lightweight boots designed to provide warmth in extreme cold. Eskimo mukluks are traditionally made with *oogruk* (bearded seal) skin bottoms and caribou tops and trimmed with fur. (Mukluk is also another name for *oogruk*.) Athabascan mukluks are traditionally made of moose hide and trimmed with fur and beadwork.

Muktuk

This Eskimo delicacy consists of the outer skin layers of whales. The two species of whale most often used for muktuk are the bowhead whale and the beluga, or white whale. The outer skin layers consist of a corky protective layer, the true skin and the blubber. In the case of beluga muktuk, the outer layer is white, the next layer is black and the blubber is pink. It may be eaten fresh, frozen, cooked or pickled.

Museums, Cultural Centers and Repositories

Visiting any of the following museums, historic sites, or other repositories offers a look into the rich diversity of Alaskan culture and history. For information about hours of operation and features of the collections, write to the addresses given or check with the Alaska State Division of Tourism, P.O. Box E, Juneau 99811; or Museums Alaska, Inc., 3779 Bartlett St., Homer 99603.

Adak Community Museum, PSC 486, Box 1313, FPO AP 96506-1271

Alaska Aviation Heritage Museum,

4721 Aircraft Drive, Anchorage 99502

Alaska Indian Arts, Inc., P.O. Box 271, Haines 99827 (historic site)

Alaska Resources Library, 222 W. Seventh Ave., Anchorage 99513

Alaska State Museum, 395 Whittier St., Juneau 99801-1718

Alaskaland Pioneer Air Museum, P.O. Box 70437, Fairbanks 99707

Alutiiq Cultural Center, 402 Center St., Kodiak 99615

Anchorage Museum of History & Art, 121 W. Seventh Ave., Anchorage 99501

Assumption of the Virgin Mary Church, Kenai 99611 (historic site)

Baranof Museum/Kodiak Historical Society, 101 Marine Way, Kodiak 99615

Bristol Bay Historical Museum, P.O. Box 43, Naknek 99633

Carrie M. McLain Memorial Museum, P.O. Box 53, Nome 99762

Charlie Hubbard Museum, P.O. Box 552, Cooper Landing 99572

Circle District Historical Society, P.O. Box 1893, Central 99730

Clausen Memorial Museum, P.O. Box 708, Petersburg 99833

Cordova Museum, P.O. Box 391, Cordova 99574

Corrington Museum, P.O. Box 382, Skagway 99840

Damon Memorial Museum, P.O. Box 66, Soldotna 99669

Dog Mushing Museum, Box 80136, Fairbanks 99708

Dorothy G. Page Museum, P.O. Box 870874, Wasilla 99687

Duncan Memorial Museum, P.O. Box 282, Metlakatla 99926

Eagle Historic Society, P.O. Box 23, Eagle 99738

Eklutna Village Historical Park, 510 L St., Suite 200, Anchorage 99501

Fairbanks Native Association Native Village, 201 First Ave., Fairbanks 99701

Fort Richardson Fish and Wildlife Center, Building 600, Fort Richardson 99505

George I. Ashby Memorial Museum, P.O. Box 84, Copper Center 99573

Heritage Library and Museum, P.O. Box 100600, Anchorage 99510

Hoonah Cultural Center, P.O. Box 144, Hoonah 99829

House of Wickersham, 400 Willoughby Ave., Juneau 99801

Husila Cultural Center, P.O. Box 70, Husila 99746

Iditarod Museum, P.O. Box 870800, Wasilla 99687

The Imaginarium, 725 W. Fifth Ave., Anchorage 99501

Institute of Alaska Native Arts (IANA), P.O. Box 80583, Fairbanks 99708

Interior and Arctic Alaska Aeronautical Museum, P.O. Box 70437, Fairbanks 99707

Inupiat History, Language and Cultural Center, P.O. Box 69, Barrow 99723

Isabel Miller Museum, 330 Harbor Drive, Sitka 99835

Jessie Wakefield Memorial Library, P.O. Box 263, Port Lions 99550

Juneau Douglas City Museum, 155 S. Seward St., Juneau 99801

Juneau Mining Museum, 490 S. Franklin St., Juneau 99801

Kake Tribal Heritage Foundation, P.O. Box 263, Juneau 99801

Kenai Bicentennial Visitors and Cultural Center, P.O. Box 1991, Kenai 99611

Klawock Totem Park, P.O. Box 113, Klawock 99925 (historic site)

Kodiak Area Native Association, 402 Center St., Kodiak 99615

Matanuska Valley Museum, Greater Palmer Chamber of Commerce, Palmer 99645

Museum of Alaska Transportation and Industry, P.O. Box 870646, Wasilla 99687

NANA Museum of the Arctic, P.O. Box 49, Kotzebue 99752

National Bank of Alaska Heritage Library Museum, P.O. Box 100600, Anchorage 99510

National Park Service, 2525 Gambell St., Anchorage 99503

Oscar Anderson House, 420 M St., Anchorage 99502

Palmer Museum, P.O. Box 45, Palmer 99645

Pioneer Memorial Park, P.O. Box 176, Fairbanks 99707

Pratt Museum, 3779 Bartlett St., Homer 99603

Rasmuson Library, University of Alaska, Fairbanks 99701

Resurrection Bay Historical Society Museum, P.O. Box 55, Seward 99664

Russian Bishop's House, P.O. Box 944, Sitka 99835

Saint Herman's Theological Seminary, P.O. Box 726, Kodiak 99615 (historic site)

Samuel K. Fox Museum, P.O. Box 273, Dillingham 99576

Saxman Totem Park and Tribal House, P.O. Box 8558, Ketchikan 99901 (historic site)

Sheldon Jackson Museum, 104 College Drive, Sitka 99835

Sheldon Museum and Cultural Center, P.O. Box 269, Haines 99827

Simon Paneak Memorial Museum, P.O. Box 21085, Anaktuvuk Pass 99721

Soldotna Historical Society, P.O. Box 1986, Soldotna 99669

Southeast Alaska Indian Cultural Center, 106 Metlakatla, Sitka 99835

Talkeetna Historical Society Museum, P.O. Box 76, Talkeetna 99676

Tanana Valley Agricultural Museum, P.O. Box 188, Fairbanks 99707

Tok Visitor Center, P.O. Box 335, Tok 99780

Tongass Historical Museum, 629 Dock St., Ketchikan 99901

Totem Bight, Ketchikan. For information, write Alaska Division of Parks, P.O. Box M, Juneau 99811 (historic site)

Totem Heritage Center, 629 Dock St., Ketchikan 99901 (historic site)

Trail of '98 Museum, P.O. Box 415, Skagway 99840

Tribal House of the Bear, P.O. Box 868, Wrangell 99929 (historic site)

U.S. Historical Aircraft Preservation Museum, P.O. Box 6813, Anchorage 99502

University of Alaska Museum, 907 Yukon Drive, Fairbanks 99775

Valdez Museum, P.O. Box 307, Valdez 99686

Visual Arts Center, 713 W. Fifth Ave., Anchorage 99501

Wales Museum, Wales 99783

Wasilla Historical Society, 323 Main St., Wasilla 99654

Whittier Historical Museum, P.O. Box 728, Whittier 99502

Wickersham House, P.O. Box 71336, Fairbanks 99707

Wildlife Museum, Elmendorf Air Force Base, Anchorage 99506

Wrangell Museum, P.O. Box 1050, Wrangell 99929

Yugtarvik Regional Museum, P.O. Box 388, Bethel 99559

Mushrooms

More than 500 species of mushroom grow in Alaska, and, while most are not common enough to be seen and collected readily by the amateur mycophile (mushroom hunter), many edible and choice species shoot up in any available patch of earth. Alaska's "giant arc of mushrooms" extends from Southeast's panhandle through Southcentral, the Alaska Peninsula and the Aleutian Chain and is prime mushroom habitat. Interior, western and northern Alaska also support mushrooms in abundance.

Mushroom seasons vary considerably according to temperature, humidity and available nutrients, but most occur from June through September. In

a particularly cold or dry season, the crop will be scant.

There are relatively few poisonous mushrooms in relation to the number of species that occur throughout Alaska. Most toxic species are not fatal to healthy adults, but may produce severe symptoms such as heart palpitations, nausea, or may act as a laxative. Even edible mushrooms may disagree with one's digestion; the only test for an inedible or poisonous mushroom is positive identification. *If you can't identify it, don't eat it.*

Muskeg

Muskegs are deep bogs where little vegetation can grow except for sphagnum moss, black spruce, dwarf birch and a few other shrubby plants. Such swampy areas cover much of Alaska.

Musk-oxen

Musk-oxen are stocky, shaggy, long-haired mammals of the extreme northern latitudes. They remain in the open through Alaska's long winters. Their name is misleading, for they do not give musk and are more closely related to sheep and goats than to cattle. Adult males may weigh 500 to 900 pounds, females between 250 and 500 pounds. Both sexes have horns that droop down from their forehead and curve back up at the tips.

When threatened by wolves or other predators, musk-oxen form circles or lines with their young in the middle. These defensive measures did not protect them from man and his gun.

Musk-oxen were eliminated from Alaska in about 1865, when hunters shot and killed the last herd of 13. The species was reintroduced to the territory in the 1930s when 34 musk-oxen were purchased from Greenland and brought to the University of Alaska at Fairbanks. In 1935–36, the 31 remaining musk-oxen at the university were shipped to Nunivak Island in the Bering Sea, where the herd eventually thrived. Animals from the Nunivak herd have been transplanted to areas along Alaska's western and northern coasts; at least five herds—approximately 1,200 musk-oxen—now exist in the state.

Recent indications are that musk-oxen from Nelson Island are spreading to the mainland and that individuals from the eastern arctic herd have wandered west into adjacent Canada.

The soft underhair of musk-oxen is called qiviut and grows next to the skin, protected by long guard hairs. It is shed naturally every spring. Oomingmak Musk Ox Producers' Cooperative maintains a musk-oxen farm at Talkeetna, where workers gather the qiviut for cottage industry use. The hair is spun into yarn in Rhode Island and sent back to Alaska, where the cooperative arranges for knitters in villages in western Alaska, where jobs are scarce, to knit the yarn into clothing at their own pace.

Each village keeps its own distinct signature pattern for scarves knitted from qiviut. Villagers also produce stoles, tunics, hats and smoke rings, which are circular scarves that fit a person's head like a hood.

A domestic musk-oxen farm is located just outside Palmer. Guided tours operate daily from May to September and bring visitors face to face with these unique arctic animals. For more information, write: Musk–ox Farm, P.O. Box 587, Palmer 99645.

National Forests

Alaska has two national forests, the Tongass and the Chugach. The Tongass occupies the panhandle or southeast portion of the state. The Chugach extends south and east of Anchorage along the southcentral Alaskan coast, encompassing most of the Prince William Sound area.

These two national forests are managed by the U.S. Forest Service for a variety of uses. They provide forest products for national and international markets; minerals; recreational opportunities; wilderness experiences; and superb scenery and views for Alaska residents and visitors.

Nearly 200 public recreation cabins are maintained in the Tongass and Chugach national forests. They accommodate visitors from all over the world and are a vacation bargain at $20 per night, including firewood and, on some freshwater lakes, a boat. (*See also* Cabins)

Wildlife and fisheries are important Forest Service programs in the national forests of Alaska. The Tongass and Chugach national forests are also home to some of Alaska's most magnificent wildlife. It is here that the United States' national bird, the bald eagle, and large brown (grizzly) bears may be encountered in large numbers. All five species of Pacific salmon spawn in the rivers and streams of the forests, and smaller mammals and waterfowl abound. The Forest Service is charged with the management of this rich habitat; the Alaska Department of Fish and Game manages the wildlife species that this habitat supports.

There are many recreational opportunities in the national forests of Alaska, including backpacking, fishing, hunting, photography, boating, nature study and camping, to list just a few. For further information concerning recreational opportunities, contact the U.S. Forest Service office nearest the area you are visiting.

The Alaska National Interest Lands Conservation Act of 1980—also referred to as ANILCA—and the Tongass Timber Reform Act (TTRA) of 1990 changed the status of certain lands in Alaska's national forests. (*See also* Land Use; National Parks, Preserves and Monuments; *and* National Wilderness Areas)

ANILCA created approximately 5.5 million acres of wilderness (consisting of 14 units) within the 17 million-acre Tongass National Forest. It also added three new areas to the forest: the Juneau Icefield, Kates Needle and parts of the Barbazon Range, totaling more than 1 million acres. The Tongass Timber Reform Act (TTRA) of 1990 amended ANILCA and designated five additional wilderness areas and an addition to the existing Kootznoowoo Wilderness.

The lands bill also provided exten-sive additions to the Chugach National Forest. These additions, totaling about 2 million acres, include the Nellie Juan area east of Seward, College Fiord extension, Copper/Rude rivers addition and a small extension at Controller Bay southeast of Cordova.

The following charts show the effect of the Alaska lands act on the Tongass and Chugach national forests:

Wilderness Units in Tongass National Forest (including acres)

Wilderness Areas Established Dec. 2, 1980 by ANILCA
  Kootznoowoo Wilderness (Admiralty Island National Monument)**, 955,921*
  Coronation Island Wilderness, 19,232
  Endicott River Wilderness, 98,729
  Maurelle Islands Wilderness, 4,937
  Misty Fiords National Monument**, 2,142,243
  Petersburg Creek–Duncan Salt Chuck Wilderness, 46,777
  Russel Fiord Wilderness, 348,701
  South Baranof Wilderness, 319,568
  South Prince of Wales Wilderness, 90,996
  Stikine–LeConte Wilderness, 448,926
  Tebenkof Bay Wilderness, 66,839
  Tracy Arm–Fords Terror Wilderness, 653,179
  Warren Island Wilderness, 11,181
  West Chichagof–Yakobi Wilderness, 264,747
Wilderness Areas Established Nov. 28, 1990 by TTRA
  Chuck River Wilderness, 74,298
  Karta Wilderness, 39,889
  Kuiu Wilderness, 60,581
  Pleasant–Lemusurier–Inian Islands Wilderness, 23,096
  South Etolin Wilderness, 83,371
Total Acreage, 5,753,211

*Kootznoowoo Wilderness includes 18,486 acres (including 24 acres of non-National Forest land) in the Young Lake Addition established by TTRA.
**Designated monuments under ANILCA; first areas so designated in the National Forest system. These wilder-nesses include only the public lands above mean high tide.

	Tongass	Chugach
Total Acreage Before ANILCA	15,555,388	4,392,646
Total Acreage After ANILCA	16,954,713	5,940,040*
Wilderness Acreage Created	5,753,211	none created
Wilderness Study	none created	2,019,999 acres
Wild and Scenic River Study	Situk River**	none created

*This lands act provides for additional transfers of national forest land to Native corporations, the state and the Fish and Wildlife Service of an estimated 296,000 acres on Afognak Island, and an estimated 242,000 acres to the Chugach Native Corporation.
**The lands act provides for a maximum of 640 acres on each side of the river, for each mile of river length.

National Guard

(*See also* Military)

The Department of Military Affairs administers the Alaska Army National Guard and the Air National Guard. The guard is charged with performing military reconnaissance, surveillance and patrol operations in Alaska; providing special assistance to civil authorities during natural disasters or civil disturbances; and augmenting regular Army and Air Force in times of national emergency. About 1,314 full-time employees work for the National Guard.

The Alaska Air National Guard has a headquarters unit located in Anchorage, a composite group made up of a tactical airlift squadron, an air refueling squadron and several support squadrons and flights. There are units based at Kulis Air National Guard Base on the west side of Anchorage International Airport, at Eielson Air Force Base in Fairbanks, and in Kotzebue, Bethel and Juneau.

Authorized staffing is 4,565 military personnel; about 35 percent are full-time technicians. When mobilized, the Air National Guard becomes an integral part of Alaska Command's Air Force component, and the Army National Guard becomes a part of Alaska Command's Army component.

The major unit of the Alaska Army National Guard, with a muster of 2,300, is the 207th Infantry Group, consisting of five Scout Battalions and detachments in almost 100 communities across the state. In addition, it has an airborne element, an air traffic control detachment and an aviation detachment.

The Alaska Division of Emergency Services administers statewide disaster preparedness and response programs. The division is the primary contact for obtaining emergency assistance from state, federal, military and independent services. Its personnel also provide guidance and financial assistance to state and local agencies to help them prepare for and recover from disasters. The agency responds to threats or occurrences of disasters, and directs disaster response in unincorporated areas where local government does not have the resources to respond adequately.

National Historic Places

(*See also* Archaeology)

A "place" on the National Register of Historic Places is a district, site, building, structure or object significant to the state for its history, architecture, archaeology or culture. The national register also includes National Historic Landmarks. NHLs are properties given special status by the secretary of the interior for the significance to the nation, as well as to the state. The register is an official list of properties recognized by the federal government as worthy of preservation. Listing on the register begins with owner's consent and entails a nomination process with reviews by the State Historic Preservation officer, the Alaska Historic Sites Advisory Committee and the keeper of the National Register. Limitations are *not* placed on a listed property: The federal government does not attach restrictive covenants to the property or seek to acquire it.

Listing on the register means that a property is accorded national recognition for its significance in American history or prehistory. Additional benefits include tax credits on income-producing properties and automatic qualification for federal matching funds for preservation, maintenance and restoration work when such funds are available. Listed properties are also guaranteed a full review process for potential adverse effects by federally funded, licensed or otherwise assisted projects. Such a review usually takes place while the project is in the planning stage: Alternatives are sought to avoid, if at all possible, damaging or destroying the particular property in question.

Southcentral

A.E.C. Cottage No. 23, Anchorage

Alaska Central Railroad Tunnel No. 1, Seward

Alaska Nellie's Homestead, Lawing vicinity

Alex (Mike) Cabin, Eklutna

American Cemetery, Kodiak

Anchorage City Hall, Anchorage

Anderson (Oscar) House, Anchorage

Ascension of Our Lord Chapel, Karluk

Bailey Colony Farm, Palmer

Ballaine House, Seward

Beluga Point Archaeological Site, North Shore, Turnagain Arm

Bering Expedition Landing Site NHL, Kayak Island

Berry House, Palmer

Brown & Hawkins Store, Seward

Campus Center Site, Palmer

Cape St. Elias Lighthouse, Kayak Island

Chilkat Oil Company Refinery Site, Katalla

Chisana Historic District, Chisana

Chitina Tin Shop, Chitina

Chugachik Island Archaeological Site, Kachemak Bay

Coal Village Site, Kachemak Bay

Cooper Landing Historic District, Cooper Landing

Cooper Landing Post Office, Cooper Landing

Copper River and Northwestern Railway, Chitina vicinity

Cordova Post Office and Courthouse, Cordova

Crow Creek Mine, Girdwood

Cunningham-Hall PT-6 NC692W Aircraft, Palmer

Dakah De'nin's Village Site, Chitina

David (Leopold) House, Anchorage

Diversion Tunnel, Lowell Creek, Seward

Eklutna Power Plant, Eklutna

Federal Building-U.S. Courthouse (Old), Anchorage

Fourth Avenue Theatre, Anchorage

Gakona Roadhouse, Gakona

Government Cable Office, Seward

Herried House, Palmer

Hirshey Mine, Hope vicinity

Holm (Victor) Cabin, Cohoe

Holy Assumption Russian Orthodox Church NHL, Kenai

Holy Resurrection Church, Kodiak

Holy Transfiguration of Our Lord Chapel, Ninilchik

Hope Historic District, Hope vicinity

Hyland Hotel, Palmer

Independence Mine Historic District, Hatcher Pass

Indian Valley Mine, Girdwood vicinity

KENI Radio Building, Anchorage

Kennecott Mines NHL, McCarthy vicinity

Kimball's Store, Anchorage

Knik Site, Knik vicinity

KOD-171 Archaeological Site, Kodiak

KOD-207 Archaeological Site, Kodiak

KOD-233 Archaeological Site, Kodiak

Kodiak Naval Operating Base (Fort Abercrombie and Fort Greely) NHL, Kodiak Island

Lauritsen Cabin, Seward Highway

Matanuska Colony Community Center, Palmer

McCarthy General Store, McCarthy

McCarthy Power Plant, McCarthy

Middle Bay Brick Kiln, Kodiak

Moose River Site, Naptowne, Kenai area

Nabesna Gold Mine, Nabesna area

Nativity of Holy Theotokos Church, Afognak Island

Nativity of Our Lord Chapel, Ouzinkie

Old St. Nicholas Russian Orthodox Church, Eklutna

Palmer Depot, Palmer

Palugvik Archaeological District, Hawkins Island

Patten Colony Farm, Palmer

Pioneer School House, Anchorage

Potter Section House, Anchorage

Protection of the Theotokos Chapel, Akhiok

Puhl House, Palmer

Rebarcheck (Raymond) Colony Farm, Palmer area

Reception Building, Cordova

Red Dragon Historic District, Cordova

Russian-American Company Magazin (Erskine House) NHL, Kodiak

St. Michael the Archangel Church, Cordova

St. Nicholas Chapel, Seldovia

St. Peter's Episcopal Church, Seward

Sts. Sergius and Herman of Valaam Chapel, Ouzinkie

Sts. Sergius and Herman of Valaam Church, English Bay

Selenie Lagoon Archaeological Site, Port Graham vicinity

Seward Depot, Seward

Sourdough Lodge NHL, Gulkana area

Susitna River Bridge, Alaska Railroad, Talkeetna vicinity

Swetman House, Seward

Tangle Lakes Archaeological District, Paxson vicinity

Teeland's Store, Wasilla

Three Saints Bay Site NHL, Kodiak Island
United Protestant Church, Palmer
Van Gilder Hotel, Seward
Wasilla Community Hall, Wasilla
Wasilla Depot, Wasilla
Wasilla Elementary School, Wasilla
Wendler Building, Anchorage
Yukon Island, Main Site NHL, Yukon Island

Southeast

Alaska Native Brotherhood Hall NHL, Sitka
Alaska Steam Laundry, Juneau
Alaska Totems, Ketchikan
Alaskan Hotel, Juneau
American Flag Raising Site NHL, Sitka
Bergmann Hotel, Juneau
Building No. 29 NHL, Sitka
Burkhart-Dibrell House, Ketchikan
Cable House and Station, Sitka
Cape Spencer Lighthouse, Cape Spencer
Chief Shakes House, Wrangell
Chilkoot Trail and Dyea NHL, Skagway
Davis (J.M.) House, Juneau
Duncan (Father William) Cottage, Metlakatla
Eldred Rock Lighthouse, Lynn Canal
Emmons House, Sitka
Etolin Canoe, Etolin Island
First Lutheran Church, Ketchikan
Fort Durham NHL, Taku Harbor, Juneau vicinity
Fort William H. Seward NHL, Haines
Frances House, Juneau
Fries Miners Cabins, Ketchikan
Gilmore Building, Ketchikan
Government Indian School, Haines
Governor's Mansion, Juneau
Holy Trinity Church, Juneau
Ketchikan Ranger House, Ketchikan
Klondike Gold Rush National Historic Park, Skagway area
Mayflower School, Douglas
Mills (May) House, Sitka
Mills (W.P.) House, Sitka
New Russia Archaeological Site NHL, Yakutat
Old Sitka NHL, Sitka
Pleasant Camp, Haines Highway
Porcupine Historic District, Skagway vicinity
Russian Bishop's House NHL, Sitka

Governor's Mansion, Juneau

St. John the Baptist Church, Angoon
St. Michael the Archangel Cathedral NHL, Sitka
St. Nicholas Church (Russian Orthodox), Juneau
St. Peter's Church, Sitka
St. Philip's Episcopal Church, Wrangell
Saxman Totem Park, Ketchikan
See House, Sitka
Sheldon Jackson Museum, Sitka
Sitka National Historical Park, Sitka
Sitka Naval Operating Base NHL, Sitka
Sitka Pioneers' Home, Sitka
Skagway and White Pass Historic District NHL, Skagway vicinity
Sons of Norway Hall, Petersburg
Totem Bight, Ketchikan
Twin Glacier Camp, Juneau
U.S. Army Corps of Engineers, Storehouse No. 3, Portland Canal
U.S. Army Corps of Engineers, Storehouse No. 4, Hyder
U.S. Coast and Geodetic Survey House, Sitka
Valentine Building, Juneau
Walker–Broderick House, Ketchikan
Wickersham House, Juneau
Wrangell Public School, Wrangell
Ziegler House, Ketchikan

Western

Adak Army and Naval Operating Bases NHL, Adak
Anangula Site NHL, Aleutian Islands
Ananiuliak Island Archaeological District, Aleutian Islands
Anvil Creek Gold Discovery Site, Nome
Archaeological Site 49 Af 3, Katmai National Park and Preserve
Archaeological Site 49 MK 10, Katmai National Park and Preserve

Atka B-24 Liberator, Aleutian Islands

Attu Battlefield and U.S. Army and Navy Airfields NHL, Attu

Brooks River Archaeological District, Katmai National Park and Preserve

Cape Field at Fort Glenn NHL, Aleutian Islands

Cape Krusenstern Archaeological District NHL, Kotzebue vicinity

Cape Nome Mining District Discovery Sites NHL, Nome

Cape Nome Roadhouse, Nome vicinity

Carrighar (Sally) House, Nome

Chaluka Site NHL, Umnak Island

Christ Church Mission, Anvik

Discovery Saloon, Nome

Dutch Harbor Operating Base and Fort Mears NHL, Aleutian Islands

Elevation of the Holy Cross Church, Naknek

Fairhaven Ditch, Imruk Lake

First Mission House, Bethel

Fort St. Michael Site, Unalakleet vicinity

Fure's Cabin, Katmai National Park and Preserve

Gambell Sites, Gambell

Holy Ascension Orthodox Church NHL, Unalaska

Holy Resurrection Church, Belkofski

Iyatayet Archaeological Site NHL, Norton Sound

Japanese Occupation Site, Kiska NHL, Aleutian Islands

Kaguyak Village Site, Katmai

Arctic Brotherhood Hall, Skagway Historic District

National Park and Preserve

Kijik Historic District, Lake Clark National Park and Preserve

Kolmakov Redoubt Site, Kuskokwim River, Aniak vicinity

Kukak Village, Katmai National Park and Preserve

Norge Storage Site, Teller

Old Savonoski Site, Katmai National Park and Preserve

Onion Portage Archaeological District NHL, Noatak vicinity

Pilgrim 100B N709Y Aircraft, Dillingham

Pilgrim Hot Springs, Seward Peninsula

Port Moller Hot Springs Village Site, Alaska Peninsula

Presentation of Our Lord Chapel, Nikolai

Redoubt St. Michael Site, Unalakleet vicinity

St. George the Great Martyr Orthodox Church, St. George Island

St. Jacob's Church, Napaskiak

St. John the Baptist Chapel, Naknek

St. John the Theologian Church, Perryville

St. Nicholas Chapel, Ekuk

St. Nicholas Chapel, Igiugig

St. Nicholas Chapel, Nondalton

St. Nicholas Chapel, Pedro Bay

St. Nicholas Chapel, Sand Point

St. Nicholas Church, Kwethluk (ROC)

St. Nicholas Church, Nikolski

St. Nicholas Church, Pilot Point

St. Seraphim Chapel, Lower Kalskag

St. Sergius Chapel, Chuathbaluk

Sts. Constantine and Helen Chapel, Lime Village

Sts. Peter and Paul Russian Orthodox Church, St. Paul Island

Savonoski River District, Katmai National Park and Preserve

Seal Islands Historic District NHL, Pribilof Islands

Sir Alexander Nevsky Chapel, Akutan

Sitka Spruce Plantation NHL, Amaknak Island

Snow Creek Placer Claim No. 1, Nome vicinity

Solomon Roadhouse, Solomon

Takli Island Archaeological District, Katmai National Park and Preserve

TEMNAC P-38G Lightning Aircraft, Aleutian Islands

Transfiguration of Our Lord Chapel, Nushagak

Wales Archaeological District NHL, Wales vicinity

Interior

Biederman (Ed) Fish Camp, Eagle area

Big Delta State Historic District, Delta Junction

Campus Center Site, Fairbanks

Central Roadhouse, Central

Chatanika Gold Camp, Chatanika

Chena Pump House, Fairbanks

Chugwater Archaeological Site, Fairbanks

Clay Street Cemetery, Fairbanks

Creamer's Dairy, Fairbanks

Davis (Mary Lee) House, Fairbanks

Dry Creek Archaeological Site NHL, Healy vicinity

Eagle Historic District NHL, Eagle

Ester Camp Historic District, Fairbanks

Ewe Creek Ranger Cabin No. 8, Denali National Park

Fairview Inn, Talkeetna

Federal Building, U.S. Post Office, Courthouse (Old), Fairbanks

Goldstream Dredge No. 8, Mile 9, Old Steese Hwy.

Harding Railroad Car, Alaskaland, Fairbanks

Igloo Creek Cabin No. 25, Denali National Park

Immaculate Conception Church, Fairbanks

Joslin (Falcon) House, Fairbanks

The Kink, Fortymile River

Lacey Street Theatre, Fairbanks

Ladd Field NHL (Fort Wainwright), Fairbanks

Lower East Fork Ranger Cabin No. 9, Denali National Park

Lower Toklat River Ranger Cabin No. 18, Denali National Park

Lower Windy Creek Ranger Cabin No. 15, Denali National Park

Main School, Fairbanks

Masonic Temple, Fairbanks

McGregor (George) Cabin, Eagle vicinity

Mission Church, Arctic Village

Mission House (Old), Fort Yukon

Moose Creek Ranger Cabin No. 19, Denali National Park

Mount McKinley National Park Headquarters, Denali National Park

St. Michael the Archangel Cathedral NHL, Sitka

Nenana Depot, Nenana

Oddfellows Hall (First Avenue Bathhouse), Fairbanks

Rainey's Cabin, Fairbanks

Riley Creek Ranger Cabin No. 20, Denali National Park

Ruby Roadhouse, Ruby

Sanctuary River Cabin No. 31, Denali National Park

Slaven, (Frank), Roadhouse, Eagle vicinity

Steele Creek Roadhouse, Fortymile

Sternwheeler Nenana NHL, Fairbanks

Sullivan Roadhouse, Fort Greely

Sushana River Ranger Cabin No. 17, Denali National Park

Tanana Mission, Tanana

Taylor (James) Cabins, Eagle vicinity

Teklanika Archaeological District, Denali National Park and Preserve

Thomas (George C.) Memorial Library NHL, Fairbanks

Tolovana Roadhouse, Tanana vicinity

Toklat Ranger Station (Pearson Cabin) No. 4, Denali National Park

Upper East Fork Cabin No. 29, Denali National Park

Upper Savage River Cabin, Denali National Park

Upper Toklat River Ranger Cabin No. 24, Denali National Park

Upper Windy Creek Ranger Cabin No. 7, Denali National Park

Wickersham House, Fairbanks

Woodchopper Roadhouse, Eagle vicinity

Yukon River Lifeways District, Eagle vicinity

Far North

Aluakpak Site, Wainwright vicinity

Anaktuuk Site, Wainwright vicinity

Atanik District, Wainwright vicinity

Avalitkuk Site, Wainwright vicinity

Birnirk Site NHL, Barrow

Gallagher Flint Station Archaeological Site NHL, Sagwon

Ipiutak Archaeological District, Point Hope

Ipiutak Site NHL, Point Hope

Ivishaat Site, Wainwright vicinity

Kanitch, Wainwright vicinity

Leffingwell Camp NHL, Flaxman Island

Napanik Site, Wainwright vicinity

Negilik Site, Barrow

Point Barrow Refuge, Cape Smythe Whaling and Trading Station, Barrow vicinity

Utkeagvik Presbyterian Church Manse, Barrow

Uyagaagruk, Wainwright vicinity

Will Rogers-Wiley Post Site, Barrow vicinity

National Parks, Preserves and Monuments

The National Park Service administers approximately 54 million acres of land in Alaska, consisting of 15 units classified as national parks, national preserves and national monuments. The Alaska National Interest Lands Conservation Act of 1980—also referred to as ANILCA (*see* Land Use)—created 10 new National Park Service units in Alaska and changed the size and status of the three existing Park Service units: Mount McKinley National Park, now Denali National Park and Preserve; Glacier Bay National Monument, now a national park and preserve; and Katmai National Monument, now a national park

and preserve. (*See* map, pages 120–21)

In 1992, Alaska's national parks, preserves and monuments experienced a slight increase of visitors over the 1,216,000 numbers in 1991. Klondike Gold Rush National Historic Park showed the biggest gain in visitations in 1992, reaching 148,019 visitors, an increase of 34 percent from 1991. Denali is still the most popular destination, with Glacier Bay the second-most visited park. Visitors from cruise ships helped boost the number of visitors to the Sitka National Historical Park to a record 142,467.

National parks are traditionally managed to preserve scenic, wildlife and recreational values; mining, cutting of house logs, hunting and other resource exploitation are carefully regulated within park monument and preserve boundaries, and motorized access is restricted to automobile traffic on authorized roads. However, regulations for National Park Service units in Alaska recognize that these units contain lands traditionally occupied and used by Alaska Natives and rural residents for subsistence activities. Therefore, management of *some* parks, preserves and monuments in Alaska provides for subsistence hunting, fishing and gathering activities, and the use of such motorized vehicles as snow machines, motorboats and airplanes where such activities are customary. National preserves do permit sport hunting.

Following is a list of National Park Service parks, preserves and monuments. The U.S. Forest Service manages another two national monuments: Admiralty Island National Monument, 937,000 acres; and Misty Fiords National Monument, 2.1 million acres. Both are in Southeast and part of the National Wilderness Preservation System. (*See also* National Wild and Scenic Rivers *and* National Wilderness Areas)

Information on the parks, preserves and monuments is available at the Alaska Public Lands Information Centers: 605 W. Fourth Ave., Suite 105, Anchorage 99501; 250 Cushman St., Suite 1A, Fairbanks 99701; and P.O. Box 359, Tok 99780.

National Park Service units are

followed by address, acreage and major features or recreations:

Aniakchak National Monument and Preserve, Superintendent, Katmai National Park and Preserve, P.O. Box 7, King Salmon 99613 (603,000 acres). Aniakchak dry caldera.

Bering Land Bridge National Preserve, National Park Service, P.O. Box 220, Nome 99762 (2,785,000 acres). Lava fields, archaeological sites, migratory waterfowl.

Cape Krusenstern National Monument, National Park Service, P.O. Box 1029, Kotzebue 99752 (660,000 acres). Archaeological sites.

Denali National Park and Preserve, National Park Service, P.O. Box 9, Denali Park 99755 (6,028,000 acres). Mount McKinley, abundant wildlife.

Gates of the Arctic National Park and Preserve, National Park Service, P.O. Box 74680, Fairbanks 99707 (8,472,000 acres). Brooks Range, wild and scenic rivers, wildlife.

Glacier Bay National Park and Preserve, National Park Service, P.O. Box 140, Gustavus 99826 (3,283,000 acres). Glaciers, marine wildlife.

Katmai National Park and Preserve, National Park Service, P.O. Box 7, King Salmon 99613 (4,090,000 acres). Valley of Ten Thousand Smokes, brown bears.

Kenai Fjords National Park, National Park Service, P.O. Box 1727, Seward 99664 (580,000 acres). Fjords, Harding Icefield, Exit Glacier.

Klondike Gold Rush National Historical Park, National Park Service, P.O. Box 517, Skagway 99840 (2,721 acres). Chilkoot Trail.

Kobuk Valley National Park, National Park Service, P.O. Box 1029, Kotzebue 99752 (1,750,000 acres). Archaeological sites, Great Kobuk Sand Dunes, river rafting.

Lake Clark National Park and Preserve, National Park Service, 4230 University Drive, Suite 311, Anchorage 99508 (4,044,000 acres). Backcountry recreation, fishing, scenery.

Noatak National Preserve, National Park Service, P.O. Box 1029, Kotzebue 99752 (6,574,000 acres). Abundant wildlife, river floating.

Sitka National Historical Park, National Park Service, P.O. Box 738, Sitka 99752 (106 acres). Russian Bishop's House, trails.

Wrangell–St. Elias National Park and Preserve, National Park Service, P.O. Box 29, Glennallen 99588 (13,188,000 acres). Rugged peaks, glaciers, expansive wilderness.

Yukon–Charley Rivers National Preserve, National Park Service, P.O. Box 164, Eagle 99738 (2,523,000 acres). Backcountry recreation, river floating.

National Petroleum Reserve

(*See also* Oil and Gas)

In 1923, President Warren G. Harding signed an executive order creating Naval Petroleum Reserve Number 4 (NPR-4), the last of four petroleum reserves to be placed under control of the U.S. Navy. The secretary of the Navy was charged to "explore, protect, conserve, develop, use, and operate the Naval Petroleum Reserves," including NPR-4, on Alaska's North Slope. (*See* map, pages 120–21)

The U.S. Geological Survey (USGS) had begun surface exploration in the area in 1901; following creation of the 23-million-acre reserve, exploration programs were conducted by the Navy. From 1944 to 1953, extensive geological and geophysical surveys were conducted and 36 test wells were drilled. Nine oil and gas fields were discovered; the largest oil field, near Umiat, contains an estimated 70 million to 120 million barrels of recoverable oil. Active exploration was suspended in 1953.

In 1974, the Arab oil embargo, coupled with the knowledge of large petroleum reserves at nearby Prudhoe Bay, brought about renewed interest in NPR-4, and Congress directed the Navy to resume its exploration program.

In 1976, all lands within NPR-4 were redesignated the National Petroleum Reserve Alaska (NPR-A) and jurisdiction was transferred to the secretary of the interior. In 1980, Congress (Continued on page 122)

NATIONAL INTEREST LANDS

(Numbers refer to accompanying map)

NATIONAL WILDLIFE REFUGE SYSTEM
1 Alaska Maritime NWR*
  Chuckchi Sea Unit
  Bering Sea Unit
  Aleutian Islands Unit
  Alaska Peninsula Unit
  Gulf of Alaska Unit
2 Alaska Peninsula
3 Arctic
4 Becharof
5 Innoko
6 Izembek
7 Kanuti
8 Kenai
9 Kodiak
10 Koyukuk
11 Nowitna
12 Selawik
13 Tetlin
14 Togiak
15 Yukon Delta
16 Yukon Flats

NATIONAL PARK SYSTEM
17 Aniakchak Natl. Monument and Preserve
18 Bering Land Bridge Nat'l. Preserve
19 Cape Krusenstern Nat'l. Monument
20 Denali Nat'l. Park and Preserve
21 Gates of the Arctic Nat'l. Park and Preserve
22 Glacier Bay Nat'l. Park and Preserve
23 Katmai Nat'l. Park and Preserve
24 Kenai Fjords Nat'l. Park
25 Kobuk Valley Nat'l. Park
26 Lake Clark Nat'l. Park and Preserve
27 Noatak Nat'l. Preserve
28 Wrangell–St. Elias Nat'l. Park and Preserve
29 Yukon–Charley Rivers Nat'l. Preserve
30 Klondike Gold Rush Nat'l. Historical Park
31 Sitka Nat'l. Historical Park

BUREAU OF LAND MANAGEMENT SYSTEM
32 Steese Nat'l. Conservation Areas
33 White Mountains Nat'l. Recreation Area

NATIONAL FOREST SYSTEM
34 Chugach Nat'l. Forest
35 Tongass Nat'l. Forest
36 Admiralty Island Nat'l. Monument**
37 Misty Fiords Nat'l. Monument**

NATIONAL WILD AND SCENIC RIVERS SYSTEM
There are 26 rivers designated wild and
scenic by the 1980 Alaska National
Interest Lands Conservation Act.

*The Alaska Maritime National Wildlife Refuge
consists of all the public lands in the coastal
waters and adjacent seas of Alaska, including
islands, islets, rocks, reefs, capes and spires.
**Admiralty Island and Misty Fiords national
monuments are part of the Tongass National
Forest, which includes 17 other wilderness areas.

Chukchi Sea

Bering Sea

Aleutian Islands

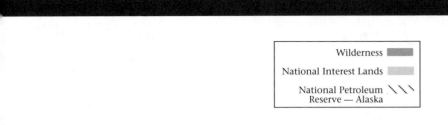

Wilderness

National Interest Lands

National Petroleum
Reserve — Alaska

Gulf of Alaska

Alaska Peninsula

(Continued from page 119)

authorized the secretary of the interior to prescribe an expeditious program of competitive leasing of oil and gas tracts in the reserve, clearing the way for private development of the area's resources.

By mid-1983, three competitive bid lease sales, involving a total of 7.2 million acres of NPR-A, had been held. Dates of the sales and the number of acres involved were: January 1982, 1.5 million acres; May 1982, 3.5 million acres; and July 1983, 2.2 million acres. As oil prices have dropped, interest from the oil companies has lessened and leases have expired. As of mid-1993, there were only two leases covering 19,388 acres.

The Interior Department, through USGS, continued exploration of NPR-A into the 1980s. Past naval explorations and those conducted by USGS resulted in the discovery of oil at Umiat and Cape Simpson, and several gas fields, including Walakpa, Gubic and Point Barrow. The North Slope Borough is developing the reserves in the Walakpa field to provide gas for heating and electrical generation for Barrow. The Borough plans to drill up to eight wells to produce the gas. Data gathered indicates NPR-A may contain recoverable reserves of 1.85 billion barrels of crude oil and 3.74 trillion cubic feet of natural gas.

National Wild and Scenic Rivers

(See also Rivers)

The Alaska National Interest Lands Conservation Act (ANILCA) of Dec. 2, 1980, gave wild and scenic river classification to 13 streams within the National Park System, six in the National Wildlife Refuge System and two in Bureau of Land Management Conservation and Recreation areas. *(See* map, pages 120–21) An additional five rivers are located outside designated preservation units. Twelve more rivers were designated for further study and possible wild and scenic classification.

The criteria for wild and scenic river classification cover more than just float trip possibilities. Scenic features, wilderness characteristics and recreational opportunities that would be impaired by alteration, development or impoundment are also considered.

Rivers are classified into three categories under the Wild and Scenic Rivers Act. The wild classification is most restrictive of development or incompatible uses—it stresses the wilderness aspect of the rivers. The scenic classification permits some intrusions upon the natural landscape, and the recreational classification is the least restrictive category. A specified amount of land back from the river's banks is also put in protected status to ensure access, use and the preservation of aesthetic values for the public.

For those desiring to float these rivers, special consideration must be given to put-in and take-out points because most of the designated wild and scenic rivers are not accessible by road. This means that voyagers and their crafts have to be flown in and picked up by charter bush planes. Because Federal Aviation Administration regulations prohibit the lashing of canoes and kayaks to pontoons of floatplanes when carrying passengers, inflatable rafts and folding canvas or rubber kayaks are often more convenient and less expensive to transport.

Further information on rivers and river running can be obtained from the Alaska Public Lands Information Centers: 605 W. Fourth Ave., Suite 105, Anchorage 99501; 250 Cushman St., Suite 1A, Fairbanks 99701; and P.O. Box 359, Tok 99780; the U.S. Fish and Wildlife Service, 1011 E. Tudor Road, Anchorage 99503; and the Bureau of Land Management, 222 W. Seventh Ave., No. 13, Anchorage 99513. Information for rivers within park units or managed by the National Park Service is also available from the particular park headquarters. *(See also* National Parks, Preserves and Monuments)

Rivers Within National Park Areas

Alagnak—Katmai National Preserve

Alatna—Gates of the Arctic National Park

Aniakchak—Aniakchak National Monument; Aniakchak National Preserve

Charley—Yukon–Charley Rivers National Preserve

Chilikadrotna—Lake Clark National Park and Preserve

John—Gates of the Arctic National Park and Preserve

Kobuk—Gates of the Arctic National Park and Preserve

Mulchatna—Lake Clark National Park and Preserve

Noatak—Gates of the Arctic National Park and Noatak National Preserve

North Fork Koyukuk—Gates of the Arctic National Park and Preserve

Salmon—Kobuk Valley National Park

Tinayguk—Gates of the Arctic National Park and Preserve

Tlikakila—Lake Clark National Park and Preserve

Rivers Within National Wildlife Refuges

Andreafsky—Yukon Delta National Wildlife Refuge

Ivishak—Arctic National Wildlife Refuge

Nowitna—Nowitna National Wildlife Refuge

Selawik—Selawik National Wildlife Refuge

Sheenjek—Arctic National Wildlife Refuge

Wind—Arctic National Wildlife Refuge

(General information on rivers not listed in refuge brochures may be obtained from respective refuge offices by addressing queries to refuge managers. Addresses for refuges are given in the brochures.)

Rivers Within Bureau of Land Management Units

Beaver Creek—The segment of the main stem from confluence of Bear and Champion creeks within White Mountains National Recreation Area to the Yukon Flats National Wildlife Refuge boundary.

Birch Creek—The segment of the main stem from the south side of Steese Highway downstream to the bridge at Milepost 147.

Rivers Outside of Designated Preservation Units

Alagnak—Those segments or portions of the main stem and Nonvianuk tributary lying outside and westward of Katmai National Park and Preserve.

Delta River—The segment from and including all of the Tangle Lakes to a point one-half mile north of Black Rapids.

Fortymile River—The main stem within Alaska, plus tributaries.

Gulkana River—The main stem from the outlet of Paxson Lake to the confluence with Sourdough Creek; various segments of the west fork and middle fork.

Unalakleet River—Approximately 80 miles of the main stem.

Rivers Designated for Study for Inclusion in Wild and Scenic Rivers System

Colville River
Etivluk–Nigu Rivers
Kanektok River
Kisaralik River
Koyuk River
Melozitna River
Porcupine River
Sheenjek River (lower segment)
Situk River
Squirrel River
Utukok River
Yukon River (Rampart section)

Related reading: *The Alaska River Guide: Canoeing, Kayaking, and Rafting in the Last Frontier,* by Karen Jettmar. Experienced wilderness guide provides vital information and more than 90 trip options for traveling Alaska's rivers. *See* ALASKA NORTHWEST LIBRARY in the back of the book.

National Wilderness Areas

Passage of the Alaska National Interest Lands Conservation Act (ANILCA) on Dec. 2, 1980, added millions of acres to the National Wilderness Preservation System. Administration of these wilderness areas is the responsibility of the agency under whose jurisdiction the land is situated. Agencies that administer wilderness areas in Alaska include the National Park Service, U.S. Fish and Wildlife Service and the U.S. Forest Service. Although the Bureau of Land Management has authority to manage wilderness in the public domain, no BLM wilderness areas exist in Alaska. (*See* map, pages 120–21)

In addition, passage of the Tongass Timber Reform Act (TTRA) on Nov. 28, 1990, designated an additional 299,721 acres of the Tongass National Forest as wilderness.

Wilderness allocations to different agencies in Alaska are: U.S. Forest Service, approximately 5,753,211 acres; National Park Service, approximately 32,848,564 acres; and U.S. Fish and Wildlife Service, approximately 18,676,320 acres.

Wilderness, according to the federal Wilderness Act of 1964, is land sufficient in size to enable the operation of natural systems without undue influence from activities in surrounding areas and should be places in which people are visitors who do not remain. Alaska wilderness regulations follow the stipulations of the Wilderness Act as amended by the Alaska lands act. Specifically designed to allow for Alaska conditions, the rules are considerably more lenient about transportation access, human-made structures and use of mechanized vehicles. The primary objective of a wilderness area continues to be the maintenance of the wilderness character of the land.

In Alaska wilderness areas, the following uses and activities are permitted:

• Fishing, hunting and trapping will continue on lands within the national forests, national wildlife refuges and national park preserves. National park wilderness does not allow sport hunting, or sport or commercial trapping.

• Subsistence uses, including hunting, fishing, trapping, berry gathering and use of timber for cabins and firewood, may be allowed but are not permitted in all wilderness areas. Contact the particular land manager for the most up-to-date rules on subsistence activity.

• Public recreation or safety cabins in wilderness areas in national forests, national wildlife refuges and national park preserves will continue to be maintained and may be replaced. A limited number of new public-use cabins may be added if needed.

• Existing special-use permits on all national forest wilderness lands for cabins, homesites or similar structures may continue. Use of temporary campsites, shelters and other temporary facilities and equipment related to hunting and fishing on national forest lands will continue.

• Fish habitat enhancement programs, including construction of buildings, fish weirs, fishways, spawning channels and other accepted means of maintaining, enhancing and rehabilitating fish stocks, may be allowed in national forest wilderness areas.

• Special-use permits for guides and outfitters operating within wilderness areas in the national forests and national wildlife refuges will continue.

• Private, state and Native lands surrounded by wilderness areas will be guaranteed access through the wilderness area.

• Use of fixed-wing airplanes, motorboats, snow machines, and nonmotorized methods of surface transportation for *traditional* activities and for access to villages and homesites will be allowed to continue.

National Wildlife Refuges

There are approximately 77 million acres of National Wildlife Refuge lands in Alaska administered by the U.S. Fish and Wildlife Service. (National wildlife refuge acreage in Alaska increased nearly fourfold with the signing of the Alaska National Interest Lands Conservation Act, ANILCA, in December 1980.) Wildlife refuges are designed to protect the habitats of representative populations of birds, fish and mammals. The 16 refuges vary widely in size. (*See* map, pages 120–21)

Public use is limited as only two of the refuges—Kenai and Tetlin—are accessible by road. Among the public recreational uses permitted within national wildlife refuges are sightseeing, nature observation and photography, sport hunting and fishing (under state law), boating, camping, hiking and picnicking. Trapping can be carried out under applicable state and federal laws. Commercial fishing and related facilities (campsites, cabins, etc.) are authorized by special-use permits.

Subsistence activities within national wildlife refuges are all protected under the lands bill. Use of snowmobiles, motorboats and other means of surface transportation traditionally relied upon by local rural residents for subsistence is generally permitted. Fixed-wing aircraft access to wildlife refuges is usually allowed, though certain areas within the Kenai National Wildlife Refuge have been closed to aircraft (a map is available from the refuge manager). A special-use permit is required for all helicopter access.

National Wildlife Refuge administrative addresses are followed by acreage and resident wildlife:

Alaska Maritime National Wildlife Refuge, 2355 Kachemak Drive, Homer 99603 (3,557,030 acres). Seabirds, sea lions, sea otters, harbor seals, walrus.

Alaska Peninsula National Wildlife Refuge, P.O. Box 277, King Salmon 99613 (3,500,000 acres). Brown bears, caribou, moose, sea otters, bald eagles, peregrine falcons, wolves, wolverines, migrating whales.

Arctic National Wildlife Refuge, 101 12th Ave., Box 20, Fairbanks 99701 (19,049,236 acres). Caribou, polar bears, grizzly bears, wolves, Dall sheep, peregrine falcons, musk-oxen.

Becharof National Wildlife Refuge, P.O. Box 277, King Salmon 99613 (1,200,000 acres). Brown bears, bald eagles, caribou, moose, salmon.

Innoko National Wildlife Refuge, P.O. Box 69, McGrath 99627 (3,850,000 acres). Migratory waterfowl, beaver, lynx, marten, moose.

Izembek National Wildlife Refuge, P.O. Box 127, Cold Bay 99571 (321,000 acres). Black brant (coastal geese), brown bears.

Kanuti National Wildlife Refuge, 101 12th Ave., Box 11, Fairbanks 99701 (1,430,000 acres). Waterfowl.

Kenai National Wildlife Refuge, Box 2139, Soldotna 99669 (1,970,000 acres). Moose, salmon, mountain goats, Dall sheep, bears, lynx, wolves.

Kodiak National Wildlife Refuge, 1390 Buskin River Road, Kodiak 99615 (1,865,000 acres). Brown bears, black-tailed deer, bald eagles, river otter.

Koyukuk National Wildlife Refuge, P.O. Box 287, Galena 99741 (3,550,000 acres). Wolves, caribou, bear, moose, waterfowl.

Nowitna National Wildlife Refuge, P.O. Box 287, Galena 99741 (1,560,000 acres). Migratory waterfowl, caribou, moose, bears, furbearers.

Selawik National Wildlife Refuge, P.O. Box 270, Kotzebue 99752 (2,150,000 acres). Caribou, migratory birds.

Tetlin National Wildlife Refuge, P.O. Box 779, Tok 99780 (700,000 acres). Migratory waterfowl, Dall sheep, moose, bear, ptarmigan.

Togiak National Wildlife Refuge, P.O. Box 270, Dillingham 99576 (4,105,000 acres). Nearly every major wildlife species of Alaska is represented.

Yukon Delta National Wildlife Refuge, P.O. Box 346, Bethel 99559 (19,624,458 acres). Migratory birds, musk-oxen and reindeer are found on Nunivak Island.

Yukon Flats National Wildlife Refuge, 101 12th Ave., Box 14, Fairbanks 99701 (8,630,000 acres). Waterfowl, moose, caribou, bear.

Native Arts and Crafts

(*See also* Baleen; Baskets; Beadwork; Masks; Potlatch; Skin Sewing; *and* Totems)

The traditional arts and crafts of Alaska's Natives were produced for ceremonial and utilitarian reasons. This work was not thought of as art in the Western sense but as objects and designs to fulfill specific functions. Native art also reflected spiritual values and the physical environment each group inhabited. Alaska's Natives are known for their ingenious use and manipulation of natural materials to supply life's needs. Roots, bark, grasses, wood, fur, skins, feathers and the sea's resources are still used to produce containers, clothing, hunting implements, ceremonial regalia and many other items.

Today, most Native utilitarian objects are modern adaptations using plastic, metal and glass. But many traditional Native designs and materials are still used to create ceremonial objects, and Alaska Native arts and crafts are widely sought by collectors, museums and tourists. This new market for their work has proven beneficial to Native artists and therefore to Native culture as a whole, which is experiencing the transition from a subsistence lifestyle to a contemporary Western economy.

The Inupiat and Yup'ik Eskimo people, like all of the Alaska Native groups, are divided geographically and linguistically. Because their coastal environment offers few forest resources, the Eskimo people have learned to rely on the tundra and the sea for cultural materials. The Inupiat of northern Alaska are known for making objects out of sea mammal parts—especially ivory, baleen and whale bone. Their ivory carving and scrimshaw work is world renowned, and more contemporary work in which stiff baleen is coiled into elegant baskets is also gaining recognition.

The Yup'ik of western Alaska also utilize sea mammal materials in their art. In addition, they rely heavily on the coastal rye grass for their intricate coiled baskets and mat work. Yup'ik ceremonial masks, which are carved primarily of wood, assembled and painted, are distinctive in the global tribal mask-making tradition. Both the Inupiat and Yup'ik groups produce warm, beautiful clothing using the furs and skins of indigenous land and sea mammals.

The Aleut people of the Aleutian Islands also make beautiful baskets from rye grass, but they use a twining technique. The Aleut are known for their traditional capes made of sea mammal gut and their bentwood hats and visors.

The Athabascan Indians of Alaska's Interior live in a region abundant with forest and river resources. They make decorative beaded clothing and other items, often on tanned, smoked moose-hide, and they form the bark of the birch tree into lightweight canoes, baby cradles and a variety of containers. They are also known for their skill sewing skins into clothing.

The Tlingit, Haida and Tsimshian people of southeastern Alaska are part of the Pacific Northwest Coast Indian culture, which extends down the coast of British Columbia and into Washington state. Each person in this culture is given at birth his or her own totemic crest—an animal form representing the family clan. These crests are reproduced in many art forms such as elaborate ceremonial regalia; carvings in wood, metal or stone; paintings or prints; and jewelry. The carvers of the Northwest Coast, best known for boldly carved monumental totem poles, record legendary happenings and honor important people or events. Their artwork, which adheres to a complex, formal design system, is highly stylized and dramatic. Fine Northwest Coast pieces such as carved and painted wood masks and bentwood boxes are sought worldwide by collectors and museums.

Native People

Alaska's 85,698 Native people make up about 15.6 percent of the state's total population. Of those, the majority are Eskimo, Indian and Aleut. Although many live in widely scattered villages along the coastline and great rivers of Alaska, 14,569 Native persons lived in Anchorage in 1990, and Fairbanks had a Native population of nearly 5,330 that year.

At the time Europeans came in contact with the Natives of Alaska in 1741, the Indian, Eskimo and Aleut people lived within well-defined regions, with little mixing of ethnic groups. All were hunting and gathering people who did not practice agriculture.

In southeastern Alaska, the salmon, deer and other plentiful foods permitted the Tsimshian, Haida and Tlingit Indians to settle in permanent villages and develop a culture rich in art. The Athabascan Indians migrated from one seasonal subsistence camp to another to take advantage of seasonal abundance of fish, waterfowl and other game. The Aleut and coastal Eskimo subsisted primarily on the rich resources of the rivers and the sea.

The Tsimshians moved in 1887 from their former home in British Columbia to Annette Island in Southeast Alaska, under Anglican minister Father William Duncan. About 1,200 now live in Metlakatla. They are primarily fishermen, as are most southeastern people.

Approximately 1,000 Haida live in Alaska, about 300 of whom live in Hydaburg on the south end of Prince of Wales Island. They migrated to the coast from Canada in the 1700s. The Haida excel in the art of totem carving and are noted for precise and delicate working of wood, bone, shell, stone and silver.

Today, about 10,000 Tlingit live throughout southeastern Alaska; approximately another 1,000 live in other parts of the state, primarily in the Anchorage area. The Tlingit, who migrated west from what is now Canada before the first European contact, commercially dominated the interior Canadian Indians, trading eulachon oil, copper pieces and Chilkat blankets for various furs. Like the Haida, they are part of the totem culture; totems provide a historic record of major events in the life of a family or clan.

Athabascan Indians, who occupied the vast area of interior Alaska, were nomadic people whose principal source of food was land animals. Hard times and famines were frequent for all Athabascans, except the Tanaina and Ahtna groups, who lived along the Gulf of Alaska and could rely on salmon as their basic food.

The Eskimo have traditionally lived in villages along the harsh Bering Sea and Arctic Ocean coastlines, and along a thin strip of the Gulf of Alaska coast, including Kodiak Island. They took salmon, waterfowl, berries, ptarmigan and a few caribou, but it was the sea and its whales, walruses and seals that provided the foundation for their existence. Houses were igloos—dwellings built partially underground and covered with sod. They did not live in snow igloos.

The Aleut have traditionally lived on the Alaska Peninsula and along the Aleutian Chain. When the Russians reached the Aleutians in the 1740s, practically every island was inhabited. Decimated by contact with the white man, there are only a few Aleut settlements, including two on the Pribilof Islands, where Natives work handling seal herds for the government.

The Aleut lived in permanent villages, taking advantage of sea life and land mammals for food. Their original dwellings were large, communal structures, housing as many as 40 families. After Russian occupation they lived in much smaller houses, called barabaras. Today many Aleuts are commercial fishermen.

Rapid advances in communications, transportation and other services to remote villages have altered Native life in Alaska. Economic changes, from a subsistence to a cash economy, culminated in the passage of the Alaska Native Claims Settlement Act. It gave Alaska Natives $962.5 million and 44 million acres of land as compensation for the loss of lands historically occupied by their people.

NATIVE REGIONAL CORPORATIONS

Twelve regional business corporations were formed under the 1971

NATIVE REGIONAL CORPORATIONS

Alaska Native Claims Settlement Act to manage money and land received from the government. (*See* map above.) A 13th corporation was organized for those Natives residing outside Alaska. Following is a list of corporations and the area or region each administers:

Ahtna Incorporated (Copper River Basin), Drawer G, Copper Center 99573 or 2701 Fairbanks St., Anchorage 99503

Aleut Corporation (Aleutian Islands), 1 Aleut Plaza, 4000 Old Seward Highway, Suite 300, Anchorage 99503

Arctic Slope Regional Corporation (Arctic Alaska), P.O. Box 129, Barrow 99723, or 313 E St., Suite 5, Anchorage 99501

Bering Straits Native Corporation (Seward Peninsula), P.O. Box 1008, Nome 99762

Bristol Bay Native Corporation (Bristol Bay area), P.O. Box 198, Dillingham 99576 or P.O. Box 100220, Anchorage 99510

Calista Corporation (Yukon–Kuskokwim Delta), P.O. Box 408, Bethel 99559 or 516 Denali St., Anchorage 99501

Chugach Alaska Corporation (Prince William Sound), 3000 A St., Suite 400, Anchorage 99503

Cook Inlet Region, Incorporated (Cook Inlet region), 2525 C St., Anchorage 99503

Doyon, Limited (interior Alaska), 201 First Ave., Suite 200, Fairbanks 99701

Koniag, Incorporated (Kodiak area), 4300 B St., Anchorage 99503

NANA Regional Corporation (Kobuk region), P.O. Box 49, Kotzebue 99752 or 4706 Harding Drive, Anchorage 99503

Sealaska Corporation (southeastern Alaska), One Sealaska Plaza, Juneau 99801

Thirteenth Regional Corporation (outside Alaska), 13256 Northup Way, Suite 12, Bellevue, WA 98005

Regional Nonprofit Corporations

Aleutian–Pribilof Islands Association, Incorporated (Aleut Corporation), 1689 C St., Anchorage 99501

Association of Village Council Presidents (Calista Corporation), P.O. Box 219, Bethel 99559

Bristol Bay Native Association (Bristol Bay Native Corporation), P.O. Box 237, Dillingham 99756

Central Council of Tlingit–Haida Indian Tribes (Sealaska Corporation), One Sealaska Plaza, Suite 200, Juneau 99801

Cook Inlet Native Association (Cook Inlet Region, Incorporated), 670 W. Fireweed Lane, Anchorage 99503

Copper River Native Association (Ahtna Incorporated), Drawer H, Copper Center 99573

Inupiat Community of the Arctic Slope (Arctic Slope Regional Corporation), P.O. Box 437, Barrow 99723

Kawerak, Incorporated (Bering Straits Native Corporation), P.O. Box 948, Nome 99762

Kodiak Area Native Association (Koniag, Incorporated), P.O. Box 172, Kodiak 99615

Maniilaq (formerly Mauneluk) Association (NANA Regional Corporation), P.O. Box 256, Kotzebue 99752

North Pacific Rim Native Association (Chugach Alaska Corporation), 3000 A St., Suite 400, Anchorage 99503

Tanana Chiefs Conference (Doyon, Limited), 201 First Ave., Fairbanks 99701

Other Native Organizations

Alaska Eskimo Whaling Commission, P.O. Box 570, Barrow 99723

Alaska Federation of Natives, 411 W. Fourth Ave., Suite 1-A, Anchorage 99501

Alaska Native Brotherhood, P.O. Box 112, Juneau 99801

Alaska Native Commission on Alcoholism and Drug Abuse, P.O. Box 4-2463, Anchorage 99509

Alaska Native Foundation, 411 W. Fourth Ave., Suite 314, Anchorage 99501

Alaska Native Health Board, 1135 W. Eighth, Suite 2, Anchorage 99501

Central Council of Tlingit and Haida Indian Tribes of Alaska, One Sealaska Plaza, Suite 200, Juneau 99801

Fairbanks Native Association, Incorporated, 310 First Ave., Fairbanks 99701

Interior Village Association, 127½ Minnie St., Fairbanks 99701

Inuit Circumpolar Conference, Barrow 99723

Norton Sound Health Corporation, P.O. Box 966, Nome 99762

Southeast Alaska Regional Health Corporation, P.O. Box 2800, Juneau 99803

Yukon–Kuskokwim Health Corporation, P.O. Box 528, Bethel 99559

Yupiktat Bista (a branch of the Association of Village Council Presidents), Bethel 99559

Native Village Corporations

In addition to the 12 regional corporations managing money and land received as part of the Alaska Native Claims Settlement Act, eligible Native villages were required to form corporations and to choose lands made available by the settlement act by December 1974. The 203 Native villages that formed village corporations eligible for land and money benefits are listed under their regional corporation.

Ahtna Incorporated: Cantwell, Chistochina, Chitina, Copper Center, Gakona, Gulkana, Mentasta Lake, Tazlina.

Aleut Corporation: Akutan, Atka, Belkofski, False Pass, King Cove, Nelson Lagoon, Nikolski, St. George, St. Paul, Sand Point, Unalaska, Unga.

Arctic Slope Regional Corporation: Anaktuvuk Pass, Atkasook, Barrow, Kaktovik, Nuiqsut, Point Hope, Point Lay, Wainwright.

Bering Straits Native Corporation: Brevig Mission, Council, Golovin, Inalik/Diomede, King Island, Koyuk, Marys Igloo, Nome, St. Michael, Shaktoolik, Shishmaref, Stebbins, Teller, Unalakleet, Wales, White Mountain.

Bristol Bay Native Corporation: Aleknagik, Chignik, Chignik Lagoon, Chignik Lake, Clarks Point, Dillingham, Egegik, Ekuk, Ekwok, Igiugig, Iliamna, Ivanof Bay, Kokhanok, Koliganek, Levelock, Manokotak, Naknek, Newhalen, New Stuyahok, Nondalton, Pedro Bay, Perryville, Pilot Point, Portage Creek, Port Heiden, South Naknek, Togiak, Twin Hills, Ugashik.

Calista Corporation: Akiachak, Akiak, Alakanuk, Andreafsky, Aniak, Atmautluak, Bethel, Bill Moores,

Chefornak, Chevak, Chuathbaluk, Chuloonwick, Crooked Creek, Eek, Emmonak, Georgetown, Goodnews Bay, Hamilton, Hooper Bay, Kasigluk, Kipnuk, Kongiganak, Kotlik, Kwethluk, Kwigillingok, Lime Village, Lower Kalskag, Marshall, Mekoryuk, Mountain Village, Napaimiute, Napakiak, Napaskiak, Newtok, Nightmute, Nunapitchuk, Ohogamiut, Oscarville, Paimiut, Pilot Station, Pitkas Point, Platinum, Quinhagak, Red Devil, Russian Mission, St. Marys, Scammon Bay, Sheldons Point, Sleetmute, Stony River, Toksook Bay, Tuluksak, Tuntutuliak, Tununak, Umkumiut, Upper Kalskag.

Chugach Natives, Incorporated: Chenaga, English Bay, Eyak, Port Graham, Tatitlek.

Cook Inlet Region, Incorporated: Chickaloon, Knik, Eklutna, Ninilchik, Seldovia, Tyonek.

Doyon, Limited: Alatna, Allakaket, Anvik, Beaver, Bettles Field, Birch Creek, Chalkyitsik, Circle, Dot Lake, Eagle, Fort Yukon, Galena, Grayling, Healy Lake, Holy Cross, Hughes, Huslia, Kaltag, Koyukuk, Manley Hot Springs, McGrath, Minto, Nenana, Nikolai, Northway, Nulato, Rampart, Ruby, Shageluk, Stevens Village, Takotna, Tanacross, Tanana, Telida.

Koniag, Incorporated: Afognak, Akhiok, Kaguyak, Karluk, Larsen Bay, Old Harbor, Ouzinkie, Port Lions, Woody Island.

NANA Regional Corporation, Incorporated: Ambler, Buckland, Deering, Kiana, Kivalina, Kobuk, Kotzebue, Noatak, Noorvik, Selawik, Shungnak.

Sealaska Corporation: Angoon, Craig, Hoonah, Hydaburg, Kake, Kasaan, Klawock, Saxman, Yakutat.

Related reading: *Shamans and Kushtakas,* by Mary Giraudo Beck, illustrations by Marvin Oliver. Tales in Tlingit and Haida mythology provide a powerful mix of history, legend and adventure. *See* ALASKA NORTHWEST LIBRARY in the back of the book.

Nenana Ice Classic

(*See also* Breakup)

The Ice Classic is a gigantic betting pool offering $240,000 in 1993 in cash prizes to the lucky winner who guessed the time, to the nearest minute, of the ice breakup on the Tanana River at the town of Nenana. Official breakup time each spring is established when the surging ice dislodges a tripod and breaks an attached line, which stops a clock set to Yukon standard time. The Nenana Ice Classic was 77 years old in 1993.

Tickets for the classic are sold for $2 each, entitling the holder to one guess. Ice Classic officials estimate over $7 million has been paid to lucky guessers through the years.

The primary intention of the Ice Classic was never as a fund-raiser for the town, but as a statewide lottery, which was officially sanctioned by the first state legislature in one of its first actions back in 1959. But over the years the contest has benefited the town. Fifty percent of the gross proceeds goes to the winners. Nenana residents are paid salaries for ticket counting and compilation, and about 15 percent is earmarked for upkeep of the Nenana Civic Center and as donations to local groups such as the Dog Mushers, to the Visitors Center and to other activities or organizations.

The U.S. Internal Revenue Service also gets a large chunk of withholding taxes on the $140,000 payroll and a huge bite of each winner's share. In 1993, there were two betting pools and a single winner of the $240,000 prize.

Another pool, the Kuskokwim Ice Classic, has been a tradition in Bethel since 1924. Initially, it was said that the winner was paid 20 fish or 20 furs, but stakes are considerably higher now, with the winner receiving 40 percent of the total ticket sales.

Breakup times for the Nenana Ice Classic from 1918 through 1993, arranged in order of day and time of breakup, are:

April 20, 1940— 3:27 P.M.
23, 1993— 1:01 P.M.
24, 1990— 5:19 P.M.
26, 1926— 4:03 P.M.
28, 1969—12:28 P.M.
28, 1943— 7:22 P.M.
29, 1939— 1:26 P.M.
29, 1958— 2:56 P.M.
29, 1953— 3:54 P.M.
29, 1983— 6:37 P.M.

April 30, 1936—12:58 P.M.
    30, 1980— 1:16 P.M.
    30, 1942— 1:28 P.M.
    30, 1934— 2:07 P.M.
    30, 1978— 3:18 P.M.
    30, 1951— 5:54 P.M.
    30, 1979— 6:16 P.M.
    30, 1981— 6:44 P.M.
May 1, 1991—12:04 A.M.
    1, 1932—10:15 A.M.
    1, 1956—11:24 A.M.
    1, 1989— 8:14 P.M.
    2, 1976—10:51 A.M.
    2, 1960— 7:12 P.M.
    3, 1941— 1:50 A.M.
    3, 1919— 2:33 P.M.
    3, 1947— 5:53 P.M.
    4, 1967—11:55 A.M.
    4, 1973—11:59 A.M.
    4, 1944— 2:08 P.M.
    4, 1970—10:37 P.M.
    5, 1957— 9:30 A.M.
    5, 1961—11:31 A.M.
    5, 1987— 3:11 P.M.
    5, 1929— 3:41 P.M.
    5, 1946— 4:40 P.M.
    5, 1963— 6:25 P.M.
    6, 1977—12:46 P.M.
    6, 1974— 3:44 P.M.
    6, 1950— 4:14 P.M.
    6, 1928— 4:25 P.M.
    6, 1954— 6:01 P.M.
    6, 1938— 8:14 P.M.
    7, 1925— 6:32 P.M.
    7, 1965— 7:01 P.M.
    8, 1959—11:26 A.M.
    8, 1966—12:11 P.M.
    8, 1930— 7:03 P.M.
    8, 1933— 7:30 P.M.
    8, 1968— 9:26 P.M.
    8, 1986— 9:31 P.M.
    8, 1971—10:50 P.M.
    9, 1923— 2:00 P.M.
    9, 1955— 2:31 P.M.
    9, 1984— 3:33 P.M.
    10, 1931— 9:23 A.M.
    10, 1972—11:56 A.M.
    10, 1975— 1:49 P.M.
    10, 1982— 5:36 P.M.
    11, 1921— 6:42 A.M.
    11, 1918— 9:33 A.M.
    11, 1920—10:45 A.M.
    11, 1985— 2:36 P.M.
    11, 1924— 3:10 P.M.
    12, 1927— 5:42 A.M.
    12, 1922— 1:20 P.M.
    12, 1952— 5:04 P.M.
    12, 1937— 8:04 P.M.

May 12, 1962—11:23 P.M.
    13, 1948—11:13 A.M.
    14, 1992— 6:26 A.M.
    14, 1949—12:39 P.M.
    15, 1935— 1:32 P.M.
    16, 1945— 9:41 A.M.
    20, 1964—11:41 A.M.

Newspapers and Periodicals

(*Rates are subject to change*)

Air Guardian, 6000 Air Guard Road, Anchorage 99502. Monthly. Annual rates: free.

Alaska Bar Rag, 310 K St., No. 602, Anchorage 99501. Bimonthly. Annual rates: $25.

Alaska Business Monthly, P.O. Box 241288, Anchorage 99524. Monthly. Annual rates: $21.95.

Alaska Commercial Fisherman, 3933 Geneva Place, Anchorage 99508. Biweekly. Annual rates: $30.

Alaska Designs, P.O. Box 103115, Anchorage 99510. Monthly. Annual rates: free to members.

Alaska Directory of Attorneys, 203 W. 15th Ave., Suite 102, Anchorage 99501. Semiannually. Annual rates: $25 per issue.

Alaska Economic Report, 3037 S. Circle, Anchorage 99507. Biweekly. Annual rates: $225.

The Alaska Geographic Society, P.O. Box 93370, Anchorage 99509. Quarterly. Annual rates: $39; outside the U.S., $49.

Alaska Journal of Commerce, P.O. Box 91419, Anchorage 99509. Weekly. Annual rates: $51.

Alaska Justice Forum, 3211 Province Drive, Anchorage 99508. Quarterly. Annual rates: free.

Alaska Living Magazine, 801 Barnette St., Fairbanks 99701. Bimonthly. Annual rates: $18; outside the U.S., $36.

ALASKA magazine, 808 E St., Suite 200, Anchorage 99501. Monthly. Annual rates: $24; outside the U.S., $29.

Alaska Media Directory, 6200 Bubbling Brook, Anchorage 99516. Annually. Annual rates: $68.

Alaska Native Directory, 3002 Spenard Road, Anchorage 99503. Annually. Annual rates: $125.

Alaska Travel News, P.O. Box 202622, Anchorage 99520. May through August. Annual rates: free.

Alaska Traveller, P.O. Box 201894, Anchorage 99520. Three issues a year. Annual rates: free.

Alaska View, 501 W. International Airport Road, Suite 16, Anchorage 99518. Monthly. Annual rates: $25.

Alaska Women, HCR 64, Box 453, Seward 99664. Yearly.

AlaskaMen, 201 Arctic Slope Ave., Suite 100, Anchorage 99518. Bimonthly. Annual rates: $24.95.

Alaskan, 134th Public Affairs Team, P.O. Box 5800, Anchorage 99503. Bimonthly. Annual rates: free.

Alaskan Guide to Healthy Living, 529 W. Ninth Ave., Anchorage 99501. Annually. Annual rates: free.

Alaskan Southeaster, P.O. Box 240667, Douglas 99824. Monthly. Annual rates: $28.

Alaskan Viewpoint, HCR 64, Box 453, Seward 99664. Quarterly. Annual rates: $10.

The All-Alaska Weekly, P.O. Box 70970, Fairbanks 99707. Weekly. Annual rates: $24.

Anchorage Bypass, P.O. Box 243512, Anchorage 99524. Weekly. Annual rates: $35.

Anchorage Chamber of Commerce Newsletter, 437 E St., Suite 300, Anchorage 99501. Monthly. Annual rates: $12.

Anchorage Daily News, P.O. Box 149001, Anchorage 99514. Daily. Annual rates: Anchorage home delivery, $114; second-class mail, $300.

Anchorage Gazette, P.O. Box 100100, Anchorage 99510. Weekly. Annual rates: $1 per issue.

Anchorage Visitors Guide, 1600 A St., Suite 200, Anchorage 99501. Annually. Annual rates: free.

Aniak Paper, P.O. Box 116, Aniak 99557. Bimonthly. Annual rates: $15.

Arctic Soldier Magazine, Public Affairs Office, HQ, 6th Infantry Division (Light), Fort Richardson 99505. Quarterly. Annual rates: free.

Arctic Sounder, P.O. Box 290, Kotzebue 99752. Weekly. Annual rates: second-class mail, $32; first-class, $75.

Arctic Star, Public Affairs Office, HQ, 6th Infantry Division (Light), Fort Wainwright 99703. Weekly. Annual rates: free.

Boat Broker, P.O. Box 22163, Juneau 99802. Monthly. Annual rates: free; $12 if mailed.

Borough Post, 3709 Spenard Road, Anchorage 99503. Weekly. Annual rates: $45.

Bristol BayTimes, P.O. Box 1770, Dillingham 99576. Weekly. Annual rates: second-class mail, $32; first-class, $75.

Capital City Weekly, 8365 Old Dairy Road, Juneau 99801. Weekly. Annual rates: home delivery, free; mail delivery, $52/year.

Chilkat Valley News, P.O. Box 630, Haines 99827. Weekly. Annual rates: $32.

Chugiak–Eagle River Star, 16941 North Eagle River Loop, Eagle River 99577. Weekly. Annual rates: $16.

Commercial Buyers Guide, P.O. Box 112955, Anchorage 99511. Biannually. Annual rates: $9.95 per issue.

Commercial Fisherman's Guide, P.O. Box 65119, Port Ludlow, WA 98365. Annually. Annual rates: $13.95.

Copper River Country Journal, P.O. Box 336, Glennallen 99588. Bimonthly. Annual rates: $25.

Cordova Times, P.O. Box 200, Cordova 99574. Weekly. Annual rates: $75.

Current Drift, 1801 Crescent Drive, Anchorage 99508. Monthly. Annual rates: free.

Daily Sitka Sentinel, P.O. Box 799, Sitka 99835. Monday through Friday. Annual rates: $75.

The Delta Wind, P.O. Box 986, Delta Junction 99737. Biweekly. Annual rates: 85¢ per issue.

Eagles Call, Box 2 NAS Adak, FPO Seattle 98791. Weekly. Annual rates: free.

Fairbanks Arts, P.O. Box 72786, Fairbanks 99707. Bimonthly. Annual rates: $15.

Fairbanks Daily News–Miner, P.O. Box 70710, Fairbanks 99707. Daily, except Saturday. Annual rates: $252.

Fairbanks Magazine, 921 Woodway, Fairbanks 99709. June through October. Annual rates: $2.25 per issue.

The Frontiersman, 1261 Seward Meridian, Wasilla 99654. Semiweekly. Annual rates: $26.

Great Lander Bush Mailer, 3110 Spenard Road, Anchorage

99503. Monthly. Annual rates: free.

Greater Anchorage Tomorrow, 437 E St., Suite 300, Anchorage 99501. Monthly. Annual rates: $12.

Haines Sentinel, P.O. Box 630, Haines 99827. Annually. Annual rates: free.

Hand in Hand: The Alaska Journal of Parenting, P.O. Box 230973, Anchorage 99523. Bimonthly. Annual rates: $16.

Homer News, 3482 Landings St., Homer 99603. Weekly. Annual rates: Kenai Peninsula Borough, $38.

Info-Juno, P.O. Box 21708, Juneau 99802. Weekly. Annual rates: $54.

Island News, P.O. Box 19430, Thorne Bay 99919. Weekly. Annual rates: $55.

Joint Venture News, 3581 Kachemak Circle, Anchorage 99515. Monthly. Annual rates: $49.

Juneau Empire, 3100 Channel Drive, Juneau 99801. Monday through Friday. Annual rates: $110.

Ketchikan Daily News, P.O. Box 7900, Ketchikan 99901. Monday through Saturday. Annual rates: $84.

Kodiak Daily Mirror, 1419 Selig, Kodiak 99615. Monday through Friday. Annual rates: $85.

The Local Paper, 1752 Tongass Ave., Ketchikan 99901. Weekly. Annual rates: free.

The MILEPOST®, 3000 Northup Way, Suite 200, Bellevue, WA 98004. Annually, available in March. Annual rates: $16.95 plus $2.50 for fourth-class postage; $4.50 for first-class mail.

Mukluk News, P.O. Box 90, Tok 99780. Bimonthly. Annual rates: $20.

Mushing, P.O. Box 149, Ester 99725. Bimonthly. Annual rates: $21.

New Alaskan, 8339 Snug Harbor Lane NTG, Ketchikan 99901. Quarterly. Annual rates: $7 outside of Ketchikan.

Nome Nugget, P.O. Box 610, Nome 99762. Weekly. Annual rates: $50.

North Pole Independent, P.O. Box 55757, North Pole 99705. Weekly. Annual rates: $25.

Northcountry Companion Visitor Guide, P.O. Box 336, Glennallen 99588. Annually. Annual rates: free.

The Northern Light, Campus Center, 3211 Providence Drive, Anchorage 99508. Weekly. Annual rates: free.

Northland News, P.O. Box 70710, Fairbanks 99707. Monthly. Annual rates: free.

Peninsula Clarion, P.O. Box 3009, Kenai 99611. Monday through Friday. Annual rates: $64.

Petersburg Pilot, P.O. Box 930, Petersburg 99833. Weekly. Annual rates: $28.

Senior Voice, 325 E. Third Ave., Suite 300, Anchorage 99501. Monthly. Annual rates: $15 seniors; $20 under 55.

Seward Phoenix Log, P.O. Box 89, Seward 99664. Weekly. Annual rates: $32.

Seward Visitors Guide, P.O. Box 89, Seward 99664. Annually. Annual rates: free.

The Skagway News, P.O. Box 1898, Skagway 99840. Biweekly. Annual rates: $30.

Sourdough Sentinel, 3rd Wing, Public Affairs, Elmendorf Air Force Base 99506. Weekly. Annual rates: free.

Southeast Alaska Business Journal, 8365 Old Dairy Road, Juneau 99801. Monthly. Annual rates: $11.95.

Tundra Drums, P.O. Box 868, Bethel 99559. Weekly. Annual rates: $32.

Tundra Times, P.O. Box 92247, Anchorage 99509. Weekly. Annual rates: $20.

Valdez Star, P.O. Box 367, Valdez 99686. Weekly. Annual rates: $45.

Valdez Vanguard, P.O. Box 157, Valdez 99686. Weekly. Annual rates: $75.

Valley Sun, 1261 Seward Meridian, Wasilla 99654. Weekly. Annual rates: free to Matanuska–Susitna Borough box holders.

Wrangell Sentinel, P.O. Box 798, Wrangell 99929. Weekly. Annual rates: $27.50.

Your Personal Guide to Anchorage, P.O. Box 1581, Anchorage 99510. Monthly. Annual rates: free.

Your Personal Guide to Fairbanks, P.O. Box 1581, Anchorage 99510. Monthly. Annual rates: free.

Your Personal Guide to Juneau, P.O. Box 1581, Anchorage 99510. Monthly. Annual rates: free.

No-see-ums

In its usual swarms this tiny, gray-black, silver-winged gnat is a most persistent pest and annoys all creatures. But, when alone, each insect is difficult to see. While no-see-ums don't transmit disease, their bites are irritating. Protective clothing, netting and a good repellent are recommended while in the bushes or near still-water ponds. Tents and recreational vehicles should be well screened.

Nuchalawoya

Nuchalawoya means "where the great waters meet"; it was originally a meeting of Athabascan chiefs held near the time of the summer solstice. Nuchalawoya today is a festival held in June at Tanana, a town located at the confluence of the Tanana and Yukon rivers. The festival is open to the public.

Obituaries

See page 209 for listings.

Officials

UNDER RUSSIA

Emperor Paul of Russia grants the Russian–American Company an exclusive trade charter in Alaska.

Chief Managers, Russian–American Company

Alexander Andrevich Baranof, 1799–1818

Leontil Andreanovich Hagemeiste, January–October 1818

Semen Ivanovich Yanovski, 1818–1820

Matxei I. Muravief, 1820–1825

Peter Egorovich Chistiakov, 1825–1830

Baron Ferdinand P. von Wrangell, 1830–1835

Ivan Antonovich Kupreanof, 1835–1840

Adolph Karlovich Etolin, 1840–1845

Michael D. Tebenkof, 1845–1850

Nikolai Y. Rosenberg, 1850–1853

Alexander Ilich Rudakof, 1853–1854

Stephen Vasili Voevodski, 1854–1859

Ivan V. Furuhelm, 1859–1863

Prince Dmitri Maksoutoff, 1863–1867

UNDER UNITED STATES

U.S. purchases Alaska from Russia in 1867; U.S. Army given jurisdiction over Department of Alaska.

Army Commanding Officers

Bvt. Maj. Gen. Jefferson C. Davis, Oct. 18, 1867–Aug. 31, 1870

Bvt. Lt. Col. George K. Brady, Sept. 1, 1870–Sept. 22, 1870

Maj. John C. Tidball, Sept. 23, 1870–Sept. 19, 1871

Maj. Harvey A. Allen, Sept. 20, 1871–Jan. 3, 1873

Maj. Joseph Stewart, Jan. 4, 1873–April 20, 1874

Capt. George R. Rodney, April 21, 1874–August 16, 1874

Capt. Joseph B. Campbell, Aug. 17, 1874–June 14, 1876

Capt. John Mendenhall, June 15, 1876–March 4, 1877

Capt. Arthur Morris, March 5, 1877–June 14, 1877

U.S. Army troops leave Alaska; the highest ranking federal official left in Alaska is the U.S. collector of customs. Department of Alaska is put under control of the U.S. Treasury Department.

U.S. Collectors of Customs

Montgomery P. Berry, June 14, 1877–Aug. 13, 1877

H.C. DeAhna, Aug. 14, 1877–March 26, 1878

Mottrom D. Ball, March 27, 1877–June 13, 1879

U.S. Navy is given jurisdiction over the Department of Alaska.

Navy Commanding Officers

Capt. L.A. Beardslee, June 14, 1879–Sept. 12, 1880

Comdr. Henry Glass, Sept. 13, 1880–Aug. 9, 1881

Comdr. Edward Lull, Aug. 10, 1881–Oct. 18, 1881

Comdr. Henry Glass, Oct. 19, 1881–March 12, 1882

Comdr. Frederick Pearson, March 13, 1882–Oct. 3, 1882

Comdr. Edgar C. Merriman, Oct. 4, 1882–Sept. 13, 1883

Comdr. Joseph B. Coghlan, Sept. 15, 1883–Sept. 13, 1884

Lt. Comdr. Henry E. Nichols, Sept. 14, 1884–Sept. 15, 1884

Congress provides civil government for

the new District of Alaska in 1884; on Aug. 24, 1912, territorial status is given to Alaska.

Presidential Appointments

John H. Kinkead (President Arthur), July 4, 1884–May 7, 1885. (He did not reach Sitka until Sept. 15, 1884.)

Alfred P. Swineford (President Cleveland), May 7, 1885–April 20, 1889

Lyman E. Knapp (President Harrison), April 20, 1889–June 18, 1893

James Sheakley (President Cleveland), June 18, 1893–June 23, 1897

John G. Brady (President McKinley), June 23, 1897–March 2, 1906

Wilford B. Hoggatt (President Roosevelt), March 2, 1906–May 20, 1909

Walter E. Clark (President Taft), May 20, 1909–April 18, 1913

John F.A. Strong (President Wilson), April 18, 1913–April 12, 1918

Thomas Riggs Jr. (President Wilson), April 12, 1918–June 16, 1921

Scott C. Bone (President Harding), June 16, 1921–Aug. 16, 1925

George A. Parks (President Coolidge), June 16, 1925–April 19, 1933

John W. Troy (President Roosevelt), April 19, 1933–Dec. 6, 1939

Ernest Gruening (President Roosevelt), Dec. 6, 1939–April 10, 1953

B. Frank Heintzleman (President Eisenhower), April 10, 1953–Jan. 3, 1957

Mike Stepovich (President Eisenhower), April 8, 1957–Aug. 9, 1958

Alaska becomes a state Jan. 3, 1959.

Elected Governors

William A. Egan, Jan. 3, 1959–Dec. 5,1966

Walter J. Hickel,* Dec. 5, 1966–Jan. 29, 1969

Keith H. Miller,* Jan. 29, 1969–Dec. 7, 1970

William A. Egan, Dec. 7, 1970–Dec. 2, 1974

Jay S. Hammond, Dec. 2, 1974–Dec. 6, 1982

Bill Sheffield, Dec. 6, 1982–Dec. 1, 1986

Steve Cowper, Dec. 1, 1986–Dec. 3, 1990

Walter J. Hickel, Dec. 3, 1990–

*Hickel resigned before completing his first full term as governor in order to accept the position of secretary of the interior. He was succeeded by Miller.

In 1906, Congress authorized Alaska to send a voteless delegate to the House of Representatives.

Delegates to Congress

Frank H. Waskey, 1906–1907

Thomas Cale, 1907–1909

James Wickersham, 1909–1917

Charles A. Sulzer, 1917–contested election

James Wickersham, 1918, seated as delegate

Charles A. Sulzer, 1919, elected; died before taking office

George Grigsby, 1919, elected in a special election

James Wickersham, 1921, seated as delegate, having contested election of Grigsby

Dan A. Sutherland, 1921–1930

James Wickersham, 1931–1933

Anthony J. Dimond, 1933–1944

E.L. Bartlett, 1944–1958

Unofficial delegates to Congress to promote statehood, elected under a plan first devised by Tennessee. The Tennessee Plan delegates were not seated by Congress but did serve as lobbyists.

Senators:

Ernest Gruening, 1956–1958

William Egan, 1956–1958

Representative:

Ralph Rivers, 1956–1958

Alaska becomes 49th state in 1959 and sends two senators and one representative to U.S. Congress.

Senators:

E.L. Bartlett, 1958–1968

Ernest Gruening, 1958–1968

Mike Gravel, 1968–1980

Ted Stevens, 1968–

Frank H. Murkowski, 1980–

Representatives:

Ralph Rivers, 1958–1966

Howard Pollock, 1966–1970

Nicholas Begich, 1970–1972

Donald E. Young, 1972–

Correspondence Addresses

The Honorable Walter J. Hickel, Office of the Governor, P.O. Box A, Juneau 99811

The Honorable John B. "Jack" Coghill, Office of the Lieutenant Governor, P.O. Box AA, Juneau 99811

Alaska's Delegation in U.S. Congress:

The Honorable Ted Stevens, United

States Senate, 522 Hart Bldg., Washington, D.C. 20510
The Honorable Frank H. Murkowski, United States Senate, 709 Hart Bldg., Washington, D.C. 20510
The Honorable Donald E. Young, House of Representatives, 2331 Rayburn House Office Bldg., Washington, D.C. 20515

Alaska State Legislature
Members of the Alaska Legislature as of the end of the 1992 session are listed below. During sessions, members of the legislature receive mail at P.O. Box V, Juneau 99811.

House of Representatives
District 1: William Williams (Democrat)
District 2: Ben Grussendorf (Democrat)
District 3: Fran Ulmer (Democrat)
District 4: Bill Hudson (Republican)
District 5: Jerry Mackie (Democrat)
District 6: Cliff Davidson (Democrat)
District 7: Gail Phillips (Republican)
District 8: Gary "Lee" Davis (Republican)
District 9: Mike Navarre (Democrat)
District 10: Joseph Green (Republican)
District 11: Jim Nordlund (Democrat)
District 12: Mark Hanley (Republican)
District 13: Cynthia Toohey (Republican)
District 14: Terry Martin (Republican)
District 15: Kay Brown (Democrat)
District 16: David Finkelstein (Democrat)
District 17: Sean Parnell (Republican)
District 18: Con "Ralph" Bunde (Republican)
District 19: Jerry Sanders (Republican)
District 20: Brian Porter (Republican)
District 21: Bettye Davis (Democrat)
District 22: Ramona Barnes (Republican)
District 23: Eldon Mulder (Republican)
District 24: Pete Kott (Republican)
District 25: Ed Willis (Independent)
District 26: Patrick Carney (Democrat)
District 27: Ronald Larson (Democrat)
District 28: Curt Mendard (Democrat)
District 29: John Davies (Democrat)
District 30: Tom Brice (Democrat)
District 31: Joe Sitton (Democrat)
District 32: Al Vezey (Republican)
District 33: Gene Therriault (Republican)
District 34: Jeanette James (Republican)
District 35: Harley Olberg (Republican)

District 36: Irene Nicholia (Democrat)
District 37: Eileen MacLean (Democrat)
District 38: Richard Foster (Democrat)
District 39: Lyman Hoffman (Democrat)
District 40: Carl Moses (Alaska Indepence)

Senate
District A: Robin Taylor (Republican)
District B: Jim Duncan (Democrat)
District C: Fred Zharoff (Democrat)
District D: Suzanne Little (Democrat)
District E: Judith Salo (Democrat)
District F: Drue Pearce (Republican)
District G: Loren Leman (Republican)
District H: Johnny Ellis (Democrat)
District I: Steve Rieger (Republican)
District J: Dave Donley (Democrat)
District K: Tim Kelly (Republican)
District L: Randy Phillips (Republican)
District M: Rick Halford (Republican)
District N: Jay Kerttula (Democrat)
District O: Steve Frank (Republican)
District P: Bert Sharp (Republican)
District Q: Mike Miller (Republican)
District R: Georgianna Lincoln (Democrat)
District S: Al Adams (Democrat)
District T: George Jacko (Democrat)

Oil and Gas

Alaska's first exploratory oil well was drilled in 1898 on the Iniskin Peninsula, Cook Inlet, by Alaska Petroleum Company. According to the Alaska Oil and Gas Association, oil was encountered in this first hole at about 700 feet, but a water zone beneath the oil strata cut off the oil flow. Total depth of the well was approximately 1,000 feet.

The first commercial oil discovery was made in 1902 near Katalla, near the mouth of the Bering River east of Cordova. This field produced until 1933.

As early as 1921, oil companies surveyed land north of the Brooks Range for possible drilling sites. In 1923, the federal government created Naval Petroleum Reserve Number 4 (now known as National Petroleum Reserve-Alaska, see National Petroleum Reserve), a 23 million-acre area of Alaska's North Slope. Wartime needs speeded up exploration. In 1944, the Navy began drilling operations on the petroleum reserve and continued until 1953, but made no significant oil discoveries. Since 1981, the U. S. Department of the Interior has leased out oil and gas tracts in the reserve.

Atlantic Richfield discovered oil in 1957 on the Kenai Peninsula, at a depth of approximately 2 miles, about 20 miles northeast of Kenai at what became known as the Swanson River Oilfield. Later, Union Oil Company found a large gas field at Kalifonsky Beach (the Kenai Gas Field) and Amoco found the first oil offshore at a location known as Middle Ground Shoals in Cook Inlet in 1962. Since 1957, the oil and gas industry has invested over $45 billion in Alaska. The money has gone toward exploration and development of North Shore oil fields, and construction of the trans-Alaska pipeline.

Currently, there are 18 production platforms in Cook Inlet, one of which produces only gas. Built to contend with extreme tides, siltation and ice floes, the Cook Inlet platforms are in one of three successful areas of offshore oil production in the United States. Hundreds of miles of pipeline with diameters up to 20 inches link the offshore platforms with onshore facilities at Kenai and Drift River. The deepest producing oil well in the state is in the Swanson River Oilfield on the Kenai

Peninsula; total depth is 17,689 feet. By late 1992, Alaska had 1,599 producing wells, according to the Alaska Oil and Gas Conservation Commission.

A fertilizer plant, the largest of its kind on the West Coast, is located at Nikiski, near Kenai. It uses natural gas as a feed stock to manufacture ammonia and urea. One refinery is located at Kenai and two at North Pole near Fairbanks. Gasoline, diesel fuel, heavy fuel oil, propane, JP-4, Jet A and asphalt are produced for use within and outside of Alaska. Crude oil topping plants located at Prudhoe Bay; Kuparuk; and at pump stations 6, 8 and 10 provide diesel oil for oil field and pipeline use. Liquefied natural gas is produced at a special Philips LNG plant and is the only LNG export facility in the U.S.

The Prudhoe Bay oil field, largest in North America, was discovered in 1968 by Atlantic Richfield Company and Exxon. Recoverable reserves are now estimated to be 12 billion barrels of oil and 26 trillion cubic feet of natural gas. Peak production of 1.5 million barrels per day has begun to decline and is transported from North Slope fields via the trans-Alaska pipeline from Prudhoe Bay to Valdez. (*See also* Pipeline)

In spring of 1988, it was estimated that one-half of the Prudhoe Bay recoverable oil reserve had been pumped. A $2 billion waterflood project was

Oil and Gas Facts (/D=per day; CF=cubic feet)

	Cook Inlet	North Slope
Producing Fields:		
Oil	6	5
Gas	12	0
Number of Active Wells:		
Oil	252	1,347
Gas	98	18
Injectors	70	547
Average Production Rates Per Well:		
Oil	186 barrels/D	1,100 barrels/D
Water	659 barrels/D	1,274 barrels/D
Gas (gas wells only)	5.0 million CF/D	0.2 million CF/D
Cumulative Production:		
Oil	1,160 million barrels	9,441 million barrels
Water	663 million barrels	3,034 million barrels
Gas (net)	4,373 billion CF	2,074 billion CF
Remaining Reserves:*		
Oil	93 million barrels	6,671 million barrels
Gas	2,827 billion CF	30,844 billion CF

*Reserve statistics taken from Dept. of Natural Resources, Division of Oil and Gas publication *Historical and Projected Oil and Gas Consumption,* October 1993.

installed to maximize oil recovery by forcing additional oil out of the reservoir rock and into producing wells. The Central Gas Facility, built at Prudhoe Bay, is currently capable of processing 5.4 billion cubic feet of natural gas and yielding more than 54,000 barrels of natural gas liquids daily. By 1994, the processing capacity will be up to 7.2 billion cubic feet daily. The facility is the largest gas plant in the world.

Two new fields, Endicott and Lisburne, are in production, with Lisburne beginning production in 1986 and currently producing 35,000 barrels. Endicott began production in February 1986, and is owned by BP Exploration (56.7 percent), Exxon (21 percent), Amoco (10.5 percent) and Union (10.5 percent). The remaining 1.3 percent is owned by ARCO; Cook Inlet Region, Incorporated; Doyon, Limited; and NANA Regional Corporation, and is the first offshore commercial development in the United States portion of the Beaufort Sea. Endicott is estimated to have 350 million barrels of oil, and in early 1990 was producing 120,000 barrels a day.

Milne Point, located 35 miles northwest of Prudhoe Bay, is a field operated by Conoco. Economically, this is a marginal field with estimated reserves of 100 million barrels. Conoco suspended drilling operations in February 1985, but resumed production in October 1990, and at the rate of 20,000 barrels per day. In 1991, production also began from the shallow Schrader Bluff formation, which added 5,000 barrels per day.

The Kuparuk River Field, 40 miles west of Prudhoe Bay, is being developed by ARCO. The field went into production in mid-December 1981; approximately 300,000 barrels a day are currently being delivered to the trans-Alaska pipeline. Alaska's North Slope oil fields amount to 25 percent of U.S. oil production and about 12 percent of U.S. oil consumption. In February 1989, ARCO and Exxon announced the discovery of a 300 million-barrel oil field at Point McIntyre, which is about two miles north of the Prudhoe Bay field. The reservoir for the field lies offshore beneath the Beaufort Sea, and if the estimates of the amount of recoverable reserves are correct, the field would be the largest domestic discovery since the discovery of the Endicott field in the late 1970s. Production start-up is to begin by the end of 1993 with an anticipated production of 75,000 barrels per day.

In 1984, Shell Western discovered oil at Seal Island, 12 miles northwest of Prudhoe Bay. Northstar Island, five miles to the west, was the site of delineation drilling in 1985, and in the same region, Sandpiper Island reported another strike in 1985. Texaco hit a strike on the Colville River Delta about eight miles northwest of the Kuparuk River field. Exploration in Navarin Basin began when Amoco drilled five wells, Exxon drilled two wells and ARCO drilled one well. The average well took 60 days to drill and the average cost per well was $20 million to 30 million. Although none of the wells is considered commercially feasible, drilling was halted by legal action.

In October 1985, the 9th Circuit Court of Appeals in San Francisco ruled that drilling must stop in Navarin Basin until a lawsuit filed by the villages of Gambell and Stebbins was fully heard. In a significant decision in early 1987, the Supreme Court overturned the 9th Circuit ruling and held that the aboriginal rights of Alaska Natives were extinguished by Section 4(b) of the Alaska Native Claims Settlement Act, and that Section 810(a) of the Alaska National Interest Lands Conservation Act (ANILCA), which provides protection for subsistence resources, did not extend to the outer continental shelf.

The Alaska Natural Gas Transportation System (proposed Alaska gas pipeline) was authorized by the federal government in 1977. Estimated cost was $10 billion with a completion date of 1983. A two-year delay in the northern part of the project was announced in May 1982 by Northwest Alaskan, the consortium building the project. Recent cost estimates for the gas pipeline have risen to more than $40 billion. A completion date is not set for the foreseeable future, due to problems in financing the project. Now, most industry observers feel that the proposed trans-Alaska gas system is the most viable idea for transporting North Slope gas to Valdez for shipment to market.

Alaska Oil and Natural Gas Liquid Production (in millions of barrels)

Year	Oil*	Natural Gas**
1972	73.6	0.608
1973	73.1	0.812
1974	72.2	0.793
1975	72.0	0.765
1976	67.0	0.770
1977	171.3	0.863
1978	444.8	0.815
1979	511.3	0.635
1980	591.6	0.735
1981	587.3	0.988
1982	618.9	0.999
1983	625.6	0.692
1984	630.4	0.678
1985	666.2	0.986
1986	681.3	1.600
1987	716.0	16.500
1988	738.1	20.300
1989	684.0	18.045
1990	647.3	18.190
1991	656.3	23.880
1992	627.3	26.910

*Oil production for the years 1902–71 totaled 396,537,603 barrels; for the years 1902–82, total production amounted to 3,682,769,004 barrels.
**Natural gas liquid production for the years 1902–71 totaled 1,312,113 barrels; for the years 1902–83, total production was 9,218,705 barrels.
Source: 1983 Statistical Report, Alaska Oil and Gas Conservation Commission, 3001 Porcupine Drive, Anchorage 99501.

Since 1987, Alaska and Texas have alternated as the number one state in oil production. The top five oil-producing states are: Alaska, Texas, Louisiana, California and Oklahoma. According to the State Division of Oil and Gas, Alaska currently provides about 25 percent of the nation's oil.

The state of Alaska receives approximately 85 percent of its general revenue from petroleum taxes and royalties, and since 1959, the state has collected more than $38 billion in oil and gas revenues. In early 1986, the price of oil dropped. Oil industry employment then declined rather than increased, and the state government was in a more tenuous fiscal situation. By early 1990, oil prices had improved, but Prudhoe Bay production had begun to decline.

While crude oil produced in the North Slope cannot be exported, there are no such restrictions on natural gas, but so far, no transportation system has been constructed for North Slope gas. In 1990, natural gas and products derived from it (ammonia and urea) made up about 12.5 percent of all Alaska exports. Most natural gas produced in Alaska is either locally consumed or reinjected back into oil wells.

Natural gas provides a relatively low-cost source of energy for certain Railbelt residents and businesses of Alaska. There are four refineries in Alaska, which satisfy 75 percent of gasoline, diesel and jet fuel consumption in the state.

Oil and gas leasing on state land in Alaska is managed by the Department of Natural Resources, Division of Oil and Gas. The secretary of the interior is responsible for establishing oil and gas leasing on federal lands in Alaska, including the outer continental shelf. In 1986, Chevron, in partnership with a Native corporation, completed its well at Kaktovik on the coastal plain of the

Arctic National Wildlife Refuge. The land was obtained in a swap with the U.S. Department of the Interior, but Congress will have to approve any further development within the boundaries of the refuge.

Oil Spill

Prince William Sound was the site of the largest oil spill in U.S. history, when the 987-foot *Exxon Valdez* oil tanker, carrying a full cargo of 53,094,510 gallons of crude oil, struck Bligh Reef on March 24, 1989. Before the tanker leak could be stopped, more than 270,000 barrels, or about 11 million gallons, of crude oil oozed into Prince William Sound. The oil, which poured out of the tanker at a rate of 42,488 barrels per hour, contaminated more than 1,500 miles of coastline in Prince William Sound, the Gulf of Alaska and lower Cook Inlet.

At the time the tanker hit the reef, the third mate was piloting the tanker.

Within 15 hours of the spill, skimmer ships began to vacuum oil off the water's surface; booms were set up strategically to prevent the oil spill from contaminating salmon fisheries. Other fishing vessels assisted in attempts to capture oiled and wounded wildlife, and transport those animals to rehabilitation centers.

Four days after the spill, the oil slick covered a 300-square-mile area, hitting islands, beaches and fish hatcheries throughout the sound, an area known for its rich commercial herring and salmon hatcheries. Oil from the tanker also was found later to have fouled beaches on the Alaska Peninsula, almost 600 miles from the spill site.

Cleanup efforts involved armies of cleaning crews, who used techniques ranging from washing rocks by hand to washing the shore rocks with highly pressurized hot water. Bioremediation was another cleanup technique, which involved applying fertilizer to oiled shorelines to accelerate oil-metabolizing bacteria. Winter storms proved to assist the cleanup of many beaches throughout the oil spill area. Cleanup efforts were resumed in the spring of 1990 and continued into 1992.

Thousands of marine mammals, birds and other wildlife perished as a result of the oil spill. Carcasses of 1,011 sea otters were recovered from the sound in 1989, and estimates of the number of otters that died range from about 3,500 to 5,500. About 31,000 birds were reported to have been killed, caused by the spill.

But scientists believe these figures represent only a fraction of the total loss, since many birds were thought to have floated out to sea, sunk, or simply have not been found. Preliminary figures fix the loss at between 350,000 and 390,000 birds, according to a report produced by the federal agencies, including the U.S. Department of Fish and Wildlife, in charge of damage assessment and restoration.

Exxon Corp. accepted full responsibility for the spill on March 25, 1989. More than 29,000 claims were filed for damages related to the oil spill. Many of the claims were from fishermen, canneries, Natives and business owners in the region whose livelihood was curtailed by the oil spill: in 1989, the red salmon season was canceled in Prince William Sound.

Litigation continues to this day as a result of the oil spill. The state of Alaska sued Exxon and Alyeska Pipeline Service Company in 1989; Exxon countersued, alleging that state officials hampered cleanup efforts. In October 1991, the state of Alaska and the federal government settled their suits with Exxon, splitting $1.25 billion. Of this amount, $900 million in civil damages is to be paid over a 10-year period ending in September 2001. Administration of the $900 million civil settlement is overseen by the Exxon Valdez Oil Spill Trustee Council, a panel of three state and three federal representatives.

It is estimated that Exxon spent about $2.5 billion on the cleanup. During the peak of operations, 11,000 people worked on the cleanup, using 1,400 vessels and 85 aircraft. Each summer since the spill, teams of specialists have surveyed the shorelines, making recommendations for further cleanup. Each year fewer shoreline segments require cleaning due to previous cleaning and the natural cleansing action of winter storms. Although some

Barrow

Prudhoe Bay

**Southern limit of
continuous permafrost**

Kotzebue

Arctic Circle

Nome

Fairbanks

**Southern limit of
discontinuous permafrost**

Anchorage

Yakutat

Ketchikan

subsurface oil persists in some areas, additional cleanup efforts may cause more stress to the environment with little benefit. Now efforts have shifted from cleaning up the spill area to restoring the area to its pre-spill condition. Environmental monitoring continues.

Exxon released its own scientific study on the oil spill in mid-1993, which concluded that no significant effects remain on the shoreline.

For further information, contact the Oil Spill Information Center, 645 G St., Anchorage 99501; (907) 276-7178. This public library specializes in materials on the *Exxon Valdez* oil spill.

Parka

Pronounced PAR-kee, this over-the-head garment worn by Eskimos was made in several versions. The work parka most often came from caribou fawn skin, while the fancy parka, reserved for special occasions, used the skin of the male ground squirrel (the male offering grayer fur than the

female). The rain parka was made from *oogruk* (bearded seal) intestine. A person's wealth was judged by the quality of his/her best parka.

Permafrost

Permafrost is defined as ground that remains frozen for two or more years. In its continuous form, permafrost underlies the entire Arctic region to depths of 2,000 feet. In broad terms, continuous permafrost occurs north of the Brooks Range and in the alpine region of mountains (including those of the Lower 48).

Discontinuous permafrost occurs south of the Brooks Range and north of the Alaska Range. Much of the Interior and parts of southcentral Alaska are underlain by discontinuous permafrost.

Permafrost affects many man-made structures and natural bodies. It influences construction in the Arctic because building on it may cause the ground to thaw and if the ground is ice-rich, structures will sink. Arctic and subarctic rivers typically carry 55 percent to 65 percent of the precipitation that falls onto their watersheds, roughly 30 percent to 40 percent more than rivers of more temperate climates. Consequently, northern streams are prone to flooding and have high silt loads. Permafrost is responsible for the thousands of lakes dotting the arctic tundra because groundwater is held on the surface.

A tunnel excavated in permafrost near Fox, north of Fairbanks, during the early 1960s is maintained cooperatively by the University of Alaska Fairbanks, and the U.S. Army Cold Regions Research and Engineering Laboratory. It is one of the few such tunnels in the world; it offers unique research opportunities on a 40,000-year-old accumulation of sediments and ice.

The tunnel is open to the general public from June 1 through August 31 each year, by appointment only, through the CRREL office.

Permanent Fund

In 1976, state voters approved a constitutional amendment to establish the Alaska Permanent Fund. This provides that a percentage of all mineral lease rentals, royalties, royalty sales proceeds, federal mineral revenue sharing payments and bonuses shall be placed in a Permanent Fund. Essentially a trust fund for all Alaskans, money from the fund may be used in income-producing investments, but may not be used for state operating expenses (interest income from the Permanent Fund can go into the state's General Fund).

In 1980, the legislature established a Permanent Fund dividend payment program that provides for distribution of the fund's earnings (interest income and capital gains on any liquidation of assets) among the people of Alaska. Eligible residents were to receive a $50 dividend for each year of residency since 1959. The U.S. Supreme Court declared the 1980 program unconstitutional on the grounds that it discriminated against short-term residents, and in 1982, a new state program was signed into law. Under the plan, an initial $1,000 dividend was paid to applicants who had lived in the state for at least six months prior to applying. Dividends are distributed each year to every resident who applies and qualifies, and the amount is decided by adding together the Fund's net income for the last five years, multiplying that number by 21 percent, and dividing that number in half.

If Alaska's Permanent Fund were a Fortune 500 company, it would rank in the top 5 percent in terms of net income. It is the largest pool of money in the country, and the only fund that pays dividends to residents. By the year 2000, it is projected that the Permanent Fund will be producing more revenues for the state than Prudhoe Bay, and as of February 1991, the principal on the Fund was at $11.6 billion. The 1993 dividend payment to residents is anticipated to be between $900 and $1,000. It will be the first time residents can choose to have the dividend directly deposited into their bank account.

Pioneers' Homes

"The state of Alaska recognizes the invaluable contributions of its older citizens and seeks to offer a place for them in which they can live in comfort and security, while remaining active members of the Alaska community. The companionship of other pioneer Alaskans whose earlier years have been spent in the exciting days of the territory is one of the advantages of living in the Pioneers' Homes." These words were taken from a state brochure describing Pioneers' Homes. The six state-supported homes offer a comfortable, secure residence for several hundred older Alaskans. The homes provide space for 294 ambulatory residents, 60 assisted-living residents and 273 nursing residents.

Applicants must be 65 years or older, have lived continuously in Alaska for 15 years immediately preceding application for admission and agree to pay the rent established by the Department of Administration. (Some exceptions are made for Alaskans who have lived in the state more than 30 years.) Race, sex, national origin and religion are not considered when determining eligibility. Some people are under the mistaken impression that to qualify for the Pioneers' Homes, one must be a member of the Pioneers of Alaska. This is not the case. Pioneers of Alaska is a private, fraternal organization and is not connected with the state-operated Pioneers' Homes.

The first Pioneers' Home was established in Sitka in 1913 for "indigent prospectors and others who have spent their years in Alaska." With the coming of statehood in 1959, the homes were officially opened to women and Alaska Natives.

For additional information about Pioneers' Homes, contact the Director of Pioneers' Benefits, P.O. Box CLMS0211, Juneau 99811; phone (907) 465-4400.

Following are the locations of the six homes:

Anchorage Pioneers' Home, 923 W. 11th Ave., Anchorage 99501; phone (907) 276-3414.

Fairbanks Pioneers' Home, 2221 Eagan Ave., Fairbanks 99701; phone (907) 456-4372.

Juneau Pioneers' Home, 4675 Glacier Highway, Juneau 99801; phone (907) 780-6422.

Ketchikan Pioneers' Home, 141 Bryant, Ketchikan 99901; phone (907) 225-4111.

Palmer Pioneers' Home, 250 E. Fireweed, Palmer 99645; phone (907) 745-4241.

Sitka Pioneers' Home, 120 Katlian St., Sitka 99835; phone (907) 747-3213.

Pipeline

The trans-Alaska pipeline designer, builder and operator is the Alyeska Pipeline Service Company, a consortium of the following seven oil companies:

BP Pipeline Company, 50.01%

ARCO Transportation Alaska, Inc., 21.35%

Exxon Pipeline Company, 20.34%

Mobil Alaska Pipeline Company, 4.08%

Unocal Pipeline Company, 1.36%

Phillips Alaska Pipeline Corporation, 1.36%

Amerada Hess Pipeline Corporation, 1.50%

Pipeline length: 800 miles; slightly less than half that length is buried, the remainder is on 78,000 above-ground supports, located 60 feet apart, built in a flexible zigzag pattern. There are more than 800 river and stream crossings. Normal burial of pipe was used in stable soils and rock; above-ground pipe—insulated and jacketed—was used in thaw-unstable permafrost areas. Thermal devices prevent thawing around vertical supports. It has 151 stop-flow valves.

Pipe: Specially manufactured coated pipe with zinc anodes installed to prevent corrosion. Size is 48 inches in diameter, with thickness from 0.462 to 0.562 inch. Pipe sections before

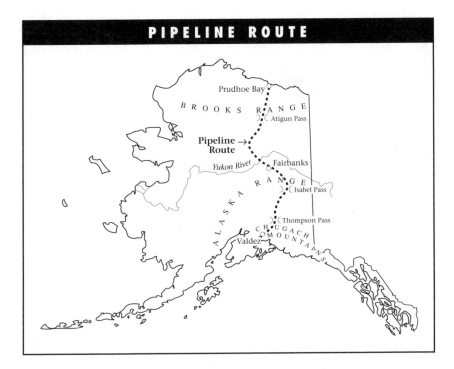

construction are in lengths of 40 and 60 feet.

Cost: $8 billion, which includes terminal at Valdez, but does not include interest on money raised for construction.

Amount of oil pumped through pipeline: As of Dec. 28, 1990, 8 billion barrels of crude oil. In 1990, the 10,000th tanker sailed from the Marine Terminal at Valdez with a cargo of Alaska North Slope crude oil destined for U.S. markets.

Operations: Control center at Valdez terminal and 11 operating pump stations along line monitor and control pipeline.

Pipeline throughput: 1.8 million barrels a day, average.

Estimated crude oil reserves recoverable on the North Slope: approximately 8 billion barrels as of Jan. 1, 1991.

Terminal: 1,000-acre site at Port Valdez, northernmost ice-free harbor in the U.S., with 18 tanks providing storage capacity of 9,180,000 barrels of oil.

Valdez ship-loading capacity: 110,000 barrels per hour for each of three berths; 80,000 barrels per hour for one berth.

Length and cost of pipeline haul road built by Alyeska: 360 miles, from the Yukon River to Prudhoe Bay, $150 million.

Yukon River bridge: first bridge (2,290 feet long) to span the Yukon in Alaska.

Important dates: July 1968, Prudhoe Bay oil field discovery confirmed; **1970,** suits filed to halt construction, Alyeska Pipeline Service Company formed; **Nov. 16, 1973,** presidential approval of pipeline legislation; **April 29, 1974,** construction begins on North Slope Haul Road (now the Dalton Highway) and is completed 154 days later; **March 27, 1975,** first pipe installed at Tonsina River; **June 20, 1977,** first oil leaves Prudhoe Bay, reaches Valdez terminal July 28; **Aug. 1, 1977,** first tanker load of oil shipped aboard the SS *ARCO Juneau*; **June 13, 1979,** tanker number 1,000 (SS *ARCO Heritage*) sails; **July 15, 1983,** 3 billionth barrel of oil leaves pump station; **Sept. 15, 1986,** 5 billionth barrel of oil leaves pump station; **April 19, 1987,** 7,000th tanker sails from Marine Terminal with Prudhoe Bay crude oil; **Feb. 16, 1988,** 6 billionth barrel arrives at the Marine Terminal; **May 2, 1988,** *Chevron Mississippi* is 8,000th tanker to load crude oil at Marine Terminal; **June 30, 1989,** 7 billionth barrel was loaded on the *Mobil Arctic,* and the 9,000th tanker sailed from the Marine Terminal at Valdez with a full load of crude oil; **Dec. 28, 1990,** 8 billionth barrel was pumped from the North Slope into the pipeline and arrived in Valdez on Jan. 1, 1991.

Place Names

Alaska has a rich international heritage of place names. Throughout the state, names of British (Barrow), Spanish (Valdez), Russian (Kotzebue), French (La Perouse), American (Fairbanks) and Native Alaskan (Sitka) origin dot the map. Some Alaska place names are quite common. There are about 70 streams called Bear Creek in Alaska (not to mention Bear Bay, Bear Bluff, Bear Canyon, Bear Cove and Bear Draw) and about 50 called Moose Creek. Many place names have an unusual history. In 1910, geologist Lawrence Martin named Sherman Glacier in the Chugach Mountains after Gen. William Tecumseh Sherman, with the explanation, "He [Sherman] said, 'War is hell'; so I put him on ice, near the Sheridan Glacier."

For a comprehensive listing, description and history of Alaska's usual and unusual place names, from Aaron Creek to Zwinge Valley, see Donald Orth's *Dictionary of Alaska Place Names,* U.S. Geological Survey Professional Paper 567.

Poisonous Plants

Alaska has few poisonous plants, considering the total number of plant species growing in the state. Nonetheless, some extremely poisonous plants are found in the state. Baneberry (*Actaea rubra*), water hemlock (*Cicuta douglasii* and *C. mackenzieana*), fly agaric mushroom (*Amanita muscaria*),

monkshood (*Aconitum* species) and false hellebore (*Veratrum* species) are the most dangerous. Be sure you have properly identified plants before harvesting for food.

Alaska has no poison ivy or poison oak, which are found in almost all other states. However, cow parsnip produces a photoreactive chemical which can cause blisters and burns.

Related reading: *Discovering Wild Plants, Alaska, Western Canada, the Northwest,* by Janice Schofield. More than 130 species are described, along with traditional uses of wild plants; includes recipes, color photographs and illustrations. *See* ALASKA NORTHWEST LIBRARY at the back of the book.

Political Parties

There are four recognized political parties in Alaska. To become recognized in the state, a political party must be an organized group of voters that represents a particular political program and that nominated a candidate for governor who received at least 3 percent of the total votes cast at the preceding general election for governor.

Alaska's four political parties are:

Alaska Independence Party, Acting Chairperson Edgar Paul Boyko; correspondence only to 2521 Old Steese Road, Fairbanks 99712; phone (907) 457-1884.

Democratic Party of Alaska, Chairperson Greg Wakefield, P.O. Box 104199, Anchorage 99510-4199; phone (907) 258-3050.

Green Party of Alaska, Chairperson Ronny Rosenberg, P.O. Box 82653, Fairbanks 99708; phone (907) 452-6476.

Republican Party of Alaska, Chairperson Pauline Martens, P.O. Box 243732, Anchorage 99524-3732; phone (907) 276-4467.

Populations and Zip Codes

According to the U.S. Census Bureau, Alaska's population grew 3.7

percent from April 1990 to July 1991 to 570,300 people. This rate increase makes Alaska the second-fastest growing state after Nevada for this same period.

From 1980–89, Alaska's population increased 31.1 percent. According to the Alaska Department of Labor, this growth was the result, in part, of the economic boom of the early 1980s driven by increased state oil revenues and federal government expenditures. The boom fueled high immigration to the state from 1981 through 1983.

Natural increase also plays a role in Alaska's population growth. In 1990, the state's birth rate was 24.4 births per 1,000 population, which was well above the national rate of 15.4. However, that trend may now be slowing. According to 1991 figures, Alaska's population under the age of 5 is growing at a rate of only 1.3 percent, almost

50 percent lower than the national rate of 2.5 percent.

Between April 1990 and July 1991, the state's population aged 46 to 64 increased 7.1 percent, compared to the national rate of 1.2 percent. Likewise, Alaska's residents 65 and older increased 7.2 percent, compared to the national rate of 2.2 percent for the same period. Alaska's residents aged 25 to 44 grew 2.9 percent, compared to 1.9 percent for the nation between April 1990 and July 1991.

Increased growth rates of older residents are attributed to a number of factors, including the financial benefits of the state's longevity bonus, property tax rebates, Permanent Fund dividend, as well as Alaska's lack of a state income tax.

The populations for cities and communities in the following lists are taken from the Alaska Department of Labor 1991 estimates (NA=Not Available):

Community	Year Incorporated	Population	Zip
Akhiok (AH-key-ok)	1972	81	99615
Akiachak (ACK-ee-a-chuck)	—	495	99551
Akiak (ACK-ee-ack)	1970	287	99552
Akutan (ACK-oo-tan)	1979	487	99553
Alakanuk (a-LACK-a-nuk)	1969	559	99554
Aleknagik (a-LECK-nuh-gik)	1973	200	99555
Allakaket (alla-KAK-it)	1975	172	99720
Ambler	1971	301	99786
Anaktuvuk Pass (an-ak-TU-vuk)	1957	246	99721
Anchor Point	—	920	99556
Anchorage (Municipality)	1920	237,193	99510
Eastchester Station	—	—	99501
Fort Richardson	—	—	99505
Elmendorf AFB	—	—	99506
Mountain View	—	—	99508
Spenard Station	—	—	99509
Downtown Station	—	—	99510
South Station	—	—	99511
Alyeska Pipeline Co	—	—	99512
Federal Building	—	—	99513
Anderson	1962	649	99744
Angoon	1963	690	99820
Aniak (AN-ee-ack)	1972	529	99557
Annette	—	46	99926
Anvik	1969	82	99558
Arctic Village	—	109	99722
Atka	1988	87	99502
Atmautluak (at-MAUT-loo-ack)	1976	267	99559
Atqasuk	1982	217	99791
Auke Bay	—	NA	99821
Barrow	1959	3,702	99723

Community	Year Incorporated	Population	Zip
Beaver	—	104	99724
Bethel	1957	4,818	99559
Bettles Field	1985	33	99726
Big Delta	—	408	99737
Big Lake	—	1,552	99652
Birch Creek	—	38	99790
Border	—	NA	99780
Brevig Mission	1969	205	99785
Buckland	1966	340	99727
Butte	—	1,909	NA
Cantwell	—	147	99729
Cape Yakataga	—	NA	99574
Central	—	48	99730
Chalkyitsik (chawl-KIT-sik)	—	86	99788
Chase	—	38	NA
Chefornak (cha-FOR-nack)	1974	330	99561
Chenega	—	95	99574
Chevak	1967	619	99563
Chickaloon	—	178	99674
Chicken	—	NA	99732
Chignik	1983	177	99564
Chignik Lagoon	—	55	99565
Chignik Lake	—	133	99564
Chiniak	—	73	99615
Chistochina	—	62	NA
Chitina (CHIT-nah)	—	53	99566
Chuathbaluk (chew-ATH-ba-luck)	1975	129	99557
Chugiak (CHOO-gee-ack)	—	NA	99567
Circle	—	88	99733
Clam Gulch	—	76	99568
Clarks Point	1971	58	99569
Clear	—	NA	99704
Coffman Cove	1989	198	99950
Cohoe	—	533	99669
Cold Bay	1982	122	99571
College	—	11,526	99709
Cooper Landing	—	253	99572
Copper Center	—	452	99573
Copperville	—	167	NA
Cordova	1909	2,171	99574
Covenant Life	—	71	NA
Craig	1922	1,387	99921
Crooked Creek	—	111	99575
Crown Point	—	63	NA
Cube Cove	—	162	NA
Deadhorse	—	33	99734
Deering	1970	158	99736
Delta Junction	1960	736	99737
Denali Park	—	NA	99755
Dillingham	1963	2,110	99576
Diomede (DY-o-mede)	1970	179	99762
Dora Bay	—	51	99950
Dot Lake	—	71	99737
Douglas	1902	NA	99824
Dry Creek	—	104	NA
Dutch Harbor	1942	NA	99692
Eagle	1901	161	99738

Community	Year Incorporated	Population	Zip
Eagle River	—	NA	99577
Eagle Village	—	34	NA
Edna Bay	—	77	99825
Eek	1970	284	99578
Egegik (EEG-gah-gik)	—	126	99579
Ekwok (ECK-wok)	1974	78	99580
Elfin Cove	—	57	99825
Elim (EE-lum)	1970	267	99739
Emmonak (ee-MON-nuk)	1964	692	99581
English Bay	—	171	99695
Ester	—	166	99725
Evansville	—	30	99726
Eyak	—	175	NA
Fairbanks	1903	32,156	9970–
Main Office	—	—	99701
Eielson AFB	—	5,875	99702
Fort Wainwright	—	—	99703
Main Office Boxes	—	—	99706
Downtown Station	—	—	99707
College Branch	—	—	99708
Salcha	—	—	99714
False Pass	1990	62	99583
Ferry	—	58	NA
Flat	—	NA	99584
Fort Greely	—	1,200	99790
Fort Yukon	1959	602	99740
Fox	—	278	99712
Fox River	—	389	NA
Freshwater Bay	—	71	NA
Fritz Creek	—	1,423	99603
Gakona (ga-KOH-na)	—	26	99586
Galena (ga-LEE-na)	1971	829	99741
Gambell	1963	546	99742
Game Creek	—	72	NA
Girdwood	—	NA	99587
Glennallen	—	463	99588
Golovin (GAWL-uh-vin)	1971	142	99762
Goodnews Bay	1970	236	99589
Grayling	1969	203	99590
Gulkana	—	107	99586
Gustavus (ga-STAY-vus)	—	258	99826
Haines	1910	1,234	99827
Halibut Cove	—	84	99603
Happy Valley	—	328	NA
Harding Lake	—	27	99714
Healy	—	500	99743
Healy Lake	—	48	NA
Hobart Bay	—	47	99850
Hollis	—	99	99950
Holy Cross	1968	273	99602
Homer	1964	3,736	99603
Hoonah	1946	793	99829
Hooper Bay	1966	890	99604
Hope	—	159	99605
Houston	1966	815	99694
Hughes	1973	54	99745
Huslia (HOOS-lee-a)	1969	203	99746

149

Community	Year Incorporated	Population	Zip
Hydaburg	1927	405	99922
Hyder	—	111	99923
Iguigig	—	35	99613
Iliamna (ill-ee-YAM-nuh)	—	94	99606
Ivanof Bay	—	30	99502
Jakolof Bay	—	27	99603
Juneau	1900	27,695	9980–
Main Office	—	—	99801
Main Office Boxes	—	—	99802
Mendenhall Station	—	—	99803
State Government Offices	—	—	99811
Kachemak (CATCH-a-mack)	1961	372	99603
Kake	1952	725	99830
Kaktovik (kack-TOE-vik)	1971	224	99747
Kalifonsky	—	299	99669
Kalskag	1975	173	99607
Kaltag	1969	235	99748
Karluk	—	75	99608
Kasaan (Ka-SAN)	1976	52	99924
Kasigluk (ka-SEEG-luk)	1982	459	99609
Kasilof (ka-SEE-loff)	—	390	99610
Kenai (KEEN-eye)	1960	6,535	99611
Kenny Lake	—	426	NA
Ketchikan	1900	8,478	99901
Kiana (Ky-AN-a)	1964	401	99749
King Cove City	1947	744	99612
King Salmon	—	688	99613
Kipnuk (KIP-nuck)	—	472	99614
Kivalina	1969	327	99750
Klawock (kla-WOCK)	1929	758	99925
Klukwan	—	129	99827
Knik	—	279	99687
Kobuk	1973	79	99751
Kodiak	1940	7,299	99615
U.S. Coast Guard Station	—	1,646	99619
Kokhanok (KO-ghan-ock)	—	152	99606
Koliganek (ko-LIG-a-neck)	—	189	99576
Kongiganak (kon-GIG-a-nuck)	—	322	99559
Kotlik	1970	499	99620
Kotzebue (KOT-sa-bue)	1958	2,886	99752
Koyuk	1970	253	99753
Koyukuk (KOY-yuh-kuck)	1973	121	99754
Kupreanof (ku-pree-AN-off)	1975	24	99833
Kwethluk (KWEETH-luck)	1975	559	99621
Kwigillingok (kwi-GILL-in-gock)	—	278	99622
LaBouchere Bay	—	133	NA
Lake Minchumina (min-CHOO-min-a)	—	32	99757
Larsen Bay	1974	149	99624
Lazy Mountain	—	820	NA
Levelock (LEH-vuh-lock)	—	101	99625
Lignite	—	101	NA
Lime Village	—	51	99627
Long Island	—	177	NA
Lower Kalskag	1969	300	99626
Lutak	—	48	NA
Manley Hot Springs	—	104	99756
Manokotak (man-a-KO-tack)	1970	404	99628

Community	Year Incorporated	Population	Zip
Marshall	1970	278	99585
McCarthy	—	26	99588
McGrath	1975	531	99627
McKinley Park	—	176	99755
Meadow Lakes	—	2,431	NA
Mekoryuk (ma-KOR-ee-yuk)	1969	189	99630
Mendeltna	—	38	NA
Mentasta Lake	—	78	99780
Metlakatla	1944	1,498	99926
Meyers Chuck	—	39	99903
Minto	—	220	99758
Moose Creek	—	611	99705
Moose Pass	—	83	99631
Mosquito Lake	—	85	NA
Mountain Village	1967	727	99632
Naknek (NACK-neck)	—	581	99633
Napakiak (NAP-uh-keey-ack)	1970	323	99634
Napaskiak (na-PASS-kee-ack)	1971	362	99559
Naukati Bay	—	83	NA
Nelson Lagoon	—	93	99571
Nenana (nee-NA-na)	1921	406	99760
New Stuyahok (STU-ya-hock)	1972	396	99636
Newhalen	1971	161	99606
Newtok	1976	213	99559
Nightmute	1974	137	99690
Nikiski	—	2,833	99635
Nikolai	1970	107	99691
Nikolevsk	—	394	99556
Nikolski	—	35	99638
Ninilchik	—	480	99639
Noatak	—	344	99761
Nome	1901	3,519	99762
Nondalton	1971	212	99640
Noorvik	1964	520	99763
North Pole	1953	1,460	99705
Northway	—	119	99764
Northway Junction	—	93	NA
Northway Village	—	109	NA
Nuiqsut (noo-IK-sut)	1975	391	99789
Nulato	1963	364	99765
Nunapitchuk (NU-nuh-pit-CHUCK)	1969	390	99641
Nyac (NY-ack)	—	NA	99642
Old Harbor	1966	298	99643
Oscarville	—	59	99695
Ouzinkie (u-ZINK-ee)	1967	216	99644
Palmer	1951	3,008	99645
Paxson	—	32	99737
Pedro Bay	—	53	99647
Pelican	1943	231	99832
Pennock Island	—	108	99928
Perryville	—	116	99648
Petersburg	1910	3,349	99833
Pilot Point	1992	64	99649
Pilot Station	1969	470	99650
Pitkas Point	—	142	99658
Platinum	1975	54	99651
Pleasant Valley	—	404	NA

Community	Year Incorporated	Population	Zip
Point Baker	—	39	99927
Point Hope	1966	680	99766
Point Lay	—	138	99759
Polk Inlet	—	121	NA
Port Alexander	1974	119	99836
Port Alice	—	27	NA
Port Alsworth	—	50	99653
Port Clarence	—	26	99762
Port Graham	—	160	99603
Port Heiden	1972	126	99549
Port Lions	1966	238	99550
Port Protection	—	56	99950
Primrose	—	63	NA
Prudhoe Bay	—	46	99734
Quinhagak (QUIN-a-gak)	1975	511	99655
Rampart	—	65	99767
Red Devil	—	47	99656
Ridgeway	—	2,114	NA
Rowan Bay	—	138	99850
Ruby	1973	163	99768
Russian Mission	1970	266	99657
St. George	1983	178	99591
St. John Harbor	—	0	NA
St. Marys	1967	458	99658
St. Michael	1969	299	99659
St. Paul	1971	771	99660
Salamatof	—	1,032	99611
Salcha	—	350	99714
Sand Point	1966	892	99661
Savoonga (suh-VOON-guh)	1969	545	99769
Saxman	1930	379	99901
Saxman East	—	490	99901
Scammon Bay	1967	360	99662
Selawik (SELL-a-wick)	1977	597	99770
Seldovia	1945	302	99663
Seward	1912	2,806	99664
Shageluk (SHAG-a-look)	1970	144	99665
Shaktoolik (shack-TOO-lick)	1969	184	99771
Sheldon Point	1974	110	99666
Shishmaref (SHISH-muh-reff)	1969	466	99772
Shungnak (SHOONG-nack)	1967	224	99773
Sitka (City and Borough)	—	8,815	99835
Skagway	1900	735	99840
Skwentna	—	90	99667
Slana	—	65	99586
Sleetmute	—	103	99668
Soldotna	1967	3,652	99669
South Naknek	—	143	99670
Stebbins	1969	442	99671
Sterling	—	3,979	99472
Stevens Village	—	98	99774
Stony River	—	49	99557
Sutton	—	310	99674
Takotna (Tah-KOAT-nuh)	—	30	99675
Talkeetna (Tal-KEET-na)	—	256	99676
Tanacross	—	105	99776
Tanana (TAN-a-nah)	1961	353	99777

Community	Year Incorporated	Population	Zip
Tatitlek	—	108	99677
Teller	1963	254	99778
Tenakee Springs	1971	98	99841
Tetlin	—	85	99779
Thorne Bay	1982	614	99919
Togiak (TOE-gee-yack)	1969	615	99678
Tok (TOKE)	—	988	99780
Toksook Bay	1972	449	99637
Tonsina	—	38	99573
Trapper Creek	—	281	99683
Tuluksak (tu-LOOK-sack)	1970	371	99679
Tuntutuliak (TUN-too-TOO-li-ack)	—	299	99680
Tununak	1975	333	99681
Twin Hills	—	71	99576
Two Rivers	—	459	99716
Tyonek (ty-O-neck)	—	160	99682
Unalakleet (YOU-na-la-kleet)	1974	732	99684
Unalaska (UN-a-LAS-ka)	1942	3,450	99685
Valdez (val-DEEZ)	1901	4,279	99686
Venetie (VEEN-a-tie)	—	203	99781
Wainwright	1962	501	99782
Wales	1964	147	99783
Wasilla (wah-SIL-luh)	1974	4,124	99687
Whale Pass	—	67	99950
White Mountain	1969	182	99784
Whitestone Logging Camp	—	150	NA
Whittier	1969	278	99693
Willow	—	285	99688
Wrangell	1903	2,539	99929
Yakutat (YAK-a-tat)	1948	552	99689

Census Populations of Major Cities

City	1900	1920	1940	1950	1970	1980	1990
Anchorage	*	1,856	4,229	11,254	48,081	174,431	226,338
Barrow	*	*	*	*	2,104	2,207	3,469
Cordova	*	955	938	1,165	1,164	1,879	2,110
Fairbanks	*	1,155	3,455	5,771	14,771	22,645	30,843
Juneau	1,864	3,058	5,729	5,956	6,050	19,528	26,751
Kenai	290	332	303	321	3,533	4,324	6,327
Ketchikan	459	2,458	4,695	5,305	6,994	7,198	8,263
Kodiak	341	374	864	1,710	3,798	4,756	6,365
Nome	12,488	852	1,559	1,876	2,357	2,301	3,500
Petersburg	*	879	1,323	1,619	2,042	2,821	3,207
Seward	*	652	949	2,114	1,587	1,843	2,699
Sitka	1,396	1,175	1,987	1,985	6,075	7,803	8,588
Valdez	315	466	529	554	1,005	3,079	4,068
Wrangell	868	821	1,162	1,263	2,029	2,184	2,479

*Population figures unavailable. Source: Alaska Department of Labor

Population by Census Areas (See map on following page)

Map

Key	Census Area	1970	1980	1990
	Alaska	302,583	401,851	550,043
1	North Slope Borough	3,451	4,199	5,979
2	Northwest Arctic Borough	4,048	4,831	6,113
3	Nome	5,749	6,537	8,288
4	Yukon–Koyukuk	7,045	6,471	6,681

CENSUS AREAS

Map

Key	Census Area	1970	1980	1990
5	Fairbanks North Star Borough	45,864	53,983	77,720
6	Southeast Fairbanks	4,308	5,676	5,913
7	Wade Hampton	3,917	4,665	5,791
8	Bethel	8,917	10,999	13,656
9	Dillingham	2,510	3,232	4,012
10	Bristol Bay Borough	1,147	1,094	1,410
11	Aleutian Islands	7,834	7,768	11,942
12	Matanuska–Susitna Borough	6,509	17,816	39,683
13	Anchorage Borough	126,385	174,431	226,338
14	Kenai Peninsula Borough	16,586	25,282	40,802
15	Kodiak Island Borough	9,409	9,939	13,309
16	Valdez–Cordova	4,979	8,348	9,952
17	Skagway–Yakutat–Angoon	2,792	3,478	4,385
18	Haines Borough	1,401	1,680	2,117
19	Juneau Borough	13,556	19,528	26,751
20	Sitka Borough	6,073	7,803	8,588
21	Wrangell–Petersburg	4,920	6,167	7,042
22	Prince of Wales–Outer Ketchikan	3,782	3,822	6,278
23	Ketchikan Gateway Borough	10,041	11,316	13,828
24	Lake and Peninsula Borough	1,362	1,384	1,668
25	Denali Borough	NA	1,402	1,792
26	Aleutians East Borough	1,301	1,643	2,464
27	Aleutians West Borough	6,533	6,125	9,478

Source: March 15, 1992, estimates, Alaska Department of Labor

Potlatch

This Native gathering, primarily an Indian custom, is held to commemorate major life events. Traditional Native foods are served, songs and dances are performed and gifts are distributed to everyone who attends. A funeral potlatch might result in the giving away of the deceased's possessions to relatives or to persons who had done favors for the deceased during his or her lifetime.

Before the U.S. and Canadian governments outlawed the practice in the 1880s, potlatches were a focal point of Native society. The host family might give away all its possessions in an attempt to demonstrate its wealth to the guests. Each guest in turn would feel an obligation to hold an even bigger potlatch. The outlawing of potlatches resulted in the disintegration of all aspects of Native culture. Potlatch restrictions were repealed in 1951.

Radio Stations

Alaska's radio stations broadcast a wide variety of music, talk shows, religious and educational programs. Many radio stations in Alaska also broadcast personal messages, long a popular and necessary form of communication in Alaska—especially in the bush. It was in consideration of these messages—and the importance of radio stations in providing the sole source of vital weather information to fishermen and hunters—that the United States and Canada agreed to grant some Alaska radio stations international communication status. The "clear channel" status provides protection against interference from foreign broadcasters. Personal message broadcasts are heard on: KYAK's Bush Pipeline, **Anchorage**; KBRW's Tundra Drums, **Barrow**; KYUK's Tundra Drums, **Bethel**; KDLG's Bristol Bay Messenger, **Dillingham**; KIAK's Pipeline of the North, **Fairbanks**; KIYU's Yukon Wireless, **Galena**; KCAM's Caribou Clatter, **Glennallen**; KHNS's Listener Personals, **Haines**; KBBI's Bay Bush Lines, **Homer**; KRBD's Muskeg Messenger, **Ketchikan**; KTKN's Public Service Announcements, Ketchikan; KVOK-KJJZ-FM's Highliner Crabbers, **Kodiak**; KOTZ's Messages, **Kotzebue**; KSKO's Messages, **McGrath**; KICY's Ptarmigan Telegraph, **Nome**; KNOM's Hot Lines, **Nome**; KJNP's Trapline Chatter, **North Pole**; KFSK's Muskeg Messages, **Petersburg**; KRSA's Channel Chatters, **Petersburg**; KCAW-FM's Muskeg Messages, **Sitka**; KSRM's Tundra Tom Tom, **Soldotna**; and KSTK-FM's Radiograms, **Wrangell**.

A complete listing of Alaska's radio stations follows:

Anchorage
KASH-FM 107.5 MHz; 1300 E. 68th, Suite 208, 99518
KATB-FM 89.3 MHz; P.O. Box 210389, 99521
KBYR 700 kHz; **KNIK-FM** 105.3 MHz; P.O. Box 102200, 99510
KEAG-FM 97.3 MHz; 3700 Woodland Park Drive, Suite 300, 99517
KENI 550 kHz; **KBFX-FM** 100.5 MHz; 1777 Forest Park Drive, 99517
KFQD 750 kHz; **KWHL-FM** 106.5 MHz; 9200 Lake Otis Parkway, 99507
KHAR 590 kHz; **KBRJ-FM** 104.1 MHz; 11259 Tower Road., 99515
KJMM-FM 94.5 MHz; 3605 Arctic Blvd., Suite 945, 99503
KKSD 1080 kHz; 1300 E. 68th, Suite 208, 99518
KLEF-FM 98.1 MHz; 3601 C St., Suite 290, 99503
KPXR-FM 102.1 MHz; 3700 Woodland Drive, No. 300, 99517
KRUA-FM 88.1 MHz; 3211 Providence Drive, 99508
KSKA-FM 91.1 MHz; 4101 University Drive, 99508
KYAK 650 kHz; **KGOT-FM** 101.3 MHz; 2800 E. Dowling Road, 99507
KYMG-FM 98.9 MHz; 500 L St., Suite 200, 99501

Barrow
KBRW 680 kHz; P.O. Box 109, 99723

Bethel
KYKD-FM 100.1 MHz; P.O. Box 905, 99559
KYUK 640 kHz; P.O. Box 468, 99559

Cordova
KCHU-FM 88.1 MHz; P.O. Box 467, Valdez 99686

KLAM 1450 kHz; P.O. Box 60, 99574

Dillingham
KDLG 670 kHz; P.O. Box 670, 99576

Fairbanks
KAKQ-FM 101.1 MHz; 3504 Industrial Ave., 99701
KCBF 820 kHz; P.O. Box 950, 99707
KFAR 660 kHz; KWLF-FM 98.1 MHz; P.O. Box 70910, 99707
KIAK 970 kHz; KIAK-FM 1025 MHz; P.O. Box 73410, 99707
KSUA-FM 103.9 MHz; P.O. Box 83831, 99708
KUAC-FM 104.7 MHz; University of Alaska, 312 Tanana Drive, 99775
KUWL-FM 91.5 MHz; P.O. Box 70339, 99707
KWLF-FM 98.1 MHz; P.O. Box 70910
KXLR-FM 95.9 MHz; P.O. Box 950, 99707

Galena
KIYU 910 kHz; P.O. Box 165, 99741

Glennallen
KCAM 790 kHz; P.O. Box 249, 99588

Haines
KHNS-FM 102.3 MHz; P.O. Box 1109, 99827

Homer
KBBI 890 kHz; 3913 Kachemak Way, 99603
KGTL 620 kHz; KWVV-FM, 103.5 MHz; P.O. Box 103, 99603

Juneau
KINY 800 kHz; 1107 W. Eighth St., 99801
KJNO 630 kHz; 3161 Channel Drive, Suite 2, 99801
KSUP-FM 106.3 MHz; 1107 W. Eighth St., 99801
KTKU-FM 105.1 MHz; 3161 Channel Drive, Suite 2, 99801
KTOO-FM 104.3 MHz; 224 Fourth St., 99801

Kenai
KCZP-FM 91.9 MHz; P.O. Box 2111, 99611
KPEN-FM 101.7 MHz; P.O. Box 103, Homer 99603

KZXX 980 kHz; 6672 Kenai Spur Road, 99611

Ketchikan
KRBD-FM 105.9 MHz; 716 Totem Way, 99901
KTKN 930 kHz; KGTW-FM 106.7 MHz; 526 Stedman, 99901

Kodiak
KMXT-FM 100.1 MHz; 718 Mill Bay Road, 99615
KVOK 560 kHz; KJJZ-FM 101.1 MHz; P.O. Box 708, 99615

Kotzebue
KOTZ 720 kHz; P.O. Box 78, 99752

McGrath
KSKO 870 kHz; P.O. Box 70, 99627

Naknek
KAKN-FM 100.9 MHz; P.O. Box 0, 99633

Nenana
KIAM 630 kHz; P.O. Box 474, 99760

Nome
KICY 850 kHz; KICY-FM 100.3 MHz; P.O. Box 820, 99762
KNOM 780 kHz; P.O. Box 988, 99762

North Pole
KJNP 1170 kHz; KJNP-FM 100.3 MHz; P.O. Box 0, 99705

Petersburg
KFSK-FM 100.9 MHz; P.O. Box 149, 99833
KRSA 580 kHz; P.O. Box 650, 99833

St. Paul
KUHB-FM 91.9 MHz; Pouch 5, 99660

Sand Point
KSDP 840 kHz; P.O. Box 328, 99661

Seward
KSWD 950 kHz; P.O. Box 405, 99664

Sitka
KCAW-FM 104.7 MHz; 2-B Lincoln St., 99835

KIFW 1230 kHz; **KSBZ-FM** 103.1 MHz; P.O. Box 299, 99835

Soldotna
KSLD 1140 kHz; 374 Lovers Lane, 99669
KSRM 920 kHz; **KWHQ-FM** 100.1 MHz; R2, Box 852, 99669

Unalakleet
KNSA 930 kHz; P.O. Box 178, 99684

Unalaska
KIAL 1450 kHz; P.O. Box 181, 99685

Valdez
KCHU 770 kHz; P.O. Box 467, 99686
KVAK 1230 kHz; P.O. Box 367, 99686

Wasilla
KMBQ-FM 99.7 MHz; P.O. Box 871890, 99687

Whittier
KCHU-FM 88.3 MHz; P.O. Box 467, 99686

Wrangell
KSTK-FM 101.7 MHz; P.O. Box 1141, 99929

Yakutat
KJFP-FM 103.9 MHz; P.O. Box 388, 99689

In addition to the preceding commercial and public radio stations, the Detachment 8, Air Force Pacific Broadcasting Squadron at Elmendorf Air Force Base (Elmendorf AFB 99506) operates the Alaskan Forces Radio Network. AFRN is the oldest broadcast network in the U.S. military. It began in January 1942 on Kodiak Island, with a volunteer crew that pieced together a low-power station from second-hand parts, borrowed records and local talent. Eventually, the servicemen generated enough interest in Hollywood and Washington, D.C., to receive "official" status. Those early efforts resulted in the Armed Forces Radio and Television Service, a far-flung system of broadcast outlets serving U.S. forces around the world.

Nearly all the programming heard at AFRN locations in Alaska originates at Elmendorf AFB, although it is not broadcast in the Elmendorf vicinity. (In addition to network programming, Fort Greely originates about six hours of programming a day at its location.) Following is a list of AFRN outlets:

Fort Greely, **AFRN-FM** 90.5 MHz, 93.5 MHz

Galena Airport, **AFRN-FM** 90.5 MHz, 101.1 MHz

King Salmon Airport, **AFRN-FM** 90.5 MHz, 101.7 MHz

Shemya Air Force Base, **AFRN-FM** 90.5 MHz, 101.1 MHz

Tok Coast Guard Station, **AFRN-FM** 90.5 MHz, 101.1 MHz

Railroads

The Alaska Railroad is the northernmost railroad in North America and was for many years the only one owned by the United States government. Ownership now belongs to the state of Alaska. The ARR rolls on 470 miles of mainline track from the ports of Seward and Whittier to Anchorage, Cook Inlet and Fairbanks in the Interior.

The Alaska Railroad began in 1912 when Congress appointed a commission to study transportation problems in Alaska. In March 1914, the president authorized railroad lines in the territory of Alaska to connect open harbors on the southern coast of Alaska with the Interior. The Alaska Engineering Commission surveyed possible railroad routes in 1914 and, in April 1915, President Woodrow Wilson announced the selection of a route from Seward north 412 miles to the Tanana River (where Nenana is now located), with branch lines to Matanuska coal fields. The main line was later extended to Fairbanks. Construction of the railroad began in 1915. On July 15, 1923, President Warren G. Harding drove the golden spike, signifying completion of the railroad, at Nenana.

The railroad offers year-round passenger, freight and vehicle service. The ARR features flag-stop service along the Anchorage-to-Fairbanks corridor, as well as summer express trains to Denali National Park and Preserve.

Passenger service is daily between mid-May and early September, and in winter, weekly service is available between Anchorage and Fairbanks. A one-day excursion to Seward is provided daily, mid-May to early September. Additionally, daily service to Whittier is offered from May through September and four days a week in winter. In 1992, 473,240 passengers rode the Alaska Railroad. For more information contact The Alaska Railroad, P.O. Box 107500, Anchorage 99510.

The privately owned White Pass and Yukon Route provided a narrow-gauge link between Skagway, Alaska, and Whitehorse, Yukon Territory. At the time it was built—1898 to 1900—it was the farthest north any railroad had operated in North America. The railway maintained one of the steepest railroad grades in North America, climbing to 2,885 feet at White Pass in only 20 miles of track.

The White Pass and Yukon Route provided both passenger and freight service until 1982, when it suspended service. In May 1988, it began operating again as an excursion train only, going from Skagway to the summit of White Pass and eight miles beyond to Fraser, British Columbia. For more information contact the White Pass and Yukon Route, P.O. Box 435, Skagway 99840.

Regions of Alaska

Southeast

Southeast, Alaska's panhandle, stretches approximately 500 miles from Icy Bay, northwest of Yakutat, to Dixon Entrance at the United States–Canada border beyond the southern tip of Prince of Wales Island. Massive ice fields, glacier-scoured peaks and steep valleys, more than a thousand named islands, and numerous unnamed islets and reefs characterize this vertical world where few flat expanses break the steepness. Spruce, hemlock and cedar, the basis for the region's timber industry, cover many of the mountainsides.

Average temperatures range from 50°F to 60°F in July and from 20°F to 40°F in January. Average annual precipitation varies from 80 to more than 200 inches. The area receives from 30 to 200 inches of snow in the lowlands and more than 400 inches in the high mountains.

The region's economy revolves around fishing and fish processing, timber and tourism. Mining is taking on increasing importance with development of a world-class molybdenum mine near Ketchikan and a base metals mine on Admiralty Island.

Airplanes and boats provide the principal means of transportation. Only three communities in Southeast are connected to the road system: Haines via the Haines Highway to the Alaska Highway at Haines Junction; Skagway, via Klondike Highway 2 to the Alaska Highway; and Hyder, to the continental road system via the Cassiar Highway in British Columbia. Juneau, on the Southeast mainland, is the state capital; Sitka, on Baranof Island, was the capital of Russian America.

Southcentral/Gulf Coast

The Southcentral/Gulf Coast region curves 650 miles north and west of Southeast to Kodiak Island. About two-thirds of the state's residents live in the arc between the Gulf of Alaska on the south and the Alaska Range on the north, the region commonly called Southcentral. On the region's eastern boundary, only the Copper River valley breaches the mountainous barrier of the Chugach and Saint Elias mountains. On the west rise lofty peaks of the Aleutian Range. Within this mountainous perimeter course the Susitna and Matanuska rivers.

The irregular plain of the Copper River lowland has a colder climate than the other major valley areas, with January temperatures hitting –16°F compared with average lows of 0°F in the Susitna Valley. July temperatures average 50°F to 60°F in the region.

Precipitation in the region ranges from a scant 17 inches annually in drier areas to more than 76 inches a year at Thompson Pass in the coastal mountains.

Vegetation varies from the spruce-hemlock forests of Prince William Sound to mixed spruce and birch forests in the Susitna Valley to tundra in the highlands of the Copper River–Nelchina Basin.

Alaska agriculture historically has been most thoroughly developed in the Matanuska Valley. The state's dairy industry is centered there and at a new project at Point MacKenzie across Knik Arm from Anchorage. Vegetables thrive in the area and Matanuska Valley is well known for its giant cabbages.

Hub of the state's commerce, transportation and communications is Anchorage, on a narrow plain at the foot of the Chugach Mountains, and bounded by Knik Arm and Turnagain Arm, offshoots of Cook Inlet. The population of this, Alaska's largest, city is closely tied to shifts in the state's economy.

Alaska's major banks and oil companies have their headquarters in Anchorage, as does the Alaska Railroad. The city's port handles much of the shipping in and out of the state. Anchorage International Airport saw over 4.5 million passengers pass through in 1991. Valdez, to the east of Anchorage on Prince Willam Sound, is the southern terminal of the trans-Alaska pipeline, which brings oil from Prudhoe Bay on the North Slope.

Interior

Great rivers have forged a broad lowland, known as the Interior, in the central part of the state between the Alaska Range on the south and the Brooks Range on the north. The Yukon River carves a swath across the entire state. In the Interior, the Tanana, Porcupine, Koyukuk and several other rivers join with the Yukon to create summer and winter highways. South of the Yukon, the Kuskokwim River rises in the hills of the western Interior before beginning its meandering course across the Bering Sea coast region.

Winter temperatures in the Interior commonly drop to –50°F and –60°F. Ice fog sometimes hovers over Fairbanks and other low-lying communities when the temperature falls below zero. Controlled by the extremes of a continental climate, summers usually are warmer than in any other region; high temperatures are in the 80s and 90s. The climate is semi-arid, with about 12 inches of precipitation recorded annually.

Immense forests of birch and aspen bring vibrant green and gold to the Interior's landscape. Spruce cover many of the slopes and cottonwood thrive near river lowlands. But in northern and western reaches of the Interior, the North American taiga gives way to tundra. In highlands above tree line and in marshy lowlands, grasses and shrubs replace trees.

Gold lured the first large influx of non-Natives to Alaska's Interior. Fairbanks, largest community in the region, was once a booming gold-mining camp. Now the city on the banks of Chena

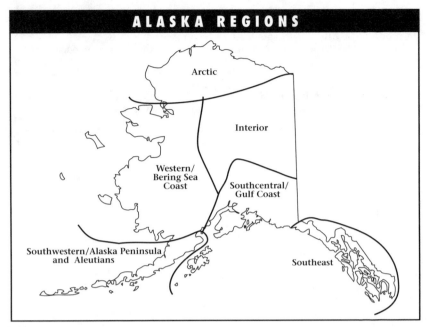

ALASKA REGIONS

Arctic

Interior

Western/
Bering Sea
Coast

Southcentral/
Gulf Coast

Southwestern/Alaska Peninsula
and Aleutians

Southeast

Slough is a transportation and supply center for eastern and northern Alaska. The main campus of the University of Alaska overlooks the city.

About 100 miles east of Fairbanks, farmers at the Delta project hope to build a foundation for agriculture based on barley. With barley for feed, Alaska farmers look for development of a beef cattle industry. At Healy, southwest of Fairbanks, the state's only operating coal mine produces coal used to generate electricity for the Interior. The rest of the Interior relies primarily on a subsistence economy, sometimes combined with a cash economy where fishing or seasonal government jobs are available.

Arctic

Beyond the Brooks Range, more than 80,000 square miles of tundra interlaced with meandering rivers and countless ponds spread out along the North Slope. In far northwestern Alaska, the Arctic curves south to take in Kotzebue and other villages of the Kobuk and Noatak river drainages.

Short, cool summers with temperatures usually between 30°F and 40°F allow the permanently frozen soil to thaw only a few inches. Winter temperatures range well below zero, but the Arctic Ocean moderates temperatures in coastal areas. Severe winds sweep along the coast and through mountain passes. The combination of cold and wind often drops the chill-factor temperature far below the actual temperature. Most areas receive less than 10 inches of precipitation a year, but the terrain is wet in summer because of little evaporation and frozen ground.

Traditionally the home of Inupiat Eskimos, the Arctic was inhabited by few non-Natives until oil was discovered at Prudhoe Bay in the 1960s. Today the region's economy is focused on Prudhoe Bay and neighboring Kuparuk oil fields. Petroleum-related jobs support most of the region's residents either directly or indirectly. Subsistence hunting and fishing fill any economic holes left by the oil industry.

The largest Inupiat Eskimo community in the world, Barrow is the center of commerce and government activity for the region. Airplanes, the major means of transportation, fan out from there to the region's far-flung villages.

The Dalton Highway, formerly the North Slope Haul Road, connects the

Arctic with the Interior. The 416-mile road is open to the public to Disaster Creek near Dietrich Camp, but north of Disaster Creek, only permit holders may travel the road. (*See* Dalton Highway)

Western/Bering Sea Coast

Western Alaska extends along the Bering Sea coast from the Arctic Circle south to where the Alaska Panhandle joins the mainland near Naknek on Bristol Bay. Home of Inupiat and Yup'ik Eskimos, the region centers around the immense Yukon–Kuskokwim river delta, the Seward Peninsula to the north and Bristol Bay to the south.

Summer temperatures range from the 30s to low 60s. Winter readings generally range from just above zero to the low 30s. Wind chill lowers temperatures considerably. Total annual precipitation is about 20 inches with northern regions drier than those to the south.

Much of the region is covered with tundra, although a band of forests covers the hills on the eastern end of the Seward Peninsula and Norton Sound. In the south near Bristol Bay, the tundra once again gives way to forests. In between, the marshy flatland of the great Yukon–Kuskokwim Delta spreads out for more than 200 miles.

Gold first attracted non-Natives to the hills and creeks of the Seward Peninsula. To the south, only a few anthropologists and wildlife biologists entered the world of the Yup'ik Eskimos of the delta. At the extreme south, fish, including the world's largest sockeye salmon run, drew fishermen to the riches of Bristol Bay.

The villages of western Alaska are linked by air and water, dogsled and snow machine. Commerce on the delta radiates out from Bethel, largest community in western Alaska. To the north, Nome dominates commerce on the Seward Peninsula, while several fishing communities take their livelihood from the riches of Bristol Bay.

Southwestern/Alaska Peninsula and Aleutians

Southwestern Alaska includes the Alaska Peninsula and Aleutian Islands. From Naknek Lake, the peninsula curves southwest about 500 miles to the first of the Aleutian Islands; the Aleutians continue south and west more than 1,000 miles. Primarily a mountainous region with about 50 volcanic peaks, only on the Bering Sea side of the peninsula does the terrain flatten out.

More than 200 islands, roughly 5,500 square miles in area, form the narrow arc of the Aleutians, which separate the North Pacific from the Bering Sea. Nearly the entire chain is in the Alaska Maritime National Wildlife Refuge. Unimak Island, closest to the Alaska Peninsula mainland, is 1,000 miles from Attu, the most distant island. Five major island groups make up the Aleutians, all of which are treeless except for a few scattered stands that have been transplanted on the islands.

The Aleutian climate is cool, with

summer temperatures up to the 50s and winter readings in the 20s and lower. Winds are almost constant and fog is common. Precipitation ranges from 21 to more than 80 inches annually. The peninsula's climate is somewhat warmer than the islands' in summer and cooler in winter.

Aleuts, original inhabitants of the chain, still live at Atka, Atka Island; Nikolski, Umnak Island; Unalaska, Unalaska Island; Akutan, Akutan Island; and False Pass, Unimak Island.

The quest for furs first drew Russians to the islands and peninsula in the 1700s. The traders conquered the Aleuts and forced them to hunt marine mammals. After the United States purchased Alaska, fur traders switched their efforts to fox farming. Many foxes were turned loose on the islands, where they flourished and destroyed native wildlife. With the collapse of the fur market in the 1920s and 1930s, the islands were left to themselves. This relative isolation was broken during World War II when Japanese military forces bombed Dutch Harbor and landed on Attu and Kiska islands. The United States military retook the islands, and after the war the government resettled Aleuts living in the western Aleutians to villages in the eastern Aleutians, closer to the mainland.

Today fishing provides the main economic base for the islands and the peninsula. Many Aleuts go to Bristol Bay to fish commercially in summer.

Religion

Nearly every religion practiced in American society is found in Alaska. Following is a list of addresses for some of the major ones:

Alaska Baptist Convention, 1750 O'Malley Road, Anchorage 99516

Alaska Moravian Church, Bethel 99559

Assemblies of God,1048 W. International Airport Road, Anchorage 99502

Baha'i Faith, 13501 Brayton Drive, Anchorage 99516

Christian Science Church, 1347 L St., Anchorage 99501

Church of God, 1348 Bennington Drive, Anchorage 99508

Church of Jesus Christ of Latter-day Saints, 13111 Brayton Drive, Anchorage 99516

Congregation Beth Sholom, 7525 E. Northern Lights Blvd., Anchorage 99504

Episcopal Diocese of Alaska, 1205 Denali Way, Fairbanks 99701

Presbyterian Churches, 616 W. 10th Ave., Anchorage 99501

Roman Catholic Archdiocese of Anchorage, 225 Cordova, Anchorage 99501

Russian Orthodox Diocese of Alaska, 414 Mission Road, Kodiak 99615

The Salvation Army, 726 E. Ninth Ave., Anchorage 99501

United Methodist Church, Alaska Missionary Conference, 3402 Wesleyan Drive, Anchorage 99508

Unity of Anchorage, 10821 Totem Road, Anchorage 99516

Reptiles

For all practical purposes, reptiles are not found in Alaska outside of captivity. The northern limits of North American reptilian species may be the latitude at which their embryos fail to develop during the summer. Three sightings of a species of garter snake, *Thamnophis sirtalis*, have been reported on the banks of the Taku River and Stikine River.

Rivers

(*See also* National Wild and Scenic Rivers)

Following are Alaska's 10 longest rivers (*see* map next page):

Map Key

1 Yukon, 1,400 miles*
2 Porcupine, 555 miles**
3 Koyukuk, 554 miles
4 Kuskokwim, 540 miles
5 Tanana, 531 miles
6 Innoko, 463 miles
7 Colville, 428 miles
8 Noatak, 396 miles
9 Kobuk, 347 miles
10 Birch Creek, 314 miles

*The Yukon flows about 1,400 miles in Alaska; the remainder is in Canada. It ranks fourth in North America in length (1,875 miles total), fifth in drainage area (327,600 square miles).

**The Porcupine, a major tributary of the Yukon River, flows from Canada into Alaska.

There are more than 3,000 rivers in Alaska. The major navigable Alaska inland waterways are as follows:

Chilkat—Navigable by shallow-draft vessels to village of Klukwan, 25 miles above mouth.

Kobuk—Controlling channel depth is about 5 feet through Hotham Inlet, 3 feet to Ambler and 2 feet to Kobuk Village, about 210 river miles.

Koyukuk—Navigable to Allakaket by vessels drawing up to 3 feet during normally high river flow and to Bettles during occasional higher flows.

Kuskokwim—Navigable (June 1 to September 30) by 18-foot draft ocean-going vessels from mouth upriver 65 miles to Bethel. Shallow-draft (4-foot) vessels can ascend river to mile 465. McGrath is at Mile 400.

Kvichak—The river is navigable for vessels of 10-foot draft to Alaganak River, 22 miles above the mouth of Kvichak River. Remainder of this river (28 miles) navigable by craft drawing 2 to 4 feet, depending on stage of river. Drains into Lake Iliamna, which is navigable an additional 70 miles.

Naknek—Navigable for vessels of 12-foot draft for 12 miles with adequate tide. Vessels with 3-foot draft can continue an additional 7.5 miles.

Noatak—Navigable (late May to mid-June) for shallow-draft barges to a point about 18 miles below Noatak village. Shallow-draft vessels can continue on to Noatak.

Nushagak—Navigable (June 1 to August 31) by small vessels of $2^1/_2$-foot draft to Nunachuak, about 100 miles above the mouth. Shallow-draft, ocean-going vessels can navigate to mouth of Wood River at mile 84.

Porcupine—Navigable to Old Crow, Yukon Territory, by vessels drawing 3 feet, during spring runoff and fall rain floods.

Stikine—Navigable (May 1 to October 15) from mouth 165 miles to Telegraph Creek, British Columbia, by shallow-draft, flat-bottom riverboats.

Susitna—Navigable by sternwheelers and shallow-draft, flat-bottom riverboats to confluence of Talkeetna River, 75 miles upstream, but boats cannot cross bars at mouth of river. Not navigable by ocean-going vessels.

Tanana—Navigable by shallow-draft

(4-foot), flat-bottom vessels and barges from the mouth to Nenana and by smaller river craft to the Chena River 201 miles above the mouth. Craft of 4-foot draft can navigate to Chena River on high water to University Avenue Bridge in Fairbanks.

Yukon—Navigable (June 1 to September 30) by shallow-draft, flat-bottom riverboats from the mouth to near the head of Lake Bennett. It cannot be entered or navigated by ocean-going vessels. Controlling depths are 7 feet to Stevens Village and 3 to 5 feet from there to Fort Yukon.

Roadhouses

An important part of Alaska history, roadhouses were modest quarters that offered bed and board to travelers along early-day Alaska trails. The majority provided accommodations for sled dog teams, as most travel occurred in winter. By 1920, there were roadhouses along every major transportation route in Alaska. Most roadhouses have vanished, though a few of the historic roadhouses survive, including: Sourdough Roadhouse on the Richardson Highway; Gakona Lodge on the Glenn Highway; Paxson Lodge at the junction of the Richardson and Denali highways; and Talkeetna Roadhouse. Several roadhouses are included in the National Register of Historic Places. Some of these historic roadhouses are occupied by modern businesses.

Rocks and Gems

(*See also* Gold; Jade; *and* Minerals and Mining)

Gemstones are not easy to find in Alaska—you have to hunt for them and often walk quite a distance. The easiest ones to collect are float-rocks that were scattered millions of years ago by glaciers. These rocks are found on ocean beaches and railroad beds, and in creeks and rivers all over Alaska. In most rock-hunting areas, every instance of high water, wind, heavy rain and a melting patch of snow and ice uncovers a new layer, so you can hunt in the same area over and over and make new finds.

The easiest gemstones to search out are in the crypto-crystalline group of quartz minerals. These gems have crystals not visible to the naked eye. They are the jaspers, agates, cherts and flints.

Thunder eggs, geodes and agatized wood (all in the chalcedony classification) occur in Alaska. Thunder eggs have a jasper rind enclosing an agate core; harder-to-find geodes usually have an agate rind with a hollow core filled with crystals; agatized and petrified woods come in various colors and often show the plant's growth rings. Sometimes even the bark or limb structure is visible on agatized and petrified woods.

Crystalline varieties of quartz can also be found: amethyst (purple), citrine (yellow), rose quartz (pink), rock crystal (clear) and smoky quartz (brown).

Other gems to search for in Alaska are: onyx, feldspar, porphyry, jade, serpentine, soapstone, garnet, rhodonite, sapphire, marble, amethyst, staurolite, malachite and covelite (blue copper).

Russian Alaska

(*See also* History)

Russian presence in Alaska began with the 1741 voyages of Vitus Bering and Alexei Chirikof. Their exploration of the Aleutian Islands and the Alaska mainland spurred dozens of voyages by Russian fur hunters, or *promyshlenniki*. By the mid-1800s, Russians had explored most of the coast of southern and southwestern Alaska and some of the Interior. Their interest in Alaska lay primarily in exploiting the rich fur resources of the region, especially sea otters and fur seals. In 1799, the Russian post known today as Old Sitka was established. That same year, a trade charter was granted to the Russian-American Company, a monopoly authorized by the Czar in 1790 to control activities in Alaska.

During the entire Russian period, which lasted from 1741 to 1867, there were rarely more than about 500 Russians in Alaska at any one time. Nevertheless, the Aleut, Eskimo and Indians whom the Russians encountered felt the devastating effects of foreign contact. Native populations declined drastically from introduced diseases. The population of the Aleut people, the first to succumb to Russian occupation, was reduced to less than 20 percent of the precontact level through warfare, disease and starvation. The Tlingit, Haida and Chugach may have been reduced by 50 percent. The Russians also brought to the new land their customs, religion and language, which, through subjugation and the efforts of the missionaries, brought great changes in traditional technologies, social patterns and religious beliefs.

In 1867, facing increasing competition and frustrated in their efforts to expand its territory, the Russians sold Alaska to the United States for $7.2 million.

Today, one of the foremost legacies of the Russian period is the Russian Orthodox Church, still a vital aspect of Native culture in Southwest, Southcentral and Southeast Alaska. Visitors to Kodiak, Sitka and smaller Native communities can see the familiar onion-shaped domes of the Russian Orthodox churches.

Related reading: *Where the Sea Breaks Its Back,* by Corey Ford. This epic story tells the history of early naturalist Georg W. Steller and the Russian exploration of Alaska. *See* ALASKA NORTHWEST LIBRARY in the back of the book.

School Districts

(*See also* Education)

Alaska's 54 public school districts served approximately 110,366 pre-elementary through 12th grade students in the 1990–91 school year. There are two types of school districts: city and borough school districts and Regional Educational Attendance Areas (REAA). The 33 city and borough school districts are located in municipalities, each contributing funds for the operation of its local schools. The 21 REAAs are located in the unorganized boroughs and have no local government to contribute funds to their schools. The REAAs are almost solely dependent upon state funds for school support.

City and borough school districts are supported by about 67 percent state, 25 percent local and 8 percent federal funding.

The Centralized Correspondence School (CCS), Alaska Department of Education, 3134 Channel Drive, No. 100, Juneau 99801-7897, provides courses by correspondence to students in grades K–12.

Following are the names and addresses of Alaska's 54 public school districts:

Adak Region Schools, PSC 486, Box 1234, FPO AP 96506-0005, Intra-Alaska Mail, Adak

Alaska Gateway Schools, Box 226, Tok 99780

Aleutian Region Schools, Pouch 790, Unalaska 99685

Aleutians East Borough Schools, P.O. Box 429, Sand Point 99661

Anchorage Schools, 4600 DeBarr Road, Box 196614, Anchorage 99519

Annette Island Schools, Box 7, Metlakatla 99926

Bering Strait Schools, Box 225, Unalakleet 99684

Bristol Bay Borough Schools, Box 169, Naknek 99633

Chatham Schools, Box 109, Angoon 99820

Chugach Schools, 165 E. 56th Ave., Suite D, Anchorage 99518

Copper River Schools, Box 108, Glennallen 99588

Cordova City Schools, Box 140, Cordova 99574

Craig City Schools, Box 800, Craig 99921

Delta/Greely Schools, Box 527, Delta Junction 99737

Dillingham City Schools, Box 170, Dillingham 99576

Fairbanks North Star Borough Schools, Box 71250, Fairbanks 99707

Galena City Schools, Box 299, Galena 99741

Haines Borough Schools, Box 1289, Haines 99827

Hoonah City Schools, Box 157, Hoonah 99829

Hydaburg City Schools, Box 109, Hydaburg 99922

Iditarod Area Schools, Box 90, McGrath 99627

Juneau City Schools, 10014 Crazy Horse Drive, Juneau 99801

Kake City Schools, Box 450, Kake 99830

Kashunamiut School District, 985 KSD Way, Chevak 99563

Kenai Peninsula Borough Schools, 148 N. Binkley St., Soldotna 99669

Ketchikan Gateway Borough Schools, Pouch Z, Ketchikan 99901

Klawock City Schools, Box 9, Klawock 99925

Kodiak Island Borough Schools, 722 Mill Bay Road, Kodiak 99615

Kuspuk Schools, Box 49, Aniak 99557

Lake and Peninsula Schools, Box 498, King Salmon 99613

Lower Kuskokwim Schools, Box 305, Bethel 99559

Lower Yukon Schools, Box 32089, Mountain Village 99632

Matanuska–Susitna Borough Schools, 125 W. Evergreen, Palmer 99645

Nenana City Schools, Box 10, Nenana 99760

Nome City Schools, Box 131, Nome 99762

North Slope Borough Schools, Box 169, Barrow 99723

Northwest Arctic Borough Schools, Box 51, Kotzebue 99752

Pelican City Schools, Box 90, Pelican 99832

Petersburg City Schools, Box 289, Petersburg 99833

Pribilof Schools, Pouch 5, St. Paul Island 99660

Railbelt School District, Drawer 280, Healy 99743

St. Marys School District, Box 171, St. Marys 99658

Sitka Borough Schools, Box 179, Sitka 99835

Skagway City Schools, Box 497, Skagway 99840

Southeast Island Schools, Box 8340, Ketchikan 99901

Southwest Region Schools, Box 90, Dillingham 99576

Tanana Schools, Box 89, Tanana 99777

Unalaska City Schools, Pouch 260, Unalaska 99685

Valdez City Schools, Box 398, Valdez 99686

Wrangell City Schools, Box 2319, Wrangell 99929

Yakutat City Schools, Box 427, Yakutat 99689

Yukon Flats Schools, Box 359, Fort Yukon 99740

Yukon/Koyukuk Schools, Box 309, Nenana 99760

Yupiit Schools, Box 100, Akiachak 99551

Shipping

Vehicles

Persons shipping vehicles between Washington and Anchorage are advised to shop around for the carrier that offers the services and rates most suited to the shipper's needs. Not all carriers offer year-round service and freight charges vary greatly depending upon the carrier, and the weight and height of the vehicle. Rates quoted here are only approximate. Sample fares per unit: northbound, Washington to Anchorage, under 66 inches in height, $934.39; over 66 inches and under 87 inches, $1,179.36. Southbound, Anchorage to Washington, any unit under 84 inches, $673.92. Fuel surcharges and terminal handling charges may be applied.

Not all carriers accept rented moving trucks and trailers, and a few of those that do accept them require authorization from the rental company to carry its equipment to Alaska. Check with the carrier and your rental company before booking service.

Make your reservation at least two weeks in advance, and prepare to have the vehicle at the carrier's loading facility two days prior to sailing. Carriers differ on what items they allow to travel inside the vehicle, from nothing at all to goods packaged and addressed separately. Coast Guard regulations forbid the transport of vehicles holding more than one-quarter tank of gas and none of the carriers listed allows owners to accompany their vehicles in transit. *Remember to have fresh antifreeze installed in your car or truck prior to sailing.*

At a lesser rate, you can ship your vehicle aboard a state ferry to southeastern ports. However, you must accompany your vehicle or arrange for someone to drive it on and off the ferry at departure and arrival ports.

Carriers that will ship cars, truck

campers, house trailers and motor-homes from Anchorage to Seattle/Tacoma include:

The Alaska Railroad, P.O. Box 107500, Anchorage 99510; phone (907) 265-2490.

Sea-Land Freight Service, Inc., 1717 Tidewater Ave., Anchorage 99501; phone (907) 274-2671, or vehicle rates hotline (907) 263-5900.

Totem Ocean Trailer Express, 2511 Tidewater Ave., Anchorage 99501; phone (907) 276-5868.

In the Seattle/Tacoma area, contact:

A.A.D.A. Systems, P.O. Box 2323, Auburn, WA 98071; phone (206) 762-7840.

Alaska Railroad, 2203 Airport Way S., Suite 215, Seattle, WA 98134; phone (206) 624-4234.

Sea-Land Service, Inc., 3600 Port of Tacoma Road, Tacoma, WA 98424; phone (206) 922-3100, or 1-800-426-4512 (outside Washington).

Totem Ocean Trailer Express, P.O. Box 24908, Seattle, WA 98124; phone (206) 628-9280 or 1-800-426-0074 (outside Washington, Alaska and Hawaii).

Vehicle shipment between south-eastern Alaska ports and Seattle is provided by:

Alaska Marine Lines, 5615 W. Marginal Way SW, Seattle, WA 98106; phone (206) 763-4244 or 1-800-443-4343 (serves Ketchikan, Wrangell, Petersburg, Sitka, Juneau, Haines, Skagway, Yakutat, Excursion Inlet and Hawk Inlet).

Boyer Alaska Barge Line, 7318 Fourth Ave. S., Seattle, WA 98108; phone (206) 763-8575 (serves Ketchikan and Wrangell).

Household Goods and Personal Effects

Many moving van lines have service to and from Alaska through their agency connections in most Alaska and Lower 48 cities. To initiate service, contact the van line agents nearest your starting point.

Northbound goods are shipped to Seattle and transferred through a port agent to a water-borne vessel for transportation to Alaska. Few shipments go over the road to Alaska. Southbound shipments are processed in a like manner through Alaska ports to Seattle, then on to the destination.

Haul-it-yourself companies provide service to Alaska for those who prefer to move their goods themselves. It is possible to ship a rented truck or trailer into southeastern Alaska aboard the carriers that accept privately owned vehicles (*see* Vehicles, *preceding*). A few of the carriers sailing between Seattle and Anchorage also carry rented equipment. However, shop around for this service, for it has not been common practice in the past—rates can be very high if the carrier does not yet have a specific tariff established for this type of shipment. *You will not be allowed to accompany the rented equipment.*

Sitka Slippers

Also known as Alaska tennis shoes, Wrangell sneakers or Petersburg sneakers, Sitka slippers are heavy-duty rubber boots worn by residents of rainy southeastern Alaska.

Skiing

Both cross-country and downhill skiing are popular forms of outdoor recreation in Alaska from November through May. There are developed ski facilities in several Alaska communities, backcountry powder skiing is available by charter helicopter or ski-equipped aircraft and cross-country skiing opportunities are virtually limitless throughout the state. It is also possible to ski during the summer months by chartering a plane to reach glacier skiing spots.

In the 1992 Winter Olympics, Hilary Lindh of Juneau turned all eyes to the state of Alaska when she won the silver medal for the downhill. This was the first individual merit Olympic medal that an Alaskan has ever won.

Anchorage

There are two major downhill ski areas in the Anchorage area: Alyeska Resort and Alpenglow at Arctic Valley. Alyeska Resort, 40 miles southeast of Anchorage, is the state's largest ski resort, offering five chair lifts with runs up to a mile long. Chair No. 3 is equipped for night skiing and a fifth chair lift is reserved for racer training. The resort also has two rope tows and cross-country skiing.

During the spring of 1993, Alyeska Resort began extensive reconstruction and remodeling. Under construction is the Alyeska Prince Hotel, a structure of more than 300 rooms, which will open early in 1995. The seven-story structure will include formal and informal restaurants, an indoor pool, exercise and health facilities, and meeting rooms.

A new, high-speed gondola capable of carrying 65 passengers at a time to a restaurant high on the slopes is to open to the public before the close of 1993.

Landscaping work is also in progress, including a lake between the hotel and the mountain base that will double as a skating rink for winter guests.

Alyeska is open year-round, with skiing from November through April and sightseeing during the summer. Hours of operation depend on daylight, except for chair No. 3.

Alpenglow, a few miles from Anchorage, is owned and operated by the Anchorage Ski Club, a nonprofit corporation. Arctic Valley is open on winter weekends and holidays. Facilities include two double chair lifts, a T-bar/Poma lift combination and three rope tows on beginner slopes.

Several smaller alpine slopes maintained by the municipality of Anchorage include: Far North Bicentennial Park; Russian Jack Springs Park, with rope tows; and Hilltop, south of town, featuring the closest chair lift to the Anchorage area.

There are several popular cross-country ski trails in the Anchorage area in city parks that are maintained by the municipality. These include: Russian Jack Springs, with nearly 5 miles of trails, all lighted; Kincaid Park, site of the first World Cup and U.S. National races in Alaska and the U.S. in March 1983, with 24 miles of trails, 6 miles lighted, and a warm-up facility; Far North Bicentennial Park, with 3 miles of trails, about 2 miles lighted; Hillside Park, with 10.8 miles of trails, 1.5 miles lighted; Tony Knowles Coastal Trail, with 9 miles of trails, none lighted; and Chester Creek Greenbelt, with 10 kilometers of trails, none lighted. Cross-country skiers can find trails in Chugach State Park and in the Turnagain Pass area in Chugach National Forest, about 57 miles south of Anchorage.

Palmer

Hatcher Pass, site of the Independence Mine State Park, north of Palmer, is an excellent cross-country ski area with several maintained trails. The lodge has a coffee shop and warm-up area. The ski area is open from October through May.

Fairbanks

Fairbanks has a few downhill ski areas, but none as large as Alyeska resort. Cleary Summit and Skiland, about 20 miles from town on the Steese Highway, both privately owned and operated, have rope tows, with a chair lift at Cleary Summit; Ski Boot Hill at 4.2 mile on Farmer's Loop Road has a rope tow; Birch Hill, located on Fort Wainwright, is mainly for military use; the University of Alaska has a small slope and rope tow; and Chena Hot Springs Resort at mile 57 on the Chena Hot Springs Road has a small alpine ski area that uses a tractor to transport skiers to the top of the hill.

Popular cross-country ski trails in the Fairbanks area include: Birch Hill recreation area, about 3 miles north of town on the Steese Expressway to a well-marked turnoff, then 2 miles in; the University of Alaska, Fairbanks, with 26 miles of trails that lead out to Ester Dome; Creamers Field trail near downtown; Salcha cross-country ski area, about 40 miles south of town on the Richardson Highway, with a fairly large trail system also used for ski races; Two Rivers trail area, near the elementary school at mile 10 Chena Hot Springs Road; and Chena Hot Springs Resort, offering cross-country ski trails for both novice and more experienced skiers.

Juneau

Eaglecrest Ski Area on Douglas Island, 12 miles from Juneau, has a 4,800-foot-long chair lift, a Platter Pull lift, a 3,000-foot-long chair lift and a day lodge. Cross-country ski trails are also available. Eaglecrest is open from November to May. A few smaller alpine ski areas are located at Cordova, Valdez, Ketchikan and Homer. All have rope tows.

Several cross-country ski races are held each year. The largest, the Alaska Nordic Ski Cup Series, determines contestants for the Arctic Winter Games and Junior Olympic competitions. The series of five races is held in Anchorage, Homer, Salcha and Fairbanks. The World Masters Cross Country Ski Championships also were held in Anchorage in February 1992, and Valdez is now home to the World Extreme Ski Championships in April.

Skin Sewing

(*See also* Beadwork; Mukluks; *and* Parka)

The craft of sewing tanned hides and furs was a highly developed skill

among Alaska's Natives. Although commercially made garments are now often worn by Eskimo villagers, women who are exceptional skin sewers still not only ensure the safety of family members who must face the harsh outdoors, but are regarded as a source of pride for the entire community.

Sewers place great importance on the use of specific materials, some of which are only available seasonally. For instance, winter-bleached sealskin can only be tanned during certain seasons. Blood, alder bark and red ochre are traditionally used for coloring on garments and footgear. Most sewers prefer sinew as thread, although in some areas sinew cannot be obtained and waxed thread or dental floss is substituted. Skins commonly used for making parkas and mukluks include seal, reindeer, caribou and polar bear. Wolf and wolverine are prized for ruffs.

Parka styles, materials used and ornamentation (such as pieced calfskin or beadwork trim) vary from village to village, and between Yup'ik, Inupiat and Siberian Yup'ik sewers. The cut of parkas changes from north to south.

In most regions, mukluk styles and material vary with changes in season and weather conditions. The mukluks advertise the skill of their makers and the villages where they were made.

The manufacture of children's toys, primarily clothed dolls and intricately sewn balls, still reflects the traditional ingenuity of skin sewers.

Skookum

Skookum is a word meaning strong or serviceable. It originated with the

Chehalis Indians of western Washington and was incorporated into the Chinook jargon, a trade language dating from the early 1800s. A skookum chuck is a narrow passage between a saltwater lagoon and the open sea. In many areas of Alaska, because of extreme tides, skookum chucks may resemble fast-flowing river rapids during changes of the tide.

Soapstone

This soft, easily worked stone is often carved into art objects by Alaskans. Most of the stone, however, is imported. Alaska soapstone is mined in the Matanuska Valley by blasting. This process creates in the stone a tendency to fracture when being worked; therefore, it is not as desirable as imported soapstone.

Sourdough

Carried by many early-day pioneers, this versatile, yeasty mixture was used to make bread and hot cakes. Sourdough cookery remains popular in Alaska today. Because the sourdough supply is replenished after each use, it can remain active and fresh indefinitely. A popular claim of sourdough cooks is that their batches trace back to pioneers at the turn of the century. The name also came to be applied to any Alaska or Yukon old-timer.

Related reading: *Alaska Sourdough: The Real Stuff by a Real Alaskan,* by Ruth Allman. *Cooking Alaskan,* hundreds of time-tested recipes, including a

section on sourdough. *See* ALASKA NORTHWEST LIBRARY at the back of the book.

Speed Limits

The basic speed law in Alaska states the speed limit is "no speed more than is prudent and reasonable."

The maximum speeds are 15 miles per hour in an alley, 20 miles per hour in a business district or school zone, 25 miles per hour in a residential area and 55 miles per hour on any other roadway.

Locally, municipalities and the state may, and often do, reduce or alter maximums as long as no maximum exceeds 55 miles per hour.

Squaw Candy

Squaw candy is salmon that has been dried or smoked for a long time until it's very chewy. It's a staple food in winter for rural Alaskans and their dogs.

State Forest

Created in 1983, the 1.81 million-acre Tanana Valley State Forest is located almost entirely within the Tanana River basin and includes 200 miles of the Tanana River. It extends from near the Canadian border approximately 265 miles west to Manley Hot Springs, encompasses areas as far south as Tok, and is interspersed with private and other state lands throughout the basin. The Bonanza Creek Experimental Forest near Nenana is located within the state forest.

Hardwood and hardwood-spruce trees dominate almost 90 percent of the forest, and 22 percent (392,000 acres) is suitable for harvest. There are 44 rivers, streams and lakes within the forest with significant fish, wildlife, recreation and water values. Nearly all of the land will remain open for mineral development.

Approximately 85 percent of the forest is located within 20 miles of a highway, making it one of the more accessible public lands in the Interior. Rivers and trails throughout the river basin provide additional access to areas in the forest. The Eagle Trail State Recreation Site is the only developed facility in the Tanana Valley State Forest and has 40 campsites. For more information, contact the Regional Forester, Northcentral District, 3726 Airport Way, Fairbanks 99701.

State Park System

The Alaska State Park system began in July 1959 with the transfer of federally managed campgrounds and recreation sites from the Bureau of Land Management to the new state of Alaska. These sites were managed by the state Division of Lands until 1970—under Forestry, Parks and Recreation until 1966, then under Parks and Recreation. The Division of Parks was created in October 1970.

The Alaska State Park system consists of approximately 116 individual units divided into six park management districts. There are 47 recreation sites, 15 recreation areas, 6 historic parks, 3 historic sites, 2 state trails, 7 state parks (Chugach, Denali, Chilkat, Kachemak Bay, Point Bridget, Shuyak Island and Wood-Tikchik), 1 wilderness park, 1 special management area, 1 preserve, and 33 marine parks. The Kenai River Special Management Area is renowned for its salmon fishing. The 49,000-acre Alaska Chilkat Bald Eagle Preserve has the world's largest concentration of bald eagles. Wood-Tikchik State Park is Alaska's most remote state park and, with 1.5 million acres of wilderness, is the largest state park in the United States.

Campsites are available on a first-come, first-served basis usually for $6 or $8 per night. Fee exceptions are Eagle River Campground (Chugach State Park) and Chena River State Recreation Site for $12, and Eklutna Lake Campground (Chugach State Park) and Willow Creek State Recreation Area for $10. Daily use of improved boat launches varies from $3 to $5. Use of sanitary dump stations is $3. These are located at Chena River SRS, Harding Lake SRA and Ninilchick SRA. A yearly camping pass is also available for $75. A yearly boat launch pass is $50. If both passes are purchased at once, total cost is $100. In addition to camping and picnicking, many units offer hiking trails, boating and fishing, as well as winter activities. Most developed campgrounds have picnic tables, firepits, water and latrines. General information on the state park system is available from the Division of Parks, P.O. Box 107005, Anchorage 99510-7005.

State park units are managed by six area offices and are listed on the following pages. Designations for units of the Alaska State Park system are abbreviated as follows: SP–State Park, SHP–State Historical Park, SHS–State Historic Site, SMA–Special Management Area, SRA–State Recreation Area, SRS–State Recreation Site, ST–State Trail, SMP–State Marine Park, P–Preserve, WP–Wilderness Park, PUF–Public Use Facility. Park units designated "undeveloped" may have camping, hiking trails and limited facilities. Parks that indicate no developed campsites or picnic sites may offer fishing or river access, hiking and other activities. (*See* map pages 174–75)

Map Key	Acreage	Campsites	Picnic Sites	Public-Use Cabins	Nearest Town
Southeast District (400 Willoughby Building, Juneau 99801)					
1 Totem Bight SHP	11	—	—	—	Ketchikan
2 Refuge Cove SRS	13	—	14	—	Ketchikan
3 Settlers Cove SRS	38	12	—	—	Ketchikan
4 Pioneer Park SRS	3	—	—	—	Sitka
5 Baranof Castle SHS	1	—	—	—	Sitka
6 Halibut Point SRS	22	—	9	—	Sitka
7 Old Sitka SHP	51	—	—	—	Sitka
8 Juneau Trail Sys. ST	15	—	—	—	Juneau
9 Johnson Creek SRS	65	—	—	—	Juneau
10 Wickersham SHS	0.5	—	—	—	Juneau

171

Map Key	Acreage	Campsites	Picnic Sites	Public-Use Cabins	Nearest Town
11 Point Bridget SP	2,800	—	—	1	Juneau
12 Chilkoot Lake SRS	80	32	—	—	Haines
13 Portage Cove SRS	7	9	3	—	Haines
14 Chilkat SP	6,045	15	—	—	Haines
15 AK–Chilkat Bald Eagle P	49,320	—	—	—	Haines
16 Mosquito Lake SRS	5	10	—	—	Haines
17 Gruening SHP	12	—	—	—	Juneau
18 Dall Bay SMP	585	—	—	—	Ketchikan
19 Thom's Place SMP	1,198	—	—	—	Wrangell
20 Beecher Pass SMP	660	—	—	—	Wrangell
21 Joe Mace Island SMP	62	—	—	—	Wrangell
22 Security Bay SMP	500	—	—	—	Petersburg
23 Taku Harbor SMP	700	—	—	—	Juneau
24 Oliver Inlet SMP	560	—	—	1	Juneau
25 Funter Bay SMP	162	—	—	—	Juneau
26 Shelter Island SMP	3,560	—	6	—	Juneau
27 St. James Bay SMP	1,022	—	—	—	Juneau
28 Sullivan Island SMP	2,163	—	—	—	Juneau
29 Chilkat Islands SMP	6,560	—	—	—	Haines
30 Magoun Islands SMP	1,135	—	—	—	Sitka
31 Big Bear/Baby Bear SMP	1,023	—	—	—	Sitka

Northern District (3700 Airport Way, Fairbanks 99709)

Map Key	Acreage	Campsites	Picnic Sites	Public-Use Cabins	Nearest Town
32 Tok River SRS	38	50	—	—	Tok
33 Eagle Trail SRS	640	45	4	—	Tok
34 Moon Lake SRS	22	15	—	—	Tok
35 Fielding Lake SRS	600	7	—	—	Delta Junction
36 Donnelly Creek SRS	42	12	—	—	Delta Junction
37 Clearwater SRS	27	18	—	—	Delta Junction
38 Delta SRS	7	22	6	—	Delta Junction
39 Big Delta SHP	10	25	5	—	Delta Junction
40 Quartz Lake SRA	600	88	6	1	Delta Junction
41 Birch Lake SRS	191	10	—	—	Delta Junction
42 Harding Lake SRA	169	125	35	—	Delta Junction
43 Salcha River SRS	61	95	5	—	Delta Junction
44 Chena River SRS	27	63	30	—	Fairbanks
45 Chena River SRA	254,080	61	13	4	Fairbanks
46 Upper Chatanika Rvr SRS	73	35	—	—	Fairbanks
47 Lower Chatanika Rvr SRA	570	80	9	—	Fairbanks

Mat-Su/Copper Basin District (HC 32, Box 6706, Wasilla 99687)

Map Key	Acreage	Campsites	Picnic Sites	Public-Use Cabins	Nearest Town
48 Denali SP	324,240	93	35	—	Talkeetna
49 Montana Creek SRS	82	89	28	—	Talkeetna
50 Willow Creek SRA	3,583	152	—	—	Willow
51 Nancy Lake SRA	22,685	98	26	12	Willow
52 Nancy Lake SRS	36	30	30	—	Willow
53 Rocky Lake SRS	48	10	—	—	Wasilla
54 Big Lake North SRS	19	60	24	—	Wasilla
55 Big Lake South SRS	16	20	10	—	Wasilla
56 Kepler-Bradley Lakes SRA	344	—	10	—	Palmer
57 Finger Lake SRS	47	41	10	—	Palmer
58 Wolf Lake SRS	23	4	4	—	Palmer
59 Independence Mine SHP	761	—	—	—	Palmer
60 Summit Lake SRS	360	—	—	—	Palmer
61 Moose Creek SRS	40	12	4	—	Palmer
62 King Mountain SRS	20	22	2	—	Palmer

Map Key	Acreage	Campsites	Picnic Sites	Public-Use Cabins	Nearest Town
63 Bonnie Lake SRS	129	8	—	—	Palmer
64 Long Lake SRS	480	9	—	—	Palmer
65 Matanuska Glacier SRS	229	12	—	—	Palmer
66 Little Nelchina SRS	22	11	—	—	Glennallen
67 Lake Louise SRA	90	60	—	—	Glennallen
68 Dry Creek SRS	372	58	4	—	Glennallen
69 Porcupine Creek SRS	240	12	—	—	Tok
70 Liberty Falls SRS	10	10	—	—	Chitina
71 Squirrel Creek SRS	350	23	—	—	Copper Center
72 Little Tonsina SRS	103	8	—	—	Copper Center
73 Worthington Glacier SRS	113	—	—	—	Valdez
74 Blueberry Lake SRS	192	15	—	—	Valdez

Chugach/Southwest District (HC 52, Box 8999, Indian 99540)

Map Key	Acreage	Campsites	Picnic Sites	Public-Use Cabins	Nearest Town
75 Chugach SP	495,204	127	82	—	Anchorage
76 Potter Section House SHS	0.5	—	—	—	Anchorage
77 Wood–Tikchik SP	1,555,200	3	—	—	Dillingham

Kenai Peninsula District (P.O. Box 1247, Soldotna 99669)

Map Key	Acreage	Campsites	Picnic Sites	Public-Use Cabins	Nearest Town
78 Bettles Bay SMP	680	—	—	—	Whittier
79 Zeigler Cove SMP	720	—	—	—	Whittier
80 Surprise Cove SMP	2,280	—	—	—	Whittier
81 S. Esther Island SMP	3,360	—	—	—	Whittier
82 Horseshoe Bay SMP	970	—	—	—	Seward
83 Sawmill Bay SMP	2,320	—	—	—	Valdez
84 Shoup Bay SMP	4,560	—	—	—	Valdez
85 Jack Bay SMP	811	—	—	—	Valdez
86 Boswell Bay SMP	799	—	—	—	Cordova
87 Canoe Passage SMP	2,735	—	—	—	Cordova
88 Decision Point SMP	460	—	—	—	Whittier
89 Entry Cove SMP	370	—	—	—	Whittier
90 Granite Bay SMP	2,105	—	—	—	Whittier
91 Kayak Island SMP	1,437	—	—	—	Cordova
92 Driftwood Bay SMP	840	—	—	—	Seward
93 Safety Cove SMP	660	—	—	—	Seward
94 Sandspit Point SMP	600	—	—	—	Seward
95 Sunny Cove SMP	300	—	—	—	Seward
96 Thumb Cove SMP	300	—	—	—	Seward
97 Kenai River SMA	2,770	138	5	—	Sterling
98 Caines Head SRA	5,961	4	4	1	Seward
99 Bernice Lake SRS	152	11	1	—	Kenai
100 Captain Cook SRA	3,466	65	70	—	Kenai
101 Crooked Creek SRS	49	75	30	—	Soldotna
102 Kasilof River SRS	50	16	—	—	Soldotna
103 Johnson Lake SRA	324	50	25	—	Soldotna
104 Clam Gulch SRA	129	116	—	—	Soldotna
105 Ninilchik SRA	97	165	—	—	Homer
106 Deep Creek SRA	155	300	—	—	Homer
107 Stariski SRS	30	13	—	—	Homer
108 Anchor River SRA	213	75	—	—	Homer
109 Anchor River SRS	53	9	—	—	Homer
110 Kachemak Bay SP&WP	368,290	8	1	1	Homer
111 Fort Abercrombie SHP	183	13	—	—	Kodiak

(Continued on page 176)

STATE PARKS

(Numbers refer to accompanying list)

P = Preserve
PUF = Public Use Facility
SHP = State Historical Park
SHS = State Historic Site
SMA = Special Management
 Area
SMP = State Marine Park
SP = State Park
SRA = State Recreation Area
SRS = State Recreation Site
ST = State Trail
WP = Wilderness Park

NORTHERN

Circle

Elliott Highway

Steese Highway

Fairbanks

Alaska

Delta Junction

Alaska Highway

Tok Junctio

George Parks Highway

Denali

Richardson Highway

Paxson

Highway

Highway

COPPER
BASIN

MAT-SU

Glennallen

SOUTHCENTRAL

Glenn

Edgerton Highway

Palmer

CHUGACH

Valdez

Richardson Highway

Anchorage

Kenai

Soldotna

Sterling Highway

Seward

Seward
Highway

Homer

KENAI
PENINSULA

Kodiak

KODIAK

SOUTH-WEST
77

Area shown in detail

Alaska Highway

Alaska Highway

Haines Highway

Klondike Highway 2

15 16 Skagway
12
Haines 14
13 29
28 11 8 9 10 17
27 Juneau
26 23
25 24
31
4 5 6 7
30 Sitka

22 20 Wrangell
21 19
1 2 3
SOUTHEAST Ketchikan
18

(Continued from page 173)

Map Key	Acreage	Campsites	Picnic Sites	Public-Use Cabins	Nearest Town
Kodiak District (SR Box 3800, Kodiak 99615)					
112 Buskin River SRS	196	15	—	—	Kodiak
113 Pasagshak SRS	20	10	—	—	Kodiak
114 Shuyak Island SP	11,000	—	—	4	Kodiak

State Symbols

Flag

Alaska's state flag was designed in 1926 by Benny Benson, a seventh-grade student who entered his design in a territorial flag contest. The Alaska Legislature adopted his design as the official flag of the Territory of Alaska on May 2, 1927.

The flag consists of eight gold stars—the Big Dipper and the North Star—on a field of blue. In Benny Benson's words, "The blue field is for the Alaska sky and the forget-me-not, an Alaska flower. The North Star is for the future state of Alaska, the most northerly of the Union. The Great Bear—symbolizing strength."

Alaska was proclaimed the 49th state of the Union on Jan. 3, 1959. The drafters of the constitution for

redesigned the original seal, which became a symbol for the new Territory of Alaska in 1912. The constitution of Alaska adopted the territorial seal as the Seal for the State of Alaska in 1959.

Represented in the state seal are icebergs, northern lights, mining, agriculture, fisheries, fur seal rookeries and a railroad. The seal is $2^1/8$ inches in diameter.

Song

Alaska's Flag

Eight stars of gold on a field of blue—
Alaska's flag.
May it mean to you the blue of the sea, the
evening sky,
The mountain lakes, and the flow'rs
nearby;
The gold of the early sourdough's dreams,
The precious gold of the hills and streams;
The brilliant stars in the northern sky,
The "Bear"—the "Dipper"—and, shining
high,
The great North Star with its steady light,
Over land and sea a beacon bright.
Alaska's flag—to Alaskans dear,
The simple flag of a last frontier.

The lyrics were written by Marie Drake as a poem that first appeared on the cover of the October 1935 *School Bulletin*, a territorial Department of Education publication that she edited while assistant commissioner of education.

The music was written by Mrs.

Alaska stipulated that the flag of the territory would be the official flag of the state of Alaska. When the flag was first flown over the capital city on July 4, 1959, Benny Benson proudly led the parade that preceded the ceremony, carrying the flag of eight stars on a field of blue, which he had designed 33 years before.

Seal

The first governor of Alaska designed a seal for the then-District of Alaska in 1884. In 1910, Gov. Walter E. Clark

Elinor Dusenbury, whose husband, Col. Ralph Wayne Dusenbury, was commander of Chilkoot Barracks at Haines from 1933 to 1936. Mrs. Dusenbury wrote the music several years after leaving Alaska because, she was later quoted as saying, "I got so homesick for Alaska I couldn't stand it." She died Oct. 17, 1980, in Carlsbad, California.

The territorial legislature adopted *Alaska's Flag* as the official song in 1955.

Other Symbols

Bird: Willow ptarmigan, *Lagopus lagopus*, a small arctic grouse that lives among willows and on open tundra and muskeg. Its plumage changes from brown in summer to white in winter; feathers cover the entire lower leg and foot. Common from southwestern Alaska into the Arctic. Adopted in 1955.

Fish: King salmon, *Oncorhynchus tshawytscha*, an important part of the Native subsistence fisheries and a significant species to the state's commercial salmon fishery. This anadromous fish

ranges from beyond the southern extremes of Alaska to as far north as Point Hope. Adopted in 1962.

Flower: Forget-Me-Not. Adopted in 1949.

Fossil: Woolly mammoth. Adopted in 1986.

Gem: Jade. (*See* Jade.) Adopted in 1968.

Marine Mammal: Bowhead whale. Adopted in 1983.

Mineral: Gold. (*See* Gold.) Adopted in 1968.

Motto: North to the Future, adopted in 1967.

Sport: Dog mushing. (*See* Dog Mushing.) Adopted in 1972.

Tree: Sitka spruce, *Picea sitchensis*, the largest and one of the most valuable trees in Alaska. Sitka spruce grows to 160 feet in height and 3 to 5 feet in diameter. Its long, dark-green needles surround twigs that bear cones. It is found throughout Southeast and the Kenai Peninsula, along the Gulf Coast, and along the west coast of Cook Inlet. Adopted in 1962.

Subsistence

Alaska is unique among states in that it has established the subsistence use of fish and game as the highest priority consumptive use of the resource. Alaska's legislature passed subsistence priority laws in 1978 and 1986. In addition, Congress passed a priority subsistence law in 1980 for federal lands in Alaska. Studies by the Alaska Department of Fish and Game have shown that many rural communities in Alaska depend upon subsistence hunting and fishing for a large portion of their diets.

Subsistence, a controversial issue and a difficult concept to define, is defined by federal law as "the customary and traditional uses by rural Alaska residents of wild, renewable resources for direct personal or family consumption as food, shelter, fuel, clothing, tools or transportation; for the making and selling of handicraft articles out of nonedible by-products of fish and wildlife resources taken for personal or family consumption; and for the customary trade, barter or sharing for personal or family consumption."

According to Alaska State Subsistence Statutes passed in 1986, only rural residents can be considered subsistence users. In addition to the rural requirement, subsistence uses can be identified by a variety of other criteria, such as long-term traditional use, local area use and frequent sharing of harvests. Subsistence also depends upon the biological status of fish and game resources, and is not authorized if harvesting will damage the resources.

In December 1989, the Alaska Supreme Court ruled that the rural subsistence preference in the state law was unconstitutional. This placed the state out of compliance with requirements of the federal law. Consequently, the federal government took over management of subsistence on federal lands in Alaska on July 1, 1990, and began to develop its own set of subsistence regulations. Although the state desires to regain this management authority, no resolution to the issue was reached in 1992.

State subsistence fishing regulations are available as a separate pamphlet from the Alaska Department of Fish and Game, P.O. Box 3-2000, Juneau 99802. State subsistence hunting regulations are included with the annually published state hunting regulations, also available from the Alaska Department of Fish and Game.

Sundog

Sundogs are "mock suns" (parhelia) usually seen as bright spots on opposite sides of the winter sun. This optical phenomenon is created by the refraction of sunlight through tiny ice crystals suspended in the air. The ice crystals are commonly called "diamond dust."

Taiga

Taiga is a moist coniferous forest that begins where the tundra ends. Taken from a Russian word that means "land of little sticks," this name is applied to the spindly white spruce and black spruce forests found in much of southcentral and interior Alaska.

Telecommunications

History

Alaska's first telecommunications project, begun in the 1860s, was designed to serve New York, San Francisco and the capitals of Europe, not particularly the residents of Nome or Fairbanks. It was part of Western Union's ambitious plan to link California to Russian America (Alaska) with an intercontinental cable that would continue under the Bering Strait to Siberia and on to Europe. Men and material were brought together on both sides of the Bering Sea, but with the first successful Atlantic cable crossing in 1867, the trans-Siberian

intercontinental line was abandoned.

The first operational telegraph link in Alaska was laid in September 1900, when 25 miles of line were stretched from military headquarters in Nome to an outpost at Port Safety. It was one part of a $450,000 plan by the Army Signal Corps to connect scattered military posts in the territory with the United States. By the end of 1903, land lines linked western Alaska, Prince William Sound, the Interior and southeastern Alaska (where underwater cable was used).

Plagued by blocks of ice that repeatedly tore loose the underwater cables laid across Norton Sound, the military developed "wireless telegraphy" to span the icy water in 1903. It was the world's first application of radio-telegraph technology and marked the completion of a fragile network connecting all military stations in Alaska with the United States and each other. Sitka, Juneau, Haines and Valdez were connected by a line to Whitehorse, Yukon Territory. Nome, Fort Saint Michael, Fort Gibbon (Tanana) and Fort Egbert (Eagle) were linked with Dawson, Yukon Territory. A line from Dawson to Whitehorse continued on to Vancouver, British Columbia, and Seattle.

In 1905, the 1,500 miles of land lines, 2,000 miles of submarine cables and the 107-mile wireless link became the Washington-Alaska Military Cable and Telegraph System. This, in turn, became the Alaska Communications System in 1935, reflecting a shift to greater civilian use and a system relying more heavily on wireless stations than land lines. The Alaska Communications System operated under the Department of Defense until RCA Corporation, through its division RCA Alascom, took control in 1971.

Alascom

Alascom, Inc., is the original long lines carrier for the state and provides a full range of modern long-distance telecommunications services to all Alaska. When Alascom purchased Alaska Communications Systems, about 5 million calls were being handled each year. Today, with more than 200 satellite communication sites in operation, Alascom handles nearly 70 million toll calls each year. To complement its satellite communications, Alascom also maintains hundreds of miles of terrestrial microwave routes. Alascom began offering service in 1991 on its new fiber optic telecommunications cable, which as part of its parent company's North Pacific fiber optic cable, links Alaska to the Lower 48 and Japan. The 17,000-circuit capacity cable can handle up to 85,000 simultaneous messages.

On Oct. 27, 1982, Alascom launched its own telecommunications satellite, *Aurora*, into orbit from Cape Canaveral, Florida. The launching marked several firsts for Alaska: It was the first telecommunications satellite dedicated to a single state; it was the first completely solid-state satellite to be placed in orbit; and it was the first satellite to be named by a youngster in a contest. Sponsored by Alascom and the Alaska Chamber of Commerce, the contest drew some 5,000 entries from schoolchildren across Alaska. The winner was 8-year-old Nick Francis of Eagle River, who chose "aurora" for the name "because it's our light in the sky to tell us we are special people."

On May 29, 1991, Alascom launched its second satellite, *Aurora II,* from Cape Canaveral. Designed to replace the original *Aurora,* which had reached the end of its life span, *Aurora II* uses a similar design updated with modern technology to increase its life span.

A typical long-distance telephone call between two points in rural Alaska may travel nearly 100,000 miles in what engineers call a "double hop," in which a signal travels from a village to the *Aurora II,* back to toll facilities in Fairbanks, Juneau or Anchorage, up again to *Aurora II* and down to a receiving antenna in another village. The signals are relayed at almost the speed of light.

Improvements over the past 10 years have made long-distance telephone service available to every community of 25 persons or more in Alaska. Live or same-day television is now available to 90 percent of the state's population. In addition to message toll service and television transmissions, Alascom also provides the following services to the residents of Alaska: discounted calling plans, computer data transmission and access, Wide Area Telecommunications

Service (WATS), fax service, national and in-state 800 toll-free numbers, dedicated line service, marine radio, foreign exchange service, and transportable satellite earth stations. Alascom is one of Alaska's largest private employers.

General Communication Inc.

General Communication Inc. (GCI) provides long-distance telephone service to national and international destinations. In May 1991, GCI began providing in-state long-distance service to Alaska customers.

GCI transmits calls via a communications satellite, tying in with the AT&T, MCI and US Sprint national phone networks.

Telephone Numbers in the Bush

Although most Alaskan bush communities now have full telephone service, a few villages still have only one telephone. For those villages, call the information number, 555-1212. The area code for all of Alaska is 907.

Television Stations

Television in Alaska's larger communities, such as Anchorage and Fairbanks, was available years before satellites were sent into orbit. The first satellite broadcast to the state was Neil Armstrong's moon walk in July 1969. Television reached the bush in the late 1970s with the construction of telephone earth stations that could receive television programming via satellite transmissions. The state funds Satellite Television Project (TVP), which supplies general programming to more than 250 rural communities. For more information about TVP, contact the Department of Administration, Information Services, 5900 E. Tudor Road, Anchorage 99507.

Tapes of programming from the LearnAlaska Instructional Television Network, which is no longer on the air, are available to teachers through the state library system.

Regular network programming

(ABC, CBS, NBC and PBS) from the Lower 48 reaches Alaska on a time-delayed basis. Most of the stations listed here carry a mixture of network programming, with local broadcasters specifying programming. Some stations, such as KJNP, carry locally produced programming.

Cable television is available in many communities, with the cable companies offering dozens of channels. At least one cable system offers a complete satellite earth station and 24-hour programming. Local television viewing in Bethel, for example, includes Channel 4 (KYUK), which carries ITV programming such as PBS's "NOVA" series and "Sesame Street," and local news; cable Channel 8, which carries regular network programming; and a half-dozen other cable channels carrying specialized programming such as movies, sports and specials.

The following list shows the commercial and public television stations in Alaska:

Anchorage
KAKM Channel 7 (public television); 2677 Providence Drive, 99508

KIMO Channel 13; 2700 E. Tudor Road, 99507

KTBY Channel 4; 1840 S. Bragaw, Suite 101, 99508

KTUU Channel 2; P.O. Box 102880, 99510

KTVA Channel 11; P.O. Box 102200, 99510

KYES Channel 5; 3700 Woodland Drive, No. 600, 99517

Bethel
KYUK Channel 4 (public television); P.O. Box 468, 99559

Fairbanks
KATN Channel 2; 516 Second Ave., 99707

KTVF Channel 11; P.O. Box 950, 99707

KUAC Channel 9 (public television); University of Alaska, 99775

KO7UU Channel 7; 3650 Braddock St., 99707

Juneau
KJUD Channel 8; 1107 W. Eighth St., 99801

KTOO Channel 3 (public television); 224 Fourth St., 99801

Kenai
UHF Channel 17; P.O. Box 4665, 99611

North Pole
KJNP Channel 4; P.O. Box O, 99705

Sitka
KTNL Channel 13; 520 Lake St., 99835

Tides

(*See also* Bore Tide)

In southeastern Alaska, Prince William Sound, Cook Inlet and Bristol Bay, salt water undergoes extreme daily fluctuations, creating powerful tidal currents. Some bays may go totally dry at low tide.

The second greatest tide range in North America occurs in upper Cook Inlet near Anchorage, where the maximum diurnal range during spring tides is 38.9 feet. (The greatest tide range in North America is Nova Scotia's Bay of Fundy, with spring tides to 43 feet.)

Here are diurnal ranges for some coastal communities: Bethel, 4 feet; Cold Bay, 7.1 feet; Cordova, 12.4 feet; Haines, 16.8 feet; Herschel Island, 0.7 feet; Ketchikan, 15.4 feet; Kodiak, 8.5 feet; Naknek River entrance, 22.6 feet; Nikiski, 20.7 feet; Nome, 1.6 feet; Nushagak, 19.6 feet; Point Barrow, 0.4 feet; Port Heiden, 12.3 feet; Port Moller, 10.8 feet; Sand Point, 7.3 feet; Sitka, 9.9 feet; Valdez, 12 feet; Whittier, 12.3 feet; Wrangell, 15.7 feet; Yakutat, 10.1 feet.

Timber

According to the U.S. Forest Service, Anchorage Forestry Sciences Lab, 129 million acres of Alaska's 365 million acres of land surface are forested, 15 million acres of which are classified as timberland. Timberland is defined as forest land capable of producing in excess of 20 cubic feet of industrial wood per acre per year in natural stands and not withdrawn from timber utilization.

Alaska has two distinct forest ecosystems: the interior forest and the coastal rain forest. The vast interior forest covers 115 million acres, extending from the south slope of the Brooks Range to the Kenai Peninsula, and from Canada to Norton Sound. Nearly 10 million acres of white spruce, paper birch, quaking aspen, black cottonwood and balsam poplar stands are considered timberland, comparing favorably in size and growth with the forests of the lake states of Minnesota, Wisconsin and Michigan. There are an additional 3.4 million acres of forest land capable of producing more than 20 cubic feet per acre per year but are unavailable for harvest because they are in designated parks or wilderness.

The interior's land management policies and the region's remoteness from large markets have limited timber use to approximately 20 sawmills, a few of which have estimated capacities of 1 million to 5 million board feet per year, but most cutting less than 300,000 board feet per year. A mill with an estimated capacity of 70 million board feet per year has been producing intermittently. There are some exports of sawlogs, cants and chips.

The coastal rain forests extend from Cook Inlet to the Alaska–Canada border south of Ketchikan, and they continue to provide the bulk of commercial timber volume in Alaska. Of the 13.6 million acres of forested land, 5.7 million acres are classified as timberland. An additional 1.9 million acres of timber stands are capable of producing more than 20 cubic feet per acre per year. These stands are in parks and wilderness and therefore are not available for harvest.

Western hemlock and Sitka spruce provide most of the timber harvest for domestic and export lumber and pulp markets. Western red cedar and Alaska cedar make up most of the balance, along with mountain hemlock and some lodgepole pine and other species. Southeastern Alaska has two pulp mills, five major sawmills and about as many smaller mills, some operating intermittently.

Lands from which substantial volumes of timber are harvested are divided into two distinct categories: privately owned by Native corporations and villages under the 1971 Native Claims Settlement Act; and publicly owned and managed federal, state and borough lands. Timber harvests from publicly owned lands are carried through short- and long-term sales offered by government agencies. Harvests on Native lands are scheduled for accelerated cutting through the early 1990s, tapering off to a lower sustained harvest in the following years.

The forest products of Alaska are also divided somewhat along the same lines as land ownership. By federal law, timber harvested from federal lands (more than 85 percent of all timber harvested on public lands) cannot be exported without processing. Consequently, while processors dependent on federal lands produce rough-sawn lumber, pulpwood and chips, the Native corporations primarily produce round logs, which find more buyers along the Pacific Rim, especially Japan. Given that the Alaska forest products industry is almost entirely dependent on the Japanese market, the processing requirement has had considerable effect on some sections of the forest industry, as it limits responsiveness to varying market conditions. Pulp mills provide a market for wood chips and for lower-quality timber from both public and private lands. A market for this utility wood is critical to all operators.

In 1991, more than 380 million board feet of timber were harvested from publicly owned or managed lands in Alaska (excluding Bureau of Land Management lands). Approximately 80 percent of the harvest was sawtimber. An estimated 450 million board feet of sawlogs, mostly for export, were harvested from private lands. In addition, there was a pulp-log harvest from private lands of about 130 million board feet. The total 1991 timber harvest in Alaska was approximately 965 million board feet, down from more than 1.1 billion board feet in 1990. Alaska timber exports in 1991 were valued at more than $515 million.

Time Zones

On Sept. 15, 1983, Transportation Secretary Elizabeth Dole signed a

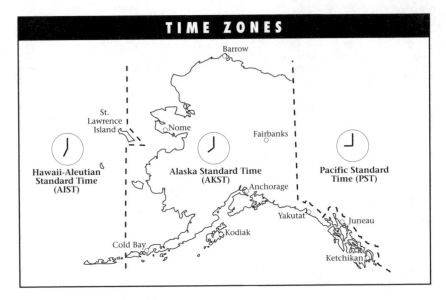

TIME ZONES

Barrow

St. Lawrence Island

Nome

Fairbanks

Hawaii–Aleutian Standard Time (AIST)

Alaska Standard Time (AKST)

Pacific Standard Time (PST)

Anchorage

Yakutat

Juneau

Cold Bay

Kodiak

Ketchikan

plan to reduce the number of time zones in Alaska from four to two. The plan, which became effective Oct. 30, 1983, when daylight saving time reverted to standard time, places 90 percent of Alaska residents on Alaska (same as Yukon) time, only one hour behind the West Coast. The far reaches of the Aleutian Islands and St. Lawrence Island enter Hawaii–Aleutian time.

Before the change, Alaska's time zones were Pacific time (southeastern Alaska), Yukon time (Yakutat) and Alaska time (from just east of Cold Bay and west of Yakutat northward, including Nome). The shift was accomplished to facilitate doing business in Alaska, improve communications and unify residents. It had the support of the governor, the state legislature and the majority of Alaskans.

Totems

(*See also* Native Arts and Crafts
and Potlatch)

In the early days of southeastern Alaska and the Pacific Northwest coast, the Native way of life was based on the rich natural resources of the land, on respect for all living things, and on a unique and complex social structure.

The totemic art of the Indians reflects this rich culture.

Totem poles, carved from the huge cedar trees of the northern coast, are a traditional art form among the Natives of the Pacific Northwest and southeastern Alaska. Although the best-known type of totem pole is tall and freestanding, totemic art also is applied to houseposts, house frontal poles and mortuary poles. Totem poles are bold statements that make public records of the lives and history of the people who had them carved and represent pride in clans and ancestors.

Animals of the region are most often represented on the poles. Commonly depicted are eagles, ravens, frogs, bears, wolves, thunderbirds and whales. Also represented are figures from Native mythology: monsters with animal features, humanlike spirits and legendary ancestors. Occasionally included are objects, devices, masks and charms and, more rarely, art illustrating plants and sky phenomena.

The poles were traditionally painted with natural mineral and vegetable pigments. Salmon eggs were chewed with cedar bark to form the binder for the ground pigment. Traditional colors are black, white and red-brown; green, blue-green, blue and yellow are also used, depending on tribal convention.

The range of colors broadened when modern paints became available. Totem art grew rapidly in the late 18th century, with the introduction of steel European tools acquired from explorers and through the fur trade. Large totem poles were a thriving cultural feature by the 1830s, having become a means by which the Natives displayed their social standing.

Totem pole carving almost died out between the 1880s and 1950s during the enforcement of a law forbidding the "potlatch," the core of Northwest Coast Indian culture. The potlatch is a ceremony in which major events are celebrated, such as marriages; guests are invited from near and far, dancing and feasting take place, property is given away and often poles are raised to commemorate the event. Since the anti-potlatching law was repealed in 1951, a revival of Native culture and the arts has taken place, and many tribes are actively carving and raising poles again. (*See* Potlatch)

Totem poles were left to stand as long as nature would permit, usually no more than 50 to 60 years. Once a pole became so rotten that it fell, it was left to decay naturally or used for firewood. Some totem poles still standing in parks today are 40 to 50 years old. Heavy precipitation and acid muskeg soils hasten decomposition, even though cedar is resistant to decay.

Collections of fine totem poles may be seen in several Alaska communities, either outdoors or in museums, including Ketchikan, Wrangell and Sitka. Carvers can be seen practicing their art at cultural centers in those towns as well as in Haines.

Tourism

Although Alaska has been attracting tourists for over 100 years, people are surprised that the visitor industry has quietly become the state's second-largest primary employer. The visitor industry employs 19,000 Alaskans directly and affects 38,000 Alaskan jobs. Over 2,500 businesses in Alaska derive most of their income from visitor sales. Tourism is a renewable resource that brings dollars to all regions of Alaska. The visitor industry is expected to play a greater role in Alaska's future as the state's petroleum production decreases.

State government has long recognized the value of the visitor industry and supports this growing segment of the state's economy through the Division of Tourism.

For the fiscal year 1994, the Division of Tourism's budget is $3.75 million for domestic market and the Alaska Tourism Marketing Council's budget is $7.5 million for international marketing. The legislature allocates these monies to promote Alaska as a visitor destination.

In 1992, tourism officials estimated that 30,000 more visitors than usual came to Alaska for celebrations surrounding the 50th anniversary of the Alaska Highway.

The continental United States provided 85 percent of Alaska's visitors in

Nonresident Visitor Volume and Impact: Summer Seasons

Year	Visitor Volume	In-State Sales (in millions)*
1985	497,300	—
1986	552,900**	$285.0
1987	515,300	—
1988	536,300	—
1989	559,300	311.4
1990	629,700	—
1991	651,700	—
1992	694,600	—

*Does not include travel to and from the state; expenditure studies done only in 1986 and 1989
**Affected by Expo '86 in Vancouver

1992, Canadian visitors formed 8.4 percent and 6.6 percent came from overseas. Of these travelers, 60 percent had independent itineraries while the remainder came on package tour programs. The most popular mode of entry for visitors was domestic air (53 percent), cruise ships (27 percent), personal vehicles (13 percent) and the ferry system (4 percent). The remainder arrived by international air (2 percent) and motor coach tours (1 percent). Total arrivals for summer 1992 were 694,600.

Alaska's scenic beauty, abundant wildlife and colorful history remain its biggest attractions. The adventure travel market is growing in Alaska, with an increasing number of visitors participating in river rafting, backcountry trekking and other wilderness experiences.

Trees and Shrubs

According to the U.S. Department of Agriculture, the number of native tree species in Alaska is less than in any other state. Species of trees and shrubs in Alaska fall under the following families: yew, pine, cypress, willow, bayberry, birch, mistletoe, gooseberry, rose, maple, elaeagnus, ginseng, dogwood, crowberry, pyrola, heath, dispensia, honeysuckle and composite.

Commercial timber species include white spruce, Sitka spruce, western hemlock, mountain hemlock, western red cedar, Alaska cedar, balsam poplar, black cottonwood, quaking aspen and paper birch.

Rare tree species include the Pacific yew, Pacific silver fir, subalpine fir, silver willow and Hooker willow.

Tundra

Characteristic of arctic and subarctic regions, tundra is a treeless plain that consists of moisture-retaining soils and permanently frozen subsoil. Tundra climates, with frequent winds and low temperatures, are harsh on plant species attempting to grow there. Soils freeze around root systems and winds wear away portions exposed above rocks and snow. Consequently, the three distinct types of Alaska tundra—wet, moist and alpine—support low-growing vegetation that includes a variety of delicate flowers, mosses and lichens.

According to a report in *Alaska Science Nuggets*, every acre of arctic tundra contains more than 2 tons of live fungi that survive by feeding on, thus decomposing, dead organic matter. Since the recession of North Slope ice age glaciers 12,000 years ago, a vegetative residue has accumulated a layer of peat 3 to 6 feet thick overlying the tundra.

Ulu

A traditional Eskimo woman's knife designed for scraping and chopping, this fan-shaped tool was originally made of stone with a bone handle. Today, an ulu is often shaped from an old saw blade and a wood handle is attached.

Umiak

An umiak is a traditional Eskimo skin-covered boat, whose design has changed little over the centuries. Although the umiak is mostly powered by outboard motors today, paddles are still used when stalking game and when ice might damage the propeller. Because umiaks must often be pulled for long distances over the ice, the boats are designed to be lightweight and easily repairable. The frames are wood, often driftwood found on the beaches, and the covering can be sewn should it be punctured. The bottom is flat and the keel is bone, which prevents the skin from wearing out as it is pulled over the ice.

Female walrus skins are the preferred covering because they are the proper thickness when split (bull hides are too thick) and because it only takes two to cover a boat. However, sometimes female walrus skins are unavailable, so the Eskimos substitute skins of the bearded seal, or *oogruk*. But *oogruk* skins are smaller and it takes six or seven skins to cover an umiak.

Once the skins are stretched over the frame and lashed into place, the outside is waterproofed with marine paint. Historically, the skin would have been anointed with seal oil or other fats, but the modern waterproofing is now universally accepted because it does not have to be renewed after each trip.

Umiak is the Inupiat word for skin boat and is commonly used by the coastal Eskimos throughout Alaska. The St. Lawrence Islanders, however, speak the Yup'ik dialect and their word for skin boat is *angyaq*.

Universities and Colleges

Higher education in Alaska is provided by the University of Alaska system and private institutions. The university system includes three regional multicampus universities, one community college and a network of service for rural Alaska. University of Alaska institutions enroll more than 30,000 people each year.

The three regional institutions are the University of Alaska Anchorage, which includes Kenai Peninsula College, Kodiak College, Matanuska–Susitna College and Prince William Sound Community College; University of Alaska Fairbanks with campuses in Bethel, Dillingham, Kotzebue and Nome; and University of Alaska Southeast with campuses in Juneau, Ketchikan and Sitka. These schools offer developmental, certificate, associate, baccalaureate and graduate degree programs. Student housing is available in Anchorage, Bethel, Fairbanks and Juneau.

University of Alaska Fairbanks research facilities include the Agricultural and Forestry Experiment Station, Center for Cross-Cultural Studies, Center for Global Change and Arctic Systems Research, Environmental Technology Laboratory, Geophysical Institute, Institute of Arctic Biology, Institute of Marine Science, Institute of Northern Engineering, Juneau Center for Fisheries and Ocean Sciences, Mineral Industry Resource Laboratory, Office of Sponsored Programs, Petroleum Development Laboratory, Polar Ice Coring Office, Transportation Research Center, Water Research Center and West Coast National Undersea Research Center.

The University of Alaska Anchorage is the home of the Alaska Center for International Business, Center for Alcohol and Addiction Studies, Center for Economic Development, Center for Economic Education, Center for Human Development: University Affiliated Program, Environment and Natural Resources Institute, Institute for Circumpolar Health Studies, Institute of Social and Economic Research and Justice Center.

Through the University's Cooperative Extension Service and Marine Advisory Program, research results are interpreted and transferred to people of the state.

For information on state colleges and universities, contact the following institutions: **University of Alaska Anchorage**, 3211 Providence Drive, Anchorage 99508: **Kenai Peninsula College**, 34820 College Drive, Soldotna 99669;

Kodiak College, 117 Benny Benson Drive, Kodiak 99615; **Matanuska–Susitna College**, P.O. Box 2889, Palmer 99645; **Prince William Sound Community College**, P.O. Box 97, Valdez 99686

University of Alaska Fairbanks, Fairbanks 99775: **Bristol Bay Campus**, P.O. Box 1070, Dillingham 99576; **Chukchi Campus**, P.O. Box 297, Kotzebue 99752; **Interior Campus**, 4280 Geist Road, Fairbanks 99775; **Kuskokwim Campus**, P.O. Box 368, Bethel 99559; **Northwest Campus**, Pouch 400, Nome 99762

University of Alaska Southeast, **Juneau Campus**, 11120 Glacier Highway, Juneau 99801; **Ketchikan Campus**, Seventh and Madison, Ketchikan 99901; **Sitka Campus**, 1332 Seward Ave., Sitka 99835

For information on private institutions of higher learning, contact the following:
Alaska Bible College, P.O. Box 289, Glennallen 99588
Alaska Pacific University, 4101 University Drive, Anchorage 99508
Sheldon Jackson College, 801 Lincoln St., Sitka 99835

Many additional schools and institutes in Alaska offer religious, vocational and technical study. For a complete listing of these and other schools, write for the *Directory of Postsecondary Educational Institutions in Alaska*, Alaska Commission on Postsecondary Education, P.O. Box FP, Juneau 99811.

Volcanoes

The state's 10 tallest volcanic peaks, nearly all of which are known to have erupted within the last 10,000 years (information from the Smithsonian Institution and the Alaska Volcano Observatory) are as follows (see map, next page):

Map Key
1 Mount Wrangell, 14,163 feet
2 Mount Spurr, 11,070 feet
3 Redoubt Volcano, 10,197 feet
4 Iliamna Volcano, 10,016 feet
5 Shishaldin Volcano, 9,372 feet
6 Pavlof Volcano, 8,261 feet
7 Mount Veniaminof, 8,225 feet
8 Isanotski Peaks, 8,025 feet
9 Mount Griggs, 7,600+ feet
10 Mount Denison, 7,500+ feet

Volcanoes on the Aleutian Islands, on the Alaska Peninsula and in the Wrangell Mountains are part of the "Ring of Fire" that surrounds the Pacific Ocean basin. There are more than 80 potentially active volcanoes in Alaska, about half of which have had at least one eruption since 1760, the date of earliest recorded eruptions. Pavlof Volcano is one of the most active of Alaskan volcanoes, having had more than 41 reported eruptions since 1760. One recent spectacular eruption of Pavlof in April 1986 sent ash 10 miles high, causing black snow to fall on Cold Bay. The eruption of Augustine Volcano (elev. 4,025 feet) in lower Cook Inlet on March 27, 1986, sent ash 8 miles high and disrupted air traffic in southcentral Alaska for several days. Most recently, Mount Redoubt erupted on Dec. 14, 1989, its first eruption since 1968. The biggest eruptions sent ash

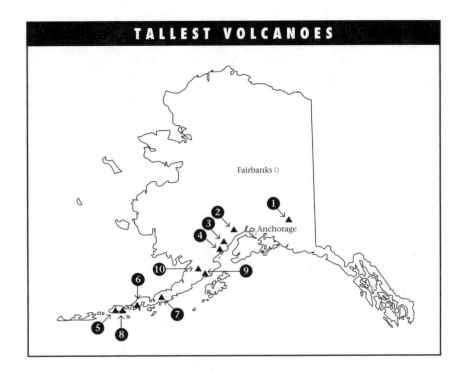

TALLEST VOLCANOES

throughout most of southcentral Alaska and disrupted air traffic. Periodic eruptions occurred from December 1989 to April 1990. Mount Spurr erupted in June, August and September 1992. Anchorage received the brunt of the ash fallout from the August eruption, which halted air traffic out of the city for several days. It was briefly interrupted again with the September eruption.

The most violent Alaskan eruption recorded occurred over a 60-hour period in June 1912 from Novarupta Volcano. The eruption darkened the sky over much of the Northern Hemisphere for several days, deposited almost a foot of ash on Kodiak, 100 miles away, and filled the Valley of Ten Thousand Smokes (now contained within Katmai National Park) with more than 2.5 cubic miles of ash during its brief but extremely explosive duration.

Waves

(See also Earthquakes; Bore Tide; *and* Tides)

Alaska's seismic history is very short, yet extremely active. Alaska responds to movement in the Aleutian–Alaska megathrust zone, where the edge of the Pacific plate descends under the North American plate. These vertical movements of the earth's crust result in vertical motion of the sea floor, which can produce great tsunamis. In fact, these crustal movements in the Alaska Peninsula, Aleutians and Gulf of Alaska can produce Pacific-wide tsunamis.

In southeastern Alaska, the Fairweather Fault lies inland. Though this fault has not triggered tectonic tsunamis as in other Alaskan areas, it can trigger nearby underwater landslides, which can cause tsunamis, even without an earthquake.

According to the Alaska Tsunami Warning Center in Palmer, Alaska has had seven tsunamis that caused fatalities in recorded history. These were of local origin and occurred between 1788 and 1964. Tsunamis originating in Alaska Pacific waters have caused all of the fatalities reported on the West Coast and in Alaska, and most of those in Hawaii. The most recent tsunami was in 1964 following the March 27, Good Friday earthquake. That wave completely destroyed three Alaskan villages before reaching Washington, Oregon and California, and continued to cause damage as far away as Hawaii, Chile and Japan.

Tsunami is taken from the Japanese words "tsu" meaning harbor and "nami" meaning great wave. Although often called tidal waves, tsunamis are not caused by tides. Generated by earthquakes occurring on or below the sea floor, tsunamis can race across the Pacific Ocean at speeds up to 600 miles per hour. Tsunamis rarely cross the Atlantic. Traveling across the open ocean, the waves are only a few feet high and can be up to 100 miles from crest to crest. They cannot be seen from an airplane or felt in a ship at sea. Once they approach shore, however, shallower water causes the waves to grow taller by increasingly restricting their forward motion. Thus, a 2-foot wave traveling 500 miles per hour in deep water becomes a 100-foot killer at 30 miles per hour as it nears the shore. The wave action of a tsunami can repeat every 15 to 30 minutes and the danger for a given area is generally not considered over until the area has been free from damaging waves for two hours.

Providing information, and timely warnings, on tsunamigenic earthquakes (those quakes measuring above 7.0 on the Richter scale and lasting 30 seconds or longer) is the job of the Alaska Tsunami Warning Center (ATWC), located in Palmer. Established in 1967, the ATWC now makes loss of life unnecessary for Alaska, Canada and the West Coast of the United States, and ensures the avoidance of such a tragedy as the April 1, 1946, earthquake at Scotch Cap on Unimak Island, Alaska. Within minutes after the quake struck, waves measuring 100 feet high completely destroyed the lighthouse on the island, killing five people. In less than five hours, the first wave hit Hawaii, killing 159 people. More recently, in March 1985, after an 8.1 quake in Chile, tsunami warnings alerted coastal Alaskans in plenty of time to take precautionary measures. Normally, tsunamis from remote Pacific sources will not be destructive in Alaska.

Another type of wave action that occurs in Alaska is a seiche. A seiche is a long, rhythmic wave in a closed or partially closed body of water. Caused by earthquakes, winds, tidal currents or atmospheric pressure, the motion of a seiche resembles the back and forth movement of a tipped bowl of water. The water moves only up and down, and can remain active from a few minutes to several hours. The highest recorded wave in Alaska, 1,740 feet, was the result of a seiche that took place in Lituya Bay on July 9, 1958. This unusually high wave was due to an earthquake-induced landslide that cleared trees from the opposite side of the bay.

Whales and Whaling

(*See also* Baleen)

Fifteen species of both toothed and baleen whales are found in Alaskan waters. Baleen refers to the hundreds of strips of flexible bonelike material that hangs from the gum of the upper jaw. The strips are fringed and act as strainers that capture krill, the tiny shrimplike organisms upon which the whales feed. Once the baleen fills with krill, whales force water back out through the sides of their mouth, swallowing the food left behind. Baleen whale cows are usually larger than bulls.

Baleen whales that inhabit Alaskan waters include blue, bowhead, northern right, fin or finback, humpback, sei, minke or little piked and gray. Toothed whales include sperm, beluga, killer, pilot, beaked (three species), dolphins (two species) and porpoises (two species). Another toothed whale, the narwhal, a full-time resident of the arctic region, is almost never seen in Alaskan waters. St. Lawrence Islanders call narwhals *bousucktugutalik,* or "beluga with tusk," due to a tusk that grows from the left side of the upper jaw on bulls only. Spiraling in a left-hand direction, the tusk can reach lengths of 7 to 8 feet on an adult.

A few facts on three of the whales indigenous to Alaska, and the whales residents and tourists are most likely to see in Alaska's waters, are interesting to note. According to the Alaska Department of Fish and Game, gray whales have the distinction of being the most primitive of the living *mysticete* ("moustached") or baleen whales. They can regularly be observed in large numbers from Alaskan shores, and are found in the North Pacific Ocean and adjacent waters of the Arctic Ocean. There are two geographically isolated stocks: the Korean or western Pacific stock, and the California or eastern Pacific stock. The California stock migrates between Baja California and the Bering and Chukchi seas, a round-trip distance of 10,000 miles, and the longest migration of any marine mammal.

Grays are mottled gray in color and covered with scars, abrasions and clusters of parasitic barnacles that are most abundant on their heads and backs, the parts that are exposed to air when they breathe.

The estimated daily consumption of an adult gray whale is about 2,600 pounds. In the approximately five months spent in Alaskan waters, one whale eats about 396,000 pounds of food, primarily amphipod crustaceans. Gray whales feed on the bottom by sucking tube-dwelling amphipods out of the sandy sediment and leaving large oval feeding imprints behind. Scientists can study these imprints and gain knowledge about the feeding habits of these whales. Muddy feeding trails are often seen when gray whales surface after feeding dives. Gray whales were called "devil fish" by early whalers because they were so aggressive and protective of their young when hunted.

Adult grays are about 36 to 50 feet long and weigh from 16 to 45 tons, with females larger than males at any given age. They have been known to live up to 70 years, but the average life-span is 40 to 50 years.

The beluga, or white whale, belongs to the *odontocetes* ("toothed") group, which includes sperm and killer whales, dolphins and porpoises. Its closest relative is the narwhal. Belugas range widely in arctic and subarctic waters, and two populations occur in Alaska. The Cook Inlet population can be found in the inlet and in the Shelikof Straits region, although some belugas have been seen east to Yakutat Bay and west to Kodiak Island. Belugas of the Western Arctic population range throughout the Bering, Chukchi and Beaufort seas. These whales winter in the ice of the Bering Sea, moving in summer over 1,500 miles to concentrated areas along the coast from Bristol Bay to the Mackenzie River delta in northwestern Canada. In Alaska, major concentrations occur in the Bristol Bay area, Norton Sound, Kotzebue Sound and Kasegaluk Lagoon. In Bristol Bay, they sometimes swim more than 100 miles per day.

Belugas are very vocal animals, producing a variety of grunts, clicks, chirps and whistles, which are used for navigating, finding prey and communicating. Because of their talkative nature, they were called "sea canaries" by whalers. Belugas are also masters of echolocation, using their sophisticated sonar to detect fish and to navigate in shallow waters or among gill nets without getting stranded. In some areas, they may dive more than 1,000 feet to feed on the bottom. At birth, belugas are dark blue-gray in color, lightening to white by the age of five or six. Adult males are 11 to 16 feet long and weigh 1,000 to 2,000 pounds; adult females are smaller, reaching 12 feet in length. Belugas can live up to 40 years.

Orcas, also known as killer whales, or blackfish, are the largest member of the dolphin family. They range from the Beaufort Sea to Antarctica and are most abundant off the Aleutians. It is thought that orcas migrate, riding cold currents south in the winter. The most unusual feature of the orca whale is the high dorsal fin on its back, which has no muscle, but may serve the whale as a keel would a boat. The fin on older males can grow to six feet in height.

Orcas are thought to be very intelligent and to possess all mammalian senses except smell. To sleep, they take catnaps on the surface of the water, and they hunt in pods using complex, cooperative patterns in an attack. Prey includes sea lions, salmon, seals, porpoises, halibut, shark, squid, belugas and other whales. Male killer whales average 23 feet in length, with females being smaller. Average lifespan is 30 to 40 years.

Whaling

Bowhead whales have been protected from commercial whaling by the Convention for the Regulation of Whaling of 1931, the International Convention for the Regulation of Whaling of 1947, the Marine Mammal Protection Act of 1972, the Endangered Species Act of 1973, and the Convention of International Trade in Endangered Species of Wild Fauna and Flora.

Commercial whaling for gray whales has been banned by the International Convention for the Regulation of Whaling since 1947. These conventions and acts have, however, allowed for a subsistence harvest by Alaska Indians, Aleuts and Eskimos.

Since 1978, the International Whaling Commission (IWC) has regulated the take of bowheads by establishing an annual catch limit for Alaska Eskimos. Also in 1978, the IWC reclassified the eastern stock of gray whales from a protected species to a sustained management stock with an annual catch limit of about 179 whales, based on the average known removals during the period 1968–77. The entire catch limit has been reserved for taking by Natives or by member governments on behalf of Natives.

Other species of large baleen whales, such as minke and fin whales, are occasionally taken by Alaska Eskimos for food. It is not necessary to report gray and minke harvests. The only toothed whale taken by Eskimos is the beluga and its harvest is monitored by the Alaska and Inuvialuit Beluga Whale Committee (AIBWC), which is currently developing a management plan.

According to the National Marine Mammal Laboratory and the Alaska Department of Fish and Game, approximate harvest figures for beluga whales for the years 1980–1992 are as follows:

Year	Beluga
1980	233–245
1981	179–231
1982	307–354
1983	226–236
1984	186–211
1985	256–352
1986	174–191
1987	133–190
1988	352–388
1989	229–259
1990	217*
1991	50*
1992	169*

*Data incomplete; not all beluga kills reported.

Wildflowers

Wildflowers in Alaska are seldom gaudy; they are usually rather small and delicate. More than 1,500 plant species occur in the state, including trees, shrubs, ferns, grasses and sedges, as well as flowering plants.

Alpine regions are particularly rich in flora and some of the alpine species are rare. Anywhere there is tundra there is apt to be a bountiful population of flowers. The Steese Highway (Eagle Summit), Richardson Highway (Thompson Pass), Denali Highway (Maclaren Summit), Denali National Park and Preserve (Polychrome Pass), Seward Highway (Turnagain Pass), Glenn Highway just north of Anchorage (Eklutna Flats) and a locale near Wasilla (Hatcher Pass) are wonderful wildflower-viewing spots. These are all readily accessible by car. Less easily accessible floral Edens are some of the Aleutian Islands, Point Hope, Anvil Mountain and the Nome–Teller Road (both near Nome), Pribilof Islands and other remote areas.

Alaska's official flower, the forget-me-not (*Myosotis alpestris*), is a delicate little beauty found throughout much of the state in alpine meadows and along streams. Growing to 18 inches tall, forget-me-nots are recognized by their bright blue petals surrounding a yellow "eye." A northern "cousin," the arctic forget-me-not (*Eritrichium aretioides*), grows in sandy soil on the tundra, or in the mountains, and reaches only 4 inches in height.

Related reading: *Discovering Wild Plants: Alaska, Western Canada, the Northwest,* by Janice Schofield. Descriptions, historical uses, harvest information and recipes of more than 130 plants. Full color photographs and drawings. *Alaska's Wild Plants: A Guide to Alaska's Edible Harvest,* by Janice Schofield. For hikers, campers and foragers, this pocket-size book is an introduction to more than 70 common edible plants. *See* ALASKA NORTHWEST LIBRARY in the back of the book.

Winds

Some of Alaska's windiest weather has been recorded on the western islands of the Aleutian chain. Overall, the causes are the same as elsewhere, incorporating planet rotation and the tendency of the atmosphere to equalize the difference between high and low pressure fronts. (*See also* Climate) A few winds occur often and significantly enough to be given names: chinook, taku and williwaws.

Chinook

Old-timers describe chinook winds as unseasonably warm winds that can cause thaw in the middle of winter. What they also cause are power outages and property damage, especially in the Anchorage bowl, where in recent years hundreds of homes have sprung up on the Chugach Mountain hillsides over which the chinook winds howl. One such wind occurred on April Fool's Day in 1980, causing $25 million in property damage and nominating the city as a disaster area. Parts of Anchorage were without power for 60 hours.

Until recently, it was not possible to predict the coming of a chinook wind. Today, however, Anchorage meteorologists can tell if the winds are gathering, when they will arrive and their relative strength. It was discerned that such a warm wind could only originate in Prince William Sound and that its speed had to be at least 55 miles per hour or faster just to cross the 3,500-foot Chugach Mountains. Other factors that need to be present are a storm near Bethel and relatively stable air over Anchorage. Meteorologists predict the coming of chinook winds 55 percent of the time.

Taku

Taku winds are the sudden, fierce gales that sweep down from the ice cap behind Juneau and Douglas, and plague residents there. Takus are shivering cold winds capable of reaching 100 miles per hour. They have been known to send a 2-by-4 timber flying through the wall of a frame house.

Williwaws

Williwaws are sudden gusts of wind

that can reach 113 miles per hour after the wind "builds up" on one side of a mountain and suddenly spills over into what may appear to be a relatively protected area. Williwaws are considered the bane of Alaska mariners. The term was originally applied to a strong wind in the Strait of Magellan.

World Eskimo-Indian Olympics

An audience of thousands watches the annual gathering of several hundred Native athletes from Alaska and the circumpolar nations competing in the World Eskimo-Indian Olympics (WEIO) in Fairbanks. Held over four days during the second-to-last weekend in July, the self-supporting games draw participants from all of Alaska's Native populations (Eskimo, Aleut, Athabascan, Tlingit, Haida and Tsimshian). Canadian, Greenlandic and Soviet Eskimos are also invited to participate, as well as Natives from the contiguous 48 states.

Spectators thrill to the sight of such feats as the knuckle hop and the ear-weight competition. Other traditional Native sports and competitions include the greased pole walk, fish cutting, stick pull, Indian-Eskimo dancing, men's and women's blanket toss, and the spectacular two-foot and one-foot high kicks. Each year the judges choose a Native queen to reign over the four-day Olympics. She reigns through the year,

making several appearances throughout the state, and represents the WEIO at the National Congress of American Indians. The judges also pick the most authentic Native costumes. Some of the more boisterous games include a lively game of tug-of-war and the muktuk-eating contest. The ear pull, because of the potential for disengaging ears from participants' heads, has been eliminated.

The games will be held on Wednesday, Thursday, Friday and Saturday evenings at the Big Dipper Recreation Arena in Fairbanks July 20–23, 1994. Advance tickets may be purchased from the World Eskimo-Indian Olympics Committee, P.O. Box 2433, Fairbanks 99707.

Yukon Quest International Sled Dog Race

(*See also* Dog Mushing *and* Iditarod Trail Sled Dog Race)

The Yukon Quest International Sled Dog Race was begun by Roger Williams and LeRoy Shank in November 1983, with the purpose of supporting a long-distance sled dog race of international character between Fairbanks, Alaska, and Whitehorse, Yukon Territory. The first race took place in February 1984, with 26 teams competing, and had a purse of $50,000.

(Continued on page 194)

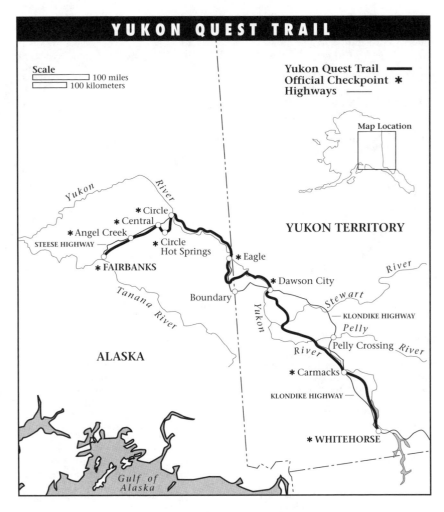

YUKON QUEST TRAIL

Scale
100 miles
100 kilometers

Yukon Quest Trail ▬▬
Official Checkpoint ✳
Highways ▬▬

Map Location

Yukon River

✳ Circle
✳ Central
✳ Angel Creek
STEESE HIGHWAY
✳ Circle Hot Springs
✳ FAIRBANKS

✳ Eagle

YUKON TERRITORY

Tanana River

Boundary

✳ Dawson City

River

Stewart River

KLONDIKE HIGHWAY

Yukon River

Pelly
Pelly Crossing *River*

ALASKA

River

✳ Carmacks

KLONDIKE HIGHWAY

✳ WHITEHORSE

Gulf of Alaska

Winners and Times

Year	Musher	Days	Hrs.	Min.	Prize
1984	Sonny Lindner, Johnson River	12	00	05	$15,000
1985	Joe Runyan, Nenana	11	11	55	15,000
1986	Bruce Johnson	14	09	17	15,000
1987	Bill Cotter, Nenana	12	04	34	15,000
1988	David Monson	12	05	06	20,000
1989	Jeff King, Denali	11	20	51	20,000
1990	Vern Halter, Trapper Creek	11	17	09	20,000
1991	Charlie Boulding, Nenana	10	21	12	25,000
1992	John Schandelmeier, Paxson	11	21	40	29,837
1993	Charlie Boulding, Nenana	10	19	09	25,000

1993 Results

Place	Musher	Days	Hrs.	Min.	Prize
1	Charlie Boulding, Nenana	10	19	09	$25,000
2	Bruce Johnson, Atlin Lake, BC	10	22	30	20,000
3	David Sawatzky, Healy	10	22	33	15,000
4	Linda Forsberg, Denali Park	10	23	11	10,000
5	Jay Caczow, Fort Yukon	11	07	11	8,000
6	Jeff Mann, Mentasta	11	10	23	6,500
7	Hans Gatt, Atlin, BC	11	11	40	5,000
8	John Peep, Fairbanks	11	14	34	4,000
9	Bill Chisholm, Two Rivers	11	19	23	3,700
10	Frank Turner, Pelly Crossing, YT	12	05	20	3,400
11	William Kleodehn, Whitehorse, YT	12	05	45	3,200
12	Tim Mowry, Fairbanks	12	13	58	3,000
13	John Gourley, Healy	12	14	02	2,800
14	Ned Cathers, Whitehorse, YT	12	19	56	2,600
15 '	Ray Brooks, Salcha	12	21	50	2,400
16	Norman Stoppenbrink, Jr., Manley	12	23	39	2,300
17	Doug Hutchinson, Fairbanks	13	04	00	2,200
18	Jim Hendrick, Fairbanks	13	05	50	2,100
19	Ed Hopkins, Eureka	13	06	33	2,000
20	Larry Grout, Fairbanks	13	06	34	1,800

(Continued from page 192)

Named for the old-time "Highway of the North," the Yukon River, the 1,000-mile trek takes between 11 and 14 days to complete, depending on the weather. It is known as one of the toughest sled dog races. During their journey between the two cities, the teams retrace the footsteps of gold rush trappers, miners, explorers and missionaries. They cross four major summits, over diverse and challenging terrain, travel 250 miles on the frozen Yukon River and cross the longest unguarded international border in the world.

The direction of the race alternates each year, and between the start and finish lines, there are six official checkpoints. The shortest distance between checkpoints is 10 miles, from Central to Circle Hot Springs, and the longest distance between checkpoints is 290 miles, from Dawson City to Carmacks. The only checkpoint at which a musher may receive help of any kind is at Dawson City, where a 36-hour layover is mandatory. Rules allow for eight dogs minimum and 14 dogs maximum at the start. Five dogs are the minimum allowed at the finish, and only four dogs can be dropped during the course of the race. Each musher may use only one sled throughout the race, and mandatory equipment includes a sleeping bag, hand ax, snowshoes, promotional material and eight booties per dog.

Yearly Highlights, 1992 and 1993

The following is a collection of the more significant news events from mid-1992 to mid-1993 . . . the high spots for a record of the times. *THE ALASKA ALMANAC®: FACTS ABOUT ALASKA* wishes to credit the *Anchorage Daily News* and the *Fairbanks Daily News–Miner* as the primary sources of information for Yearly Highlights.

Anchorage Times Is Sold, Shut Down

The *Anchorage Times* ceased publication with the June 3, 1992, edition, leaving the state's largest city with one newspaper.

The afternoon newspaper sold its publishing equipment, but not its downtown building and land, to the rival morning *Anchorage Daily News* under an agreement concluded June 1.

Until the sale, Anchorage had been the smallest city in the U.S. with two competing newspapers.

The victory of the *Daily News* marked one of the most abrupt reversals of fortune in modern daily journalism. The paper was near colapse when McClatchy Newspapers Inc., a Sacramento-based chain, bought it in 1979. Circulation was about 12,000 daily, compared with nearly 50,000 for the *Times*. The *Anchorage Daily News'* total paid circulation for the period ending March 31, 1992, was 60,874 daily and 82,641 Sunday. The *Anchorage Times'* circulation was 44,057 daily and 42,256 Sunday. McClatchy publishes 11 daily newspapers.

For a Big Fish, Cast Your Lure in July

July is a month of records for sport-fishing in Alaska. According to the July 1993 issue of *Alaska* magazine, no fewer than four state records have been claimed during this peak period.

• The state record Arctic grayling was caught in July 1982 by Paul Kanitz. Kanitz hooked his 4-pound, 13-ounce trophy in Southwest Alaska's famous Ugashik Narrows.

• Fred Thynes hauled in a 32-pound chum salmon at Caamano Point near Ketchikan in July 1986.

• During this month in 1974 on the Kenai River, where fishermen often stand elbow to elbow in pursuit of fish, Chuck Leach took a record, 16-pound sockeye (red) salmon.

• In salt water, James McKenzie claimed the state's biggest ling cod in July 1991. McKenzie made his 66-pound catch in Resurrection Bay out of Seward.

Research Vessel Measures Amount of Nuclear Waste Dumped by Russia

During the summer of 1992, the University of Alaska Anchorage's research vessel *Alpha Helix*, based in Seward on Resurrection Bay, worked with an international scientific team to measure the extent of nuclear waste dumping by the former Soviet Union.

Senator Frank Murkowski, R–Alaska, commented that as much as 20 times the amount of radiation released by the Chernobyl nuclear power plant melt-down in 1986 has been released into Russia's northern Arctic. The concern is that pollution will work its way into the Arctic Ocean, contaminating marine life. Additional monitoring is under construction for 1993.

Mount Spurr Erupts, Dumps Ash on Anchorage

Mount Spurr erupted for the second time in 1992, sending an ash plume 60,000 feet into the air, halting air traffic out of Anchorage and raining ash from the Matanuska Valley to Yakutat in southeastern Alaska. The explosion, which occurred at 4:41 P.M. on Tuesday, August 18, came with almost no warning. Pilots flying over the volcano were reporting a plume with ash before scientists noticed the growing tremors on the peak. Mount Spurr's June 27th eruption also came with relatively little warning.

Anchorage received the brunt of the ash fallout, which darkened the sky and buried the city in up to ¼ inch of the stuff. Residents with respiratory ailments were encouraged to stay indoors to avoid exposure to the ash. Air filters and surgical masks were out of supply in a matter of hours. Visibility during the ashfall was almost zero, hampering traffic. Many city and government offices operated on reduced schedules. Three thousand weary travelers were stranded at Anchorage International Airport. Normal air traffic did not resume until several days after the eruption.

A week after the explosion, cleanup crews were still trying to remove the ash.

Summer of the Bears

From the rugged, wild land of the Interior to the greenbelts of Anchorage, Alaskans found brown and black bears overrunning human turf like never before. The encounters ranged from comedic to tragic, including two fatal attacks in which bears apparently preyed on people.

The 1992 season began with a surge of young bears entering Anchorage's outskirts. In the areas surrounding the city, biologists estimated a population of five to 10 brown bears and 35 to 40 black bears—about as many as the area can support. Consequently, a bumper crop of 2-year-old cubs began wandering into town, raiding barbecues and garbage bins, meandering through neighborhoods and parks.

Elsewhere in the state, bear encounters sometimes turned dangerous. Three brown bears attacked two hunters in the Alaska Range, mauling one of the hunters. Another brown bear tried to tear its way into a trailer full of sleeping gold miners on a claim near Central before it was shot dead.

But the most extraordinary and frightening events took place in early July when a woman vacationing at a cabin in Glennallen was chased outside, killed and partially eaten by a black bear. Two days later, a 6-year-old boy walking with his mother and sister in the Alaska Peninsula community of King Cove was attacked, killed and also partially eaten by a 400-pound brown bear.

These incidents, though out of the ordinary, heightened fears throughout Alaska. In the weeks that followed, numerous bears were killed in the Glennallen area.

Bear Research Could Alter Human Approach to Health

If science could only figure out how bears do it, humans might be healthier. So writes Carla Helfferich of the Geophysical Institute, University of Alaska

Fairbanks, in a column about how bears pull off some metabolic marvels.

First of all, Helfferich points out, black bears in hibernation manage to recycle calcium and urea. Second, polar bears, since they feed on nice fat seals and on whale blubber, should, by the human model, have terrifically high levels of blood cholesterol. But studies show that the fat-gorging polar bear has very healthy blood.

In fact, blood taken from bears during the seal-free season showed levels of cholesterol nearly 25 percent higher than blood taken from them while they had plenty of seal blubber to chew. The level of triglycerides, a fatty substance implicated in clogging arteries, is nearly 50 percent higher while bears fast than while they're feeding.

A well-fed bear's blood has plenty of omega-3. Bears don't eat fish, but seals do, and the bears apparently benefit from the seal's healthy diet.

Barrow Residents Haul in a Record 20 Whales in Fall Season

Eskimo residents of Barrow support about 14 whaling teams, each with a captain and crew. The village is limited to 18 strikes per season, but Barrow was doing so well that neighboring villages who didn't sight whales decided to pass on some of their strikes. So even after Barrow got its limit, the hunt was able to continue.

Barrow harvested a record 20 whales in the fall of 1992. Piles of muktuk pieces the size of sofa cushions were stacked before almost every house in town. The largest whale brought in was a 50-foot female bowhead.

Biologists are present to survey every whale killing, measuring and taking samples to determine the health of whaling stock.

However, when the smell of whale butchering is on the wind, polar bears leave their pack ice habitat and venture onshore, often coming right into town. So many polar bears were summoned by the delicious odors that residents could often see a half dozen at a time, and authorities often found it necessary to use blank cartridges to disperse the enormous animals.

Eventually 20 to 30 polar bears began dining near Barrow. Later the ice pulled away from shore, stranding the bears on the mainland. No humans were injured, but at least three bears were killed before the bears finally dispersed.

Anchorage Loses Another Piece of its Past

Heavy equipment demolished a World War II-vintage log cabin on a bluff above Cook Inlet. Preservationists had tried for years to save the one-story cabin in Bootlegger Cove. The cabin was built by U.S. soldiers in 1942 as an anti-aircraft lookout. It housed a gasoline-powered searchlight designed to pinpoint enemy airplanes flying overhead at night. An anti-aircraft gun emplacement was built into the bluff below.

"We really worked hard to save it," Kerry Hoffman, former director of Anchorage Historic Properties, told the *Anchorage Daily News.* "But you just can't save every single thing."

The site of the cabin is not far from the Oscar Anderson House, a popular tourist destination. The Oscar Anderson House, Anchorage's first wood frame house, was built in 1915 by Oscar Anderson, the 18th Caucasian settler to set foot in Anchorage's tent city.

Flight Specialist Is Hero

Flight Service Specialist David Long, an employee of the Federal Aviation Administration in Deadhorse, was on duty on the cloudy night of Oct. 26, 1992, when the pilot of a Cessna 207 radioed that the electrical systems of her plane were malfunctioning. The pilot was not able to navigate, and she also reported smoke in the cockpit.

Long immediately responded to the call for assistance by setting in motion emergency procedures and using directional finding equipment to determine the plane's location.

He relayed compass headings to the pilot to get her on course to Deadhorse. Knowing she did not have much visibility, Long persistently provided weather conditions at Deadhorse airport and updated headings for her. According to the FAA, Long kept his cool and calmly and professionally guided the pilot in as she broke through the clouds at 600 feet.

As a result of his rescue of the distressed pilot, Long will be awarded the Flight Assist of the Year Award by the FAA at a ceremony in the summer of 1993 at the agency's headquarters in Washington, D.C.

Recycling Builds a Shimmering Wall in Kodiak

Recycling, the Richter scale and the Russian Orthodox church all play a part in Stacy Studebaker's 120-foot-long, 6-foot-high glass bottle and mortar wall. Studebaker began building in August 1991, and has completed all but 30 feet.

The project recycles more than 9,000 glass bottles and 300 bags of mortar. That's quite a feat when one considers Kodiak's maritime climate and that cement work can only be done on dry days when the temperature rises above 40°F.

The overall effect is a colorful, shimmering, translucent surface worked in an undulating pattern. The top is not level, but pleases the eye with wavelike scallops. Marbles and glass bricks, distributed at random, add interest.

Stacy collected the bottles from friends, neighbors, and dumpsters. Her favorite bits are the red glass votive candle holders that the Russian Orthodox Church donated to the project by the boxful.

According to the *Kodiak Daily Mirror,* a local structural engineer has deemed the wall earthquake proof.

"Nirvana Dragon" Found in Dutch Harbor

According to a story in the Dec. 16, 1992, *Anchorage Daily News,* an important find of ancient marine mammal bones has been uncovered by construction crews in Dutch Harbor.

The site appears to be a graveyard for a pod of hippolike prehistoric creatures called Behemotops. The 30 teeth and bones recovered so far indicate that the remains of at least four Behemotops are present.

A construction crew building a road along Unalaska Valley's Nirvana hillside turned up the fossils. When they were compared to photographs from the Smithsonian Institution, they appeared to be a Desmostylid, a type of animal fairly common along the Pacific Rim 10 million years ago. Behemotops is one kind of Desmostylid.

Unalaska poet Jerah Chadwick, coordinator of the University of Alaska Fairbanks' Aleutian-Pribilof Islands regional program, was alerted to the find. Chadwick noted that local school kids called the creature "the Nirvana dragon."

"Dragon isn't only easier to say," Chadwick said "it's something the kids could more easily identify. It became known as the Nirvana dragon because of where it was found."

History and Good Food Go Up in Smoke

Sourdough Roadhouse, the oldest existing roadhouse in Alaska, burned to the ground on Dec. 27, 1992. The log structure was located near the entrance to Sourdough Creek Campground at Milepost 147.5 of the Richardson Highway.

Built in 1903 and placed on the National Register of Historic Places in 1974, the roadhouse was still operating in the original building. As late as the 1970s, owners still opened holes in the ice on the Gulkana River and hauled drinking water back to the roadhouse, where the only power available came from a generator.

Reportedly former roadhouse owner Hazel Waechter maintained a fox farm in the 1920s and early 30s, and sold fox pelts to early tourists braving the primitive conditions of the trail that eventually became the Richardson Highway.

"It was like losing an old friend, a part of my family and its ties to Alaska," lamented Bureau of Land Management state office archaeologist Robert King.

Denver Cyclist Defies Cold to Win 365-mile Bicycle Classic

After pedaling his bicycle nonstop for nearly 26 hours through swirling wind, deep snow and darkness, Bob Fourney of Denver, rode into Fairbanks in a snowstorm. Thus he became the winner of the Anchorage to Fairbanks Witner Bicycle Classic, a 365-mile race between the two cities at a most inhospitable time of year.

"I'm glad that's over," Fourney sighed as he stepped off his bike and saluted one of his support crew members with a high-five. Fourney had hoped to break the 24-hour mark but was satisfied with his 25-hour, 57-minute finish in what he called "the harshest bicycle race in the world." His prize was $2,000.

Runner-up was Hubert Schwarz of Germany, whose time was about 5½ hours behind Fourney.

Snow fell for all but about two of the hours that Fourney traveled the George Parks Highway. In Trapper Creek, he hit sleet. South of Healy, the road disappeared in a sea of white windblown drifts.

"I felt like I was riding in the Red Sea and it was closing in behind me," Fourney said. "This was scary."

Fourney is a four-time veteran of the Iditabike Race. He plans to trade in his bike for a dogsled and train for the 1,161-mile Iditarod Trail Sled Dog Race, which he says would be "a walk in the park" compared to the Bicycle Classic.

He trained for the Bicycle Classic by riding 280 miles and back again, in temperatures of 30 to 40 below zero.

Planned Wolf Hunt Backfires

The *Anchorage Daily News* bestowed its 1992 Soapy Smith Award to the Alaska Department of Fish and Game. "In announcing a plan to kill wolves, state biologists touted the benefits to tourism of larger caribou herds and more moose for visitors to see," the award read. "But it quickly became clear that tourism would be the big loser if the wolves were killed. Environmental groups and animal lovers protested, threatening boycotts and canceled reservations, leaving state officials scrambling to repair the damage."

(The Yukon Territory apparently had no tourists to lose, as it finalized its plans to do away with wolves, eventually killing 53.)

Jefferson Randolph "Soapy" Smith was a legendary gold rush con man who set up phony telegraph stations and ran a crooked gambling outfit in Skagway.

When Sun Comes Up in Barrow, Kids Write Fan Letters

On Jan. 22, 1993, the sun finally came up in Barrow for the first time in two months, but was only up for 27 minutes or so.

Kids at Ipalook Elementary School celebrated the occasion. Kindergarten teacher Mary Craumer-Morris had each student write a letter to the sun, but it was too cold outside (minus 20 or so) for the kids to read them outside.

"We shook our special sun noise-makers," Craumer-Morris said, "but we couldn't make the sun come out from behind the clouds. We think it is important for children to have a sense of the place in which they live."

Six-year-old James Aiken was glad the sun was back, and he had his priorities straight: "When the sunshine comes up and the sun comes we're going to go boating, and after we go boating we're going to go hunting," Aiken said. "And when we come back from hunting, my mom's going to hug me because she misses me."

Mount McKinley National Park Celebrates its 76th

Originally dedicated as Mount McKinley National Park, Denali National Park and Preserve celebrated its 76th anniversary in February 1993. The park is Alaska's most popular tourist destination, with half a million visitors a year.

Here's one "Denali story" that can't be topped: Harold Herning worked as a ranger in the park from 1936 to 1944. One bright moonlit night, he awoke to the sound of a sled dog barking outside park headquarters. He pulled on his underwear, stepped into a pair of moccasins and ran outside.

At the warehouse, Herning saw what looked like a big dog trying to crawl under a pile of lumber to get at a batch of new puppies. Herning grabbed the rear haunches of the intruder and pulled.

"Come out of there, Mike, you S.O.B!" he yelled, figuring he had his hands on a regular escapee from the local kennel.

The animal whirled to face him. It was a wolf.

"He was more surprised than I was," Herning recalled. "I'll never forget watching him go into the brush. And I'll never forget how coarse that hair felt."

Alaska Gift Shop the First to Tap Into Global Market

The folks at the Alaska Peddler gift shops in Juneau usually come close to hibernating each winter as cruise ship traffic halts and tourists are scarce in the state's capital. But not this year. Owners Lynn and Jerry Renowned decided to try something new to boost business in the off season. They still closed two of their three shops and kept their customary two employees, but they added close to 2 million people to their market. Most of their new customers have never seen the inside of their store. It's safe to say that most have probably never even seen Juneau or any other part of Alaska.

These new customers shop from the comfort of their homes and offices in the Lower 48, Canada and beyond by utilizing on-line computer commercial networks. The networks offer consumers electronic "shopping malls" with a wide range of services and products.

Officials Scratch Two Mushers in Iditarod Trail Sled Dog Race

In an unprecedented act, two mushers were "scratched" from the 1993 Iditarod Sled Dog Race, the 1,161-mile race from Anchorage to Nome. The mushers were disqualified for leaving their teams and accepting snow-machine rides from race trailbreakers in a storm.

Paxson musher John Schandelmeier, the leading rookie in the race, and three-time finisher Beverly Masek, filed protests. Schandelmeier was in 22nd place as the promising rookie in the race when he was scratched. Masek was scratched from the race March 18 after accepting a ride to Safety, where she was examined by a paramedic and spent the night, returning to her team the next day by snowmachine.

Adding to the confusion was the death of Sugar, one of Masek's dogs, while her team was being led by a snowmachine to a shelter cabin. At first it was thought that Sugar had been dragged to death. But an autopsy showed that the dog died of a heart attack.

Both mushers finished the race, but were not counted as contestants.

Killer Whales Amuse Audience Near Kodiak Channel

Three killer whales played catch with their 2,000-pound lunch as if it were a volleyball. After they'd tenderized their prey a bit, they dined.

The powerful black-and-white whales battered about a one-ton Steller sea lion in the channel area near Ursin's Seafoods on Shelikoff Street in Kodiak before deciding it was time to eat. "Right after the incident, they headed south and were followed by sea gulls so they must have had the sea lion with them," Ken Allread told the *Kodiak Daily Mirror.*

Allread thought the whales were gone for the day, but they later returned and took a digestive cruise around in front of the canneries.

Seward Native Association Returns to its Roots

When Seward began holding its "mountain marathon" races in 1915— races to the top of the 4,603-foot peak and back—it seemed only natural to name the peak Mount Marathon.

Eventually that became the name of the local Native Association, too.

However, recently the Mount Marathon Native Association approved a name change more in keeping with its origins. The association is now the Quteckak Tribal Council. The name was approved at an annual meeting attended by about 80 members.

The new name, pronounced kew-tek-ak, is derived from Aleutiiq, the language spoken by early natives who traveled by kayak in Resurrection Bay. It translates as "big beach," referring to the alluvial fan on which the city of Seward is located.

Spaniards Explore Arctic by Kayak, Skis, Snowshoes and Dogsled

Three Spanish explorers kayaked into the port of Valdez in March 1993, concluding an expedition that started in Greenland in February 1990. The explorers traversed the Canadian Arctic during their 8,700-mile journey across the top of the world.

The trio traveled by skis, snowshoes and dogsled. The entire three-year trek was completed in the tradition of Amundsen—without benefit of motorized transportation.

Expedition leader Ramon Hernando de Larramendi, 27, told the *Anchorage Daily News* that Natives in 70 villages in Greenland, Canada and Alaska provided clothing, food and dogs.

De Larramendi, an anthropologist, was the only member of the expedition who stayed with it from start to finish. He said research carried out during the journey would be used in a comparative study of the Native peoples of the Arctic.

A significant discovery of the trip was two mummified Eskimos at a rocky grave on the eastern shore of Greenland. The bodies are believed to be 500 years old.

The route within Alaska included the Arctic National Wildlife Refuge and Kotzebue. The final leg was from Whittier to Valdez.

The other two men finishing the trip with de Larramendi were Manuel Olivera and Antonio Martinez. Valdez was selected for the finish of the trip because the port was the northernmost point reached by Spanish explorers in the 18th century. In 1790, Salvador Fidalgo sailed into the port while seeking for the elusive Northwest Passage connecting the Atlantic and Pacific.

Dog Mushing Brings Money to Fairbanks Economy

Dog mushing has moved into a new era since gold miners carried provisions and received mail by dogsled. More than just a way to get around, more than simply sport, mushing has become a full-fledged business in Fairbanks.

Only in Fairbanks can mushers race their dogs across miles of groomed snow trails from September until May. Fairbanks is musher mecca: there are feed stores, custom-built dogsleds and harnesses, a local designer of sports clothes that weather subzero trail conditions, specialized veterinarians, top-breed sled dogs and trucks to haul them in.

For fans of the sport, there are drive-your-own dogsled rides, exclusive tours of the 1,000-mile Yukon Quest and Iditarod Trail races and front-line viewing spots for dogsled races run by sprint mushers from all over the globe.

All this translates into a $3 million to $4 million annual business for

Fairbanks. The business has broken money trails into hotels, restaurants, gift shops, airlines, car rental shops and even the downtown Dog Mushing Museum.

Though winter visitor traffic by no means rivals summer tourism in Fairbanks, mushing enthusiasts say the Fairbanks winter "package" of dog mushing, northern lights and skiing will someday be as important as the summertime tourist draw.

According to state tourism officials, who use dog mushing to lure visitors to Alaska, the trend may already be underway. In the winter of 1992, 273,500 people visited the state, a 20 percent jump from the winter before.

"Northern Exposure" Writers Bone Up on the Real Alaska

Two scriptwriters from the television show "Northern Exposure" headed north to Rampart on the Yukon River in April 1993 to soak up some local color. Previously they had relied on books and on stories they'd read in the *Wall Street Journal* for their knowledge about life in Alaska.

Andrew Schneider and Diana Frolov, visiting from Hollywood where it never snows, noted that groceries on the show should be priced higher. In Rampart, a village of 50 people, a stalk of broccoli and a hand of bananas can ring up $9 and no change.

The writers went ice fishing and visited with students. They interviewed locals about how they cope with the approach of winter, part of the plot of an upcoming episode. University of Alaska Board of Regents member Mary Jane Fate went along on the Rampart trip, to show Schneider and Frolov the mix of the old ways and new technology in bush-village life—the side-by-side existence of ice-fishing, computers and snowmachines.

The writers also toured Fairbanks, bantered with local media and visited Nenana for a dogsled ride. All along the way they made notes for future scripts.

Set in the fictional Alaska town called Cicely, "Northern Exposure" is filmed in Roslyn, Wash., a town an hour-and-a-half drive from Seattle.

That doesn't matter, Schneider told the Associated Press: "We look at Alaska as a state of mind. More than a real place. Our town is like a science fiction place. It's anything you want it to be."

Russian Cupids Aim Their Arrows at Nome, Alaska

For the past six months, singles in Nome and Provideniya have been meeting each other. The result: five Nome-Provideniya couples have married or become engaged since October 1992.

Why are Cupid's arrows flying high over the Bering Strait?

Some say it's love.

When it's 10 below zero and the wind is gusting, visiting Russian women seem oblivious to the weather as they teeter along in dress shoes and skirts. Their grooming is a contrast to the Carhart-clad or parka-wrapped women of Nome.

Nome men look and look again. "It's like the 1950s the way these women present themselves in their high heels and makeup," said Nome bachelor Mark King.

Proximity has something to do with it, too. Provideniya is only 250 miles away—closer to Nome than either Fairbanks or Anchorage.

Teacher Merle Arin married his Russian girlfriend in March. Chick Trainor became engaged to Alexandria Belkina, who cooked delicious food. Then there's Russian surgeon Viktor Trukov; he and his American bride Stefanie are expecting a baby in the fall.

Is this the real glasnost—kiss and dwell?

Record Herring Run Expected in Prince William Sound Is a No-Show

The Alaska Department of Fish and Game predicted that about 134,133 tons of herring would return to Prince William Sound for the fishery, which opened and closed this week. But only about one-third of the expected fish have so far returned to spawn along the sound's coastline.

Fishermen also reported observing lesions and white spots on the herring, according to an April 1993 story in the *Cordova Times*. Samples taken in Stockdale Harbor showed 22.1 percent of the fish were diseased. The highest incidence of diseased fish was in the

Montague Island area, which was heavily oiled in the 1989 *Exxon Valdez* oil spill.

Some of these adult herring would have grown from eggs laid during the oil spill. It was speculated that the oil affected the immune systems of the herring and that they are less able to fight off infections as adults than herring who were not inundated with crude oil.

Samples of herring were sent to Fish and Wildlife laboratories in Wisconsin for testing.

Bold Snowboarder Goes to Extremes on Mount Eccles Run

Teal Copeland, a 17-year-old Cordova High senior, impressed the entire town with his snow-boarding expertise. Zigzag tracks from the very top of Mount Eccles down a narrow chute called "the Lady of the Mountain," because of the resemblance of the shape of the snow to a reclining woman, showed that Copeland knew his stuff.

The hike up to the peak took him two and a half hours. His trek took him below the Bear on the Mountain (another local feature), over a sweeping cornice and along the backside of the west ridge line. His bold line down the mountain was the most recent of a handful of descents through the 70-degree chute.

"I had to side slip over some of the rocks," the sun-burned Copeland told the *Cordova Times*. "But once I was past that stretch, it was perfect corn snow."

"It only took five minutes to get down, but it was totally worth it," he added. "It was a great ride."

Copeland has been skiing since he was a child, but has been snow boarding only for five years. He was one of the first Cordovans to use a snow board.

Alaska Legislature Votes to Phase Out Longevity Bonus

In a move that will not make them popular with older Alaskans, the House approved legislation to phase out the longevity bonus program, which gives $2,150 a month to Alaskans 65 and older regardless of need.

Payments to those already enrolled in the program would decrease to $225 a month and would continue indefinitely. But the amount for new applicants would be decreased every year until 1996, when no more new applicants would be accepted.

The program was begun in 1972 to reward those who had lived in Alaska before statehood and to provide retirement income for self-employed persons such as miners, fishermen and trappers. When a 1994 court decision struck down the long-term residency requirement, the program was opened up virtually to all elderly Alaskans.

Current enrollment in the longevity bonus program is about 23,000 Alaskans. Elderly Alaskans earn $1.3 billion a year in retirement and other income and spend about 80 percent of it in the state.

Early Herring Arrival in Bristol Bay Surprises Seiners

The early arrival of herring at Togiak beat fishermen to the grounds. The herring opening was set by the Alaska Department of Fish and Game for Tuesday, April 27, the earliest opening in the season since 1987.

The 1992 herring season started May 20. During the 1992 opener 260 purse seiners and 230 gillnetters were reported on the grounds near Dillingham on Bristol Bay.

An aerial survey on Monday, April 26, 1993, estimated 116,000 tons of herring on the grounds. But only 25 purse seiners were out on the herring grounds by 8:30 A.M., Tuesday, April 27.

Even the staff of the *Bristol Bay Times* was surprised by the early herring. In announcing its annual herring pool guessing game, the newspaper said all entries postmarked by May 1 would be accepted. The unpredictable silvery fish showed up almost a week before deadline.

Exxon Report Says Post-Spill Future of Sound Looks Rosy

Scientists hired by Exxon Corporation to study the 1989 Alaska oil spill of an estimated 11 millions gallons of crude gave an upbeat assessment in April 1993, the first day of a four-day scientific conference held in Atlanta. The report said that "what little oil remains in Prince William Sound is swelling the abundance of life along the shore."

"What remains is not toxic," claimed Exxon scientist Hans Jahns.

The report said scientists have found a greater abundance of mussels, snails, barnacles and other intertidal creatures, an increase they attributed to "an increased food supply" of organisms that are capable of eating oil residue.

Riki Ott, a marine biologist from Cordova, accused the scientists of reaching conclusions "bought and paid for by the company that caused the spill," according to a story in the *Anchorage Daily News*. "I wish that truth ruled the day," Ott said before an audience of about 100 scientists. "What we have is corporate bullies trying to intimidate us."

Warm Month in Interior Hatches Early Aspen Leaves

The month's hot and dry weather brought spring to the Interior weeks earlier than normal in 1993. Every day of April had above-normal temperatures, according to the National Weather Service.

Green leaves began sprouting on hillside birch and aspen during the final days of the month—extremely rare for April. The average temperature was 41.1 degrees, 10.4 degrees above normal. It was the second-warmest April on record in Fairbanks, broken only by April 1940.

The warm spell was particularly welcome since it followed the third snowiest winter on record.

Pribilofs Battle the Threat of Rats to Seabirds

The rat doesn't need to wait for a sinking vessel to jump ship. In fact, rats have jumped ship and infested some 80 percent of the world's islands, where they increase and multiply and drive out native bird species, particularly nesting seabirds. The Norway rat now infests at least 20 Aleutian islands and several Alaska ports. The U.S. Fish and Wildlife Service has launched a letter campaign to ascertain how extensive the problem is in Alaska.

"An infestation of rats, on certain islands, would cause a bigger and more permanent devastation of colonial nesting seabirds than the *Exxon Valdez* oil spill, which probably killed at least 500,000 birds," the F&W letter said.

The agency is helping two rat-free island communities, St. Paul and St. George in the Pribilofs, to train their port managers in the art of "rat patrol."

Some of the infestations date back to military occupation during World War II, while others go back to sailing ships of the late 1700s.

The Pribilofs, with millions of seabirds and fur seals sought by tourists and subsistence hunters alike, can't afford to let rats invade, says St. Paul city manager Larry Merculieff. Harbor workers will be trained in rat control.

Dead Murres in Seward Prompt Collection for Study

Between mid-April and the end of May 1993, more than 200 dead murres were collected near Seward's small-boat harbor. The collection of carcasses began after residents reported seeing apparently confused birds wandering about parking lots and swimming in rain puddles. Murres usually keep away from inhabited areas.

The murres showed up when diseased herring occurred, and theories abounded that there was a connection.

Samples of carcasses collected by federal biologists were being tested to try to determine the cause of the die-off.

Former UAF Biologists Finally Get Their Due

Two researchers who 32 years ago lost their jobs over Project Chariot, a federal nuclear testing project proposed for the Arctic coast, were finally recognized for their contributions.

Former University of Alaska Fairbanks biologists Leslie Viereck and William Pruitt lost their teaching jobs at UAF in 1961 after they publicly protested against Project Chariot. On May 9, 1993, the two were awarded honorary doctorate degrees in science by UAF for the very research work that cost them their jobs.

Project Chariot would have set off up to six nuclear bombs under Cape Thompson, near the village of Point Hope, to blast out a man-made harbor.

The idea was to open up access to coal and other mineral deposits in the region for trade with Japan, said a story in the *Fairbanks Daily News–Miner*.

Viereck, Pruitt and 80 other scientists were contracted by the U.S. Atomic Energy Commission in the late '50s to research whether a nuclear blast equal to 2.4 million tons of dynamite would harm Point Hope's human inhabitants, flora and fauna. The explosion would have been 143 times greater than that at Hiroshima. Viereck and Pruitt soon realized the project would be unhealthy, but the AEC kept insisting Project Chariot was perfectly safe and that the radiation from the nuclear blast would float harmlessly out to sea.

Pruitt's research found that radiation from nuclear testing had already penetrated the Arctic food chain. Eskimos ate caribou, which fed on lichens that absorbed radiation from the air.

Viereck helped prove that Cape Thompson had a richer, more varied flora than other parts of the Arctic, with 293 species of flowering plants, 50 species of mosses and 57 species of lichens. He is known throughout the state as co-author of the "bible" of Alaska's trees and shrubs. In October 1992, he published a book on vegetation classifications in Alaska, a 15-year project.

Pruitt, 70, is currently professor of zoology at the University of Manitoba, Canada.

Permits Required for Chilkoot Hikers

Although hikers each season on the historic 33-mile Chilkoot Trail only number a tenth of the 30,000 stampeders who crossed over during the Klondike gold rush, the National Park Service decided in 1993 that it must require backcountry permits for hikers of the trail.

In 1992, 3,000 backpackers hiked the trail, which cuts through the Klondike Gold Rush National Historical Park spanning Alaska and British Columbia.

The Park Service told the *Juneau Empire* that issuing permits will help keep track of hikers and trail use. Heaviest use of the trail is during a 10-week period between mid-June and the end of August.

Average Alaskan is Young, Male

According to a new report released this month by the Department of Health and Social Services, Alaskans are young, work in dangerous occupations and have a tendency toward binge drinking.

Alaska has the second-youngest population in the country, according to the 1990 census. The median age is 29.2, more than three years younger than the national median age of 32.9. Alaska also has a higher birth rate than the U.S. norm, with 24.4 births per 1,000 residents in 1990.

Accidental injuries were the third leading cause of death in Alaska in 1990. Suicide rated higher in Alaska than in the rest of the United States. Alaska also had the highest annual rate of work-related deaths in the nation. Nearly half were from drowning, and nearly a third were from airplane crashes.

The report found Alaskans at risk for death from three major causes: cancer, heart disease and accidental injuries.

Although Alaskans are less sedentary than citizens nationwide, they are also more likely to smoke and be overweight.

Native Conference Plans Own Chamber of Commerce

In an effort to direct dollars to businesses that support Alaska Native causes, Tanana Chiefs Conference plans to form its own chamber of commerce. Called the Interior Chamber of Commerce, its membership will be comprised of businesses that clearly support Native rights such as subsistence and tribal sovereignty.

Tanana Chiefs conference, a non-profit Native corporation headquartered in Fairbanks, will invite businesses to join the new chamber and distribute the membership list in its 43 villages. Village residents will be encouraged to shop at those businesses endorsed by TCC. The purpose is to provide direction to villages about businesses that support Native causes.

Blind Woman Scales Denali

Fifty-four-year-old Joni Phelps, blind since the age of 30, scaled Mount McKinley. According to the National

Park Service, she is the first blind woman to reach the summit. She began the trek with her two 29-year-old sons on May 15, 1993.

Phelps, who lives in Pennsylvania, has relied on a guide dog since she became blind, but she never gave up her love of the outdoors and has traveled the world enjoying scuba, rock climbing and kayaking. She prepared for this trip by working with a trainer all winter long, lifting weights and learning to tie knots and stop herself in a fall by using her ice ax.

Alaska One of the Last Bastions of the U.S. Merchant Marine

The MV *Great Land,* like other cargo ships, journeys nearly 3,000 miles each week back and forth across a gulf that can be one of the world's roughest seas. The giant floating warehouse is part of Alaska's maritime lifeline to Lower 48 suppliers. Measuring more than 2½ football fields in length, the ship is often filled with more than 3 million pounds of cargo bound for merchant's shelves from Anchorage to Barrow.

In the Lower 48, trucks and trains form the supply lines that feed the great urban centers of nearly every state in the union. It is a world of 24-hour diners that straddle the interstates, hard-driving truckers and leathernecked train engineers who lead freight caravans across deserts and prairies.

But Alaska looks to ships such as the *Great Land* to stock almost everything that appears in stores. Without the weekly sailing of the *Great Land* and other cargo ships and barges, corn flakes would soon disappear from grocery shelves, toothpaste from drugstores and Big Macs from McDonald's.

In 1992, cargo ships and tugs pulling barges hauled more than 3 billion pounds of cargo to southcentral Alaska ports. That trade helps create jobs for more than a thousand workers in Alaska and Washington: longshoremen who load and unload the ships, truckers who shuttle goods between ports and warehouses, and sales and office people.

Alaskan Dinosaurs Highlighted by Release of "Jurassic Park"

Release of the "Jurassic Park" movie by Universal Studios has generated new interest in dinosaur bones and other fossils.

As a result, the Bureau of Land Management, a division of the U.S. Department of the Interior, is working with author Michael Crichton and Universal Studios to develop a series of television and radio public service announcements concerning the search for such fossils. The announcements are scheduled to appear nationwide throughout the summer.

According to BLM director Jim Baca, "Few Americans realize that dinosaurs such as *Tyrannosaurus rex* and *Stegosaurus* have all been found on BLM lands. The public service announcements will familiarize the American people with their paleontological legacy and encourage them to preserve and protect these valuable resources for future generations to study and enjoy."

Although Colorado, Utah and Wyoming may be known to many Americans as containing treasures of dinosaur fossils, there are seven types of dinosaurs known to have existed in Alaska, with several others suspected but not proven. All of the fossil remains discovered in Alaska to date are from the late Cretaceous period of 75 million to 70 million years ago.

Of the seven types, six have been found on the North Slope of Alaska in the vicinity of the Colville River on BLM-managed lands. The six include a Tyrannosaurid dinosaur, a half-scale version of the famous *Tyrannosaurus rex;* three relatively small meat eaters, Troodontid, Saurornitholestes, and Hypsilophodontid; a Pachyrhinosaurus, a three-horned cousin of Triceratops; and Hadrosaurid dinosaurs, which are duck-billed plant eaters.

The seventh type, a Nodosaurid Ankylosaur, which somewhat resembled a giant armadillo, was found in the western Talkeetna Mountains north of Anchorage.

Remarks BLM-Alaska state archaeologist Dr. Robert King, "Alaska dinosaurs are of international scientific interest. It is a mystery how they survived so far north where plant growth ceased during the winter months. Whether they migrated southward or hybernated in some fashion is a real puzzle to paleontologists."

The Alaska State Museum in Juneau and the University of Alaska Museum in Fairbanks both have dinosaur exhibits. BLM has a small display of Hadrosaurid dinosaur bones and a mammoth tusk in the Alaska Resources Library in the Anchorage Federal Office Building.

Rangers Evacuate Bumper Crop of McKinley Climbers.

Three climbers were evacuated in one day from Mount McKinley, the National Park Service said.

Akira Sakaguchi, 34, of Japan, was evacuated on the afternoon of June 16 when he was diagnosed with gastrointestinal bleeding.

A second climber, Shyam Blon, 32, of Nepal, made it up to the 20,000-foot level before being stricken with severe headaches. Blon was diagnosed with a probable blood clot in his lungs and shuttled by helicopter to Talkeetna.

A third climber, Bertha Ramirez, 41, of Mexico, had fallen 100 feet in an avalanche. Fellow climbers rescued Ramirez but said she had stopped breathing for five minutes. Park rangers stabilized her. She was later shuttled to Providence Hospital in Anchorage and listed in fair condition.

It is being suggested that climbers post a financial bond to cover potential rescue efforts from Mount McKinley. Climbers do not contribute toward the cost of having rescue assistance available, nor are they required to have rescue insurance.

The cost of rescuing climbers and removing bodies from Mount McKinley during 1992 was $431,345. The cost was divided almost evenly between the National Park Service and the military, which rescued 23 people and recovered 22 bodies at McKinley that year.

McKinley's high altitude and remote location make rescues costly. The park service pays $1,200 a day to station a high-altitude helicopter and pilot at McKinley and $450 an hour to fly the craft during a rescue mission. Critics contend the adventuresome should pay to play.

"The Dorm" of Matanuska Farm Colony is Preserved

A 90-by-30-foot dorm that once housed nurses, teachers, secretaries and other skilled, single workers recruited to help members of the Matanuska Farm Colony in the 1930s is being restored by Janet Kincaid of Palmer.

Locals see a two-story, pink-and-white eyesore, but Kincaid imagined the building reborn as a Colony Inn. Kincaid estimates her renovation bills will top $300,000. However, if the work meets historic preservation standards, Kincaid would be allowed to deduct up to 20 percent of the project's cost from her federal income taxes.

"It's exciting to be part of history," says Kincaid. "The colony was a tiny piece of American history that didn't happen anywhere else."

The dorm and other nearby buildings were hurriedly built in the fall and winter of 1935 by crews hired under President Franklin Roosevelt's massive public works program. During the summer of 1935, 200 families, mostly on relief, were moved by rail and ship from depressed towns in the Midwest to claim acreage on the new colony. They hoped to covert wilderness to prosperous farms with help from Uncle Sam.

Matanuska Colony did not thrive, but many of its distinctive barns and houses still stand.

Alaska University Will Train Russian Journalists

The University of Alaska Fairbanks received an $80,222 grant for a training program for Russian journalists.

The innovative program will bring 10 Russians (four print journalists, four television reporters and two faculty members of Yakutsk State University) to the Fairbanks campus in July and August 1993. They will take courses at the university and work with local media outlets.

Baby Musk-ox Is Nursed Back to Health by Lamb "Angel"

Panik the musk-ox was in trouble. The fuzzy female calf, No. 414 at the Musk-ox Farm in Palmer, was hardly 10 days old when she collapsed in the field where she was staying with her mother and was taken to a veterinary clinic for intravenous feeding. The calf was thin, listless and suffering from diarrhea.

By the time she was released from the clinic, the calf had become a social outcast to her herd, and was in danger of not thriving because of loneliness. A black poodle used as a playmate didn't help. Then the farm came up with the notion of borrowing a lamb.

Angel, a two-month-old white lamb, was brought over from a dairy farm in Point MacKenzie. The beginning of a friendship and a healthy musk-ox began when the calf and lamb competed for the bottle. The pair nurse together, sleep together, munch on weeds together and frolic together.

"She may have survived without the lamb, but she wouldn't be as happy," veterinarian Ron Williams told the *Anchorage Daily News.*

Alaska Demands $29 Billion From Feds

Governor Walter J. Hickel announced in July 1993 that the state of Alaska has filed suit in the U.S. Court of Federal Claims, charging that the federal government's violations of the Alaska Statehood Compact have cost the state more than $29 billion.

"When we were admitted to the Union in 1959, one of the main concerns Congress had was that Alaska had to have the economic viability needed to pay for state government," said Hickel.

According to the governor, Alaska's economic viability was to be achieved through the development of 103 million acres of state lands and by receiving 90 percent of the revenue from federal lands. Since statehood, however, more than 100 million acres of federal land have been withdrawn from development. Among other charges, the lawsuit contends that by withdrawing critical lands from mineral leasing, Congress has "taken" Alaska's interest in the revenue derived from those lands in violation of the Fifth Amendment to the U.S. Constitution.

This lawsuit is one in a series of major challenges to the federal government that the state has pursued under Hickel's direction. Alaska also seeks to overturn the federal ban on foreign export of Alaska North Slope crude oil.

Hickel said the $29 billion figure is not an arbitrary one. "That's our starting point, but we believe the loss has been far more than that. For example,

Prudhoe Bay is only 200,000 acres and has been worth in excess of $100 billion so far."

Record Heat in Anchorage

Summer 1993 was exceptionally warm and dry across southcentral Alaska. From June 1 to August 9, rainfall in Anchorage was less than one inch, the least amount of precipitation for this period since recordkeeping began in 1916.

Seven times that summer Anchorage reported a temperature of 75 degrees or higher—the most since the summer of 1953. Normally during any given summer, Anchorage could expect from zero to three days of highs reaching 75 degrees.

Reeve Still Plans to Fly to Japan

Reeve Aleutian Airways' plan to start international service from Anchorage to Chitose airport in northern Japan is still in the works, though the initial starting date for service has been delayed and the timing indefinite.

Problems in getting permission for mid-route refueling at Shemya Air Force Base and competition from MarkAir on other Reeve air routes were some of the causes for postponing the start of service.

"The potential of that market is still there," said Dick Reeve, company president.

Local Stores Scramble to Compete With National Retailers in Anchorage

With national retailers such as Costco and Eagle Hardware opening or expanding their stores in Anchorage, local store owners were gearing up for an explosion of competition in 1993. University of Alaska Anchorage marketing professor Betsy Boze said the retail boom is a hot topic among her students, many of whom are in business in Anchorage. "I think a lot of your little mom and pops are going to get killed because they just can't compete with the big chains," she said. "That's not news because it's been happening all over the country for years, but it is new to Anchorage."

But many retailers remember the crunch of the late 1980s when many of their competitors went out of business.

Adjustments in prices, selection and service were made by those who survive today in a retail economy that only recently became home to membership warehouses. For small retailers, the fine-tuning continues.

Iditarod Loses Major Race Sponsors

The Iditarod Trail Sled Dog Race, having lost two major sponsors and possibly a third, reduced its purse for the 1994 race by approximately 25 percent, it was announced in August 1993.

Dodge and ABC television will not renew their contracts for next year. Alascom is currently in negotiation with the Iditarod committee. The loss of two major sponsors has cost the Iditarod—which had a $1 million race budget in 1993—nearly $200,000. The companies are pulling out because of pressure from the Humane Society, which has been concerned about dog care in the race, according to Iditarod board president Matt Desalernos.

Obituaries

We recognize the significant contributions of just a few of the many Alaskans who died this year, from June 1992 through May 1993. Due to limited space, we are including some of the more prominent Alaskans who left a special mark on the state's history in business, politics and social development.

ANABLE, Edmund A., 89, a Jesuit priest who served in Alaska for more than 53 years, died June 24, 1992, in Spokane, Wash.

A native of New York, Anable entered the Society of Jesus in 1924 and was ordained in 1936. He asked to be assigned to Alaska Catholic missions, and was sent to St. Marys, arriving by steamboat in 1938. During his service there, he built a 56-foot hull for a new mission boat to deliver supplies and passengers to Catholic missions along the lower Yukon River.

In later years he worked at mission schools in Pilgrim Hot Springs and Holy Cross and served as pastor in Nome.

Conscientious, a hard worker and handy with tools of all sizes, Anable established a cannery to process Native-caught salmon at St. Marys. He retired in 1981, and served as pastor of Immaculate Conception Church and Sacred Heart Cathedral in Fairbanks.

BOLIMA, Sterling, Native leader of Angoon, died May 20, 1993, in Seattle after a month-long battle with cancer.

Bolima is credited with saving much of Admiralty Island from development. Angoon is located on the west side of Admiralty Island, south of Juneau.

Bolima represented Angoon's native corporation in Washington, D.C., during negotiations leading up to congressional passage of the Alaska National Interest Lands Conservation Act in 1980.

In ensuing amendments to the act, he engineered trades of land with other native corporations and the federal government to help create a national monument on the island. In return, the village corporation received lucrative timberland on Prince of Wales Island.

Born to a Tlingit mother in Sacramento, Calif., Bolima moved to Alaska in the early 1970s.

CARLSON, Phyllis Ina Downing, 83, local historian and pioneer Alaska resident, died July 6, 1993, at her home in Anchorage.

She was born Sept. 6, 1909, in Seattle and moved to the territory of Alaska in 1914 to join her father who was building a railroad from Cordova to the copper mines at Kennicott. When she graduated from Cordova High in 1928, she was one in a class of seven. After earning a teaching certificate, she taught in a one-room log cabin at Cooper Landing.

Carlson later taught in the Athabascan village of Tyonek on the west side of Cook Inlet. She was honored twice there for her contributions as a teacher, historian and friend. She and her husband Carl ran the post office, community store, radio and telephone system and helped operate the community sawmill.

The couple moved to Anchorage in 1939. After World War II, she and Carl returned to Cordova where she produced her own radio program, "Woman to Woman." She wrote a 1966 *Encyclopedia Americana* article on Anchorage and was widely published as a freelance historian in local and national magazines.

Carlson was one of the few journalists to have interviewed Benny Benson, the young man who designed Alaska's flag as a child. She also wrote about her acquaintance with Tyonek's chief Simeon Chickalusion, the man who moved the village north when the old beach village site flooded in the 1930s.

In the early 1960s she moved to Woody Island near Kodiak to work as a secretary for the Federal Aviation Administration. She was there when the earthquake hit. She returned to Anchorage in 1965. She retired from the Alaska reference desk at Z.J. Loussac Library in 1974.

In 1988 she was named a Woman of Achievement by Alaska Press Women.

She is survived by three daughters.

CHARLEY, Walter, 84, an Ahtna Athabascan elder who contributed to the passage of the 1971 Alaska Native Claims Settlement Act, died Oct. 22, 1992, in Glennallen.

Born at Wood Camp on the Copper River, Charley came from a long line of

Native leaders. He worked on the building of the Copper River and Northwestern Railroad and the trans-Alaska oil pipeline, and also participated in Native issues statewide.

Serving as president of the Chitina village corporation and of Ahtna Inc., a regional Native corporation, he also served as a former commissioner of Wrangell-St. Elias National Park.

His wife, Mamie, survives.

CHISUM, Gerald Cayle "Jack," 75, Alaska aviation innovator, died July 22, 1992, in Phoenix, Ariz.

Born in Kansas, he hopped a freight train to the West Coast after high school, working first in Oregon and then in Dutch Harbor. He survived the Japanese bombing of Dutch Harbor while a member of the U.S. Army Signal Corps, and later supervised the crew that salvaged the first crashed Japanese Zero fighter plane.

After the war, Chisum started Powerline Construction Co., which brought electricity to rural areas in Oregon, Washington, Idaho and Alaska. He homesteaded on Island Lake on the Kenai Peninsula in the 1950s, and started Chisum Flying Service, a statewide charter and guide service.

Always creating, Chisum adapted helicopters for heavylift construction and used the aircraft to set steel towers and fight fires. In the 1960s, he worked as a helicopter pilot for geologists in Saudi Arabia.

His company furnished C-130 civilian cargo planes for oil-spill cleanup efforts in Kuwait and supplied heavy-lift helicopters for the *Exxon Valdez* oil spill in Alaska. He lived by the motto, "If you're going to do something, go all the way and be the best."

DEMIENTIEFF, Nicholas Ephram, 83, died May 5, 1993, in Fairbanks.

He was born July 7, 1909, in Holy Cross. He was married to Nellie Mae Bressler in Holy Cross in 1930. The couple had 10 children.

Demientieff was a trapper, mail carrier, reindeer herder and captain of his own river freighting firm, Demientieff Navigation Co. His family and friends operated the *Beaver, Sea Wolf,* and *St. Francis* river tugs along with other riverboats and barges on all tributaries of the Yukon.

After World War II, the Department of the Army gave him a letter of commendation for freighting fuel from Nenana to Glennallen.

His determination and ambition to be a good provider showed in his success as a businessman, and he always taught kindness and treated his family with loving care.

DOW, Russell W., 72, a power plant operator, photographer and historian, died Aug. 10, 1992, in Spokane. Born in New Hampshire, he moved to Alaska in 1933 at the age of 18, traveling with the Harvard Mountaineering Club and assisting with survey work conducted by world-renowned Boston cartographer Bradford Washburn.

He and his wife homesteaded in the Butte area of Palmer in 1947. Dow worked as a miner, cook, logger, truck driver and cannery worker before becoming an operator at Eklutna Power Plant. His early photographs of Alaska appeared in many books and magazines, including *National Geographic.*

FRANKLIN, John, 63, former public safety commissioner and longtime fire fighter of Anchorage, died June 4, 1993, at Troublesome Creek, on his way home from a final visit to Denali National Park and Preserve.

Franklin succumbed after battling lung cancer for a year. In keeping with his wishes, his family took him to Denali earlier in the week to spend his last days at a campsite overlooking a river. He and his wife Allene worked as volunteer hosts at the park in 1992.

Mountain climbers who had read about Franklin's final visit sent him a rock from the summit of Mount McKinley. "That rock never left him. He died with it," Allene Franklin said. "I don't think anybody could ever have a better ending than he did."

KENNEDY, Elizabeth Margaret "Kay," 87, a pioneer Alaskan journalist whose career broke ground for women, died April 2, 1993, of cancer at her home in Fairbanks.

Born in South Dakota on Dec. 24, 1905, she traveled to Wyoming in the late '20s where she taught school, worked on a dude ranch and became the first woman in the state to become a bonded hunting guide. She earned a degree in geology from the University of Wyoming in 1931 and five years later ventured to Alaska, where she was a freelance correspondent for news services, magazines and newspapers.

In the late 1930s, she became the first civilian employee at Ladd Field, now Fort Wainwright. She went on to write for the Great Falls (Mont.) *Leader* and the Denver *Post* before returning to Alaska in 1949. She was then employed by the *Alaska Daily Empire* in Juneau and the *Fairbanks Daily News-Miner*.

She is credited with proposing a Fairbanks summer celebration in 1954, an event that grew into the city's annual Golden Days festival. Over the years she helped found the Farthest North Press Club and in 1961 served as the first president of Alaska Press Women. She wrote *Sunset* magazine's first travel guide to Alaska. Kennedy received an honorary doctorate of letters from the University of Alaska in October 1992 for contributions to the school and the state.

The University of Alaska Rasmuson Library archives was given Kennedy's collection of materials on Alaska aviation.

KUKOWSKI, Richard J. "Dick," 58, a longtime Anchorage resident, died April 22, 1993, at his home.

Shortly after graduation from high school in Minnesota, he came to Anchorage and worked for Walter Hickel. He managed the Anchorage Travellers Inn owned by Hickel. In Hickel's book, *Who Owns America,* Hickel wrote: "In business in Alaska, I always hired the young person who was looking for a break to prove himself. In 1954, I hired Dick Kukowski to manage the Anchorage Travellers Inn. I did not realize it at the time, but he was only 19, so Johnny Woods, the bartender, would not let him into the cocktail lounge. When he finally turned 21, Dick walked into the lounge and announced to Johnny, 'Give me a drink, and I'm still the boss.' "

Kukowski moved to Fairbanks in 1955 to manager Hickel's Fairbanks Inn. In 1961, he entered the U.S. Army and was stationed at Fort Richardson. He was discharged in 1963. He then accepted a job with Union Oil and lived and worked in Whittier. In 1971, he founded Urethane Specialties Co. which he and partners operated until 1978.

In January 1981, he was hired by the Alaska Department of Labor as a compliance officer for the Labor Standards and Safety Division, Section of Occupational Safety and Health. He brought knowledge of operations in the construction and oil industries to bear on his job.

In 1990, he commanded a boat doing surveillance of work crews performing oil spill cleanup in Prince William Sound. He also volunteered for the Anchorage Police Department, and was a member of Anchorage Moose Lodge.

LINGO, Dorothy Troy, 91, pioneer Alaska resident and former newspaperwoman, died June 4, 1993, at her Anchorage home.

Lingo first came to Alaska with her parents when she was six months old and lived in Skagway for two years. She then returned to Washington state and attended school in Port Angeles and Seattle.

In 1912, the family returned to Alaska when her father, John Troy, purchased the *Daily Alaska Empire* (now the *Juneau Empire*). John Troy also served as territorial governor from 1933 to 1939, and Dorothy often acted as hostess at the governor's house during that period.

Lingo began her newspaper career when she worked as a reporter on the family newspaper in Juneau from the time she was in high school until her marriage in 1935, and again from 1941–44.

She became one of the original agents with Northwest Airlines when the company began operating into Anchorage in 1946.

Lingo was a member of Pioneers of Alaska Auxiliary 34 and Gamma Phi Beta Sorority. She helped found the Girl Scouts in Anchorage. She was known as a wonderful hostess, an avid bridge player, and a great friend to many.

She is survived by her only child, Joan Moore, two grandsons and six great-grandchildren.

MUNZ, William, 82, a pioneer bush pilot who led a daring 1948 effort to rescue the crew of a downed U.S. Air Force bomber on the Seward Peninsula, died Feb. 16, 1992, in St. George, Utah.

"He was one tough cookie, tougher

than flying leather," commented Dick Gelleher, who purchased Munz's northern flying service in 1962.

Munz came to Nome in 1936 and worked as a dragline operator in a mine. He spent many years on the Seward Peninsula and had a role in establishing jade mining in the Kobuk area. He also served as an Alaska territorial representative from the Nome area.

Munz is credited with rescuing six crewmen from a downed B-29, nicknamed the "Clobbered Turkey," which crashed on the Seward Peninsula at Christmastime in 1948. Bad weather hampered the military's search and rescue and some of the crewmen froze to death before Munz and fellow pilot Jack Whaley found the plane. For his part in the rescue, Munz received the Air Medal, the Air Force's highest civilian honor.

NESETH, Eunice Von Scheele, 85, a lifelong Alaska teacher, historian, artist and museum curator, died Oct. 5, 1992, in Kodiak.

Born in Afognak, the daughter of a Swedish nobleman and a woman of Russian-Aleut descent, she earned an education degree and taught school in the Aleutian Islands, Dillingham and Kodiak.

In 1970 she and her husband Henry became caretakers of Kodiak's Baranov Museum. That same year Eunice began teaching Attu basket-weaving, thus preserving an intricate, endangered art. Her wealth of historical knowledge aided many authors writing about Kodiak's past.

ONGTOWASRUK, Clarence, 74, died Nov. 10, 1992, at his Wales residence.

He started school at age 12, completing eight grades in three years. His military service included a stint in the U.S. Army from 1942 to 1948, and time in the Alaska Territorial Guard. He worked as a district magistrate, a newspaper writer for the *Tundra Times* and *Nome Nugget*, was the first airline agent for Nome Flying Service, a reindeer herder, an assistant manager for the Wales Native Store, an ivory carver and a substitute teacher for the Bureau of Indian Affairs.

He learned how to read music,

played five instruments and was a church organist and choir director.

RHODE, Helen E., 73, grande dame of Alaska wildlife photography, died Sept. 9, 1992, in Anchorage.

Born in Oklahoma, Rhode earned a degree in education from Texas Women's University. During World War II, she worked with the defense industry in Seattle, where she met her future husband, Cecil, a famed wildlife cinematographer and lecturer.

After the war, the couple moved to Cooper Landing where they built a home beside Kenai Lake on land that Cecil had homesteaded in the 1930s. Whenever she wasn't substitute teaching at Cooper Landing school, Rhode learned what she called "the game of wildlife photography" by accompanying her husband on wilderness photo shoots. Thereafter, for a good two decades, the photo credit "Photos by Helen and Cecil Rhode" frequently appeared on photos of Alaska in books and magazine articles.

The couple began taking pictures of Denali National Park in the 1950s. After Cecil died in 1979, Helen continued her photography adventures. In spring and summer, she'd take pictures on the Kenai Peninsula. In fall she'd head north to Denali Park and photograph wildlife from the roadside. Her photos appeared in many national magazines, including *Alaska, National Wildlife, National Geographic* and *Audubon*.

SCHULTZ, Ransom "Tony," 83, veteran bush pilot, known to other aviators as the "mercy pilot" of Alaska, died June 24, 1993, in Fairbanks.

Rancy Acord, a longtime friend and fellow pilot, said Schultz was known to risk his life to save others. "If the weather was bad, some pilots would turn the trips down," Acord told the *Anchorage Daily News*. "With Schultz, any emergency that seemed real difficult, he would always volunteer and he would always make it."

Schultz was born in South Dakota and came north to Valdez in 1938 on the steamship *Yukon*, lured by his father's tales of working the beaches of Nome for gold.

From Valdez he flew as a passenger with Noel Wien to Fairbanks and soon owned his own open-cockpit two-seater. He would eventually log 34,000 air miles in a commercial aviation career that got off the ground in 1941 with Alaska State Airlines, a forerunner to Alaska Airlines. In 1954, he joined Wien Airlines, for whom he worked until his retirement in 1966.

Not all Schultz's flights were rescues. Over the years he hauled mail, convicts and corpses. One flight involved a U.S. marshal who went to Chevak to escort a man wanted for murdering his wife.

A witness and the dead woman's body also made the trip. Schultz solved the over-booking problem by seating the witness on the husband's lap, and strapping a seat belt around them both.

SEVECK, Helen Rock, 87, sister of the late newspaper editor, Howard Rock, and an Eskimo dance performer and promoter of Alaska tourism in her own right, died Dec. 31, 1992, in Fairbanks.

Born in Point Hope, she married Bob Tuzroyluk in 1923. The couple lived a traditional subsistence lifestyle at Point Hope, raising eight children. During this period Helen became the village's first health aide.

After she was widowed, Helen married Chester A. Seveck Sr. in 1958. The following year the photogenic couple signed a movie contract to play parts in the motion picture "Ice Palace," starring Richard Burton.

For 20 years the Sevecks promoted Alaska for Wien Airlines. Their fur-ruff-encircled faces were featured on many posters, calendars and brochures. They performed Eskimo dances before thousands of tourists and celebrities, including President Ronald Reagan, and appeared on the Art Linkletter, Steve Allen and Groucho Marx television shows.

In her spare time, Seveck made traditional Eskimo garments and received many awards for her skin sewing.

Seveck is survived by her son and four daughters, many grandchildren and great-grandchildren and two great-great-grandchildren.

SIMPSON, Jack Raymond, 83, Anchorage businessman, died March 24, 1993, at home in Anchorage.

He was born Dec. 18, 1909, in Condon, Ore., and married Nova Hedin in 1936 in Portland. The Simpsons moved to Alaska in 1952 where he started Northern Insurance Adjusters in Anchorage. The business grew statewide. Simpson sold it in 1971.

Simpson served in the Alaska Legislature from 1966 to 1968 under Governor Walter Hickel, and was a lobbyist in Juneau during the late 1960s. He then served as special assistant to Governor Keith Miller.

He was a former member of the Anchorage Human Rights Commission and served on the Alaska State Commission on Employment Security for Governor Jay Hammond. He helped found the Governor's Prayer Breakfast in the 1960s.

He is survived by his wife, Nova, and sons Erik and Mark.

SOURS, Lena Suuyuk, died April 16, 1993, in Kotzebue. She was born and raised in a sod hut in the late 1800s in a seasonal camp now known as Kotzebue. Sours was one of northwestern Alaska's best-known Inupiat elders. Her age was estimated at 108 to 110.

Sours and her reindeer herder husband, the late Burton Aglavialuuraq Sours, traveled extensively throughout northwestern Alaska during their lifetimes.

In her prime, Sours spent spring and summer months gathering and storing food to sustain the couple's 12 children. She spent the cold, dark months sewing, by candlelight, all her family's clothing. "We all lived in a one-room log cabin, and Mom did all the work," said Charlie Sours, one of her four surviving children.

According to the Chukchi News and Information Service, Sours served as a midwife for much of her life. Her generation still practiced traditional shamanism in her childhood, but with the arrival of Western missionaries she adopted Christianity and taught Sunday school, gave singing lessons at the Friends Church and organized the annual Christmas program.

She was well known for her fur parkas, traditionally sewn from the pelts of ground squirrels she hunted herself in the spring, traveling to squirrel camp by dog team.

In an interview in 1992, Sours credited genes, sober living, an active life—including plenty of walking—and Eskimo food for her longevity. Some of her Eskimo stories, in Inupiaq and English, were recorded and broadcast on the local public radio station.

"She was really the last survivor of our distant past," Judith Allen, the bilingual coordinator for the station, told the *Anchorage Daily News.* "She was the last survivor of the Kotzebue tribe. She knows the time before the missionaries. . . . Many of the elders when they get older, when they pass 80 or 90, are bound to start forgetting. She was always very clear."

STANFIELD, Alexander B. "Stan," 80, Alaska pioneer and watercolor artist, died April 1, 1993, in Anchorage.

Stanfield was born Feb. 4, 1913, in Gooding, Idaho. He moved to Alaska in 1940 to work with the Goodnews Bay Mining Company. He served in the Alaska Territorial Guard during World War II, then moved to Anchorage and founded a travel service.

In 1956, Stanfield became a men's clothier, then worked as a commercial artist for Anchorage Cold Storage and Carrs Quality Food Centers. He was a member of the Anchorage Elks and the Pioneers of Alaska.

He is survived by his wife, Patricia, five children, 18 grandchildren and five great-grandchildren.

STOLPE, Dr. John Raymond, 59, longtime Anchorage dentist, died suddenly of a heart attack April 24, 1993.

Stolpe was born in Michigan, earned his DDS at the University of Detroit in 1958, joined the U.S. Public Health Service and was assigned to Nome. He left his fiancee, Carol Courtney, in Detroit for what was to be a one-year stint. Three months later, Carol joined him with a wedding dress packed in her trunk. The couple spent their honeymoon seal hunting in Teller.

After two years in Nome, Stolpe was reassigned to New York. Ten more moves in 14 years followed, including tours in Anchorage and Sitka. Stolpe was co-director of the Public Health Service's Indian Health Service Dental Branch, stationed in Washington, D.C., in 1973, when he asked to return to Alaska as chief area director, Dental Services Branch, a position he held for 10 years.

He was responsible for changing dental health care delivery in rural Alaska from dogsleds to airplanes, and helped design equipment suitable for transport in bush planes. He was a persistent advocate of ensuring that funds were spent on direct patient care rather than administration.

He was also an avid fisherman, sailor and reader of mysteries.

VOKACEK, Anna May, 88, died Jan. 8, 1993, at her Finger Lake home north of Wasilla.

Born in Valdez, Vokacek served as a U.S. commissioner in Kodiak before going to work for Pacific Northern Airlines. She worked for the territorial court system and in the late 1950s helped set up the present-day superior court system in Anchorage. She was the superior court's first clerk, serving from 1960 until she retired in 1974.

She leaves her husband, Mill, and two children.

Suggested Reading

Beaman, Libby. *Libby, the Sketches, Letters and Journals of Libby Beaman, Recorded in the Pribilof Islands 1879–1880.* Tulsa: Council Oak Books.

Blackman, Margaret B. *During My Time: Florence Edenshaw Davidson, A Haida Woman.* Seattle: University of Washington Press, 1982.

——————. *Sadie Brower Neakok: An Inupiaq Woman.* Seattle: University of Washington Press, 1989.

Caras, Roger. *Monarch of Deadman Bay: The Life and Death of a Kodiak Bear.* Boston: Little Brown, 1969.

Davidson, Art. *In the Wake of the Exxon Valdez: The Devastating Impact of the Oil Spill.* San Francisco: Sierra Club Books, 1990.

Davidson, Art (text); Art Wolfe (photography); Galen Rowell (foreword). *Alakshak: The Great Country.* San Francisco: Sierra Club, 1989.

Elliot, Nan. *I'd Swap My Old Skidoo for You.* Issaquah, Wash.: Sammamish Press, 1989.

Fitzhugh, William W., and Susan A. Kaplan. *Inua: Spirit World of the Bering Sea Eskimo.* Washington, D.C.: Smithsonian Institution Press, 1982.

Garfield, Brian. *The Thousand-Mile War: World War II in Alaska and the Aleutians.* Garden City, N.Y.: Doubleday, 1969.

Greiner, James. *Wager the Wind.* New York: St. Martin's Press, 1982.

Hirschmann, Fred, and Kim Heacox. *Bush Pilots of Alaska.* Portland: Graphic Arts Center Publishing Co., 1989.

Haines, John. *The Stars, The Smoke, The Fire: 25 Years in the Northern Wilderness, a Memoir.* St. Paul: Graywolf Press, 1989.

Holm, Bill. *Spirit and Ancestor: A Century of Northwest Coast Indian Art.* Seattle: University of Washington Press, 1987.

Jonaiti, Aldona, ed. *Chiefly Feasts: The Enduring Kwakiutl Potlatch.* Seattle: University of Washington Press, 1992.

London, Jack. *The Call of the Wild.* New York: Macmillan, 1904.

Lopez, Barry. *Of Wolves and Men.* New York: Scribner's, 1978.

McPhee, John. *Coming into the Country.* New York: Farrar, Straus & Giroux, 1977.

Muir, John. *Travels in Alaska.* Boston: Houghton Mifflin, 1915.

Murie, Adolph. *A Naturalist in Alaska.* Tucson: University of Arizona Press, 1990.

Murie, Olaus. *Journeys to the Far North.* Palo Alto: The Wilderness Society and American West Publishing, 1973.

Murray, John. *The Republic of Rivers.* New York: Oxford University Press, 1990.

Nelson, Richard. *The Island Within.* San Francisco: North Point Press, 1989.

Oswalt, Wendell. *Bashful No Longer.* Tulsa: University of Oklahoma Press, 1990.

Potter, Jean. *The Flying North.* Sausalito: Comstock Editions, 1986.

Ray, Dorothy Jean. *Eskimo Art.* Seattle: University of Washington Press, 1977.

Smith, Barbara Sweetland, and Redmond J. Barnett. *Russian America: The Forgotten Frontier.* Tacoma, Wash.: Washington State Historical Society, 1990.

Stuck, Hudson. *The Ascent of Denali: A Narrative of the First Complete Ascent of the Highest Point in North America.* Lincoln: University of Nebraska Press, 1989. (Originally published in 1914.)

Tabbert, Russell. *Dictionary of Alaskan English.* Juneau: The Denali Press, 1991.

Webb, Melody. *The Last Frontier.* Albuquerque: University of New Mexico Press, 1985.

Wickersham, James. *Old Yukon: Tales—Trails—and Trials.* Washington, D.C.: Washington Law Book Co., 1938.

Woolcock, Iris. *The Road North: One Woman's Adventure Driving the Alaska Highway.* Anchorage: Greatland Graphics, 1990.

Young, S. Hall. *Alaska Days with John Muir.* New York: Fleming A. Revell, 1915.

Alaska Northwest Library

Many North Country books are suggested as related reading throughout THE ALASKA ALMANAC®: FACTS ABOUT ALASKA. Following is our Alaska Northwest Library. These books are available in bookstores or direct from Alaska Northwest Books™, An imprint of Graphic Arts Center Publishing Company, Catalog and Order Dept., P.O. Box 10306, Portland, OR 97210. Call 800-452-3032. Mail orders require a postage and handling fee.

Abalone Summer, by John Dowd. Two 11-year-olds encounter danger and intrigue, discovering ancient Haida villages and burial grounds in the remote coastal wilderness of the Queen Charlotte Islands. *Abalone Summer* offers young readers a gripping adventure tale. 128 pp., $9.95.

Alaska Bear Tales, by Larry Kaniut. Dramatic encounters between bears and humans. 324 pp., $12.95

The Alaska River Guide: Canoeing, Kayaking, and Rafting in the Last Frontier, by Karen Jettmar. Provides vital information for beginners or experienced whitewater kayakers for traveling Alaska's rivers. Includes more than 90 trip options, with detailed maps and descriptions, photographs, information on local services, put-in sites, and much more. 304 pp., $16.95

Alaska Sourdough, by Ruth Allman. Handwritten recipes "by a real Alaskan." 198 pp., $9.95

Alaska Wild Berry Guide and Cookbook. How to find and identify edible wild berries, and how to cook them. 212 pp., $14.95

The Alaska–Yukon Wild Flowers Guide. Large color photos and detailed drawings of 160 species. 227 pp., $16.95

Alaskan Igloo Tales, by Edward L. Keithahan. Arctic oral history written down in the early 20th century, with illustrations. 144 pp., $12.95

Alaska's History: The People, Land, and Events of the North Country, by Harry Ritter. Lively, concise and entertaining, this pocket-size guide to Alaska's history tells you about the adventuresome people and exciting events that have shaped the Great Land. Historical photographs, maps and drawings included. 144 pp., $10.95

Alaska's Wild Plants: A Guide to Alaska's Edible Harvest, by Janice J. Schofield. For hikers, campers, and foragers, plant lovers and visitors to the region, this book is an introduction to more than 70 of the most common edible wild plants. Includes color photographs and recipes. 96 pp., $12.95

Alaska's Wilderness Medicines, by Eleanor G. Viereck. Use of trees, flowers and shrubs for medicinal and other purposes. 116 pp., $9.95

Along the Alaska Highway. Photography by Alissa Crandall, text by Gloria J. Maschmeyer. Compelling color photographs and engaging text combine to reveal the people and landscape along this epic highway. 96 pp., $16.95

Artists at Work: 25 Northwest Glassmakers, Ceramists and Jewelers, by Susan Biskeborn. Photographic portraits by Kim Zumwalt. This book examines the lives and art of these nationally recognized regional artists. Black-and-white photographs bring the reader close to the creative process by capturing the subjects in their work environments, and color photographs display the beauty of the art they produce. 172 pp., $24.95

Baby Animals of the North, text and illustrations by Katy Main. A children's book about wildlife in the Last Frontier guaranteed to captivate the young and young at heart. Color illustrations. 36 pp., laminated board with dust jacket, $13.95

Baidarka, by George Dyson. The history, development and redevelopment of the Aleut kayak. Illustrations and photographs. 231 pp., $19.95

Caprial's Seasonal Kitchen: An Innovative Chef's Menus and Recipes for Easy Home Cooking, by Caprial Pence. One of America's brightest young chefs, Caprial Pence secured a four-star rating for Fullers restaurant in Seattle. In her first cookbook, Pence invites the home chef to discover the secrets of her innovative cooking style. 240 pp., hardbound, $19.95; softbound, $12.95

Capture of Attu. The Aleutian campaign of World War II, as told by the men who fought there. 80 pp., $6.95

Chilkoot Pass: The Most Famous Trail in the North, by Archie Satterfield. A guide for hikers and history buffs. 224 pp., $9.95

Cooking Alaskan, by Alaskans. Hundreds of time-tested recipes, including a section on sourdough. 512 pp., $16.95

Discover Alaska, foreword by Art Davidson. A comprehensive guide to America's Last Frontier and all its spectacular contrasts, including historical views and colorful photographs. 64 pp., $8.95

Discovering Wild Plants: Alaska, Western Canada, the Northwest, by Janice Schofield. Facts, pictures and illustrations detailing more than 130 plants. 368 pp., hardbound, $34.95; softbound, $26.95

Doris Dingle's Crafty Cat Activity Book, by Helen Levchuk, illustrated by John Bianchi. Doris Dingle, one of the world's great cat lovers, shares her years of feline know-how in this book of toys and games guaranteed to keep your cat entertained. 96 pp., $12.95

The Emerald Sea: Exploring the Underwater Wilderness of the Pacific Northwest.

Photographs by Dale Sanders, text by Diane Swanson. Arresting color photographs and natural history text make *The Emerald Sea* is a breathtaking introduction to one of the richest underwater habitats on earth. More than 120 color images are included. 160 pp., hardbound, $34.95

Eye of the Changer, by Muriel Ringstad. This excellent children's book is a Northwest Indian tale. 96 pp., $9.95

Garden Touring in the Pacific Northwest: A Guide to Gardens and Specialty Nurseries in Oregon, Washington, and British Columbia, by Jan Kowalczewski Whitner. Travelers and gardeners in search of an unspoiled landscape or a beautifully planned and executed garden will find this guide to 92 noteworthy gardens and 46 specialty nurseries invaluable. Includes site history and garden design along with practical details about hours, fees, directions, eating facilities and more. 192 pp., $15.95

Going Wild in Washington and Oregon: Seasonal Excursions to Wildlife and Habitats, by Susan Ewing. Author Ewing suggests nearly 100 unique seasonal outings where you can view wildlife in their own surroundings. Along with lively natural history, each trip includes information on optional viewing times, directions, equipment and more. All trips can be made by ordinary vehicles, and no extensive hiking is required. 224 pp., $14.95

Golf Courses of the Pacific Northwest, by Jeff Shelley. A comprehensive guide to year-round golfing at golf courses and driving ranges in Washington, Oregon, northern Idaho, the greater Sun Valley area, and northwestern Montana. 344 pp., $19.95

The Great Bear, edited by John A. Murray. A collection of essays about the grizzly by such contemporary writers as John McPhee, Roger Caras and A.B. Guthrie. 248 pp., $14.95

The Great Northwest Nature Factbook, by Ann Saling. Hundreds of fascinating facts on the remarkable animals, plants and natural features in Washington, Oregon, Idaho and Montana. 200 pp., $9.95

The Great Southwest Nature Factbook: A Guide to the Region's Animals, Plants, and Natural Features, by Susan J. Tweit. For residents and visitors alike, *The Great Southwest Nature Factbook* is a take-along guide to the natural wonders of Arizona, New Mexico, southern Colorado, and Utah. 224 pp., $14.95

Grizzly Cub: Five Years in the Life of a Bear, by Rick McIntyre. A true story of a young bear's first five summers, as recorded in words and 56 color photographs by Denali National Park ranger Rick McIntyre. 104 pp., $14.95

Guardians of the Whales: The Quest to Study Whales in the Wild, by Bruce Obee. Photographs by Graeme Ellis. Before the 1970s, little was known about the life patterns and behavior of whales in the wild. But a few intrepid researchers took to the waters to photograph and study these creatures in their habitats. *Guardians of the Whales* weaves the most up-to-date research with stunning color photographs and tells the personal stories of the researchers who have begun to unfold the mysteries of gray, humpback, minke, and killer whales. 184 pp., hardbound, $34.95

Guide to the Birds of Alaska, by Robert H. Armstrong. Updated and expanded; the perfect guide to 437 species found in the 49th state. Revised edition, 349 pp., $19.95

A Guide to the Queen Charlotte Islands, by Neil G. Carey. This revised 10th edition provides all the maps and information needed when visiting these rugged islands. 104 pp., $10.95

Heroes and Heroines in Tlingit–Haida Legend, by Mary Beck. Nine Native legends from the Northwest Coast, with introductions that compare the characters in Tlingit and Haida tradition with classical mythology. Illustrated. 126 pp., $12.95

Heroes of the Horizon, by Gerry Bruder. Author Bruder relates the heroic adventures of 28 veteran bush pilots who flew in Alaska's golden age of aviation, from the 1930s through the 1950s. 280 pp., $12.95

Hibrow Cow: Even MORE Alaskan Recipes and Stories, by Gordon R. Nelson. The former Alaska State trapper's recipes and humorous tales in his fourth cookbook. 215 pp., $9.95

The Hidden Coast: Kayak Explorations from Alaska to Mexico, by Joel W. Rogers. Author Rogers provides an enticing introduction to the splendor of seldom-seen rugged coastal spaces accompanied by stunning color photographs. 168 pp., $19.95

I Am Eskimo: Aknik My Name, by Paul Green with Abbe Abbott. Documentary of Eskimo life at the turn of the century, with illustrations. 96 pp., $12.95

Iditarod: The Great Race to Nome. Photography by Jeff Schultz, text by Bill Sherwonit. Foreword by Joe Redington and preface by Susan Butcher. Powerful photographs provide a dramatic visual record of the courageous human and animal competitors; the text chronicles the origins of the trail and follows the racers on the world's longest sled dog race. 144 pp., $19.95

In the Shadow of Eagles, by Rudy Billberg, as told to Jim Rearden. A true aviation pioneer recounts the adventures of his flying days from a barnstormer to an Alaska bush pilot. 352 pp., $12.95

Journeys Through the Inside Passage, by Joe Upton. Writer and fisherman Joe Upton shares his seafaring adventures along the misty coves and rugged coast of British Columbia and Alaska. 192 pp., $12.95

Kootenay Country: One Man's Life in the Canadian Rockies, by Ernest F. "Fee" Hellmen. A compelling account of the author's life fishing, hunting and guiding in the rugged Kootenays of British Columbia. With photographs and a map. 222 pp., $9.95

The Last Light Breaking: Living Among Alaska's Inupiat Eskimos by Nick Jans. Author Jans weaves together 23 essays to bring a rare perspective on America's last great wilderness and its people—the Inupiat Eskimos, an ancient culture on the cusp of change. 224 pp., hardbound, $21.95

Living by Water, by Brenda Peterson. A collection of essays reflecting on the ways water shapes the lives and spirits of the inhabitants—animals and humans—near the shores of Puget Sound. 144 pp., hardbound, $15.95; softbound, $9.95

The Lost Patrol, by Dick North. First book to unravel the tragedy of the Mounted Police patrol that perished in the winter of 1910–11 in the Northwest Territories. 149 pp., $9.95

Lowbush Moose (And Other Alaskan Recipes), by Gordon R. Nelson. A former Alaska State trooper adds special flavor to mouthwatering family recipes by telling the stories behind them. 210 pp., $9.95

Martha Black, by Martha Black. The story of a pioneer woman from the Dawson goldfields to the halls of Parliament. 149 pp., $9.95

More Alaska Bear Tales, by Larry Kaniut. A keen naturalist and seasoned storyteller, author Larry Kaniut in his second book recounts more true encounters between bears and humans. 296 pp., $12.95

The Nature of Southeast Alaska, text by Robert H. Armstrong, Richard Carstensen and Rita M. O'Clair; illustrations by Richard Carstensen; photographs by Robert H. Armstrong and Rita M. O'Clair. An intimate guide to southeastern Alaska's plants, animals and habitats by authors who know the area's most guarded secrets. 256 pp., softbound, $17.95

No Room for Bears, by Frank Dufresne, illustrated by Rachel S. Horne. The author, one of the country's most admired nature writers, weaves together personal adventure tales with bears, along with sketches of the evolution, varieties, and folklore of this extraordinary animal. An outdoor classic. 256 pp., $12.95

Nome Nuggets, by L.H. French. A soldier of fortune's account of the 1900 Nome gold rush. 64 pp., $5.95

Northwest Landscaping, by Mike Munro. This practical guide helps you create the garden you've always wanted, with plenty of practical, hands-on advice. 192 pp., $16.95

Northwest Sportsman Almanac. Edited by Terry W. Sheely. Coffee-table beautiful, tackle-box informative guide to outdoor recreation. 304 pp., hardbound, $34.95; softbound, $19.95

Once Upon an Eskimo Time, by Edna Wilder. A one-year (1868) vignette in the 121-year life of an Eskimo woman. 204 pp., $12.95

Out Among the Wolves: Contemporary Writings on the Wolf, edited by John A. Murray. Editor Murray has gathered together the best writings on the wolf, giving passionate testimony to this mythical creature's place in the wilds of North America. 248 pp., $14.95

Pacific Halibut: The Resource and The Fishery, by F. Heward Bell. An impressive book on the history of this fish and fishery. 279 pp., hardbound $24.95; softbound $19.95.

Potlatch: Native Ceremony and Myth on the Northwest Coast, by Mary Giraudo Beck; illustrations by Marvin Oliver. Author Beck paints a vivid portrait of this colorful, dramatic Northwest Coast Indian ceremony in which communities marked important events, such as funerals and weddings. 128 pp., $12.95

Raven: A Collection of Woodcuts. Dale De Armond woodcuts, Tlingit tales of Raven. Signed, numbered, limited edition. 115 pp., 12 x 12, $100

Rie Munoz, Alaskan Artist. An illustrated selection of her work. A high-quality collection of limited-edition prints from one of Alaska's foremost artists. 80 pp., $19.95

Ring of Tall Trees, by John Dowd. Dylan's family has just moved to the farm they've always wanted. But a logging company has plans to clear-cut the old-growth forest that surrounds their farm. Calling on Native ritual and myth for help, Dylan and his friends work to save the trees. *Ring of Tall Trees* presents this timely topic in a balanced and informative manner, making this story as appealing to adults as it is to children. For ages 7 to 12. 128 pp., hardbound, $14.95

Riversong Lodge Cookbook: World-Class Cooking in the Alaskan Bush, by Kirsten Dixon. For more than 10 years, Kirsten Dixon and her husband, Carl, have offered travelers the adventure of the Alaska wilderness and the pleasures of the Riversong Lodge kitchen. The 160 recipes in this book are easy to prepare and celebrate Alaska's bounty, 272 pp., hardbound, $22.95

Roots of Ticasuk: An Eskimo Woman's Family Story, by Emily Ivanoff Brown. Handed down from parent to child to grandchild, this story tells of Eskimo customs and taboos and of attempts to westernize a proud culture. 120 pp., $9.95

Seattle Brews: The Insider's Guide to Neighborhood Alehouses, Brewpubs, and Bars, by Bart Becker. Here at last is the definitive guide to fine, handcrafted beer in Seattle. Come on a guided tour of 100 Seattle area alehouses, brewpubs, and bars. Includes a brief history of local brewing, how to cook with beer, and brewpub listings from Alaska to California. 180 pp., $9.95

Seattle Emergency Espresso: The Insider's Guide to Neighborhood Coffee Spots, by Heather Doran Barbieri. Espresso cravers can now find more than 100 espresso carts, coffeehouses, and cafes. This definitive guide to the local espresso scene also includes profiles of the major roasters, recipes for coffee-time treats, and an introduction to espresso's unique language. 180 pp., $9.95

Seattle Picnics: Favorite Sites, Seasonal Menus, and 100 Recipes, by Barbara Holz Sullivan. Discover little-known gardens and stunning urban grottos around Seattle while enjoying unusual and easy-to-prepare picnic fare. 304 pp., $10.95

S'gana: The Black Whale, by Sue Stauffacher. *S'gana* is the story of a boy's struggle to save a dying killer whale. In the process, he makes discoveries about himself and his Haida Indian past. For ages 7 to 12. 224 pp., hardbound, $15.95

Shadows on the Koyukuk: An Alaskan Native's Life Along the River, by Sidney Huntington, as told to Jim Rearden. Born 78 years ago to an Athabascan mother and white trader/trapper father on the Koyukuk River in interior Alaska, Sydney Huntington's life was shaped by tragedy and adventure. In this compelling account, Huntington tells his story simply as a document of change and a tribute to the livability of Alaska's wildlands and the people who inhabit them. 240 pp., $12.95

Shamans and Kushtakas, by Mary Giraudo Beck. Nine gripping tales of the battle between the forces of good and evil: a powerful mix of history and legend to dramatize the values and traditions of Tlingit and Haida societies in Southeast Alaska. 128 pp., $12.95

Skagway Story, by Howard Clifford. Skagway in the late 19th century. 180 pp., $9.95

Skystruck: True Tales of an Alaska Bush Pilot, by Herman Lerdahl with Cliff Cernick. From early bush pilot to major airline captain, the remembrances of a lifetime of adventures. 192 pp., $9.95

To the Top of Denali: Climbing Adventures on North America's Highest Peak, by Bill Sherwonit. A comprehensive collection of Mount McKinley climbing stories, written for armchair adventurers and seasoned climbers alike. 368 pp., $10.95

Toklat: The Story of an Alaskan Grizzly Bear, by Elma and Alfred Milotte. A children's book about a grizzly and her three cubs. 124 pp., $9.95

Trapline Twins, by Miki and Julie Collins. Tales of the unique lifestyle of identical twin girls in Interior Alaska, trapping, dogsledding, canoeing and living off the land. 224 pp., $12.95

Travelers of the Cold: Sled Dogs of the Far North, by Dominique Cellura. The author traces the history of man and sled dog beginning with Eskimo legend, to the growing interest in the sport of sled dog racing. The strength and character of these animals are captured in beautiful color photographs. 172 pp., hardbound, $32.95

Two in the Far North. Margaret Murie's classic adventure about life on the Alaska frontier. In this edition, Murie extends her story to today's Alaska wilderness and parks issues. 396 pp., $12.95

The War Canoe, by Jamie S. Bryson. A compelling novel about a young Tlingit's coming of age in an Alaska that is enriching its present by recapturing the wisdom of its Native past. 198 pp., $9.95

Where the Sea Breaks Its Back, by Corey Ford; illustrated by Lois Darling. Walk with early naturalist Georg W. Steller in an epic story of exploration during the days of Russian Alaska. 224 pp., softbound, $12.95

Wild Echoes: Encounters with the Most Endangered Animals in North America, by Charles Bergman. Author Bergman's powerful encounters with endangered species, together with his interviews with experts in the field, bring the reader closer to understanding our role in their survival. 336 pp., $12.95

Winging It!, by Jack Jefford. Pioneer Alaska aviator Jack Jefford was a "pilot's pilot," one who daily faced the dangers of bush flying, helped settle a frontier, and who now tells his own story. 320 pp., $12.95

Winter Watch, by James Ramsey. For 266 days, the author tested himself against the solitude and isolation of an Arctic winter while living in an old log cabin. 154 pp., $9.95

Index

THE ALASKA ALMANAC®: FACTS ABOUT ALASKA has subject categories organized alphabetically for easy reference. Following is an index to the many topics discussed.